Disclosing a Portion

The inner mechanics of the Torah

Disclosing a Portion

The inner mechanics of the Torah

Laitman
Kabbalah
Publishers

Michael Laitman, PhD

Disclosing a Portion: the inner mechanics of the Torah

Published by Laitman Kabbalah Publishers

www.kabbalah.info info@kabbalah.info
1057 Steeles Avenue West, Suite 532, Toronto, ON, M2R 3X1, Canada

2009 85th Street #51, Brooklyn, New York, 11214, USA

Printed in Canada

ISBN - 978-1-897448-97-7

Library of Congress Control Number: 2014911292

Layout: Chaim Ratz
Cover Design: Inna Smirnova
Translation: Chaim Ratz
Editors: Mordakhay Kholdarov, Mary Pennock
Proofreading: Noga Burnot, Mary Miesem
Copy Editor: Claire Gerus
Executive Editor: Chaim Ratz
Printing and Post Production: Uri Laitman

FIRST EDITION: DECEMBER 2014

First printing

Table of Contents

Introduction

In today's world, the Torah (Pentateuch) is a method that is yet to be recognized for what it truly is. In these pages you will find the stories of the Torah as they unfold through the weekly portions (*Parashot*). Dr. Laitman's unique interpretation of the stories relies on the truths revealed in *The Book of Zohar*, which holds the secrets of the Torah. These secrets reveal a deep and very personal level of the stories, providing us with new tools to understand our own lives and the lives of those we love.

Here, for the first time, the stories of the Torah are interpreted as every person's private spiritual work. Within these pages you will find that the Torah is more than the saga of the Israeli nation. It is the inner tale of you and me, of all of us, and all of humanity. It is here that the connections among us as individuals and as a society can most clearly be seen.

Dr. Laitman's innovative interpretation relies on the authentic sources of Kabbalah and reveals new senses within us that help us connect to one another, understand one another, and truly implement the Torah's fundamental law: "Love your neighbor as yourself." In so doing, the book is a tool that can help us establish more positive, stronger relationships between us based on mutual concern and a lack of malice.

The Torah offers us a profound spiritual message, revealing how we can develop our souls and achieve the purpose of Creation.

The "wisdom of truth," known as the "wisdom of the hidden," or the "wisdom of Kabbalah," holds within it all the secrets of the world. As such, the stories in the Torah offer us rich new levels of understanding.

Through them, we see the gradual process of our personal inner development alongside the collective process of growth known as Tikkun Olam (correction of the world). Today, Tikkun Olam is precisely what we need as we face multiple crises on personal, societal, and global levels.

Indeed, these crises are a result of man's departure from Nature's laws, while the Torah presents a complete, precise plan that shows us how we can adjust ourselves to these laws and prevent or relieve crises. As a global society, we must unite as one, with one heart, or even as one family, and thus make ourselves compatible with the laws of Nature. This message in the Torah is what makes it so important to all of us in these trying times.

Beresheet

(In the Beginning)

(Genesis, 1:1 - 6:8)

Portion Summary

***Beresheet* (In the Beginning) is the first portion in the Torah (Pentateuch). It tells the story of the creation of the world in six days, and the rest on the seventh day. It talks about the creation of man, his arrival at the Garden of Eden, and the creation of woman. This portion also narrates the stories of the sin of the Tree of Knowledge, Cain and Abel, the generations from Cain to Lamech, the ten generations from Adam to Noah, the corruption that engulfed their generations, and the renewed hope that emerged with the birth of Noah.**

Commentary

Beresheet contains more stories than any other portion in the Torah. In many ways it is also the deepest, as it discusses the basis of our being—the creation of the soul.

The common soul was created out of the will to receive delight and pleasure, or simply, "the will to receive." That will is the soul's core, and it is affected by six qualities: *Hesed*, *Gevura*, *Tifferet*, *Netzah*, *Hod*, and *Yesod*. These qualities penetrated the substance—the will to receive—and designed it in synchrony with the upper force, the Creator. The reason why man is called "Adam" is that the word comes from *Adamah*, from the verse, *Adameh la Elyon* ("I will be like the most high," Isaiah, 14:14). This refers to Adam's similarity to the Creator—the sublime bestowal, sublime love—the upper force that gave birth to him.

Adam is the structure of the soul that is equal in form to the Creator, and is in *Dvekut* (adhesion) with Him in the Garden of Eden. A garden means "desire," and the garden is the part of the creature, Adam's substance—it is the will to receive. Eden marks the degree of bestowal, the degree of *Bina*. Adam, who is on the degree of *Bina*, is in the Garden of Eden.

This does not pertain to our world or to the universe we know, but rather to the common soul that the Creator created. From the very beginning, the common soul has undergone a special preparation, "the sin," because at its inception it was part of the upper force. This means that the soul had no authority of its own, nothing to its name, or any sense of independent existence. In a sense, the soul was like an embryo in its mother's womb—on the one hand, it exists, on the other hand, it is part of its mother and each of its actions is ruled by that superior entity.

Such is the structure of the soul. While it exists in the Garden of Eden, the garden itself does not permit independence. "Independence" means that a person is beyond another's control, in a state of preparing to assume self-control. The structure of the soul is the creature, the created being.

The word, *Nivrah* (creature), comes from the word, *Bar* (outside). In order to allow the structure of the soul to actually become a creature, it must be taken out and removed from the Creator. Put differently, it must be made opposite from the Creator, and this oppositeness is obtained through the sin.

Explaining the Sin

The soul consists of two forces: Cain and Abel. Abel wants to exist by raising the *Hevel* (breath/vapor), meaning the Reflected Light, or bestowal, the giving force. Cain is the opposite, wanting to draw all the pleasures, all the lights, inward, into the soul.

Cain—the quality that draws the pleasure, the light to itself, and not for the sake of the Creator, draws it until Abel, the desire to bestow, disappears. This act is called "Cain's killing of Abel."

The *Kli* (vessel) of the soul that receives light *not* for the sake of the Creator shatters into pieces, bits of self-centered desires. Each such desire is an individual soul that becomes enveloped in a wrapping similar to a *Klipa* (shell/peel). During the formation process of these broken souls, additional falls and descents occur along the spiritual degrees. They bring us to where we are in this world, each of us being a part of the single, common soul that was created.

It is precisely because we are detached from one another by our egos—immersed in the will to receive instead of in the will to bestow—that we now have an opportunity to correct. Because we were already corrected in the past, we can begin today to correct the ruin and sin that took place in the past. Although we aren't the ones who committed the sin, our souls are prepared within to enable us to carry out the correction.

This correction is called "repentance," constituting a return to precisely the state we were in while in the Garden of Eden. We must hurry and achieve that state, however, because the whole world is already moving toward connection, an essential process of unity and the perception of ourselves as a single soul. And finally, when we are all in bestowal and mutual love, we will succeed in returning to the structure, the state we maintained prior to the sin. In so doing, we will obtain the state we were in while in the Garden of Eden, and we will rise once more above the reality of this world.

Our current reality will disappear because it only exists when we are immersed in the will to receive in order to receive. When we have the intention to bestow, however, we can no longer exist in our current reality. Rather, our existence becomes completely spiritual and leads us back to the state we were in prior to our creation.

QUESTIONS AND ANSWERS

What is the meaning of Creation and what preceded it?

"Creation" refers to the creation of man and the world. The creation of the world preceded the creation of man by five days. The qualities *Hesed*, *Gevura*, *Tifferet*, *Netzah*, and *Hod*, are the first five days, and the quality called *Yesod*, the collection of the previous five, is the sixth day. *Yesod* ties them all together and becomes the *Yesod* (foundation) for the creation of man.

The wisdom of Kabbalah describes many actions preceding the creation of the world, such as "existence from existence" and "existence from absence." These are the two forces that create all the states: the four phases of Direct Light, the worlds, *Adam Kadmon*, and *Atzilut*. However, we don't relate these actions to our world because the creation of our world and of man are connected only to the world of *Atzilut*.

What is the Meaning of *Beresheet* (In the Beginning/ Genesis)?

In Kabbalah, the word *Beresheet* (in the beginning/Genesis) doesn't indicate the first act that took place in Creation. *Beresheet* indicates that Creation began from heaven and from earth, meaning from two opposite qualities. Heaven is the quality of bestowal, and earth is the quality of reception. Every other state of the creatures derives from those two qualities.

Why does the Torah tell the story from the middle and not from the beginning?

The Torah tells us only the part that is relevant to our correction. It is useless to learn what doesn't belong to our correction because we neither feel it nor understand it, nor do we have those levels or qualities. The structure of Creation is vast, yet we learn only a fraction of it–that which is necessary for us to organize ourselves for the present time. This is exactly how we expose children to the world, as a gradual process, showing them more and more of the world as they mature so they can grasp and use their knowledge to their benefit.

What is a soul?

The soul is the will to receive that is already corrected into bestowal. Although its nature, its substance, is the will to receive pleasure, above that substance is a correction that man makes–working for the sake of others.

If there are only two forces in Nature–the will to receive and the will to bestow–where is everything else?

Indeed, there are only two forces, and degrees of the same two forces, meaning manners and levels of connection between them. The degrees relate to the still, vegetative, animate, and speaking levels.

The two forces in our world manifest as positive and negative forces. We know them as "electrons" and "protons," and their various combinations form the different substances. These substances not only become solid, meaning "still"; they also become plants, or "vegetative."

Plants possess a structure of absorption, emission, metabolism, and so forth. The next level, the "animate" level, demonstrates a structure that perceives itself as existing, moving, and growing.

Next develops the "speaking" level, the structure of a human being, unique in the story of Creation. Yet, in the end, everything is composed, in various states of development, of electrons and protons.

What is a woman and what is a man?

The will to receive within the soul is called a "woman," and the will to bestow within the soul is called a "man" (*Gever*), from the Hebrew word, *Hitgabrut* (overcoming), because it overcomes the will to receive.

What is the meaning and purpose of the stories in *Beresheet*?

The stories in *Beresheet* should not be taken literally, as tales of a man and a woman who sinned, stories of snakes and apples, and so forth. In fact, the stories describe the qualities of the will to receive and the will to bestow.

All the qualities of bestowal and reception we read about in this Torah portion are our own foundations. Initially, our soul is one soul, a desire to receive filled to the brim with light. It is in perfect congruence with the light, the will to bestow, and is therefore at the degree of the Garden of Eden—the degree of *Elokim* (God).

This has nothing to do with our world, nor with anything we see and feel here and now. All the qualities described in the portion are forces of the upper dimension, from which the soul declines in quality, yet not as low as the corporeal world.

All the falls of the soul are preparations for our present situation. We, along with the universe, develop from the state in which the soul broke and received the will to receive, when the ego began to develop. We have been developing from that point ever since. However, it appears that we have been developing in only one dimension. Now, from our generation onward we are beginning to evolve in a more qualitative manner, ascending in our mental development.

As we are discovering the negativity in our lives, we are beginning to feel that life could and should be better, that our development is leading us to a dead end. Today when we study the Torah, we study it not only as a historic document, but rather we aim to use it to help us move toward our designated goal. That is, we must rise once more to the level, the state, and the qualities that we had in the Garden of Eden. This is actually our goal.

Today we are experiencing many crises because these forces disclose to us the depravity of our situation, and that we must correct ourselves and rise. This Torah portion, *Beresheet*, sheds light on our lives, on the world, and on the irreversible process we are going through.

What is the difference between our time and the time of Noah?

In Noah's time, people weren't as connected as they are today. It's true that we have always been egoists, striving to succeed and to profit for ourselves. However, in the past, Nature didn't press us as it is doing now, and we could do what we wanted.

The wisdom of Kabbalah teaches us that we have been advancing very well using our egos to build our society. However, we now have reached the end of the road, although most of us have yet to recognize it. Our planet's resources are dwindling, and we are interwoven in a network that binds us together against our will. We recognize that something is stopping our progress and preventing us from doing what we want. And when we cannot continue our business-as-usual approach to life, we become alarmed, and call it a "crisis."

Today we are feeling these crises in family ties, in our culture, in education, science, and the economy. We have the sense that we are no longer in control of the world we live in. We've always run it according to the whims of our egos, but now we can't. The world is closing in on us, forcing us to become congruent with one another. Bit by bit, the state that existed in the Garden of Eden is manifesting itself–a state in which we are tied to one another in mutual guarantee. In the Garden of Eden we were connected "as one man with one heart," as a single family, a single soul. Now we must achieve that state, but we are not equipped for it; we're broken.

How can a story such as that of Cain and Abel set an example?

The story of Cain and Abel doesn't serve as an example of good things. From the moment contradicting forces appeared in Adam, he was driven to sin. Now we must return to the state we were in prior to his sin. The states we are experiencing today are compelling us to do it. We won't be able to escape it. Life will pressure us until we seek a solution, and the solution will be to adapt ourselves to the state of infinity that existed when we were all connected as one.

From *The Zohar*: The World Was Divided into 45 Kinds of Color and Light

"*Adam HaRishon* followed the serpent down, and descended to know all that there is below. That is, he went down to extend the illumination of the left from above to everything that is below, to the place of the missing *Malchut*, like the serpent, since extension of the illumination of the *Zivug* (coupling) from above downward is the prohibition of the tree of knowledge. Therefore, because he came to draw from above downward, he was promptly attached to the *Klipot* (shells/peels)."

Zohar for All, *Beresheet*, 2, item 287

Is the serpent the cause of all troubles?

The serpent is indeed the cause of all our problems. The serpent represents our every thought and desire to use others to the maximum. It is always in us, whether we're aware of it or not.

It is not our fault that we are like that. We are at fault for only one thing: for being idle. We suffer not because we were born egoists or unkind, but because we are lazy about correcting ourselves. It's as if we were children who received certain qualities at birth and cannot be blamed for it. However, if a child can do something about those traits but avoids doing it, society's attitude toward him changes.

What we can do today?

We can begin to learn about the new world we live in, where nothing works as it did: this includes the economy, industry, commerce, family, and education.

Today's young people don't know what to study—or if they should study at all. They can't even decide if they should have children!

People are faced with an unclear environment, where things appear blurry and unpredictable. We must examine and learn from Nature what is happening to us, but most people prefer not to hear about it. That reluctance to listen stems from the ego—the serpent.

We are facing a huge problem. The pressures are still not serious enough for people to understand that big troubles await us if we do not change. Therefore, we must circulate the information about the new world and make people aware in order to make things easier for them, *before* they suffer the consequences.

Moreover, if we advance before we face these blows, we'll be like smart children who understand that otherwise they will suffer. Thus, we need to study harder and improve ourselves, or we will be forced to study and improve, regardless of our choice.

The challenge is for all of us, as this network keeps closing in on us, and the tighter it gets, the more difficulties we will experience. Economists will be unable to affect the world's economic crisis—only if all of us unite can we bring change to the world. If we can do this, the monetary system, unemployment, industry, health, and the rest of the systems will be reorganized and improved. Without that mindset, no system will advance favorably.

Terms

Beresheet

Beresheet (in the beginning) means that the Creator created six qualities and man. Within man are all the qualities by which to become similar to the Creator. In fact, this is the work of Creation—to build the substance, the will to receive. These qualities permeate the will to receive so that the structure as a soul will attain the state of the Creator.

The *Shabbat* (Sabbath)

This is Man's final correction, when he returns to the Garden of Eden. It is a state in which we reunite into a single soul.

The Garden of Eden

In the Garden of Eden, we are all in mutual bestowal, in complete mutual guarantee.

The Woman

The "woman" is the will to receive within us, which we must connect with the man within us so that the will to receive will have the intention to bestow. We are immersed in our will to receive, a desire that is initially egoistic and that is intended to resemble the Creator, to bestow upon Him.

The Serpent

The "serpent" is the evil inclination, the angel of death. The serpent will become a holy angel when all the will to receive is corrected.*

The Tree of Knowledge

The "Tree of Knowledge" is the greatest light. It was initially received in order to receive, thus causing the breaking of the soul. In the future, we will receive that light, but with the intention to bestow.

Summary

We are truly in *Beresheet*, in the beginning. Humanity is finally beginning to understand where we are, as studies of sociologists and other social scientists indicate. Let us hope that we will soon realize that we simply must unite, that this is the only way to build a new, corrected world. By doing so, we will gain physical as well as spiritual benefits.

This is why the year begins with *Beresheet*, "in the beginning," as it contains both the end and the beginning. Within this portion, encoded in the word *Beresheet*, is the entire process that we must, and will, experience.

* "The serpent is the evil inclination; it is the angel of death" (*Beresheet*, 440).
"The Creator provides His corrections to all until even the angel of death returns to being very good" (*Zohar for All*, *Mishpatim* (Ordinances), 165).

Lech Lecha

(Go Forth)

(Genesis, 12:1-17:27)

Portion Summary

The portion, Go Forth, begins with Abraham being commanded to go to the land of Canaan. When Abraham reaches the land of Canaan, hunger forces him to go down to Egypt, where Pharaoh's servants take Sarai, his wife. In Pharaoh's house, Abraham presents her as his sister, fearing for his life. The Creator punishes Pharaoh with infections and diseases, and he is forced to give Sarai back to Abraham.

When Abraham returns to the land of Canaan, a fight breaks out between the herdsmen of Lot's cattle and the herdsmen of Abraham's cattle, after which they part ways.

A war breaks out between four kings from among the rulers of Babylon, and five kings from the land of Canaan. Lot is taken captive and Abraham sets out to save him.

The Creator makes a covenant with Abraham—"the covenant of the pieces" (or "covenant between the parts")—the promise of the continuation of his descendants and the promise that they would inherit the land.

Sarai cannot have children, so she offers Abraham her maid, Hagar, and they have a child named Ishmael.

Abraham makes the covenant of circumcision with the Creator and is commanded to circumcise himself and all the males in his household. His name changes from Abram to Abraham, and his wife's name changes from Sarai to Sarah.

At the end of the portion, the Creator promises Sarah that she will have a son whose name will be Isaac.

Commentary

All the stories of the portion we read happen within us. In the correct perception of reality, this world does not exist, nor do history, geography or the story of the portion. All of them are occurrences that take place within us.

The wisdom of Kabbalah explains that perception of reality is a profound matter, relating to our innermost psychology, our senses, and our physical structure.

The Torah describes honestly the way we developed. Everyone and everything that is described reflects our mental forces. Abraham, for instance, is the tendency to develop toward spirituality, the desire to approach and discover the Creator.

The story of Abraham in Babylon is really the revelation that only one force exists and runs the world, and the desire to discover that force. Those of us who wish to discover who is managing our fate and why, or asks, "What is the meaning of my life?" are at the same starting point as was Abraham, and the force of Abraham is alive and working within them.

Abraham realized that he had to advance to the next state. In fact, he felt Nature prodding him forward, telling him, "Go forth from your land and from your kindred, and from your father's house, to the land that I will show you." There you will find the balance and will be able to realize yourself.

Maimonides and other Kabbalists wrote that this is how Abraham moved to the land of Canaan with his entire household, and thousands of the people who left Babylon along with him, and which he had established as the "house of Abraham." When Abraham reached the land of Canaan, he had arrived at a new desire, called "Canaan."

The word, *Eretz* (land), comes from the word, *Ratzon* (desire). Abraham discovered that this desire did not sufficiently elevate him; he was hungry and did not know what would sustain him and keep him at this point of the land of Canaan. Because this was a land of bestowal, and he was still not in a state where he could achieve bestowal, a new situation formed, compelling him to become attached to the will to receive. This is what made him go down to Egypt.

A great desire appeared at this point, where one feels that more steps with the intensifying ego are required, as the ego is shifting from a state of "Babylon is not enough." As the ego grows, it demands satisfaction. But this arouses fear that if one should work with the ego with the intention to bestow ("Abraham"), it will not be enough to keep oneself, and thus one might ruin the intention.

This is why people are unwilling to work with their egos, the obstruction that is growing within. The desire within tells that person, "This is my sister, not my wife." A person becomes ready to completely abstain from the whole of the desire, called "Sarah," and remain solely in the intention to bestow, called "Abraham."

Because of our growing egos, we lack a sense of fulfillment. Instead, we feel increasingly deficient and empty. "Pharaoh" is the state imprinted within us that asks, "What do I get out of it?" It seems that the current state is worse than the one we were in before, which is why Pharaoh tells Abraham to take back the desire ("Sarah") because he wanted to remain in corporeality, as he was, while that desire, Sarah, extended from spirituality.

These two parts within us are in a constant struggle. They alternate: first, Abraham grows and falls, and then Pharaoh grows and falls. It resembles how we walk, stepping with the right foot, then the left foot. It makes little difference what we call these two parts within us because they acquire different names at different degrees.

When Abraham and his entourage returned to the land of Canaan, a problem arose between the herdsmen of Lot's cattle and the herdsmen of Abraham's cattle. The word, *Lot,* means "curse." The question actually is, "Which way should one go, in the direction of the aim to receive, or in the direction of the aim to bestow?" When faced with this choice, we become perplexed and do not know what to do. This is the quarrel over the place and the wells in the story of Lot, describing the choice to distinguish between the two forces–reception and bestowal.

This story teaches us that during our spiritual development there are many events where we must look into our egos and see how it is intensifying in us.

And yet, while we must disagree with the direction of the evil, we must also refrain from destroying it. Rather, we should abstain from it, as Abraham abstained from Lot, who later saved him from Sodom.

These are the changes that happen within us. We use our bad *Kelim* (vessels), as well as our good ones, meaning our good qualities and our bad qualities, as well as all our thoughts because we learn from them.

When Abraham concludes the quarrel with the herdsmen of Lot's cattle, he wages war on the four kings who live in the country. Once again we see that as we develop, we are in a constant struggle. The kings are our great forces, our great desires. They do not allow us to enter the land of Canaan and encircle Canaan. Therefore, when we wish to achieve a certain spiritual degree in which we begin to feel the Creator, the common force of Nature, and the eternity and perfection in Nature, those *Malchuts*, those "kings," are standing in our way, blocking it.

Following this war, the Creator appears to Abraham and says to him that he is making a covenant with him. He promises that this land will truly belong to the quality of Abraham that is growing and developing atop the quality of Pharaoh, the wars, and on top of Lot.

Now that quality is powerful enough to enable one to enter the land of Canaan. This is the quality that allows one to achieve the purpose of Creation, the revelation of the Creator, and to achieve *Dvekut* (adhesion) with the Creator.

In order to actually attain the next degree, the contact with the Creator, we need a force that will "beget" the next degree. It is we who beget the new states, but the will to receive, which is "Sarah," still cannot be the force that is giving birth under the quality of Abraham. The quality of Abraham is still weak in its intention to bestow, and cannot deliver us from the will to receive. However, it *can* do it with the right line, the force of the right, but only with that part of it called "Hagar." The offshoot of that is "Ishmael," a force that belongs to the right of *Bina*, called the *Klipa* (shell/peel) of the right.

In the end, following the covenant and the numerous corrections, Abraham comes to a state where he can also work with Sarah, the overall will to receive. This is when Sarah gives birth, hence the great joy reflected in the portion.

QUESTIONS AND ANSWERS

Abraham is told to go from Babylon to Canaan. What does it mean to move from one desire to the next, and what does it feel like to be in the land of Canaan?

We are in a process of constant changes, except that we are not aware of it. The Torah speaks of the changes we go through consciously, after having decided that we really want to change our desires. The will to receive has been our entire substance, and we shift from one desire to the next, from place to place. There is a maxim that says, "Change of place, change of luck." A "place" is the desire from which we observe the world. The desire is everything; it is the foundation from which we embark on every action.

Each name or word mentioned in the Torah actually denotes a desire. In the wisdom of Kabbalah, we speak of *Aviut* (thickness), *Masach* (screen), and *Reshimot* (recollections) that determine the state of the *Neshama* (soul). Here, too, we are speaking of the same changes we go through, except the terminology is different.

"Go forth" means that we should always feel that the beginning of the path is *Yesod* (foundation), and we advance precisely when shifting from state to state. We must carry out those instructions and move from state to state until we arrive at the end of our correction. Therefore, "go forth" is the act that the Creator expects us to perform.

This means that we can move forward only if we understand that change can only happen through unity. The whole difference between spiritual degrees is the level of connection we achieve, which allows us to connect all the elements within us to attain our goal.

Nothing is created without a reason. We need all our mental powers, including Pharaoh, Lot, Abraham's cattle, Lot's cattle, the kings that are in the land, Balaam, Balak, Haman, the wicked, as well as the righteous. In the end, the Torah teaches us how to connect all our mental powers and become a whole individual.

What is the meaning of the land of Canaan with regard to our desires?

Canaan is a land that existed prior to the land of Israel. It is one of the degrees, the one before the land of Israel.

Is a person already on the way to spirituality if the point in his or her heart has awakened?

Yes. Once the point awakens in a person's heart, he or she cannot stay in Babylon. Such a person must leave Babylon and ascend to the degree of the land of Canaan. One progresses along with those who join in—those desires that one *can* work with—and rises to another degree, where one thinks in the direction of bestowal and *Hesed* (mercy), in the direction that Abraham symbolizes.

From *The Zohar*: Go Forth, to Correct Yourself

Since the Creator saw his awakening and his desire, He immediately revealed Himself to him and told him, "Go forth," to know yourself and to correct yourself. Meaning, he should stop weighing the upper forces but raise *MAN* and extend a high *Zivug* on the *Masach* that appeared to him, by which he will be rewarded with extending *Daat* for himself and correct himself.

Zohar for All, *Lech Lecha* (Go Forth), item 28

Attaining a higher degree is done by the *Aviut* (thickness) of the new desire, and through the intention over that desire. If a person performs a *Zivug de Hakaa* (coupling of striking), he or she achieves the revelation of the upper light at the degree in which the *Zivug* was made.

What does it mean that the Creator "saw his awakening"?

A person receives the awakening from the overall plan of Creation. Each of us has a time in which we begin to awaken. The general "engine" of all the souls turns like a counter and issues orders to each one. All of a sudden, you wake up, you have a desire, and you are being led. You are awakened to spirituality once or twice or thrice in life, and you must respond; you must take the initiative and begin to advance on your own.

What happens when a person discovers that he or she cannot advance any longer?

When you suddenly begin to feel that you cannot advance in spirituality, it means you are once again falling into the egotistical desire ("Pharaoh"). You are descending to Egypt once again.

This, however, is what should happen. You need to intensify your ego in order to advance, as this is all your matter. It is all the substance of Creation—the great will to receive. Without Pharaoh, you will not be able to reach Mount Sinai.

You have to have a "mountain" of evil and hatred, which you took from Pharaoh. All the desire that appeared in you became a mountain around which you feel your hatred of others. When you reach this point, you tell yourself, "I *have* to have the Torah; I have no choice; I have to have the force that will correct me, which is called 'the light that reforms.'"

Progress is always made from two directions: on one side is the growing egotistical desire; on the other side is the intention to bestow.

What is the *Klipa* of the right, and why did Abraham, the quality of *Hesed*, beget a *Klipa*?

The quality of Abraham is only just beginning; it is not entirely corrected. That is, it is the initial desire of a person, which is clear, lacking *Aviut*. When one connects *Aviut* to oneself in order to advance, the right and left connect through one's scrutiny of the desire. A person must scrutinize with which desires one can work, and with which desires one still cannot. The latter will be corrected when one reaches more advanced degrees.

Moreover, by begetting his son with his partial desire, called Hagar, the conditions change. Sarai becomes Sarah, and Abram becomes Abraham. These are not just different names. Through these corrections, we arrive at a state where we are working with a new, different desire known as "Sarah," and a new, different intention known as "Abraham," who together beget the beginning of the nation.

Is Isaac the beginning of the nation?

Not only Isaac. There are three lines altogether: the left, right, and middle line, which is Israel. Additionally, there are two *Klipot* (shells/peels): Ishmael on the right and Esau on the left. It does not mean that they are completely flawed, but only that in time they, too, will be corrected.

The *Klipa* of the right, Ishmael, is still fighting against everyone, even today.

It will remain so until the end of correction, until we all mingle together and unite.

Does circumcision mean "cutting" into the desire?

Yes, but circumcision is more than just cutting; it is also the *Klipot*, which are desires that you cannot work with. For now, they are *Klipot* until they become *Kedusha* (holiness). The problem is in you; you cannot work with such intense desires with the aim to bestow, since if you receive pleasures you will take them for yourself instead of bestowing them to others.

What does it mean to make a covenant with the Creator?

Making a covenant with the Creator means that a person makes whatever pledge is required. The covenant is a special, inner reorganization that allows one—along with one's forces—to attain a state where one will never make mistakes, through all the future degrees, provided one maintains a certain principle.

Is the Creator going to help me because of the covenant?

The covenant means that the Creator *is* helping you. The Creator = Nature. "I, the Lord, do not change" means that from now on you recognize a certain principle. If you stick to it, you are guaranteed to avoid any mistakes, any deviations, and any sins. Your spiritual advancement is always toward a degree that you still do not know. Therefore, you must be certain that when you advance, you will not fail. The covenant is the force that takes you safely from one degree to the next.

There are two covenants: the covenant of the pieces and the covenant of circumcision. Circumcision has become a Jewish conduct in the corporeal world, and it is a commandment to this day. Some say it is a cruel tradition. What is the spiritual root of circumcision?

The root lies in the need to be rid of the will to receive that one cannot correct. It is what we do all the time, including with Sarah, Hagar, and so forth. On the one hand, we scrutinize the will to receive, which is growing. On the other hand, we realize we must "cut out" some of it, similar to the end of the *Partzuf* (face). We need to decide that we cannot deal with this part for the time being. This is also what the positive and negative ("do" and "do not do") *Mitzvot* (commandments) refer to. Why "do" and "not do?" Because there is a will to receive that we cannot use.

Therefore, in every situation, we must distinguish between the desire we use and the desire we do not use. The "place" of our scrutiny is called the "*Rosh* (head) of the *Partzuf*," and this is the primary scrutiny that we must always make before every decision.

Is the foreskin the desire that we cannot use?

Yes, the foreskin, the exposing, and the drop of blood are all the corrections that engage in the intensity of the desire and its nature. We cannot currently work in favor of others, nor also in our own favor, since we are not in spirituality and we do not use them. The decision to refrain from using them is called "circumcision."

It is mentioned that Lot is taken captive. Who captured him and what is captivity?

He was taken captive by the egotistical desire of Sodom. Sodom, compared to the state we are in, is a state of great righteousness, and we even dare to say, "Sodomite rule."

Do you mean that we are worse than "Sodomite rule?"

Yes. The Sodomite rule is, "Let mine be mine and let yours be yours." I do not touch you, and you do not touch me. Even if I can steal something from you, I won't. Or even if I can use you, I will avoid it. I do not sell you something bad or manipulate you through advertisement. In short, I do not exploit you.

"Sodomite rule" does not sound so bad!

Of course. If we were in Sodomite rule today, this would be a step forward for us. It is with good reason that Lot was included in it. After all, he was close to Abraham; these qualities are not so far from one another. Abraham came to save him because the quality of Sodom is required in order to elicit anything for correction. This is why when Abraham came to Sodom, he scrutinized the desires that could be salvaged from them while the rest, which could not be scrutinized, had to go through the upheaval of Sodom.

TERMS

Go Forth

Go forth from your desire, regardless of how fine it may seem to you. You must come to a new state, a new degree. Each time, "Go forth" indicates that you will constantly be in motion, going upward.

Canaan

Canaan is the land of Israel before it has been fully corrected.

Hunger

"Hunger" means I cannot satisfy my will to receive if I am as an Egyptian, or that I cannot satisfy my desire to bestow if I am as a Jew, seeking unification with the Creator.

Sister

There are several names that we use to refer to the will to receive. Among them are "sister," "wife," and "servant." The word, "sister," refers to the will to receive you can use with filling of *Hochma* (wisdom), as it is written, "Say unto wisdom, 'You are my sister'" (Proverbs, 7:4).

Maidservant and Woman

A "maidservant" is when a person uses the desire to bestow in order to bestow. A "woman" is when a person fills her with receiving in order to bestow, from which it is already possible to bear children.

Fertility, Birth

The two above words refer to when you beget your next degree, your next state.

Covenant

A covenant is when you acquire the willpower, understanding, sensation, and support, when you are assisted in shifting from state to state without failing. If there is love between us today, we make a covenant to sustain it tomorrow, as well. The covenant helps us when we really want it to happen tomorrow. It is a force in Nature that helps us maintain our state.

Summary

The key message of the portion is truly, "go forth." We move from state to state only through the changes in our desires. Each moment we examine and scrutinize our desires in order to decide which desires we can use, and which ones we still cannot, which desires we should "kill," and which ones we should "cut off" from ourselves.

I always scrutinize how I can advance through love of others and toward the love of the Creator. "Go forth" is the way that guides me, and it is the only one that I walk.

Noah

(Genesis, 6:9-11:32)

Portion Summary

The portion, Noah, speaks of sinful people and the Creator, who sends a flood to the world. "Noah was a righteous man, perfect in his generations" (Genesis, 6:9). This is why he was chosen to survive the flood.

But he did not survive alone. Rather, he was commanded to build an ark and move into it with his kin and one pair of each animal. They were to remain in the ark for forty days and forty nights until the flood stopped.

The Creator made a covenant with Noah and his family that the flood would never return. As a token of the covenant, He placed the rainbow in the sky.

The end of the portion speaks of the tower of Babel, about the people who decided to build a tower whose head reaches the heaven. The Creator responded by confusing their language so they would not understand one another, and finally dispersing them throughout the country.

Commentary

The portion, Noah, is long, intense, and contains more details and events than other portions. As this portion takes place at the beginning of the Torah, it also marks the beginning of our spiritual path, the most important time in our spiritual development.

These initial stages unfold quite quickly, unlike subsequent events when we begin to actually correct our qualities meticulously. Later on, the events described are far more detailed, as we will see in those that later unfold in the Torah.

Our development takes place entirely over our egotistical will to receive, which we must turn into bestowal. Today we are still in the midst of a process where all of humanity must begin to work with their egos to forge the right connections among people. The struggle to overcome the ego is always a big problem, and appears as waves of a great sea, called *Malchut* of *Ein Sof* (*Malchut* of infinity).

Each time, the ego arises and we do not know what to do, so our only option is to hide in a box, in an ark. This is not merely an escape; it is actually a correction. We build around ourselves a kind of bubble, the quality of bestowal, and hide in it from all of our terrible egotistical qualities. This is how we advance.

When the ego manifests, we walk into the ark, where we adjust our corrections in order to rise above the ego and avoid using it. In the ark, we disconnect from the surrounding world, where terrible things are happening. As we do so, the self-centered desires ferociously bang on our ark's hull, attempting to pull us into many places and directions, into the depths of the sea. And yet, we stay inside the ark, focused on the desire to remain in the quality of bestowal.

The stay in the ark lasts forty days and forty nights. This is the difference between *Malchut* and *Bina*, because all of *Malchut*, all the desires, are included in *Bina*. We check ourselves by asking the crow, but the crow does not answer. The dove, however, does answer because it is from the side of *Rachamim* (mercy), from the right, from the side of peace.

When we receive the answer that all of our desires are controlled by the quality of bestowal, it is a sign that we have survived the flood. It is an indication that all of our desires and qualities, which are called "one's kin" (the family that is in the ark), have passed the first stage of correction and we are now able to continue with the corrections. The purpose of the whole process, this flow, is for us to correct our egotistical, broken souls and bring them to a state where they are in pure bestowal, and thus in complete equivalence of form, in *Dvekut* (adhesion) with the Creator.

When we go out into the air, to the dry land, the Creator says that He will make a covenant with us regarding everything that we are about to undergo. The covenant is for the future, when similar events might occur, so that we will know that we can use the forces we have used in the past.

The covenant testifies that we cannot correct ourselves and that we are compelled to use the same forces we did in the past. This is why we do not like the token of the rainbow in the sky.

Here is an example: Let us assume that we are in a quarrel and we remember that we used to be friends. Then, for the sake of that past relationship we make peace again. Thus, the rainbow–the covenant–is not a good sign because it marks our entrance into a time of weakness, where further troubles are ahead, for which we will need this covenant.

Noah's time marks the beginning of a new development. There are ten generations from Adam to Noah. These are the ten *Sefirot*, and there are ten more generations (*Sefirot*) from Noah to Abraham. There are many qualities in us that grow within us and then appear, until we again recognize our own egotistical qualities. Apparently, we have forgotten the qualities of bestowal we had while in the ark, so we can no longer cover them with *Hassadim*, the quality of *Hesed* (mercy), and with love of others, to be as one family, as it was with Noah in the ark when the whole world was as a family. At that time, everyone was under the canopy of *Hassadim*, under a canopy of love, collaborating in mutual guarantee.

Now as our egotistical desires grow once more, they lead us back to Babel–a state where we see our egos soar, attempting to have and control everything. The great egoist who controls the person is Nimrod. This is a force that is willing to do anything.

Nimrod wants to control our lives. He does not want to be above, in the quality of bestowal, but only in the quality of reception, as we can see all around us in our world today.

Everything that happened at Noah's time had to happen because of the rule, "I have created the evil inclination; I have created for it the Torah as a spice" (*Kidushin*, 30b), because "the light in it reforms them." In other words, we need to discover the evil in us, and from that revelation of evil we will discover its antidote, since we will not want to remain in the evil. This is why we need to obtain the light that reforms, the special light that the wisdom of Kabbalah tells us how to obtain so we may correct ourselves with it.

All the stories of the Torah prior to Noah's, such as that of Cain and Abel, describe how the ego intensified. We learn about it from *The Zohar*, which tells us about the true meaning of the stories of the Torah. *The Zohar* tells us openly what is simply implied in the Torah. It reveals to us what hides behind every human story, and what the Torah is actually telling us in its narratives. It is with good reason that the wisdom of Kabbalah is called the "wisdom of truth."

The Torah speaks of our souls, about how we must bring that soul out of hiding. We must discover the soul at every degree of its *Aviut*, at every stage of its shattering, and we must correct it. Within the corrected soul, we must feel our spiritual lives and remain in them, as it is written, "You will see your world in your life" (*Berachot*, 17a). We must discover the spiritual world, the Creator, the "me" that is found in the spiritual world, and we must do it here and now, while we are in this world.

However, to enter the next world we must first discover our broken souls. In this process, our souls will grow on the left line. This means that over the ten generations from Adam to Noah, great desires of the will to receive have developed in the soul. At the stage where we finish with the left line—following the Creator's decision—the right line comes along and begins to correct the left. The left line is the corrupted, broken *Malchut*, while the right line is *Bina*, the qualities of bestowal, qualities of love, giving, and mercy.

Subsequently, ten new generations arrive, the ten *Sefirot* from Noah to Abraham—intended to correct the previous generations from Adam to Noah—meaning ten *Sefirot* of *Ohr Yashar* and ten *Sefirot* of *Ohr Hozer*. Abraham comes after those twenty generations and receives the beginning of the soul at a level where he can already understand and recognize its purpose. This is why he breaks the statues and begins to fight his own huge ego, which appears to him as Nimrod, as Babylon. With Nimrod on the left, and Abraham on the right, we can begin to fight for the correction of the soul.

All these names and incidents describe what happens to our souls. The Torah speaks of what each of us should go through, and we will gradually discover how we actually go through those stages.

Questions and Answers

Is a flood a bad thing? Today, words such as "tsunami" and "flood" arouse terror.

Yes, it is bad in spirituality, too. A flood implies "evil waters," or *Gevurot*. Water is essentially *Hassadim*, but when connected to an ego that controls it, it becomes dangerous water.

In this story, as well as in the story of the tower of Babel, we learn that the Creator decided to confuse the people; He caused them to sin, and then seemingly punished them.

Of course, nothing happens without Him, for "there is none else besides Him." What matters is how we react, accept, and partake of what is happening. In each situation, we must be His partners and understand His works. It is like a mother playing with her baby. The mother wants the baby to understand her and play with her as she is playing with her child. Therefore, of course the Creator is behind the whole process, but the question is whether we know how to react to what unfolds correctly at each moment.

Can we react like that baby?

If we look at babies, we will see that they are never at rest. They are constantly striving to grasp the world, examining and learning from it. Childhood is the time of building the man, the time of man's corrections. After age twenty, everyone begins to grow old and dwindle.

The phases one goes through—the evil water, Noah, and Abraham—put us in terrible restlessness. But in the end, we will all have to go through this process to correct our souls.

That is why the whole Torah, from "In the beginning" to "Israel," was written for us, so that we can experience it in our inner work. When we correct the soul, we enter the next world.

What is Noah's Ark, and how does one enter it?

The ark is the quality of *Bina*. We are told how *Bina* is built, learn of her qualities and of how the *Sefirot*, *GAR* of *Bina* and *ZAT* of *Bina*, connect—meaning the first three *Sefirot*—*Keter*, *Hochma*, and *Bina*. Then we learn of the seven lower *Sefirot*—*Hesed*, *Gevura*, *Tifferet*, *Netzah*, *Hod*, *Yesod*, and *Malchut*. We are also told about the three parts of *Bina*—the one that belongs to the upper one, the one that belongs to *Bina* herself, and the one that belongs to the lower ones. *Bina* is a quality that receives from above and builds herself in order to pass on downward, like a mother who receives from the father and turns what she received into something suitable for the baby.

What does "being in *Bina*" mean?

"Being in *Bina*" means receiving the upper illumination. Everything comes from the influence of the upper light, and we cannot find it alone or within ourselves. When we receive this illumination from within, we feel we are inside a special force where the ego cannot harm or deflect us from our path. We are completely protected there, as though in a bubble or a box. It is still not attainment, since we are protected inside the box like a baby in the womb, but then the womb opens and the baby emerges.

Once we are born we discover that our egos have grown tremendously. This is already the time of Babylon, and in this state, Nimrod and Abraham grow within.

Initially, Abraham is controlled by Nimrod. But when he sees that his ego is working against him and he must break free, Abraham exits Nimrod's authority and tries to establish his quality of *Hesed* as the ruler of the ego. Although he cannot currently do it, since he must disconnect himself from it, he finally escapes and turns toward the land of Canaan.

What did the tower of Babylon stand for then? And is it different now?

The tower of Babel is the ego that appears in us, smothering us and not allowing us to live. On the one hand there is Nimrod, who wants to grow as high as the sky; on the other hand there is Abraham, who sees that this goal is impossible.

In that state, they part ways. The majority of the qualities follow the ego, with Nimrod. The qualities that can be cut off from the temptation that lies in the tower of Babel—and be corrected by Abraham—are those that we must begin to correct. These qualities (Abraham's) join our journey toward the land of Canaan, in the partial correction of the soul.

Today, nearly 4,000 years later, we—the "descendants of Abraham" and the "descendents of Nimrod"—are reassembling to create a joint connection. We have built the Tower of Babel once again—our global financial and economic empire. While on the one hand everything is falling apart, on the other, we, the "descendants of Abraham," are trying to do something to correct it. However, so far no one is listening.

Today we have no choice because we are past the whole process that *The Book of Zohar* details. Now we must complete the correction so Abraham can govern Babylon, the ego.

Today the world's powers do not think about changing man. They focus on changing the economic and financial systems to satisfy the ego even more. They do not think beyond it, not even as it was at the time of Noah—entering a bubble of mutual bestowal and avoiding contact with the ego.

They do not think of ceasing the wars and competition because their only interest is to profit from it. To date, none of the world's powers are ready to listen, since the financial system is a projection of our egotistical connections, hence all the crises along the way. All we can do is learn a great deal from it.

The current crisis is the last one because it describes the totality of the egotistical connections between us, which are about to break down. The message of unity can be circulated when many people talk about the crisis and its cause. It is possible that this period will end well, but it is also possible that it will decline into a war; it depends on the people on Abraham's side.

So we are the "addition" to the tower of Babel?

We belong to Abraham's group, the one that left Babylon and moved with Abraham to the land of Canaan. The others, the egoists, belong to the group that came from Nimrod, from Babylon. We must go through this period of the last recognition of evil, which is the war of *Gog uMagog*, after which we will achieve the final correction of the common soul.

Does the confusion of the languages mark the collapse of the financial system?

The confusion of the languages has been here since Babylon and has lasted until today. It arose because the singular, great ego shattered into myriad pieces to all its inclinations, and each part leaned and pulled to itself. The external manifestation of this is the confusion of the languages.

From *The Zohar*: And the Lord Smelled the Sweet Savor

"After the flood, 'I will not again,' since now the revelation of the evil has been completed, for I no longer need to add fire to disclose the *Din* (judgment), for the evil has been revealed sufficiently. 'For the inclination in a man's heart is evil from his youth,' and he must not be scolded, and all of the Creator's punishments are but corrections."

Zohar for All, Noah, item 243

"And all of the Creator's punishments are but corrections." If we truly relate to life this way and accept that everything happens for the purpose of correction, we should only know how to take part, how to make ourselves part of this flow, even if just a little, in order to experience a spiritual life filled with abundance.

Terms

Noah

"Noah was a righteous man, perfect in his generations," meaning that quality of bestowal that is now appearing in a person. Noah is righteous, from the right side, *Hesed*, in relation to that flood, in relation to those egotistical desires.

Flood

On the one hand, the flood is water. On the other hand, it is water with the force of *Gevura*, the power of fire, the destructive egotistical power. It is an incorrect connection between left and right, where the left, the ego, dominates the right.

The Ark

The "ark" is the quality of *Bina*, bestowal, *Hassadim* (mercy). It is a mother who tends to anyone who joins her and is under her influence.

Forty Days and Forty Nights

This period marks the difference between *Malchut* and *Bina*. *Bina* is called "blocked *Mem*" (final *Mem* in Hebrew). *Mem* is forty in *Gematria* (numeric values given to each letter in the Hebrew alphabet). The ascent from the quality of reception into the quality of bestowal, from *Malchut* to *Bina*, means ascending to the degree of forty.

The Crow

The "crow" is the part of the left that requires correction, compared to the "dove," which is from the right. Therefore, when the dove governs instead of the crow, when it returns with an olive leaf, it is clear that the correction has been completed and the ego is entirely under the domination of bestowal.

An Olive Leaf

The olive is used for many things, such as oil for lamps. Oil itself is one of the foundations of life. It is light of *Hochma* that can be inside the light of *Hassadim*, when we have entered a state that allows us to keep developing. Our development takes place through the light of *Hochma*, although the correction is done by the light of *Hassadim*. These are always two opposing forces.

Rainbow

The rainbow marks the covenant. If I make a covenant with you, it is not because we enjoy being together, because in that state there is no need to sign anything. Rather, it is a guarantee for tomorrow. We fear or anticipate that our relationship may deteriorate; therefore, by fore-signing we are forced to maintain good and proper relations.

In Hebrew, a rainbow is called "an arch in the cloud." The cloud does not symbolize a good situation, but the arch, the connection between us that is over the cloud, ties us in a way that allows us to continue. We need that covenant, which is an everlasting pledge.

The Tower of Babel

This is the gigantic ego that intensified during the time of Nimrod. The ego is constantly growing: it appears in the form of evil waters, waters in *Gevurot* at the time of Noah, then the Tower of Babel, and then Pharaoh, the Romans and the Greeks. The ego constantly grows and wears different facades.

VaYera

(The Lord Appeared)

(Genesis, 18:1-22:24)

Portion Summary

The portion, *VaYera* (The Lord Appeared), begins with the story of the three angels who came to Abraham and told Sarah she would have a son. Sarah laughed because she thought she was too old to bear children. Yet, she did have a son, whose name was *Ytzhak* (Isaac), named after her *Tzhok* (laughter).

The angels continued on their way to destroy the cities of Sodom and Gomorrah, as many sins were being committed there. Lot and his family were allowed to escape, but Lot's wife did not obey the angels' orders. She turned around to look and became a pillar of salt. Lot and his two daughters made it to a cave. Lot's daughters were certain that they were the only survivors in the world, so they tricked their father into having children with them.

Later in the portion, following Sarah's request, Abraham expelled Hagar and Ishmael to the desert; the Creator commanded Abraham to sacrifice his son, Isaac, and in the last moment, an angel stopped the execution. Abraham took a ram that he found caught in a thicket and offered it to the Creator instead of his son.

Commentary

In "A Preface to the Book of Zohar," one of Baal HaSulam's introductions to *The Book of Zohar*, he offers a special explanation of our perception of reality. The explanation details how we perceive the reality we live in, and how we depict the place where we are now as an image of emotions portrayed as solid, as gas, and as liquid.

The Zohar and the wisdom of Kabbalah explain that we perceive reality by reacting to something outside of us, which we do not know, and which we turn into various colors and materials. However, we need to acquire additional senses and rise to a higher perception of reality, above our senses. This is how we will discover the upper world.

The Book of Zohar speaks to us in the "language of the branches," using the terms of our world. It tells us how we can obtain and be impressed with the new form, which is higher than our world. Sometimes our concepts seem real to us, such as a "pillar of salt," the upheaval of Sodom and Gomorrah, or the story of the three angels, since "a verse does not extend the literal" (*Masechet Yevamot*, 24a). Yet, we should strive to see these concepts as relationships between us in the common soul.

The events of the portion are not merely historic tales; they are sources that deal with the connections between us. The role of these sources is to teach those who wish to advance and rise to the new perception of reality. They show how to scrutinize our desires, qualities, forces, and the connections between them. In this way, we can design from them the perception of reality that is called, "the portion, *VaYera*."

With each portion, we must rise higher until we arrive at the entrance to the land of Israel, where all our desires aim to bestow, in *Dvekut* (adhesion), so we may begin the actual work. The Torah reveals the light that reforms, so we may advance from receiving the Torah to entering the land of Israel—a state where we can work with the entire substance of Creation with all our desires in the proper way. The word, *Eretz* (land), comes from the word, *Ratzon* (desire), and the word, *Ysrael* (Israel), comes from the words *Yashar El* (straight to God).

The three angels are three forces that exist within us: right, left, and middle, by which we advance. There is the Abraham within us, the right line. Abraham has the *Klipa* (shell/peel) of the right, Hagar and Ishmael, and the *Klipa* of the left, Isaac and Esau, with whom we attain the middle line, Jacob, at the conclusion of the process of correction.

We sort out all of our mental forces from the qualities that aim toward giving, and from the qualities that aim toward receiving. In the middle, between them, is the balanced combination of the forces: the force of *Hesed* (mercy)–right–is Abraham, and the force of *Gevura*–left–is Isaac, while the forces of the angels are Michael on the right and Gabriel on the left.

We need to sort out the depth of the desires with which we can work because we cannot work with all our desires in order to bestow. Although each *Mitzva* (commandment) along the way aims toward "Love your neighbor as yourself," we still need to sort out all our desires and see whether we can achieve the love of others with them. If we cannot, we will avoid using them until we reach the next, higher state.

This is why Abraham had to cut–some to the right and some to the left–as in the case of the strife between the herdsmen of Lot's cattle and the herdsmen of his cattle. There, it was quite clear who was to the right and who was to the left. In a state of Sodom, there is a mixture once again, which requires similar scrutiny.

On the one hand, Lot must be taken out of there. On the other hand, Lot's "female" desire must be removed. A male is the force of bestowal, while a female is the force of reception. Therefore, following the scrutiny, since it was not possible to work with Lot's desire, his wife became a pillar of salt. We use salt to add flavor to our food. Without it, our food would be tasteless, but we use it only on condition that it is lifeless. Water is a state of semi-dead, semi-living. Salt, which is essentially one mineral, is extracted from the ground when it is completely lifeless; it is neither a vegetable nor an animal.

This is the way one scrutinizes more and more degrees. In the tying of Isaac, we scrutinize how to tie up the left line and how to prevent it from using its powers to the fullest. Abraham, the force of the right, holds the left line and binds it, preventing it from being used. He does it by cutting out his own animal part, but leaving his speaking part. The rest can be sacrificed as an offering.

Another form of scrutiny is through deportation of the part of the right that cannot join the left. This manifests in the expulsion of Hagar and Ishmael. Through serious inner work, we scrutinize with which forces of the soul we can work, and advance from portion to portion, from degree to degree.

Concerning our time, the Sodom and Gomorrah issue resembles America's current approach, which says, "Let mine be mine; let yours be yours." In other words, there are democracy and freedom for the individual, and each one is to oneself. Clearly and unequivocally, we do not presently come into a connection where "I am for you and you are for me." Today, there is no emotional commitment to help or bond with others. It is just as it was in Sodom and Gomorrah.

Right from the start, we are told that if we want to advance on the path of correction of the soul, we need to change how we relate to one another. Our relationships must be oriented toward connection. "Let mine be mine; let yours be yours" is the Sodomite rule. Even if it seems to us that it is a respectable attitude, where no one messes with one's neighbors' business, that attitude contradicts the purpose of Creation, which is to be "as one man with one heart" (RASHI, Exodus, 19b), to unite into a single system. This is why today Nature is presenting us with an integral, circular system where we are all inevitably connected, the complete opposite of the Sodomite rule.

The portion, *VaYera*, teaches us what we can elicit from the quality of Sodom, even if Lot's wife, her two daughters, and Lot himself stand in our way. It does not matter that we will have to continue to correct them in relation to their sins in the cave. What matters is that right at the start of our correction we must abandon the rule, "Let mine be mine; let yours be yours."

Today, the world is in precisely the same situation. This is why we must destroy the previous relationships between us that were based on money and on the egotistical connection of give and take. Instead, we must fashion a system that is similar to the integral system currently appearing worldwide, a system where we are interdependent. Our dependence is similar to that of a family, where there are no monetary considerations, but rather emotional ones, where we draw closer to each other and become "as one man with one heart."

Today, the Sodomite rule of "Let mine be mine; let yours be yours," characterizes the fall of both communism and capitalism. Presently, we are not in a state of "Give what you can and take what you need," as the communists proclaimed. Instead, we are in a process where we must exit Sodom without destroying it altogether. Rather, we must overturn it and rebuild it from the previous discernments, since everything is created for a reason.

Even things that appear to be the worst possible can be turned into good, depending on how we use them. For example, a poisonous snake contributes its venom to produce many medicines. In fact, the snake is the symbol of medicine.

It is written in *The Book of Zohar* that when a deer wants to give birth to the soul, the serpent comes and bites her, and only then does she deliver. It is impossible to give birth to anything–whether to a new degree or to a new soul–without the serpent's bite.

Today we are in a very special situation, a tipping point, an inversion we must go through. It is similar to an inversion in childbirth, when the head of the fetus turns to a position where its head turns downward. This is how we emerge from one world to the next. That inversion symbolizes our attitude toward the world and toward each other; everything becomes inverted.

This is also the inversion of Sodom and Gomorrah, which we must go through in our relationships–from "let mine be mine; let yours be yours." If we recognize it and understand it, we will go through it easily. Otherwise, we will experience it as an affliction from the forces of Nature.

Currently, the Torah is compelling us to relate to others by the rule, "That which you hate, do not do to your neighbor" (*Masechet Shabbat*, 31a). We must be very clear about this attitude, and not mistakenly compare it to Sodomite rule, "Let mine be mine; let yours be yours."

"That which you hate, do not do to your neighbor" does not mean that you only avoid harming others. Instead, it means you must *relate* to others so that you cannot harm them, *despite* your ego and your will to receive. This attitude is called "desiring mercy." Yet, this is still not an attitude of love. Rather, it is as old Hillel said to the gentile (one who wishes to draw nearer to the truth). This is only the first part, said on one leg. In the next stage, as Rabbi Akiva says, we treat others in the manner of "Love your neighbor as yourself" (Jerusalem Talmud, *Nedarim*, Chapter 9, 30b). These are the two stages, and we must now execute at least the first one.

It is therefore clear that the world is entering the path of correction coercively, feeling the shattering, the crisis, and the problems. These are the days of the Messiah, in which a new world is being born before us.

Questions and Answers

The state of Sodom and Gomorrah, of "Let mine be mine; let yours be yours," seems better than our current situation. At least in Sodom, people did not steal from one another. Are we really in a worse situation than that of the Sodomites?

Our situation is far worse than in Sodom and Gomorrah! The western ideology of "Let mine be mine; let yours be yours," actually says, "Do not interfere with others' businesses." It stresses the privacy and freedom of the individual. This attitude is what created our truly adverse situation, so we need to get past this and move on. Our progress toward the new world is mandatory, behooved by Nature.

Do we need to feel others in order to advance to the new world?

Yes, this is the very reason why we passed through the stage of the desert. The entire forty years in the desert was a stage where we rose above our egos, trying not to be disrespectful to one another. This manifested in all the sins that the children of Israel committed in the desert. Each sin had its own correction, repeatedly and ceaselessly.

In this process, disclosing the deep, corrupt desires that the children of Israel transcended ("That which you hate, do not do to your neighbor") is the beginning of everything. This is how we must deal with those in our world. It is a very difficult task because we must rise above our desires and above our nature.

Why did the Creator command Abraham to slaughter his son?

"Slaughtering" refers to slaughtering one's approach to life, which is intended to be an enjoyment of the world. To enjoy it means to enjoy exploiting the world.

Do you mean enjoyment at the expense of others?

We always compare ourselves to others, everything that we will have to ruin inside of ourselves, and what we will build as a completely new attitude toward others.

From *The Zohar*: And God Tested Abraham

"It certainly should have said Abraham, for he needed to be included in the *Din* because previously, there was no *Din* in Abraham and he was all *Hesed*. But now water became mingled with fire, *Hesed* with *Din*. Thus far, Abraham was incomplete, and he was crowned to pass judgment and correct the *Din* in its place, since there is illumination of *Hochma* only in the left line. Hence, before Abraham was included in Isaac, left line, he was incomplete, meaning he lacked illumination of *Hochma*. And through the tying, Isaac was mingled and was thus crowned with illumination of *Hochma* and was completed. This is why it writes that in the tying, he was crowned to pass judgment, and thus the *Din* was corrected, meaning the illumination of the left in its place, when he was included in Abraham's place, in *Hesed*."

Zohar for All, *VaYera* (The Lord Appeared), item 490

It seems that there is a problem here from the perspective of Creation in relation the Creator. On the one hand, the Creator needs to create something outside of Him, a *Nivra* (creature), from the word, *Bar*, (outside) of the degree. On the other hand, to do good to the creature, the Creator must elevate it to a degree where the creature is exactly like the Creator. How, then, can these opposites merge into one in a person who is similar to the Creator, though not identical?

To do that, there is a need to create in man all the desires whose nature is opposite from that of the Creator. The 613 desires in man are then built through the 613 lights of the Torah, which are called "613 ways of the Torah." When we begin to work with those desires to receive in them in order to bestow upon the Creator, this is when we correct ourselves and receive in order to bestow, which is actual bestowal.

It follows that we must undergo extensive corrections once we rise above those desires we have refrained from using. This is the beginning of Abraham's correction in relation to Isaac. The scrutiny is done by the middle line–we recognize how much it is possible to receive from it, and how much it is not possible. In other words, as we ascend the ladder of degrees, we constantly scrutinize our use of the will to receive in order to bestow.

Yet, it is clear to us that we have desires called "Lot's wife," which we must "put on hold." Salt does not become spoiled; it can be used after a long time. This is also how we use all the discernments within us, all of our desires.

Along the way, we perform a kind of covenant: "circumcision, exposing, and the drop of blood."* We do not use the biggest desires in the soul, the foreskin, but leave them for the end of correction, when we will have the strength to use them correctly, so as to do good to others. If we use them now we will only harm others. Therefore, we make all the corrections in between, called "Lot's wife."

A "woman" is the will to receive, one's ego, poised toward the desire to bestow. It can be connected to the will to receive, called "Lot and his wife." Lot is the desire to bestow. However, the will to receive cannot work with the will to bestow, which is why a person must temporarily "freeze" the will to receive, and the desire to bestow seemingly "rides over it" until the next degree, when it wakes up.

Terms

Angel

An "angel" is a force of Nature, such as gravity or electromagnetism. An angel is one of our soul's forces. The forces of our souls contain right, left, and middle, Gabriel, Michael, Uriel, Raphael, and so on.

Laughter

"Laughter" is the connection to a higher degree to which we still cannot connect through our cognizance and understanding. We laugh at opposites when we have no time to scrutinize them at that moment.

Sodom and Gomorrah

Sodom and Gomorrah are desires expressing an attitude toward others called "Let mine be mine; let yours be yours." It is an attitude

* For a more extensive explanation, see Baal HaSulam's *Beit Shaar HaKavanot*.

that is not conducive to connecting; hence, when the next degree arrives—the beginning of our connection with others—we cannot work with others and must leave them. At the same time, we are committing to take out the desires that belong to us with us, meaning Lot. In the next degree, the upper light comes in and begins to tend to us, to our souls, inverting these desires that we will later use for further degrees.

Not Looking Back

It seems quite simple to not look back. "Let bygones be bygones," we are told, and "what happened was meant to happen" because "there is none else besides Him" (Deuteronomy, 4:35), "I am the first, and I am the last" (Isaiah, 44:6). The previous moment was not up to us and should have happened as it did. We must not regret it; we must look only forward.

A Pillar of Salt

A "pillar of salt" is a desire that we do not use. It is a desire that we put on hold until we can tend to it. This includes all the desires we cut out and seemingly throw away—Ishmael, Esau, Sodom and Gomorrah, a pillar of salt, and so forth. Every time we seemingly kill kings or nations it actually represents corrections within us. These desires all awaken, then wait to be used properly after some time, and especially toward the goal of correction.

Expulsion

"Expulsion" is a desire we do not use. We expel it, depart from using that desire.

Tying

"Tying" refers to limiting the use of the desire in a certain way so that after some time we will be able to use it. It is like the world of *Akudim* (tied), in which we first close in all the light of *Ein Sof* (infinity), or it is like the four species on *Sukkot*.

From *The Zohar*: And Behold, Three Men

"All three angels are required. One is for curing him from the circumcision, which is Raphael, who is the healer. One was to tell Sarah that she would have a son. This is Michael, since he is appointed over the right side and all the blessings and the good from the right side were given into his hands."

Zohar for All, *VaYera* (The Lord Appeared), item 54

Chayei Sarah

(The Life of Sarah)

(Genesis, 23:1-25:18)

Portion Summary

In the portion, *Chayei Sarah* (The Life of Sarah), Abraham gives a eulogy after Sarah's death at the age of 127. He buys a lot for her grave from Ephron the Hittite for four hundred shekels of silver and buries her in the Cave of Machpelah, in Hebron.

Abraham objects to Isaac marrying a woman from the Canaanites, and sends Eliezer, his servant, to Aram Naharaim to find a wife for his son. When Eliezer approaches a well, he meets Rebecca and asks her to give him water. She gives him water and offers water to his camels, as well. Eliezer takes her offer as a sign that she is the right woman for Isaac, and so he brings her to Canaan.

After the death of Sarah, Abraham marries Keturah, who bears six children, whom Abraham sends eastward. Abraham dies at the age of 175 and bequeaths all that he has to Isaac.

The end of the portion elaborates on the generations of Ishmael, and on his passing at the age of 175.

Commentary

We need to remember that the Torah describes what happens within as we reveal our souls, our innermost part. The revelation of the soul is gradual and manifests in the stories of the Torah. Abraham is the initial force with which we reveal our souls, and opens the internality to discover the upper world. He is the first force of overcoming, the force of bestowal, along with that force's female, Sarah, which is suitable for the degree of Abraham.

To know with which desires we can work, and with which we cannot, we must sort out our self-centered desires, leaving the unworkable ones for the next degrees where the desire is stronger. To scrutinize the desire called "Isaac," we must first remove the desire with which we cannot work and sort it with another female, with Hagar, from whom comes Ishmael, the *Klipa* (shell/peel) of the right.

The Isaac degree within us emerges only afterward, and is an extension of the Abraham degree. It is written about Isaac, "For in Isaac will your seed be named" (Genesis, 21:12). This means that Abraham's rise to a higher degree is named Isaac. At the Isaac degree, we should reexamine our desires and sort out with which desires we can work, and with which we cannot.

We cannot scrutinize alone, as that person (Abraham) comes from only one force, one side, from the force of *Hesed* (mercy). Abraham is still without *Gevura*, and must first acquire the degree of Isaac, the foundation of *Gevura*. This is the point where the force of Eliezer comes to our aid. Eliezer is like the upper light—scrutinizing our desires and bringing us to the degree where we can sort the next stage of correction from all of our desires. That stage is called "Rebecca."

Judging by superficial signs, such as the incident with the camels, it seems that Rebecca has the force of *Bina*. Her force is not only *Kelim* (vessels) of *Galgalta Eynaim*, but is also *Kelim* of *AHP*, vessels of reception, so she can water the camels. Thus, it is possible to keep progressing with her and to continue the correction and opening up of our souls. This is why it is said that through the force of Eliezer, Abraham could find the appropriate force of overcoming for Isaac, and that force is the force of reception, called "Rebecca." She is the one from whom the next stage, the next degree, will be built.

Following Abraham and Sarah, the next stage is Isaac and Rebecca. Isaac, too, takes Rebecca to the land of Canaan and does not leave her in Aram Naharaim.

Following Isaac, Abraham makes additional scrutinies with Keturah and the six children whom he sends to the land of the east.

Each time we scrutinize desires, the scrutiny takes place at several degrees. We can use some of the desires in order to bestow and achieve love of others. Other desires are "put on hold" and we avoid using them. Instead, we use another part of the desires in such a way that their correction will precede the actual corrections. Such are the "children of the concubines."

At the end of days, meaning these days, we can see that everything is coming back to that force called "Abraham," which is reawakening in us. We are correcting in humanity the *Kelim* that were broken off from the children of Israel and the *Kelim* from the nations of the world. Among these are the ten tribes (which also have their influence) and the children of the concubines. We will also see that throughout history, the world has been going through a process of corrections.

We begin to notice that the desires awakening for correction in our souls are but a seed that was sown in previous generations, in previous states, and which are now being corrected. We experience events in life that remind us of past states and that help us understand the novelty and the uniqueness of the current time and how we should relate to it.

The degree of Abraham lives in the desire known as "Sarah" (after whom the portion is named) and scrutinizes it. Once the

Abraham degree is sorted, the end of the degree–Abraham's death, Sarah's death, and the Cave of Machpelah–has arrived.

These are the most important elements because all our corrections until the end of correction are included in a special correction known as *Tzimtzum Bet* (second restriction). There are two restrictions over our will to receive, preventing us from using it in order to receive for ourselves, but only in order to bestow upon others.

We must live in such a manner that we will lead normal lives while seeing beyond. Today, people live differently. One or two hundred years ago, people worked and earned their living in proportion to their work. This is why few were wealthy.

However, today, in the age of technological developments, we produce and earn far more than is necessary for our sustenance. This is why so many things, such as tourism and leisure activities, are developed. We keep purchasing, wasting what we have earned on what is not necessary for sustenance.

There are two restrictions on the will to receive, which is why we are currently experiencing the shattering and ruin of our previous existence. We call it the "global financial and economic crisis." First, we need to understand that we must leave for ourselves only what is necessary for our sustenance, giving the rest to the common treasury, to the nation, to the correction of the entire world. This is how every person will achieve *Tzimtzum Bet* (second restriction).

Instead of taking for ourselves, we must strive to give to others. The current crisis will compel us to understand it and thus progress, and in this way we will go through the crisis easily, pleasantly, and quickly. If we do not wish to understand it, we will experience the transition to the next degree as painful, the same way we are beginning to feel about the current crisis, with all the problems it is causing us.

The Cave of Machpelah symbolizes the approach of connecting *Malchut* with *Bina*. The whole of *Malchut*, the entirety of the will to receive, is included in *Bina*, in the desire to bestow, which works only in this manner. *Malchut* receives from *Bina* only what it needs in order to exist and work similar to *Bina*, meaning in bestowal. This is the correction we will have to make throughout humanity–reaching the quality of the Cave of Machpelah.

Questions and Answers

What is a cave and what is the meaning of the word, *Machpelah*, from the word, *Kaful* (double)?

A cave is a hole in the earth. The word, *Eretz* (earth), comes from the word, *Ratzon* (desire). Initially, our desire is as it is written, "The inclination in a man's heart is evil from his youth" (Genesis, 8:21) because "I have created the evil inclination" (Jerusalem Talmud, *Masechet Berachot*, 27b), while the corrections are made through the spice of Torah, through the light that reforms. If we feel a corruption, an ill will, a state where each wants only for self and is careless of others, it is opposite from our initial goal–to achieve bestowal upon others. This truly buries us, so we feel compelled to correct ourselves.

The correction is done through the proper study of the wisdom of Kabbalah. With Kabbalists' guidance, we draw the light that reforms from the study, which is why the wisdom of Kabbalah is called the "Law of Light," as well as the "Internality of the Torah," and the "Torah of Truth."

Through the proper study of the wisdom of Kabbalah, a force awakens in us and begins to help sort out our desires, our internality. We remove everything from all the desires, passions, and qualities with which we are born, in order to build a soul, a *Kli* (vessel) for the sensation of the upper world.

That drop of semen exists in each of us, and we can open it, nurture it, and rear our own souls from it. The soul is the part of God above within us. However, it is buried under all the desires, thoughts, and problems we are in because of our egos.

The "Cave of Machpelah" means that we are making two major corrections in the transition from not receiving for ourselves to receiving only for the benefit of others. In other words, our entire lives must be in a state of "Love your neighbor as yourself."

This state is called *Machpelah* (multiplication) because the process of correction is done in two stages. First, we correct *Malchut*, since first we receive for ourselves only what we need in order to survive. Subsequently, we receive everything else, only in order to bestow. Essentially, this is the entire correction until we finish opening up our souls and building them. Abraham performed the first correction, which brought him to the degree of *Adam HaRishon*. This is why he is called the "Father of the Nation."

Can people who are not studying Kabbalah settle for only basic sustenance?

No, it would only spoil them because it would make them think that they are righteous and do not need to study. The problem is that we think we understand how to perform the corrections. But to correct, we need the light that reforms, which is what sorts out our desires and directs us as to what we should do.

The light is what teaches us and leads us on our way. If we do not evoke the inner force called Torah, (the instructions for what to do with ourselves) we will not know how to advance. Thus, we have no choice but to study the wisdom of Kabbalah, through which we will advance favorably. This is why it was hidden for centuries and why it is being revealed specifically now.

Will I ever actually discover these forces, Sarah, Abraham, and Eliezer?

Of course you will discover all these forces within you! The right *Nukva* (female), the most corrected, is Sarah.

What is a burial, and does it matter where we bury the desire?

We bury the desire and stop using it by elevating it to the degree of *Bina*. It is written, "These are the righteous, who in their death were called 'living'" (Babylonian Talmud, *Masechet Berachot*, 18a).

That is, when you bury a desire, you bury its intention to receive and you use the desire in order to bestow. You raise it to the degree of the Cave of Machpelah, which is a very high degree.

Even when this desire is in the ground, as in a cave, you use it to bestow. These are very big corrections because the desire is not dead, but alive. It is the intentions that die, but the desire itself never dies. Therefore, "burial" does not refer to the desires themselves, but to how we use them.

When Abraham reaches a degree where he knows how to correct all of his desires–his *Nukva*, called "Sarah"–he achieves the degree of "associating *Rachamim* (mercy) with *Din* (judgment)." In that state he enters the Cave of Machpelah. The *Machpelah* means that the level of this world ascends to the level of the next world.

It is said that Sarah lived 127 years, and that Abraham lived 175 years; what is the meaning of age?

These numbers are not referring to age but to degrees. These are degrees where we can correct our souls in this manner.

Is Abraham's degree 175?

Yes, but we do not know how to count those degrees, such as the story of Methuselah or of Adam, who lived for so many years. We also do not know what it means that Abraham purchased the cave for four hundred shekels of silver. *Kesef* (silver/money) means *Masach* (screen), and the four hundred shekels are the full amount that Abraham paid for the field he bought from Ephron.

Abraham insisted on purchasing instead of receiving; what is the meaning of purchasing? Did he purchase a desire?

"Purchasing" is expressed in payment. Abraham paid with his money and with his labor so he could acquire the will to receive so as to make it work in order to bestow. Labor is the only way to open up the will to receive and use it to attain the revelation of the upper one.

In our entire universe, we are using only one percent of our will to receive. This is why we perceive only this world. We will perceive the upper world only when we open up the will to receive by two percent, then three, and so forth up to 100 percent. The more you open the desire, the more of reality you can perceive.

There is a hidden reality, and as our desires grow from day to day and from year to year, we uncover the world and discover more phenomena and more revelations in the world. Each day we make new discoveries; science develops and so do we. However, these discoveries and developments are very narrow and quite insignificant.

We do not perceive the world itself, but only what is in our interest, since this is our nature. If we wish to acquire the great desire, we must pay with great labor. That desire contains still, vegetative, animate, and human, meaning speaking. These are four stages, and each of them is at a level of one hundred, which add up to 400 (shekels of silver). *Kesef* (silver/money) means labor.

We will have to purchase the entire desire for four hundred shekels of silver. In other words, first we need to acquire *Masachim* (screens) to work with what manifests only in order to bestow. This is why we have grown up to a certain level, to a certain satiation in our development, and have reached a crisis. We will not develop beyond that; we will stop here until we understand that we can either descend, or continue to develop ourselves in a new *Kli* toward the upper world, which is aiming entirely toward bestowal upon others.

Is there a difference in the level of ego between a person who craves power, and leaders such as the Prime Minister?

No, because that ego is on the same human level. Here, however, we are speaking of a completely different ego, one that needs to be a ruler and to understand what happens *above* this life, above life and death. This is an ego we do not understand; it is the left line, *Klipot* (shells/peels), which is actually against Godliness.

The two forces begin to manifest in us. The upper force, the Creator, appears on the right side, and the opposite force appears on the left, with you in between, containing both. This is why it is called the "Cave of Machpelah" (multiplication), since we are connecting the two forces, the good as well as the bad.

Is the will to receive eternal?

It is as eternal as the Creator; it is never cancelled. Without it, there would be no creature. The Hebrew word, *Nivra* (creature), comes from the word, *Bar* (outside), meaning outside of the degree. The desire is what separates us from the Creator. But when we use it with the intention to bestow, we resemble the Creator and achieve *Dvekut* (adhesion) with Him, which is the purpose of Creation.

Some people are said to be from the children of Keturah, and some are said to be from the children of Abraham; is there truth to these sayings?

Yes, there is. The whole world came from the Babylonians, who did not want to receive Abraham's teaching through Nimrod because they were going through corrections that made them reject it, which is a correction, too. A person who rejects something has a certain viewpoint; it goes through a certain "filter." Therefore, a person who moves from Babylon through the wars in Canaan, Egypt, and in other places, is either from the children of Keturah or from the ten tribes that have scattered throughout the world and are doing our work there, although we do not know how it is done.

If we conduct DNA tests we will see that everyone has mingled with everyone, and each of us contains a bit of everyone else. This is why now that we have reached the end of the mingling, when each of us has the ability to belong to the correction at our own levels, we are moving into a crisis that leads us to scrutinize our spiritual situation. This is the current degree of humanity.

On the one hand, it is said that everything is happening within us. On the other hand, we are living in this world, and it is what we perceive. Is there a formula by which we can act in our everyday experiences?

Yes there is. Some people feel that they are living in a movie that is being "projected" within them. They relate to the world outside of them but feel it from within. It is like watching a movie and entering it, living in it like the rest of the characters, unable to pass judgment on it.

We can even tell ourselves that it is a film being projected before us, that we are in it, and we can watch ourselves from above and see how we are dealing with everything that is happening. We can also tell that the picture we see is really unfolding within us, and that we need to react to it. This is when we ascend from the degree of the film to the degree of *understanding* the film, to understanding the one who is projecting the film within us, according to our reactions to it. In other words, it depends on how we relate to the world, and it is best to relate to it as realistically as possible.

From *The Zohar*: Four Hundred Shekels of Silver

"When Abraham entered the cave ... he saw a light there, the dust was thrown before him, and two graves were revealed to him. Then a man of his form stood up from his grave, and saw Abraham and laughed. With that, Abraham knew that he was destined to be buried there.

...Adam told him, 'The Creator hid me here, and I have been hiding since.' Until Abraham came, Adam and the world were incomplete. This is why he needed to hide himself, so the *Klipot* would not grip him. But when Abraham came to the world, he corrected him and the world, and he no longer needed to hide himself."

Zohar for All, The Life of Sarah, items 105-106

Terms

Years

The words, *Shanim* (years) or *Shanah* (year), come from the word, *Shoneh* (repeating), when we repeat the corrections but on a higher level. There is a ladder of 125 rungs. There are five worlds, with five *Partzufim* (faces) in each world, and five *Sefirot* in each *Partzuf*. 5x5x5 are the 125 rungs, or degrees where we need to repeat the corrections, each time on a more advanced step. This is how we go from stage to stage, from degree to degree, until the end of all the corrections, where we are included in the world of *Ein Sof* (infinity), in *Dvekut* (adhesion) with the upper force and in complete similarity with it.

The Cave of Machpelah

The "Cave of Machpelah" is the great *Tikkun* (correction) of *Malchut* that is included in *Bina*. This is how it can correct itself in equivalence of form with *Bina*. *Malchut* is the will to receive, and *Bina* is the desire to bestow. When *Malchut* and *Bina* equalize with one another, then we have inserted the force of *Bina* throughout the earth, the desire, down to the state called a "cave."

Burial Site

A "burial site" is a place where we bury our egos. We do not bury the will to receive, but only the *intention* to receive, the qualities that work in our favor and against others. When we bury qualities that make us feel good, such as the desire to exploit, defeat, or see others as inferior, we bury the will to receive. Thus, we do not bury the desire, but only its egotistical form that manifests in us.

Marriage

"Marriage" is a state wherein we can repeatedly take various egotistical qualities from our will to receive, correct them, and thus cover them. This is the meaning of the wedding ceremony, with the *Huppah* (wedding canopy) being the *Masach* (screen). *The Zohar* explains it very clearly in the essay, "The Night of the Bride."

From *The Zohar*: And Isaac Brought Her into the Tent

"'And he took Rebecca, and she became his wife, and he loved her.' But since all the people in the world love their wives; what is the difference for which it writes specifically of Isaac, 'And he loved her'?

The awakening of the male's love toward the *Nukva* is only from the left line, as it is written, 'Let his left hand be under my head.' And darkness–left line, night–and *Nukva* are as one, since the left always awakens the love toward the *Nukva* and grips her."

Zohar for All, The Life of Sarah, items 251-252

Intentions to bestow are masculine. If, next to the masculine side–the side that overcomes, there are strong intentions to bestow on the left hand–he takes the entire side of the woman, the will to receive, and can use it in order to bestow. This is called the "beginning of the proper *Zivug* (coupling)," "Let his left hand be under my head, and his right hand shall embrace me" (Song of Songs, 8:3). The actual *Zivug* is what we read in *Simchat Torah* (the Joy of Torah).

Toldot

(These Are the Generations)

(Genesis, 25:19-28:9)

Portion Summary

The portion, *Toldot* (These Are the Generations), begins with the wedding of Isaac and Rebecca. After twenty years of infertility, Rebecca conceives and the Creator tells her she will have two sons. The first is Esau, and the second, who is holding unto his brother's heel, is Jacob. Esau becomes a hunter and Jacob studies Torah.

The first confrontation between the twins arises over the selling of the birthright. Esau returns empty-handed from a hunt, and Jacob offers him lentil stew in return for the birthright. Esau agrees. After some time, Esau discovers that Jacob deceived him.

Later in the portion, Isaac digs two wells, both of which are taken by the Philistines. A third well remains in Jacob's hands, and he calls it "Rehovot." Finally, Avimelech and Isaac make a covenant between them.

The second confrontation between the twins happens when their father wishes to bless them. Isaac wants to bless Esau, his firstborn, and Rebecca asks Jacob to dress as Esau in order to

receive the blessing of the firstborn. When Esau discovers that Jacob received his blessing, he wants to kill him, so Rebecca sends Jacob to Haran, to her brother, Lavan.

Commentary

The drama before us is, in fact, the process of man's spiritual development. The story deals with man's most fundamental forces, although it has been turned into a novel.

The Creator created the will to receive. That desire is the entirety of the substance of Creation. It is possible to use the will to receive for one's own favor or in favor of others. In fact, all of Creation is prone to using the desire in favor of others, as it is written in the Jerusalem Talmud, "Love your neighbor as yourself; it is a great rule in the Torah" (*Masechet Nedarim*, Chapter 9, 30b). This is the law of the whole of reality, the whole of Nature.

On the one hand, we must use the will to receive and satisfy it however we can. On the other hand, the act of satisfying, in which we draw everything to ourselves, must be *for the benefit of others*. This seems contradictory, but it is vital to use the ego, the will to receive, solely in a direction that is good for everyone. We cannot understand that contradiction, which is why we cannot understand the Torah, making its meaning hidden from us.

The portion seemingly explains this contradiction by saying that although Abraham loved Ishmael, he sent him away. Isaac, who loved Esau—the will to receive, all the substance of Creation—acted similarly, though Esau is our entire nature, which we need and use in everything we do in life.

We must learn to use Esau with the aim to bestow, a state where our egos turn from evil inclination into good inclination. "Love your neighbor as yourself" means that you first act only according to the "as yourself," meaning as you love yourself. Subsequently, you turn the intention into love of others.

This inversion does not happen through actions because an act in our desire is to receive. Rather, it is done by receiving in order to bestow upon *others*. Then, all that exists in the world, all the lights and bounty traverse each and every one of us and flow to the rest of the world. In this manner, everyone is nurtured..

Today, as we are discovering how interconnected we all are, we have an opportunity to understand that only through good connections between us will we receive all the satisfactions we so crave. It will happen only when we satisfy *others*; this is when we enjoy.

This is the meaning of the birthright. The firstborn is the one on top, in the *Rosh* (head). The head must have the intention to bestow, to benefit others, to love, which is called "Jacob," who is studying Torah, which is bestowal.

The portion discusses our need for the *Kelim* (vessels) of Esau, just as on Purim we speak of the lights of Haman that we receive clothed by Mordechai, which is the end of correction. It is like the Haman Pockets, where pockets are his *Kelim*. Esau, the hunter, brings all the egotistical desire under the reign of bestowal, Jacob's Torah. This is the right way to use our egos, our will to receive.

This makes the combination of Esau and Jacob appropriate. Isaac, the older one, the bigger degree, actually loves the next degree, which is entirely as Esau, a will to receive that is surfacing. In each new degree, its strong will to receive appears first, and subsequently the correction takes place. In other words, when an "Esau" is born in you, you gradually correct it through Jacob until you can use it.

An example of the right combination is the "three wells." Two wells, right and left, are not a good combination. The third well is truly *Rehovot* (wide/broad), "For now the Lord has made room for us" (Genesis, 26:22), which enables us to draw great benefit from it.

Jacob receives all the light that comes from the higher degree, from the patriarchs, since Esau cannot receive the blessing. In fact, Esau relinquishes it because otherwise he would starve. Only through Jacob—who is operating correctly with Esau's *Kelim*, our desires—can everyone be satiated because Jacob directs all his desires toward the benefit of others.

After the stealing of the birthright, a war breaks out between Jacob and Esau because they are completely different. Finally, they find the third well, the third line, founded by both of them.

We have the same problems in our world. On the one hand, we exist in our egos. On the other hand, the emerging global, integral system compels us to be tied to one another. However, we do not know how to connect the two ends. Each of us wants everything for his or her self, but the emerging integral nature does not allow it; it "argues" that we are all connected.

Thus, we are all as was Esau, facing the emerging nature that is as Jacob. Now we must complement the two. We need to dig the third well through the upper one, Isaac, in order to resolve the crisis.

Questions and Answers

Sarah was barren for many years, and so was Rebecca. Suddenly, they became pregnant. What is the meaning of barrenness and pregnancy, and the transition between them?

In the spiritual world, birth implies the advent of a new degree. In other words, we take the part of our desires that we can aim to bestow upon others and correct them into love of others. The "offspring" of this operation is called a "son."

This is why we spend many years searching for how to sort out our egotistical desires, how to take from them only the ones on which we can build our next degree. Thus, Rebecca's barrenness for twenty years represents ten *Sefirot* of *Ohr Yashar* (Direct Light) and ten *Sefirot* of *Ohr Hozer* (Reflected Light), until they all comprise a complete structure that becomes a birth.

In the birth of a new degree, we always beget both Esau and Jacob. Jacob cannot be born without Esau because there cannot be an intention to bestow without something on which to establish it. Likewise, Esau cannot be born without Jacob because there is nothing we can do with only our egos. Thus, both have to be born together.

This is why "sin crouches at the door" (Genesis, 4:7): first, the self-centered will to receive that must grow is born, and subsequently the desire to bestow arises. Both desires, or both sons, grow. One becomes a hunter, being with animals, with nothing but egotistical vitality. The hunter works with the ego, the will to receive, and enhances it. The other desire has the aim to bestow and brings us to contemplate how to use our nature to ascend to greater achievements beyond this life, to a higher degree.

When the desires grow and reach the higher degree, a struggle unfolds between them, within us, between right and left. It is settled by means of the third well. Esau must sell his birthright to Jacob or he will starve to death and never be able to receive the upper light. Likewise, Jacob cannot do without Esau because without him he has no *Kelim* in which to receive the upper light. Thus, they need each other.

Once Esau is born—our ego, as it is written, "I have created the evil inclination"—the second one is born, Jacob, and corrects it, as it is written, "I have created for it the Torah as a spice." Both Jacob and Esau eventually achieve the complete correction. They use all of Esau's *Kelim* and all of Jacob's intentions, similar to Haman and Mordechai. In this way, everyone achieves completion in the third line, the third well.

What is the "birthright" and how can it be transferred or sold?

"Birthright" means being the leader. Who is leading, the intention or the desire? According to the Torah, the firstborn inherits everything the father has. There is no meaning to being the firstborn other than that. It may very well happen that the second or third child will succeed more because they have learned from the experiences of the elder.

Clearly, the evil inclination comes first, meaning the desire that the Creator created, as it is written, "I have created the evil inclination." Initially, we are all evil; we all emerged from the breaking of the vessels; we are all egoists. Only afterward do we correct ourselves according to our free choice.

The firstborn is always Esau. However, we see that we cannot succeed with our Esau. We can see through today's crisis that we are in an impossible situation; there is nowhere to go. It will not be long before we have nothing left in the world, not even food. We are in "search mode," in Esau's field, but we cannot find any fulfillment in it.

The wisdom of Kabbalah teaches us how to understand things before they happen. Having no other choice, we must turn to Jacob and ask him to take over, to accompany us, and to manage us, since Jacob knows the ways of the Creator. He is studying Torah and he is in the light. Jacob has revealed the Creator and knows how to achieve love of others. In a global, integral world, we have to establish such connections, too, but we do not know how to do this correctly in order to sustain ourselves. This is why, eventually, the Jacob in us steps forward and manages us, meaning he becomes the elder.

So why did Esau feel deceived and seek revenge?

Esau is the evil inclination. Until it is corrected, it will always appear as such, crueler and crueler. These are the "pangs of the Messiah," where our egos, our desires to receive, appear so we may gradually correct them.

From *The Zohar*: And the Boys Grew – for He Had a Taste for Game

"This was so even while in Rebecca's intestines; each went to his own side, since when she engaged in good deeds or when she went past a place where it is good to perform the *Mitzvot* of the Torah, Jacob would rejoice and rattle to get out. And when she went near a place of idolatry, that wicked one would rattle to get out. For this reason, when they were created and came out to the world, each of them was separated and went and was drawn to his befitting place."

Zohar for All, Toldot (These Are the Generations), item 74

Man is born wanting nothing but to devour everything in sight. Even when we are little, each of us wants everything. The more we grow and expand our fields of vision, the more we want to dominate and rule over everything. It is natural and good because the ego has to grow.

In our evolution as human beings, we grew over millennia using our Esau desire. This desire grew and drew us forward, but now the world is compelling us to keep advancing, but with our Jacob desire, not the Esau one.

We are the will to receive and we always chase pleasures, but we are still not happy. Worse yet, we are sinking into depression and anxiety.

For thousands of years we thought that we were obtaining the best, that we were building the "American Dream." Now we are discovering that we are not happy because Esau is no longer leading us. All over the world we are discovering that the Esau in us can no longer hunt anything. It did not happen on the first day when he went out into the field because the world had developed and become a successful hunter while Jacob was studying Torah.

But since the day the Kabbalists arrived, matters have changed. They were sitting quietly and engaged in nothing but connection with the upper source of the light that reforms, that corrects us, while the rest of the world continued to develop with technology, which only caused people to want everything in a never-ending race to acquire.

Today Esau is returning from the field, tired and hungry, and is asking to be fed. It will not be long before decision-makers understand the gravity of our situation and seek advice. They will seek it even in the wisdom of Kabbalah, and that is when we will work together.

It is not such a simple matter because we are talking about cunningness. Even Jacob is considered a fraud because he deceived Esau twice.

It is not actual deceit because Esau was hungry. Today, we have no choice; we have completed the Esau stage and we must begin the period when Jacob is ahead. Esau did not vanish; he is just working with Jacob's method, and it is specifically with that method that he finds fulfillment.

If you are hungry and want to fill yourself, the way is to connect to the nature that is now emerging. We are all connected; we have no choice. The world and Nature are showing themselves as mutually connected. We must work accordingly and stop our self-centeredness and biases. We need to truly begin to build ourselves differently through education, and we must explain to every person in the world how much we are all interdependent, and that only through our connections will we be able to sustain ourselves.

Why did Jacob steal the birthright?

Jacob did this because Esau could not understand; he is the evil inclination. Esau is not merely the will to receive in order to draw, to satisfy itself. Esau sees that he has no choice, that he has no more meat to eat, so he is compelled to ask for the lentil stew. His consent to eat the stew expresses the transformation of his fulfillment.

What is the meaning of the lentil stew?

It means taking pleasure in giving, in satisfying others, and then all the lights will pass through us. We will live in such a way that we receive for ourselves only what we need for ordinary life, and focus our minds and hearts on connecting to others and on satisfying everyone.

Each of us ties him or herself to another, and this is the mutual guarantee. It is a major psychological shift. If we connect in this way to one another, each of us will be filled in both body and mind. But for that, we must alter our internal structures.

It is as though we must deceive ourselves. We must choose which way we want to go. We can take the path of suffering; this will leave us hungry and empty-handed mentally and physically, and will eventually force us to change. Nature, too, will force us because everything has been set up this way for us, deliberately, so we would understand.

Alternatively, we can choose the other way—to change voluntarily. The minute we place Jacob in the lead and Esau in the back, everything will harmoniously and perfectly fall into place on every level: the economy, water, ecology, and so forth.

In the end, Esau still wants to kill Jacob. He does not calm down, but only intensifies.

It has to be this way. The ego must constantly grow within us. In the next degree we will rise to an even greater level of egotism and discover that we must fight additional wars.

In other words, we are learning a method here.

These two forces, right and left, meet at higher degrees each time. Each time, they reach a temporary agreement until the end of correction, when we are all using the singular, huge ego that the Creator created. Then, we turn it into bestowal.

Nothing has changed throughout history; the same two forces keep fighting each other.

Of course things do not change in any of us, or in all of us together. However, we must enjoy this revelation. We must want this situation to appear even more. It is truly a great delight when we know what is happening and are thus in a state of connection, searching, and implementing these two forces. Thus, one builds the middle line each time and learns to use one's nature correctly, toward connection with the world, with others. In this solution, one finds the connection with the upper force.

From *The Zohar*: The Blessings

"Blessings mean giving strength for the end of correction, as it is written, 'And go out to the field and hunt game for me,' with a

Hey (in the word "hunt" in Hebrew). This implies the correction of *Malchut de Tzimtzum Aleph*, whether in Esau's way or in Jacob's way, to perpetuate that way forever.

It is known that because of the breaking of the vessels, 320 sparks fell from holiness to the *Klipot* (shells), and that afterward the Emanator corrected some of them. And because of the sin of the Tree of Knowledge, they fell into the *Klipot* once more, and our whole work in Torah and *Mitzvot* is to take those 320 sparks out of the *Klipot* and bring them back to holiness. They are the MAN that we raise."

Zohar for All, *Toldot* (These Are the Generations), item 147

We raise MAN through the 288 sparks. We cannot correct the stony heart (32 desires), and it is corrected only at the end of correction.

What does it mean to raise *MAN*?

Raising MAN means to increase the connection between us. Only through such a request—called "prayer for many"—does the force known as "The Light that Reforms" comes from above and connects us. In this connection between us, in the new, corrected *Kli* (vessel), we discover the upper world, our spiritual, eternal life here and now.

It appears from the story that Rebecca favors Jacob, and Isaac favors Esau. Why is this so? In many families we find that fathers favor the son, and mothers favor the daughter; what is the spiritual root of this phenomenon?

The root of it is that first we reveal the evil inclination, the ego, which is called "the son," "the firstborn." In each new degree, the evil inclination grows first, and the father is happy about it because he wants his son to initially grow without the corrections, to be strong, to want to "devour" the world. This is the foundation, the will to receive that is ready for correction, although this will is not yet ready to be used. Henceforth, the correction will come from Rebecca, the mother.

It is as we learn in the upper *Partzufim* (plural of *Partzuf*), upper *Aba ve Ima* (Mother and Father) from whom emerge the forces of correction. *Ima* comes from the side of *Hesed* (mercy); hence, her favored son is Jacob, the quality of Jacob. She keeps him the way *Bina* gives birth to *ZON*. Conversely, within the father is the force of his *Hochma*, which acts against the vessels of reception. This comes from the side of Isaac, the father. The mother, the power of *Hassadim* (mercies), the force of *Bina*, corrects these *Kelim*.

We also need to keep in mind that Isaac is the left side of Abraham, who emerged as the left line, in relation to Abraham. This means that his very essence is to bring to the world the force called "Isaac," the force of our egos, to discover it, so he is certainly closer to Esau.

Terms

Barrenness

"Barrenness" is the inability to give birth to the next degree. It is possible to give birth only with the right combination of the ego and the intention to bestow upon others.

Pregnancy

"Pregnancy" is a state where we are ready to give birth to the next degree. It includes nine months of conception, as well as other things. These comprise nine *Sefirot* of *Ohr Yashar* (Direct Light) and *Malchut*, where in the tenth we deliver.

Birth

"Birth" is admission into a new degree, new bestowal. It is the ability to connect with everyone on a new level. Accordingly, we receive the revelation of Godliness on the next level.

The Right of the Blessing

"Having a right" means being cleansed. The more we can work with our egos in order to bestow, the more cleansed we will be. Our egos may be thicker, but we overcome them and become purer. Thus, one develops opposite the other.

Selling the Birthright

Knowing that our egos are unfit to be used spares us great pains. It will also bring us into the willingness to sacrifice our egos in order to work under the intention to bestow.

In other words, the evil inclination also becomes the good inclination. The difference between them is only in the question, "For whom am I working, in whose favor? Is it in my own favor, or in favor of others?" This is a psychological problem. If we are working in favor of others, we can succeed only through the influence of the environment, through special education. Then, we suddenly discover that everything has opened up before us; the channels of bounty have opened and the world fills with abundance.

Lentil Stew

The "filling by the upper light" means to be filled with the intention to bestow. Esau, who cannot reach that, is willing to bow down, to be small in order to receive fulfillment from Jacob. He has no choice because he is hungry. In other words, the vessels of reception are all empty; there is no way to receive sustenance from them.

Rehovot (wide/broad)

"For now the Lord has made room for us" (Genesis, 26:22). We receive light of *Hochma* dressed in light of *Hassadim* without any limitations. This is called "light of *Hassadim* in illumination of *Hochma*." This is how we receive it until the end of correction. Afterward, the light of *Hochma* is received in full because we awaken the stony heart.

VaYetze

(And Jacob Went Out)

(Genesis, 28:10-32:3)

Portion Summary

The portion, *VaYetze* (And Jacob Went Out), begins with Jacob leaving Beersheba and heading for Haran. He stops for the night and dreams of a ladder "set up on the earth, with its top reaching to heaven; and behold the angels of God ascending and descending on it" (Genesis, 28:12). The Creator appears before him and promises him that the earth on which he is lying will be his, that he will have many sons, and that He will watch over him. The next morning, Jacob sets up a monument in that place and calls it "Beit El" (House of God).

Jacob comes to a well near Haran, where he meets Rachel and her father, Laban the Aramean. He offers to work for Laban for seven years in return for permission to marry Rachel. At the end of the seven years Laban deceives Jacob and gives him her sister, Leah, instead. He compels Jacob to work for him for seven more years, after which he gives him Rachel. Jacob marries her.

Leah has four sons from Jacob, while Rachel is barren. Rachel gives to Jacob her maidens, who give birth to four more of his sons. Leah delivers two more sons, until finally Rachel conceives and gives birth to Joseph.

Jacob asks Laban to pay him for his work and Laban gives him some of the flock, although they had a different agreement. Jacob shows the flock the troughs, and they conceive and deliver. Some of the lambs are born striped, some are speckled, and some are spotted.

Jacob feels that Laban is not treating him as before. At the same time, an angel appears before Jacob and tells him to return to the land of Israel. He leaves without notifying Laban, and Rachel steals the idols. Laban chases them in search of the idols, and catches up with them on Mount Gilead, where he rebukes him for fleeing and stealing the idols.

Finally, the men make a covenant on the mountain. Jacob is preparing to enter the land of Israel, sees angels accompanying him, and calls the place, *Mahanaim* (two camps).

COMMENTARY

Kabbalah always interprets stories as stages in a person's inner growth, according to man's purpose in this world: to discover the Creator and to achieve His degree, meaning to achieve *Dvekut* (adhesion).

Thus far, all the portions relate to man's initial point, Abraham, which is scrutinized through study, the group, connection with the teacher, and books of Kabbalah. Subsequently, we discover the next stage, Isaac, followed by Ishmael, and then by Esau.

The portion, *VaYetze* (And Jacob Went Out), speaks of Jacob, who is the middle line. Abraham is the right line, and Isaac is the left line. Jacob is special in that the middle line contains all the qualities–the good as well as the bad. In the middle line, the evil inclination and the good inclination merge in order to achieve the degree of the Creator, our goal.

The work in the middle line is done entirely in faith above reason, in bestowal, above the ego. This is the quality of Jacob in us, and this is how it develops. Jacob leaves Beersheba, meaning a certain place, an inner state, and heads for Haran, another stage along the way. On the way there, he must shift from state to state through the day and the night. In other words, Jacob experiences spiritual ascents and descents.

Each ascent means that we rise above our stony hearts, above the stone Jacob had placed under his head, and perform a special operation known as "sleep," which means raising MAN. Subsequently, in a dream–in connecting to our higher degree–we discover "Jacob's ladder," which is the ladder of degrees. The ladder consists of 125 degrees that we climb up to the house of God.

While we still cannot see the entire ladder, we see that it reaches to heaven. This is the discovery of the beginning of the way, obtained in the middle line. This is why the Creator appears before Jacob and tells him that He is giving him an *Eretz* (land), meaning *Ratzon* (desire), with which he will now begin to work.

In other words, the whole of the desire will be sanctified, work in order to bestow, approach the Creator, and Jacob is guaranteed that he will achieve it. This is why Jacob sets up a monument in that place at the foot of the ladder, and determines that this is the house of God (Beit El). Henceforth, he ascends directly to the purpose of Creation.

As always, when we begin to work with the desire, we begin to change. On the one hand, more of the evil inclination appears. On the other hand, we correct it through the good inclination.

An empty desire is called a "pit." When it is full, it is called a "well." We see in stories in the Torah that special states of ascent from one state to another take place next to wells. This happens with Abraham, Isaac, Eliezer, Moses, and Zipporah.

From *The Zohar*: And He Looked, and Behold a Well in the Field

"When Jacob sat by the well and saw that the waters were rising toward him, he knew that his wife would come there. It is the same with Moses: when he sat by the well and saw the waters rising toward him, he knew that his wife would come there. And so it was: Jacob's wife had come there, as it is written, 'While he was speaking with them, Rachel came with her father's sheep. ... And it came to pass, when Jacob saw...'

"And so it was with Moses, as it is written, 'And the shepherds came and drove them away,' and his wife, Zipporah, came there, since the well caused them that. The well is the upper *Nukva*. And as they met in the upper *Nukva*, they met with the *Nukva* in this world."

Zohar for All, *VaYetze* (And Jacob Went Out), item 95

The Zohar puts a special emphasis on the parallels between Jacob and Moses because here, an extension of the middle line has been built. In the previous wells that our fathers dug, they were still in the right or left lines. Here, however, they are in the middle line.

According to the wisdom of Kabbalah, Jacob's arrival at Laban's (in Hebrew, *Lavan* means white) indicates the upper whiteness, a very powerful light, the light of *Ein Sof* (infinity). Although it is written that Laban was wicked, this was because he appeared opposite the whole of the will to receive before it was corrected. This is why he is called "wicked."

Obviously, Laban is very interested in Jacob. He agrees, and he is very pleased because it is actually the governance of the Creator appearing from above, both opposite the good inclination and opposite the evil inclination. This governance acts in everyone.

Laban, the upper light, the governance opposite the whole of the desire that the Creator created, wishes for the entire desire to be corrected in us, not merely the small part known as Rachel, the small *Nukva* (female), but also Leah, the big *Nukva*. This is why Laban immediately goes for the entire desire, opposite his upper whiteness. This is the desire for which he seeks correction.

This is why he deceives; it is the governance of the Creator. This is how He tricks us each and every time, manipulating us, and we understand that this is precisely how we are straightened out: through ostensible deceits. The "deceit" is because we ourselves are twisted.

The result is that we are compelled to take whatever is available, understanding that even if this is not the beloved *Nukva*, we must still take it and rise to it, despite the difficulty and the mismatch with our own degrees.

Questions and Answers

Is *Nukva* a deficiency, a big desire?

Yes, *Nukva* is a deficiency. It is written* that a man's wife is as his own body. The body is called a *Nukva*, the desire (in the soul) with which we work.

In the story about the striped, speckled, and spotted, it seems that Jacob knew how to set up the genetic process. The work here is in three lines–striped, speckled, and spotted–which are the three worlds.

"Striped" refers to the world of *Adam Kadmon*, the highest world, where Laban is most dominant. Then comes "Speckled" (world of *Nekudim*), where the breaking took place. This is where the black dots over the white background come from. It is specifically through these that we receive the revelation. The "Spotted" world is that of *Atzilut*, opposite Adam's soul. Through it, we correct ourselves and discover the entire Godliness.

Jacob, the middle line, set up his work in such a way that the evil inclination and the good inclination conjoin, meaning the

* Babylonian Talmud, *Masechet Bechorot*, 35b

intention to bestow merges with the egotistical desire to receive. Jacob can work on the stone, on the stony heart; he can connect within him all three worlds–striped, speckled, and spotted. Through this work in the middle line, we truly ascend to Beit El, the house of God.

It is clear that in this manner, Rachel cannot bear children due to lack of *Hassadim*, the lack of clothing for the light of *Hochma*. The light of *Hochma* cannot reach the small *Nukva*, only the big one, Leah. Yet, we can still advance. Delivering more and more *Kelim* (vessels) on the current degree, we correct our will to receive for the next degrees, called our "sons."

Thus, Jacob has four sons from Leah, then more sons from Rachel's maidens, and finally Rachel gives him Joseph.

When Jacob asks for the pay he deserves, he wants to receive the upper light in order to bestow into his *Kelim*, but Laban insists that everything is his own. Indeed, the entire will to receive that was created, was created opposite the great upper light, which is Laban. Jacob is still not ready for it because he is still called "little Jacob"; thus, he must fight and ascend many degrees more before he becomes great and merits the name, "Israel."

Therefore, it is inevitable that Jacob and Laban will part. Jacob seemingly escapes from Laban, and Rachel steals the idols because they are her powers, her *Kelim*, which will have to be corrected.

What is the meaning of Rachel's theft?

In spirituality, "stealing" means receiving what does not belong to us (in relation to our current state), but for which we will pay later. We cannot receive what we do not deserve. There is no bias in spirituality; everything works according to the rule, "They borrowed from Me and I collect" (Babylonian Talmud, *Masechet Beitza*, 15b). In other words, we can receive now and pay later because we cannot do it with our current strength. This is how we grow.

Children deserve to receive everything from the family, although they do not bring in any income. In the next degree, when the children become parents, they will repay.

Jacob flees and Laban catches up with him near Mount Gilead, where they eventually make a covenant. Along the way, Jacob follows the middle line, which is seemingly inconvenient for Laban because he wants disclosure in all the *Kelim.* However, it is clear that the disclosure must be limited, in small portions. This is why there was a conflict between Jacob and Laban, and why they made the covenant. Man and the upper force form a special system in which we gradually advance until we achieve congruence with the upper force.

Who are the angels who appear in the portion when they ascend and descend on the ladder, and when they accompany Jacob?

"Angels" are forces in us on the way toward the revelation of the Creator in the corrected *Kelim*, according to the Law of Equivalence of Form. We constantly acquire new forces over the will to receive, according to the ego, until we are corrected into aiming to bestow, moving from hate to love.

The way to reach the Creator is through "Love your neighbor as yourself." This is the great rule; it is our entire correction–the love of others. When we advance on this path and constantly ascend, we have assisting forces. On the Eve of the Sabbath we say (as written in the Sabbath service text), "Come in peace, angels of peace, angels of the upper one." This symbolizes the end of correction.

Is it a force from within or are these forces that the Creator operates?

These are forces that the Creator operates, which is why they are called "angels." Angels are as the still, vegetative, and animate in this world that help us sustain ourselves. An angel might be a horse or a donkey, forces that accompany us and help us carry out tasks, but which are managed by the human degree in us.

When a person finds an angel, is it a discovery of the force that operates on the person?

It is a discovery of forces by which to continue rising from degree to degree.

The Creator seems to always appear in dreams. What is a dream?

A "dream" is a higher degree to which we currently cannot rise. However, we can connect to it by annulling our *Kelim*: our minds, our brains, and our emotions. It is as though we enter a state of *Katnut* (smallness/infancy), usually lying down, in order to achieve a higher degree.

When we put a stone under our heads, we thus cancel all our perceptions and desires, and walk into a dream. That is, we enter a state of *Katnut* specifically in order to obtain a higher degree, since everything we have acquired in the previous degree is unfit for the higher degree.

In spirituality there is a gap between degrees. Each higher degree is the complete opposite of its predecessor. This is why there is the concept of going through the night, through a dream, and struggling with the angels, particularly with Esau's angel. Each time, we must overcome the ego and sort out with what we should continue to the next degree, and what we should refrain from using in the meantime.

We can see many connections here to the upper degree: a dream is a connection; the stolen idols are a loan for the next degree; Laban is a degree that is still unattainable. Is everything a type of connection here?

The connection happens specifically now, when Jacob wants to enter the land of Israel, when *Malchut* connects with *Bina*, when the will to receive connects with the intention to bestow, when such a great correction unfolds in the desire. It is therefore clear why he calls the place *Mahanaim* (two camps), a place where the Creator is already present. It is the actual beginning of the ladder, which one reaches through the "angels of the upper one."

From *The Zohar*: And Behold a Ladder Was Set On the Earth

"A ladder implies that he saw that his sons were destined to receive the Torah on Mount Sinai, since *Sulam* (Ladder) is Sinai because Mount Sinai is, as it is written, 'Set on the earth with its top,' its merit, 'Reaching to heaven.' All the *Merkavot* (structures/chariots) and the camps of high angels were descending there along with the Creator when He gave them the Torah, as it is written, 'And behold the angels of God ascending and descending on it.'"

Zohar for All, *VaYetze* (And Jacob Went Out), item 70

We climb up the ladder of degrees only by using the ego, the will to receive, the hatred, Mount Sinai. The ladder is built according to the exact same principle as that of the Tower of Babel. It is the whole of the ego that the Creator created because "I have created the evil inclination." When we correct it, we rise above it through the "spice of Torah," using all of the Torah, all the light, Laban, meaning the upper whiteness. We use these to correct ourselves until we reach Heaven, a state where our entire will to receive is as bestowal, love.

Does this portion relate to what is happening in the world today? Are we, too, facing a degree we do not understand?

Today, all of us throughout the world must understand that first and foremost, we are connected; there is no way out of it. Because we are connected, we must understand that it is impossible to keep using only the left line, the egotistical line by which we have been growing thus far, and by which the entire world has been progressing. Rather, now we must also find the right line within us and build the middle line out of the two. This is why the situation we are in right now is akin to standing at the foot of the ladder.

Compulsion, on the one hand, and the dissemination of the wisdom of Kabbalah, on the other hand, will ultimately bring us to a state where we will feel that we have two angels, one on the right, and one on the left. This is when we will ask, "Come in peace, angels of peace." We will ask them to come, make peace, and put some order between us, as well as turn the egotistical qualities in each of us into qualities of bestowal. Thus, we will be able to connect to one another through those angels. All the corrections are from above. When they arrive, our desire becomes the house of God, Beit El.

According to the story in the portion, it seems that things were easier in the past. There were only Jacob and his father. Today, there are many people and it is very difficult to communicate.

The Torah seems to present nothing but a story, but it is one we must actualize in our world. The Torah narrates it as an allegory, and we need to know how to use it.

Do we have a place where we can act?

Today the whole world is one big Esau. To counter this, we must "extract" those people who engage in the interior part of the Torah, who are from the right side. It is said about them, "For you are the least of all the nations" (Deuteronomy, 7:7). However, they are the ones with the method.

Those from the left should also be extracted, and from the two of them together, the middle line needs to be built, "For they shall all know Me from the least of them unto the greatest of them" (Jeremiah, 31:33). Each of us, and the entire world must rise up to Beit El.

We see that there is another falsehood here. How can a Kabbalist know for certain that we are not being fooled again, being tricked into the next degree? Or is this how it should be?

Why not? Jacob places his entire reason as a stone under his head and wants to climb up a ladder in a dream. He cannot climb up the ladder except in his dream.

Does this mean that otherwise the ego will not let it happen?

We dedicate ourselves to this ascent; it is how we will rise to the upper degree; otherwise, we will not be able to leave the previous one. It always happens under the force of bestowal from above, from the force of reception known as "faith above reason."

When we study, it sometimes feels as if we truly are completely operated, but it is very difficult to feel this in our everyday lives.

This is why we have a means called a "group," where we learn how to nullify ourselves before others in the group, before love of friends, love of others. In this manner, we learn to leave our minds and hearts, and to connect with the others "as one man with one heart," literally in one desire, until we cannot tell our own from that of others. We simply become one with everyone.

Can that state exist in a family or between spouses?

It can, provided that the whole world is drawn toward it. We learn how to act this way in a group because toward the group, we can measure this state. We can advance with people with whom we study and work in mutual spiritual work. When everyone in the group strives for it, each member acquires all the powers that exist in the group and can ascend. Any other way is impossible.

Terms

Jacob's Ladder

"Jacob's Ladder" is the middle line by which one should walk; it is the golden path. This is the line in which one connects all of one's elements, the good and the bad.

In fact, nothing is bad. If we know how to use the bad correctly, we turn it into good and helpful. This is why Jacob's Ladder is our desires, which are initially the evil inclination, as it is written, "I have created the evil inclination." However, if we connect these desires to "I have created for it the Torah as a spice," this combination creates the middle line.

On the one hand, we constantly correct worse and worse desires, since "one who is greater than his friend, his desire is greater than him"(*Masechet Sukkah*, 52a). The more we advance, the more we discover how evil we are. A greater force comes to us, the force of the light that we discover, which we must expose and with which we correct ourselves. When the two connect in the degrees, we grow "richer," both from the desire and from the light that corrects the desire.

Thus, the sum total of one's soul grows (in the connection between them), and in it, the Creator increasingly appears. This is how we attain the middle line, until we actually reach Beit El.

Love

"Love" means that instead of my own desire to enjoy, I take others' desires and satisfy them. Love means using all my capabilities to satisfy others. Love is self-annulment; I have no desires of my own, nor anything that I want to do for myself. I am only for others.

When we connect with each other in this manner of love, we acquire all the souls, all the other desires, which then become our own. When we satisfy them, we obtain infinity (*Ein Sof*).

Seven Years

"Seven years" means seven degrees: there are six degrees of *Zeir Anpin*, called "the Holy One, blessed be He," and the seventh is *Malchut*. Together they are seven degrees that must achieve unity. Seven is always a complete number. There is also the number ten, which is *Gadlut* (adulthood), but usually, the structure consists of seven.

Reward

In our world, "reward" means that I satisfy myself. In spirituality, "reward" means that I have an opportunity to satisfy others.

From *The Zohar*: His Thought Was of Rachel

"If He set His heart upon man, He will gather his spirit and his breath unto Himself." The will and the thought draw the extension and do the deed with everything that is needed. This is why in prayer, a desire and a thought to aim in are required. Similarly, in all the works of the Creator, the thought and the contemplation does the deed and draw extensions to all that is needed."

Zohar for All, *VaYetze* (And Jacob Went Out), item 189

We cannot avoid thoughts, falls, disappointments, and mistakes altogether. It is introspection, similar to what we do at the beginning of each year. We need to always do it, and it is good that now we are going through such a process throughout the world. Humanity is finally beginning to understand how wrong its ways have been. It is possible that from this state we will all rise to Beit El.

VaYishlach

(And Jacob Sent)

(Genesis, 32:4-36:43)

Portion Summary

In the portion, *VaYishlach* (And Jacob Sent), Jacob wants to make peace with Esau after running away from him and being with Laban for many years. Esau sends angels to Jacob, who inform him that Esau is headed toward him with four hundred men.

Jacob is alarmed by the looming encounter, and at night an angel appears before him. Jacob struggles with him and defeats him, but is hurt in his thigh sinew. The angels alert Jacob that his name has changed as of that moment from Jacob to Israel. When Esau comes, they embrace and make peace, and Jacob moves to the area of Shechem.

Later, the portion speaks of Dinah, Jacob's daughter, who is abducted by Shechem–the son of Hamor, the Hivite–who wants to marry her. Jacob's sons allow the marriage on condition that all the men in the city circumcise themselves. Once they perform the circumcision, Jacob's sons kill all the men, bring Dinah back, and loot the city.

The Creator instructs Jacob to move to Beit El, where He blesses Jacob with many descendants and the inheritance of the land. At the end of the portion, Rachel dies when she delivers her second son, Benjamin. Isaac also dies and is buried by his sons, Esau and Jacob.

COMMENTARY

This portion deals with the very deep scrutinies we make within our souls to correct ourselves from the intention to receive, from the soul's egotistical form. We need these scrutinies for the soul because it was broken in a process known as "the breaking of the vessels," the ruin.

Once we achieve the degree of Jacob, which is still a degree of *Katnut* (infancy), we discover that it is impossible to move forward. Having risen above the ego, above the will to receive, and having reached a state of *Katnut*, called *Galgalta* and *Eynaim*, we have nothing with which to advance. In order to advance, we must find within ourselves additional inclinations, additional broken *Kelim* (vessels). Upon their correction, we can rise along with them. In other words, whenever we are in a certain state, we must first descend and mingle with the negative, and only then rise to the positive.

The portion speaks of precisely that state. That is, those who reach Jacob's state and cannot advance further must reconnect with the evil inclination that is still not corrected. We head toward the Esau within despite fearing that the egotistical desire might overpower us, that perhaps we will not be able to come out of that state.

This calls for special preparation. The Torah narrates that Jacob divided everything, the women, the children, and all the people with him. In other words, we are to set our desires straight, arranging all of our qualities in preparation for the disclosure of the flaws within. Thus we can properly cope with them.

Questions and Answers

It is written that Jacob comes out with a gift, a prayer, and with war. He prepares every tactic.

True, he divides his entire household. He is told that Esau is headed toward him with four hundred men. Four hundred is a complete measure, four *Behinot* (discernments), and each *Behina* (singular of *Behinot*) is a hundred-fold its power.

On the one hand, Jacob fears such power. On the other hand, he knows he has no choice. To advance toward *Dvekut* (adhesion) with the Creator, he must go through those stages.

At night, Jacob struggles with Esau's minister and undergoes a special correction, which appears in him as a flaw in the thigh sinew. But he discovers that that flaw actually keeps him. For this reason, he receives a blessing that all the revelations he will have from the part of Esau in him–symbolizing his negative qualities–will appear only in a manner of cause and consequence, to the extent and in the form that he can correct without failing. Although additional failures await him ahead, such as with Dinah, he is guaranteed that in the end it is precisely the big ego that the Creator has created in him that will assist his progress.

Therefore, following his meeting with Esau, Jacob moves to Shechem equipped with greater forces, and is now about to rise from the degree of Jacob, which is the *Katnut* of the soul, having only vessels of bestowal, to *Gadlut* (adulthood), to Israel.

"Israel" means that all of one's desires, all the qualities that have appeared thus far, are aiming straight toward the Creator. One who aims to resemble the Creator, to cling to the Creator, and therefore performs actions in Jacob's Ladder, reaches a state called *Yashar El* (straight to God), *Ysrael* (Israel). Going in another direction, it will be as it is written, "They are all as beasts" (Psalms, 49:13). If we do not engage in correcting the soul using the wisdom of Kabbalah, we are all as the "nations of the world," as Esau, uncorrected.

Dinah, Jacob's daughter, is already connected to the next degree. This is why Shechem finds her so attractive. There is rape here and coercion, which means that vessels of bestowal come under the vessels of reception. Although she is in *Din* (judgment), as her name, Dinah, implies, a great will to receive comes over her. This is why there are only two corrections that Jacob's sons can perform: the first is the circumcision of Shechem's sons; the second is killing them. This indicates the departure of the upper light from within those *Kelim*, which renders them dead.

What does the looting of the city imply?

A "city" is a place of the will to receive in *Kelim* that compels you to detach the will to receive from the light of life. Otherwise, you will not shift into correction of the will to receive. In our world, if you kill someone it is considered a felony. In the spiritual world, when the upper force takes all the pleasures from our desires, from our *Kelim*, removing the sensation of life and vitality, and we feel as though we are dead, that sensation of death helps us achieve life. In this life, we connect to the upper light and fill ourselves with eternal pleasures in attainment of Godliness, and we feel our eternal, complete life.

The killing mentioned in the portion relates to the question of why we are killing. It is similar to a person with cancer. That person fights to kill the tumor. Therefore, it depends what type of killing we are talking about, to which discernments within us we relate. In this case, the killing of the city is in one's best interest; it is a correction.

Would it not be enough to settle for the circumcision?

No. Circumcision is when you divide your desires into good and bad. If after the circumcision there are still desires that cannot be corrected, you must detach them for the time being from the light, and this is the killing. By that you save Dinah, who must be connected to the middle line for the time being, and to Jacob, by which he ascends to Beit El (the house of God).

The Creator says to Jacob, "Now you are ready to rise to the next degree, called "Beit El." When Jacob arrives he receives the blessing, vessels of bestowal, the forces with which he can maintain the degree and achieve the revelation of spirituality on that level.

Jacob receives the blessing that the whole earth, the entire desire, will be his. That is, in the end he will gradually be corrected, and then "the whole earth is before you" (Genesis, 13:9). Thus, even if the desires are dominated by other nations, meaning they are not connected to bestowal and love of others, one can correct them into having the aim to bestow.

The end of the portion speaks of the death of Rachel and Isaac.

Both Esau and Jacob take part in Isaac's burial. This is the correction of the previous degree, which must be buried. "Burial" is the construction of the next degree atop the previous one.

Jacob and Esau are conflicting qualities. What does it mean that they embrace?

There are many levels of connection between qualities, even among conflicting qualities. "Nearing" means an embrace of the right, an embrace of the left, a kiss, a high *Zivug* (coupling), and a low *Zivug*, such as "His left is under my head, and his right shall embrace me" (Song of Songs, 2:6). In other words, there are many kinds of corrections of the evil inclination.

Jacob is willing to embrace Esau, to come in contact with him after the corrections he has undergone at night. One who goes through these corrections–in very complicated situations, at night, with Esau's minister–is ready to cope with the evil inclination, to sort it, and to correct those parts that one can now correct and rise to a higher level.

There are always exits and entrances, like Jacob, who leaves and returns to the land of Israel, who escapes Esau, has experiences, and is now strong enough to cope.

What did Jacob go through in Laban's house?

This is how we come out, degree by degree. If we are on a certain degree and need to climb up to the next spiritual degree, we must take some more of the ego, of the will to receive, and correct it into working in order to bestow. The newly corrected desire joins the soul, and thus we ascend a degree. In the degree that has now grown, we receive additional revelation of Godliness, a greater connection with Godliness, and the ascent continues until we reach the final state, where our entire soul is corrected.

Why is Jacob certain now that he will have the strength to cope with Esau?

Jacob receives a blessing from Esau's minister and connects to that force in a manner similar to the story with Laban. He receives that strength from the left and can correct it into working in order to bestow. It is called a "blessing." A blessing means that alongside the revelation of the ego comes the upper light, which helps us sort out the will to receive and the new, corrupted desire. We can then scrutinize which part of the desire can be added to the new state and which part cannot. Then, with the new addition, a person achieves a new degree.

The Creator blesses Jacob with many children. What does this mean spiritually?

"Many children" means that the Creator blesses us with correcting all of our desires, which will rise out of the big *Malchut* of *Ein Sof* (infinity), out of the entire Creation, so we may correct them into working in order to bestow. This is why he is called "Israel," *Yashar El* (straight to God). He dominates the whole of Creation in a tendency toward mutual bestowal.

From *The Zohar*: You Shall Not Plow With an Ox and an Ass

"The only desire of the degrees of impurity is to attack the holy degrees. They all lurked and attacked Jacob, who was holy, as it is written, 'and Jacob came whole.' First, the serpent bit him, as it is written, 'he touched the hollow of his thigh.' It is said about Esau's minister that he was riding a serpent. Now the *Hamor* (ass) bit him, Shechem, the son of Hamor, which is the *Klipa* of the right."

Zohar for All, *VaYishlach* (And Jacob Sent), item 146

We must always consider the negative forces as an opportunity to rise to the next degree. There is no evil in the world, not even now with all the troubles and problems that are emerging. The important thing is to know how to use these forces correctly, as the Torah teaches us. Our problem is that we are not working according to the Torah. If we acted according to the wisdom of Kabbalah, which explains how to perform these corrections, we would see the world as nothing but opportunities for better conditions.

Who makes the correction, the Creator or the surrounding light?

The surrounding light makes the correction, but the person needs to draw it. Why did we receive this instruction? (After all, Torah means instruction.) Although the light in it reforms, it follows our drawing, according to our understanding of how we need to be corrected. We must do all the acts of scrutiny, division, and sorting within ourselves and with the general reality, and then ask for the correction. Although we do not have the power of correction, we, like little children, must constantly work to understand and sort things out as they should be. This is our work.

If angels are forces, what does it mean to struggle with an angel? Is it a person fighting gravity or magnetism?

We are told–as is written in the abovementioned excerpt from *The Zohar*–that an angel comes either from the right or from the left.

There are different angels that we must deal with in a certain manner in order to add them to the middle line, called Adam (man).

The important thing is how we relate to the states, correct?

What else is needed? We are in Nature, which in *Gematria* is *Elokim* (God). The laws of Nature and the commandments of the Creator are one and the same. The Torah teaches us how to use everything within us, all the elements, and their internal, as well as external qualities.

Especially now we are in such a confused world that no one knows what to do; we have no idea what tomorrow will bring and life seems vague and threatening. If people knew what is written about life in the Torah, they would understand that we have an opportunity to rise to the next degree, to a completely different level, to the revelation of Godliness. The world is already quite close to a great and special correction.

Is the correction up to the Creator or up to us?

The correction is up to us. There is one goal before us and two ways to get there. The left way is the path of suffering. The right (side) way is the path of Torah, the path of the light that corrects. The left way means going with the rod that develops us and compels us to advance. The right way means drawing the light that reforms.

In any case, our egos, the will to receive, the evil inclination in us, must be corrected. How it will happen depends on our approach to correction, and on our understanding that everything that appears before us is only so we may correct ourselves, meaning to make us draw the light that reforms.

This brings us back to the wisdom of Kabbalah, which we must use because it is the interior of the Torah, the law of truth, the law of the light. And precisely by using it correctly, we can draw the light that reforms. This path will spare us blows because we will advance nicely and easily from degree to degree up Jacob's ladder.

From *The Zohar*: And Jacob Sent Angels

"'For He will give His angels charge over you, to keep you.' When a person arrives in the world, the evil inclination immediately comes along with him and always complains about him, as it is written, 'sin crouches at the door.' Sin crouches—this is the evil inclination. 'At the door'—the door of the womb, meaning as soon as one is born."

Zohar for All, VaYishlach (And Jacob Sent), item 1

This is how we are born, with a small, self-centered will to receive. Even after we develop, we are still little animals, as it is written, "They are all as beasts" (Psalms, 49:13). Although it appears to us that there are very wicked people in the world, this is not considered wickedness. "Wickedness" appears when a person truly wants to harm the public, to harm humanity. An ordinary person is neither good nor bad; he is inconsequential. Such a person is operated by Nature, and there is nothing that comes inherently from the person.

Today the inclination toward evil appears throughout the world because *Elokim* (God), which in *Gematria* is Nature, is showing us that the whole world is interconnected. Therefore, we, too, must be connected. Through this connection we will reach equivalence of form, *Dvekut* (adhesion) with the Creator. If we resist that connection and act to the contrary, egotistically, becoming more closed within and removed from others, this is precisely how we can become wicked.

The evil inclination first appears when the world begins to manifest itself as circular, connected, integral, and global. Yet, we have not "jumped in"; we have not united and have not connected. We are still immersed in our egos, in the evil inclination, the exact opposite of the condition that the Creator is presenting before us.

We are at the threshold of destruction, yet people will not change their views.

This is the problem. This is why the wisdom of Kabbalah is surfacing after thousands of years in concealment. The idea is that through Kabbalah, the people of Israel will understand that it has a very important role to play, being "a light for the nations" (Isaiah, 42:6), and that it must correct itself. We are merely a transition for the correction of the entire world. If we do not realize the correction in time, the whole world will demand it of the Jews without even knowing why, and hatred toward the Jews will intensify. Therefore, we should act fast.

What exactly is it that we need to correct?

We need to be a society that is conducted in mutual guarantee, living by the conditions that existed at the foot of Mount Sinai, where all were ready to unite "as one man with one heart." Thus we will become a nation, and only under that condition will we continue to exist.

For now, we truly exist by the grace of God "on probation" until we implement mutual guarantee, as mentioned in Baal HaSulam's essay, "A Speech for the Completion of *The Zohar*." But our time might run out, and we may receive no further extensions. Then we will not be able to live in the land of Israel; we will have to flee because this land will reject us once again, as it is written in the Torah, in *The Zohar*, and in many other places.*

Today we have a great opportunity when we join to demand the correction in the world. Although we do not know what it is, we, as owners of the method and being in possession of the Torah, must reveal it to everyone, but first and foremost, to ourselves. This is why we must unite, be "as one man with one heart," connect together as a nation, connect to *Yashar El*, and be "the nation of Israel." We need

* "When Israel do not engage in Torah, the left intensifies and the power of the idol worshipping nations grows. They suckle from the left, rule over Israel, and inflict upon them laws that they cannot endure. Because of that, Israel were exiled and scattered among the nations" (*Zohar for All*, *BeShalach* (When Pharaoh Sent), item 306).

to stick to the middle line and begin to rise with it toward *Dvekut* with the Creator, toward greater and greater bonding between us in "love your neighbor as yourself," meaning in brotherly love. Once we lost that love and the Temple was ruined, so we must return to that state and pull after us the rest of humanity.

So is Jacob connection, and Esau separation? And is our task to overcome separation through connection?

Precisely. These are two conflicting forces, and we need to "enthrone" the Jacob in us over the Esau in us, and do the same in our society. People need to understand the message, the essence, the purpose of this conflict, and act accordingly.

Terms

Struggle

The "struggle" is an internal one between the ego, which pulls us toward worldly pleasures such as food, sex, family, money, respect, knowledge, and power, and the purpose of life, which is to discover the upper realm, to which we need to rise, to a complete, eternal life.

Also, we need to do it now, as it is written, "You will see your world in your life" (*Masechet Berachot*, 17a). Here in our lives is where we discover the eternal life of the soul, which is why we live in two worlds. We need to come to a state where the death of the body does not feel to us as death at all. It is not as if we have lost anything of ourselves; rather, we remain because we discover that the upper degree of life is several times greater than the sensations of the physical life.

This is the goal we should achieve, and we can only achieve it through a struggle by a group and a society, and by studying the right sources. To rise above the physical, corporeal life, we must not slight it, but use it in order to rise.

Reconciliation and Peace

"Reconciliation and peace" mean that for now, we cannot cope with our evil inclination and turn it into a good inclination, using it in order to bestow. First, we have to turn the qualities that existed in us as negative–which we were using only for our own pleasure and against others–into qualities of bestowal upon others.

Is there no conflict between the two qualities?

There is no conflict. It is written that the angel of death becomes a holy angel.* We neither kill, nor slight or delete anything in ourselves. We only correct the way we use our qualities.

Israel

Ysrael (Israel) means *Yashar El* (straight to God). It means that we aim directly toward the quality of the Creator. The quality of the Creator is love and bestowal, and we constantly strive to reach it. We have several means to do that: teachers, books, groups, and friends. If we use them properly, according to the method explained in the books, the one that Abraham was the first to speak and write about, we can perform the corrections quite easily. In this way each of us–and all of us together–will become Israel. A person from Israel is each of us, and all of us together are the people (or nation) of Israel.

Circumcision

A "circumcision" is like a covenant. When we perform a correction in our will to receive, we must always put aside those desires that we still cannot correct, and deal only with those that we can add to *Bina*, to bestowal. Therefore, out of all our desires (which are divided into 620 desires), we cut off the part that is in order to

---

* *Zohar for All*, *Mishpatim* (Ordinances), item 165; *Zohar for All*, *Beresheet* (Genesis), item 440.

receive. That which exists in us for now, and which we cannot correct, is put in the dust.

This act symbolizes our inability to correct that part. However, it will be corrected at the end of correction. It is the stony heart, which must be corrected, as it is written that we should actually perform the correction on the heart.

From *The Zohar*: If You Faint in the Day of Adversity

"But one out of a thousand is the evil inclination, which is one of those 1,000 damagers, which stand at the left, because he rises up and takes permission, and subsequently descends and puts to death. Hence, if a man walks on the path of truth, that evil inclination becomes his slave, as it is written, 'Better is he that is a lowly one who has a servant.' At that time, he rises and becomes an advocate and speaks before the Creator in favor of the man."

Zohar for All, *VaYishlach* (And Jacob Sent), item 185

VaYeshev

(And Jacob Sat)

(Genesis, 37:1-40:23)

Portion Summary

In the portion, *VaYeshev* (And Jacob Sat), Jacob dwells in the land of Canaan. The protagonist of this portion is Joseph, Jacob's youngest son. Joseph was gifted with a knack for prophetic dreams. In one of them, he sees himself ruling over his brothers. He tells them about it and brings their envy against him.

His brothers lead the cattle to Shechem to graze there, and his father sends him to them. On his way he meets a man and asks him about his brothers: "I seek my brethren" (Genesis 37:16). By the time Joseph finds his brothers, they are already conspiring to kill him because of their envy. Reuben manages to prevent them from committing the murder. Instead, the brothers decide to throw Joseph into a pit, planning to sell him to the Ishmaelites. A convoy of Midianites that passes by takes Joseph with them down to Egypt.

When Joseph arrives in Egypt, he hides in the home of Pharaoh's captain of the guard, Potiphar. Potiphar's wife tries to

seduce Joseph but he refuses her. She avenges by claiming that Joseph tried to force himself on her. Joseph is thrown into the dungeon as a result.

In the pit, Joseph meets Pharaoh's two officials, the chief cupbearer and the chief baker. He discloses to them his gift for interpreting dreams. He interprets their dreams and predicts that within three weeks the chief cupbearer will be released, and the chief baker will be hanged. Joseph asks the chief cupbearer that once he is released, he will go to Pharaoh and tell him that Joseph is jailed for no reason and ask for his release.

Commentary

This portion contains a profound spiritual message. It narrates the correction of the soul, which is man's purpose in life, and the reason why the Torah was given. Initially, the evil inclination appears, as it is written, "I have created the evil inclination, I have created for it the Torah as a spice" (*Masechet Kidushin*, 30b), for "the light in it reforms it" (*Eicha*, "Introduction," Paragraph 2).

"Reforming" means returning to a state of "love your neighbor as yourself." That is, it brings us back to the quality of bestowal, to similarity with the Creator. This is what we should achieve, as it is written, "Return, Oh Israel unto the Lord your God" (Hosea 14:2).

The Torah demonstrates how the ego, the will to receive, keeps changing until it is corrected. In the example shown in this portion, we see how all our qualities connect, then separate, manifesting imbalance among them until they beget more advanced qualities that are closer to bestowal.

Jacob is the beginning of the quality of bestowal within us. Abraham, Isaac, and Jacob are the three patriarchs. Jacob is actually the senior, containing both the desire to receive and the desire to bestow within us, as we can only elicit the middle line using both. The middle line, Jacob, is still not attributed to the level of implementation in us, but to the level of decision- making.

The expression of Jacob's level of implementation is his sons, from Reuben, the eldest, to Joseph, the youngest. And precisely in this hierarchy do the qualities within us hang down. This is how the ego, in all its (still incorrect) forms, is corrected. The one who completes them is Joseph, the righteous. He gathers all the previous qualities into the quality of *Yesod* (foundation), which is called "the righteous Joseph," or "a righteous, the foundation of the world" (Proverbs 10:25).

On the one hand, Joseph is using all his previous qualities—*Keter*, *Hochma*, *Bina*, *Hesed*, *Gevura*, *Tifferet*, *Netzah*, *Hod*, and *Yesod*—but on the other hand, he needs to lead them into *Malchut*. *Malchut* is the egoistic will to receive, Pharaoh, Egypt, symbolizing the entirety of our egos.

Once we have reached a state of discovering within these qualities of bestowal—from Abraham, the quality of *Hesed*, through *Gevura*, *Tifferet*, *Netzah*, *Hod*, and through *Yesod*, who is Joseph—it is time for us to part from the fathers and belong to the will to receive. First, we need to permeate the will to receive, and then the will to receive will permeate us.

Once we are permeated with both qualities—reception and bestowal—we must see that first, the quality of bestowal enters the quality of reception and begins to correct it. Only then does it begin to remove from the quality of reception the part of the will to receive that can be corrected.

It is similar to an educator working with a band of criminals. He can take several of the more advanced members of the group who are willing to work with him, and bring them into correction. In other words, when we enter the will to receive, we are entering exile. And when exiting it, we come out with "great substance," meaning with several "felons" who desired correction and consider it redemption. Once they are corrected, they have "great substance" because they have acquired additional power in the general quality of bestowal.

Thus, through all those exiles and redemptions, we correct the entire evil inclination. This is also how we understand the whole process, how we come to know the plan of Creation, and how we become similar to the Creator. Joseph, the last of the qualities of bestowal, undergoes many processes in order to detach from the quality of bestowal and prepare to enter the quality of reception, i.e., Egypt.

This is the reason for his contention with his brothers. They hate him and reject him because they cannot understand what he wants. They do not understand how the youngest son can be the greatest. But Joseph is different from them.

Banim (sons) is three times *Yod-Hey-Vav-Hey*, in three lines. These are the twelve sons. Not only is Joseph the greatest because he is willing to connect with them, but the others also bow to him, surrender to him. As long as they do not enter *Malchut*, while he is already mingled with Egypt, they accept it because they see how that situation will later be realized in the will to receive for the purpose of correction.

It follows that we go through stages that seem to us completely incorrect and bad, just as we do not understand his brothers' conduct with Joseph. Jacob is suffering and helpless. The brothers wish to kill Joseph and lie to Jacob, but strangers save Joseph from the pit, although their intention is to sell him.

This is how we become detached from our previous qualities. We accumulate those previous qualities within the qualities of *Yesod*, the quality of Joseph, and we separate ourselves from using them. Put differently, we leave the land of Canaan and enter Egypt.

In Egypt, when we come in contact with the will to receive, when the quality of bestowal enters the will to receive, the will to receive immediately senses how much it can gain and profit from it. If it were just another form of reception, it would not matter all that much. But if we can bestow in order to receive, then we are like merchants. We calculate every manner of bestowal that we add to the will to receive by connecting to everything, and through negotiation we can gain profits from them for ourselves.

In this manner, we discover that the quality of Joseph can be very lucrative to the will to receive. One feels shrewder, more powerful, more useful, and more successful than others. One does not behave aggressively in order to receive, but rather obtains by deliberation: "I will sell you this and you will sell me that." This is a development of the ego.

That is why, when the quality of Joseph mingles with our will to receive, as Joseph mingled with Egypt, it brings great profits to those who are with him in Egypt, meaning to our self-centered forms.

In fact, the profit is so great that we develop a desire to use it in order to receive, but the human in us cannot agree to it. This is what happened when Joseph arrived at the house of Potiphar. When he arrived, it was fine, but with his wife it was past the limit. Here, the human in us sees there is a desire to exploit it in order to receive, meaning to cut us from our foundation, and this is something to which we cannot agree. When we disagree with it, we feel helpless, imprisoned, and incarcerated.

That sensation lasts a long time and grows through the alien "forces," the chief cupbearer and the chief baker, in the state of being in prison. These qualities within us are in touch with the Joseph within us. They bring us to Pharaoh and accompany us. The quality of the chief baker is destroyed because it belongs to the ego's forces of bestowal, with which Joseph understands he cannot work.

But the ego's forces of reception—the chief cupbearer, which is tantamount to wine—are the ones that awaken. The chief cupbearer does not save Joseph right away, but only after we awaken from the fall, from the descent.

In order to rise from one degree to the next, we dream. A dream is a state of losing the previous state and attaining a new one. We need to be inverted to be reborn.

We experience three states: lying down, sitting, and standing. "Lying down" is the state of dreaming. When in that state, our head, body, and legs are all on the same level, indicating that we have neither intellect nor wisdom. But it is precisely in this form that we acquire the *Kelim* (vessels) of the next degree and become inverted, just as a newborn baby emerges from its mother's womb. While in the womb, it is with its head up, but toward birth it turns upside down, and once it is out, it turns upward once again.

"Lying down" means losing all our *Mochin* (light of *Hochma*, wisdom). This is how we should transfer from one state to the next. On the one hand, we lose our previous degree, and on the other hand, we begin to acquire the next degree, which becomes a whole new world for us. This is the inner vision with which we begin to understand the meaning of "tomorrow," the next degree into which we enter.

This degree is nothing like the dreams in our world. Rather, here the Torah is telling us about the entrance to a higher level. In the dream state, we see ourselves in more advanced forms, know how to use such qualities as the chief cupbearer, the chief baker, and Pharaoh, and can advance with them because they are already formed within.

In the end, when Joseph is incarcerated because of Potiphar's wife, he discovers within him the qualities of the chief cupbearer and the chief baker. Precisely because he kills the chief baker and nurtures the quality of the chief cupbearer, he arrives at the house of Pharaoh.

Throughout the evolution of the generations there is hatred between brothers—between Cain and Abel, between Isaac and Ishmael, and between Jacob and Esau. This hatred is defined as *Klipa* (shell/peel) and *Kedusha* (sanctity/holiness). In this portion, there are twelve brothers, Jacob's sons, which are man's qualities, but there is such hatred among them that they are willing to kill the quality called "Joseph."

However, the hatred is only toward Joseph. The brothers understand one another. Each of them represents a different quality within us. We have many qualities, but no knowledge how to integrate them in the middle line. We cannot understand how to work with the various qualities together, meaning with our egos, our will to receive.

The interesting thing about Joseph is that he tells his brothers, "A person has an egoistic desire, not the qualities of bestowal that you have. That is, I can connect your qualities to the egoistic desire; I know how to do it." Therefore, each one who represents a certain quality knows that through bestowal he will achieve something, from the right or from the left—to *Hesed*, to *Gevura*, to *Tifferet*, to *Netzah*, to *Hod*, except for *Yesod*.

The entire structure of twelve brothers, twelve sons of Jacob, is that they all work above the ego, above the will to receive, bestowing in order to bestow. It is so because the middle line, Jacob, who still belongs to the head, to the degree of the patriarchs, begets all the qualities of the brothers except for that of Joseph, and they are all in bestowal, too, from below upward.

Questions and Answers

So why did Jacob understand it and even love Joseph?

Jacob loved Joseph because he was a continuation of himself; they were both in the middle line—Jacob in *Tifferet* and Joseph in *Yesod*.

What does it mean that each brother represents a certain quality?

The twelve sons of Jacob are qualities that relate to bestowal. Actually, they are eleven, because Joseph has no quality; he is a collection of those qualities.

The idea behind the quality of Joseph in us is that we can take all those qualities, merge them in different combinations, and use them with our egos. In other words, we can begin to work with the ego so it would work with those qualities and support them. In this manner, we can correct ourselves. These qualities do not understand how it is possible to steal in order to bestow.

What is a quality? Is stealing a quality? Are anger and laziness qualities?

Hesed, for instance, is the quality of bestowal. In a state of *Hesed*, a person is in *Hassadim* (mercy). Such a person gives, contributes, and does all that he or she can. This begs the question, "How can one's ego join one's *Hesed*?" A person can give, but only if it is in order to gain profits. In fact, this is how Joseph is used in Egypt, first in Potiphar's house, then with Pharaoh.

Joseph brings them the quality of *Hassadim* and they use it. Egypt becomes rich and thriving through Joseph because all the egoists understand that bestowal makes everyone benefit egoistically.

However, the qualities of bestowal themselves do not understand how it is possible to use the ego in order to support them. This is the essence of the contrast between Abraham and Isaac, who loved Ishmael because the pure quality cannot maintain its clean form and at the same time connect with *Malchut*, the will to receive.

There is a very special and complicated process here of hatred and misunderstandings between them. But Joseph can connect the qualities of bestowal to the will to receive so that, eventually, it will benefit the qualities of bestowal. The brothers—qualities of bestowal within us—do not understand how this is possible, so they object. We, too, do not understand how this is possible.

The wisdom of Kabbalah teaches us how to use the qualities of bestowal correctly in order to correct our egos. Besides Kabbalah, no one deals with it because no one has the three-line method. All religions, faiths, and methods are seemingly above the ego; we ostensibly rise above the ego as though we are not selfish, and are all in bestowal.

Does that mean that the "self" lives *between* the two lines?

Yes, but only the qualities of Joseph and Jacob. Jacob is in this quality in the middle line in the head, and Joseph is at the end of the middle line, at the entrance to *Malchut*, because he is *Yesod*. In Joseph there is contact with the house of Pharaoh from the start, and then with Pharaoh himself. This is why he is misunderstood; the brothers cannot understand what he wants to do. They think that his contact with the ego, the will to receive, will harm them.

We are the same inside, as is human society. We can see that everyone hates the wisdom of Kabbalah. No one understands what it does, nor even knows what it's for because Kabbalah deals with strange things—man's correction, the correction of the soul. It seems unreasonable to take those sublime qualities—bestowal and Godliness—and connect them to the ego, to desires to steal, rape, to the worst levels of the ego. But it is for this reason that this method is called "the wisdom of Kabbalah (Heb: reception)": it teaches how to use the worst will to receive in order to achieve love precisely through it.

No other methods can achieve man's correction, a state of "Love your neighbor as yourself." This is why everyone forgets this rule of the Torah and does not deal with it. Only the wisdom of Kabbalah corrects us. We must remember that all those who work "above" the ego, every religion and faith, do not understand how it is possible to correct man's ego, so they perform superficial gestures without diving into the ego and genuinely tending to it. They do not deal with the essence: "I have created the evil inclination; I have created for it the Torah as a spice."

In this portion, we see for the first time how difficult it is to deal with it. Henceforth, there will be a reason for all the ruins, transgressions, the problems in the desert, and all the wars. The problem that still remains is how to properly join the qualities of bestowal with the qualities of reception in us, to correct our egos.

Can we deduce from that regarding what is happening in the world today? After all, today the world is enslaved to our egos. Who is today's Joseph?

Today's Josephs are those who have the method for correcting the ego, which is appearing in the world through the upper force. In other words, it is those who study the wisdom of Kabbalah, as it is written, "I have created for it the Torah as a spice," because "the light in it reforms it." The method of the light is the wisdom of Kabbalah, and it is very difficult to explain it to the world. It is also difficult to accept that there is a way to correct the ego, the mutual hatred, the crises we are experiencing, which are the results of our egos.

Joseph was not trying to explain anything; he was simply sold into slavery, went to Egypt, and mingled there. Why do we need to explain it today?

Today this is what we need to do: explain by disseminating the wisdom of Kabbalah, which is called "the Messiah's *Shofar* (horn)." We must circulate it and spread it throughout the world because by doing so we become included in the nations of the world, as was Joseph in Egypt. In this manner we plant the seeds of bestowal that will make everyone begin to understand the reason for all the troubles until they, too, can rise.

These troubles are intensifying and there is no way to avoid them because our hanging down, our evolution, is continuing. The present state of affairs is a cause for war. The war of *Gog uMagog* stems from the same reason, as do all our wars. We are standing at a tipping point, and this portion is very pertinent and meaningful.

The focal point of the problem is unfounded hatred among brothers, and this is the state we are in today. On the one hand, it seems as though there is nothing we can do; hatred exists amongst people, as well as toward the wisdom of Kabbalah. Moreover, it is expected to intensify, as it is hard for people to understand the wisdom of Kabbalah despite all the explanations. On the other hand, this very point reveals the two opposites within us: the soul and the body. It is impossible to disconnect them, and Joseph is the point that connects them.

Terms

Joseph

Joseph is *Yesod*, a quality that includes all our good qualities, the qualities of bestowal. It is a collection of all the qualities of bestowal, and because it has nothing of its own but the collection of prior qualities, it can connect with the quality of reception.

This quality can connect within it all the qualities of bestowal at its upper part, and all the qualities of reception at its lower part. It is Joseph because it collects all the qualities within it.*

Joseph is also called "the foundation of the world," since the world truly appears in this quality, a collection of two forces–bestowal and reception–where the Creator and the creature meet.

The Striped Tunic

The striped tunic is three stripes, which are actually two, seemingly black and white, because it is made of wool, which is both black and white. However, out of the black and white emerges a middle line that does not really exist. It does not exist in the tunic, but it is the

* The name Joseph comes from the word *Osef* (collecting/gathering).

human who makes it. When wearing the striped tunic, a person becomes the middle line between the two stripes.

I Seek My Brethren

Joseph understands that without the power of all the qualities above him—his brothers—he will not be able to handle Egypt. This is why when he meets them in Egypt he says, "How good and how pleasant it is for brothers to also sit together" (Psalms, 133:1). It means that now it really does become apparent how good it is that they are mingled in Egypt, and that there is an opening for the correction of Egypt, a door for the correction of man's ego.

From *The Zohar*: And a Man Found Him

"Joseph was the upper covenant, *Yesod de* (of) ZA. As long as the covenant, which is Joseph, existed, Divinity existed as it should, peacefully in Israel. Since Joseph, the upper covenant, left the world, for he was sold into slavery, the covenant and Divinity and Israel were all exiled."

Zohar for All, *VaYeshev* (And Jacob Sat), item 104

Miketz

(At the End)

(Genesis, 41:1-44:17)

Portion Summary

The portion, *Miketz* (At the End), begins with Pharaoh's dream about seven healthy, well-fed looking cows coming up from the Nile, followed by seven meager, malnourished-looking cows. In a second dream, Pharaoh sees seven plump, wholesome-looking ears of grain, followed by seven ears that were thin and scorched. As with the cows, the thin ears eat the plump ones.

None of Pharaoh's counselors could interpret his dreams. The chief cupbearer, who was saved, remembered Joseph and his gift for deciphering dreams. He took the opportunity and asked to bring Joseph out of prison. Joseph came and solved Pharaoh's dream. He said that there would be seven years of wealth and abundance in Egypt, immediately followed by seven years of hunger, and that Pharaoh should prepare for them.

Joseph also suggested how Pharaoh should prepare for them. Pharaoh appointed Joseph in charge, second only to the king, so he would set up the warehouses.

Indeed, the seven plentiful years were followed by seven years of famine, and the entire nation turned to Joseph to relieve their hunger and help them through it. Everyone, including Jacob's sons, who were in the land of Israel, came to Egypt to avoid the hunger.

Jacob's sons came to Joseph, but they did not recognize their own brother. At first, Joseph thought they were spies. Afterward, he sent Simeon to prison and said to his brothers, "Go back, but without Simeon." Joseph hid a goblet in Benjamin's belongings and declared that if the thief who stole the goblet was caught, he would be put to death, and everyone would be punished.

The brothers returned to Jacob and told him of Joseph's request that their brother, Benjamin, should go down to Egypt with them. Initially, Jacob refused to send Benjamin back to Pharaoh because he had already lost Joseph and Simeon, but he finally agreed to let him go.

The portion describes the different predicaments that Joseph put his brothers through, causing them to separate, but the brothers reinforced their unity.

The portion ends with everyone being in Egypt. Benjamin is accused of stealing the goblet, and Joseph decides to keep him as a slave.

Commentary

These stories represent different states that we must go through as we advance in the correction of our souls. The Torah tells us how we must perform the correction.

There is no need to correct our bodies because they are part of the animal kingdom and exist as do all other animals. We must get our souls, however, out of the current state, and this portion narrates how we should approach the correction and achieve the birth of our souls.

It is written, "I have created the evil inclination; I have created for it the Torah as a spice" (*Masechet Kidushin*, 30b). In other words, our foundation is the evil inclination, our ego. When we recognize the ego and begin to work with it, we experience firsthand the entire process the Torah describes.

The previous portions dealt with the point in the heart that awakens and develops in a person. This portion deals with how that development takes place. We all come from a broken *Kli* (vessel), which must be corrected and connected. This is the correction by which we achieve the rule, "Love your neighbor as yourself; it is the great rule of the Torah,"* referring to the connection of all of us into a single *Kli*, when all the people are as one.

First, the people of Israel will achieve unity. Subsequently, they will serve as "a light for the nations" and will connect everyone to that *Kli*. Thus, "They shall all know Me from the least of them to the greatest of them" (Jeremiah 31:33). Knowing means attaining, as it is written, "And the man knew Eve, his wife" (Genesis 4:1). This is the goal we must reach, and it is achievable only through unity.

When we connect, we discover how wicked we are, how undesirable connection is to us, and how we prefer to avoid it. Who among us thinks these days about brotherly love, about "love your neighbor as yourself"? Although it is written in the Torah, although it is the great rule on which the entire Torah stands, no one engages in the actual implementation of this idea.

We have virtually forgotten that single rule, without which the whole Torah is meaningless. The portion explains how we should approach the correction stage by stage. All the *Mitzvot* (commandments) in the Torah are but internal corrections of ourselves toward achieving this principle—the great rule of the Torah, and shifting from love of man to love of God, as Baal HaSulam wrote in *Matan Torah* (the Giving of the Torah) and *The Arvut* (the Mutual Guarantee).

* "Love your neighbor as yourself. Rabbi Akiva says, 'It is a great rule in the Torah'" (Jerusalem Talmud, *Seder Nashim*, *Masechet Nedarim*, Chapter 9, p 30b).

Love of man is the *Kli* within which appears the Creator's upper light, and the revelation of the Creator to the creatures is the purpose of Creation, as it is written, "And they shall all know Me, from the least of them to the greatest of them."

Whether we want to or not, we go through states in which we descend to a state called Pharaoh. In that state, the ego appears. Pharaoh, the ego, appears precisely when we want to unite, when we understand that the purpose of Creation is to obtain connection, unity. The more we try to accomplish it between us, the more we discover Pharaoh within us. Pharaoh is a great and important degree in our progress toward attainment of the spiritual degree, the human level.

Life as we know it is on the animate level. To reach the human level, we must be connected like *Adam HaRishon* (Adam, the first man), who included the whole of humanity within him. Adam's soul divided into 600,000 souls, which then multiplied so that in each of us there is a spark of *Adam HaRishon*. The human level is the level of collecting those sparks in each of us. However, we are still on the animate level and must elevate ourselves from the animate level to the speaking level.

The portion explains that we can rise to the speaking level by recognizing Pharaoh within us, with the egoistic desire that wants only to receive and to give nothing. We approach it and come to know it precisely when we are in a state that he "feeds" us, and we are helpless against him.

It is the same in our lives today: if we leave our egos, we will have nothing to eat. If, for example, we abolish all competitiveness between us, the envy, lust, and pursuit of power and respect, the world will stop developing. Therefore, we need these forces, as it is written, "Envy, lust, and honor deliver man out of the world."* These forces deliver us from this world, and into a higher, more spiritual world.

* Mishnah, *Seder Nezikin, Masechet Avot*, Chapter 4, p 27.

We must come to know Pharaoh, our ego, in a deeper sense. We must bring ourselves to want it, although we naturally do not. That desire contradicts our natural inclination.

If we aim toward connection with people, understanding that the purpose of Creation is to achieve love and connection, we seemingly oppose it. Therefore, the ego necessarily appears in us. On the other hand, the ego understands that we must use all of our good qualities.

This situation instigates a split into two forces–the force of Jacob and the force of Pharaoh, or the force of Joseph and the force of Pharaoh. Gradually, we learn to discern between those two forces in us and understand how they complement one another, how Joseph mingles with Pharaoh, and how Pharaoh mingles with Joseph.

Joseph is "the righteous Joseph." He is *Yesod*, who collects all of our qualities of bestowal–the giving and the love. Pharaoh is the correction of all the bad, egoistic qualities. These two qualities must unite in order to complement one another, so the bad qualities become as good ones, so the evil inclination becomes as the good inclination, as it is written, "The angel of death is destined to become a holy angel."*

These processes happen within us. We notice that we are confused, like Pharaoh, who is confused by his dream. A dream is a very high indication of one's progress. It occurs when we are confused and disoriented. In the transition from state to state, we do not understand what is going on, having left the previous state, but not yet reached the recognition, the new understanding, and therefore we are confused.

When we engage in self-scrutiny, or even in more superficial research, we experience periods where we are still not in control of the new perception. At the same time, we must leave the previous perception or we will not be able to rise to the new level. This is why that state is called "a dream." Similarly, in our world, between each

* Mentioned in *The Writings of Rabash*, Vol 1, "What Is Torah and Work in the Path of the Creator?"

two days there must be night, darkness, departure of the intellect, reason. The dream comes to help us prepare to perceive what the new day holds in store for us.

Here we can see the mingling that exists between spiritual qualities, the qualities of the Creator and the qualities of the person, the creature. The qualities of the Creator, who aims only to bestow, are called "the right side." The qualities of the creature, who aims entirely to receive, are "the left side." The connection between them occurs when Jacob and his entire household go down to Egypt.

Jacob is in Egypt and mingles with the Egyptians in order to later elicit all the *Kelim* (vessels), to elicit all the power from the ego, except for the ego itself. This state is called "And afterward they shall come out with great substance" (Genesis 15:14).

The entire portion deals with the descent into that state. We may have good desires, but are still be unable to progress with them because these desires are too thin.

When we begin to study, we uncover a desire to advance and understand ourselves, to know the reality that governs us, the upper reality. On the one hand, we feel we do not have this power. On the other hand, we feel that the process we are going through is pre-installed in us, so it is inevitable that we should discover the evil inclination, Pharaoh, within us. Our good qualities are included in our egoistic qualities, and this is called "for the famine was in the land of Canaan" (Genesis 42:5). Therefore, we have no choice but to go down to Egypt.

When we do not see spirituality as a strong foundation, we become included in our will to receive. The will to receive then grows and becomes crueler and more intense, to the point that it seems as though it is about to swallow us. But when we advance in the right direction, we find that Joseph already exists within our will to receive.

Joseph is already in Egypt, and through it we become included in the ego. This is why there is always a kind of partition between the qualities of bestowal and the qualities of reception.

Joseph says to Simeon that the brothers are spies, and sends the rest of the brothers to their home land. However, they have no choice but to return to Egypt because we have no choice but to work with the ego, the will to receive, or there will not be any progress.

The ego was created against us, and if we do not invert it to work to bestow, we will not be able to enter Creation and discover the upper world.

In fact, we work only with our own qualities. This is why this wisdom is called *Hochmat HaKabbalah* (the wisdom of reception), since we receive within the vessels of reception the *Kelim* that were once cruel. We will feel the spiritual world only after we correct our *Kelim*.

As just said, the brothers returned to Joseph for the second time. However, this time Joseph gave them a *Kli*, the goblet he received from Egypt. He handed it over to the house of Jacob, thus pulling all of them back, and all the children of Israel went down to Egypt. Joseph connected to Egypt in a special way—in the quality of *Yesod* that characterized him. This quality concentrates within it all the upper qualities that enter *Malchut*—our will to receive—through it.

Joseph married the daughter of one of Pharaoh's spiritual advisors, Osnat, and had two sons, Ephraim and Menashe. This meant that with the entrance of the children of Israel to Egypt, Pharaoh began to change. It seems as though a connection was made that worked in Pharaoh's favor, since the whole world came to him, to *Malchut*—the only one who can provide nourishment. But this nourishment was actually received from the first nine *Sefirot*, not from *Malchut*.

The first nine *Sefirot* are included in *Malchut* because they first have to be included in Pharaoh, *Malchut*. We absorb these qualities as those who are acquiring good, new qualities and good behavior, and use them in order to receive. We use what we acquired for our own benefit—deceiving people, penetrating good environments and stealing wherever possible.

We must go through such a period when our good qualities are "captive." Although we use them for our own pleasure, they still gradually work on us, just as with the children of Israel in Egypt. When the children of Israel came to Egypt, they connected to Pharaoh so that afterward, when the plagues would come over Pharaoh, they would still feel that they could no longer stay with the general will to receive and work in favor of their egos, and then they would run with great substance.

The connection is between the qualities of the Creator and the qualities of the creature. The nine *Sefirot* of the Creator enter the tenth *Sefira* (singular for *Sefirot*), *Malchut*, the quality of the creature, our ego, but it does not happen instantaneously, but gradually.

Questions and Answers

In this portion, Joseph tests his brothers, separating them. They overcome it and reunite, then he separates them again. It seems that currently the world is in a similar situation: we understand that we have to connect, but we can't, due to our egos. What can we learn from this portion about the direction that the world should take?

This portion serves as a big warning sign, especially to the people of Israel. The people of Israel have to come down to Pharaoh. That is, we must go out to the world and help it rise. If we fail to do so, it will be bad because this is not the way of Torah.

We must direct all of our teaching, all the light toward disseminating the wisdom of Kabbalah throughout the world. It is called the "Messiah's horn."

It is written in *The Zohar* that only through the power of *The Book of Zohar* will the children of Israel come out of exile. However, we are still not in exile; we must first enter it. Exile is when we want to connect but do not know how to do it because something is stopping us. We search for the ego, which is stopping us, and we must find the Pharaoh within us and between us. This is why we must first connect among us as much as we can, as in "all of Israel are friends."*

We must circulate the Integral Education of "Love your neighbor as yourself" throughout the nation and explain in a scientific manner everything that Kabbalah discloses–that we must obtain unity and mutual guarantee, or our situation will be desperate. We must convey to the world the same message, too, or the whole world will come to us with demands. They will not even know why, but they will be right because it is according to the laws of Nature. This demand of the world is "the war of *Gog uMagog*," the war of the end of days.

This is why the house of Jacob goes down to Egypt, and this is what we, too, must do. We should begin with connecting among us, with feeling our inner Pharaohs, and we must begin to tend to them. We must study the Torah in such a way that it becomes a reforming light for us. In other words, we will draw light to us through our desire to unite.

When we study Torah, we aim only for connection. We do not aspire for knowledge or wit, but only for unity among us. It is the rule that the Torah requires of us: "Love your neighbor as yourself; it is the great rule of the Torah." It is the only reason why the Torah was given.

"I have created the evil inclination; I have created the Torah as a spice because the light in it reforms it." We must observe it, and today the whole world demands it of us.

Thus, we will finally arrange our nation. Our nation was founded on the unity of exiles from Babylon around Abraham. Maimonides writes that they connected based on the rule, "Love your neighbor as yourself," and that this is why they became a nation. Once we lost that principle, we stopped being a nation. Instead, we have become a collection of exiles. We are still in exile, in a kind of collection, so we must circulate these words and notify everyone as quickly as we can.

---

* Mishnah, *Shekalim*, *Ikar Tosfot Yom Tov*, Chapter 8, Mishnah 1.

If we circulate through all the nations the method for connecting everyone in mutuality, as Nature requires, as the current crisis is demanding, according to the wisdom of Kabbalah, we will see how differently everyone begins to relate to us. They will be willing to connect and to help.

What do years of abundance and years of hunger mean, and why is the number seven mentioned twice?

It is a process we must go through, in ascents and descents, once on the animate level and once on the vegetative level. It is similar to the shattering of the two Temples. In a descent from above, from the degree of Jacob, we need to descend once on the level of *Mochin* of *Haya*, and once on the level of *Mochin* of *Neshama*. It is the same as with the two Temples, the First Temple and the Second Temple, the same as the ruin that happened to us in the spiritual world, the world of *Nekudim*.

Will every person have to experience it personally?

To an extent, each and every one of us experiences this process. But when we advance together toward connection, it is not a problem; we can go through this entire process with joy.

If we disseminate the wisdom and the world hears and understands, will it still be necessary for the world to go through this process?

It is the recognition of evil. This is how we come to know our disease. Just as a physician uses diagnosis to determine a person's illness and prescribe the proper medicine, we "diagnose the evil" and rise to a higher degree. Therefore, we need not be afraid. If we all march toward mutual guarantee and unity, we will have no problems because even things that seem undesirable will work toward our attainment of the degree that has been prepared for us—*Yashar El* (straight to God), toward unity.

TERMS

Years of Abundance and Years of Hunger

"Years of abundance and years of hunger" are the ups and downs that we must go through, which divide into years. The number seven represents the *Sefirot Hesed*, *Gevura*, *Tifferet*, *Netzah*, *Hod*, *Yesod*, and *Malchut*.

These years connect *Zeir Anpin*, which contains six *Sefirot*, with *Malchut*. This connection creates a new *Kli* between the qualities of the Creator and the qualities of the creature.

The wisdom of Kabbalah refers to the six qualities as "the Holy One blessed be He." The seventh quality is the *Shechina* (Divinity), which is currently Pharaoh, also known as "Divinity in exile." After the correction, Pharaoh becomes a holy place–in order to bestow–the place of our souls, the place of connection between us.

The Sages of Egypt

The sagacity of Egypt is called "external wisdom." It maintains that you need not change within in order to obtain all the good in this life and in the spiritual life, and you can settle for the intellect. Study without changing; don't think about the correction of the heart, about your ego, that you need to change; study a couple of pages and you will be happy. This, in essence, is the wisdom of Egypt, as it is written, "there is wisdom in the nations–believe."*

Grain and Hunger

"Hunger" is a sensation of the will to receive that cannot satisfy itself. The grain matches the degree of hunger from which you are suffering. This refers to two degrees–the degree of *Mochin* of *Haya*, and the degree of *Mochin* of *Neshama*.

* "If one should tell you, 'there is wisdom in the nations, believe; there is Torah in the nations, do not believe" (Midrash Rabah, *Eicha*, Parasha 2, Paragraph 13).

Brothers

"Brothers" means connection. When the desires to receive connect in common intentions and common *Masachim* (screens), when all wish to unite in order to obtain the sublime goal, they are called "brothers." This is why there is *Malchut*, Egypt, Pharaoh, and above it the entire house of Jacob. The symbol of the house of Jacob is the twelve brethren, *HaVaYaH* (*Yod-Hey-Vav-Hey*) times three lines, four letters times three lines, which are the twelve brothers.

A Meal

The filling of the *Kli* happens when there is food and drink. As on Purim, it requires two portions. This is all the light, the flavors that spread from the *Peh* (mouth) of the *Partzuf* downward. The inner light that spreads through the *Partzuf* is called "a meal." If we do it in *Partzufim* that are integrated together, it is like the law of communicating vessels, where everyone fills up to the same level, which is called "a meal of brothers." This is why it is the only condition where the term, "When brothers also sit together" (Psalms 133:1) holds true.

From *The Zohar*: And the Men Were Afraid because They Were Brought into Joseph's House

"The good inclination needs the joy of Torah, and the evil inclination needs the joy of wine, adultery, and pride. This is why man needs to always anger it from that great day, judgment day, the day of account, when all that protects a person are the good deeds that he does in this world so they will protect him at that time."

Zohar for All, *Miketz* (At the End), item 198

VaYigash

(Judah Approached)

(Genesis, 44:18-47:27)

Portion Summary

In the portion, *VaYigash* (Judah Approached), Joseph asks his brothers to leave Benjamin, having discovered the silver goblet that he himself hid in his belongings. Judah explains to Joseph that he cannot leave Benjamin behind because he is responsible for him, and he promised his father to bring him back safely. Judah tells Joseph that they had already lost one brother, unaware that Joseph is the one managing the event behind the scenes.

Joseph decides to expose himself to his brothers. He tells them how his being sold into slavery turned out for the best, and that now he can support his family because he is in charge of all of Egypt. After the reconciliation, Joseph sends the brothers to Jacob with carts and goods, and asks Jacob to come to Egypt.

At first, Jacob cannot believe the story. But once the brothers present him with Joseph's gift, he is delighted and wants to go to Egypt to see Joseph before he dies. On the way to Egypt, Jacob stops and offers sacrifices. The Creator appears to Jacob and promises

him that his descendants will be a great nation in Egypt, and that eventually they will all return to the land of Israel.

Jacob and his sons arrive in Egypt, in the land of Goshen, where Joseph meets them. He bursts in tears when he sees his father after all those years. Joseph tells them that Pharaoh wants to meet them.

To prepare for the meeting, Joseph tells the family to say that they are shepherds and wish to live in a separate place from the Egyptians, in the land of Goshen. Joseph introduces his father and brothers to Pharaoh, who agrees that they will live in the land of Goshen.

The hunger continues and Joseph provides for everyone. The Egyptians and all the others give up their money and eventually themselves as slaves to Pharaoh.

At the end of the portion, Joseph establishes a system of taxation by which Pharaoh holds all the assets; he provides the Egyptians with seeds for their crops, and they give him one fifth of the crop.

Commentary

The portion describes both the internal process of man's development, and the general process of the correction of the world. Man and the world are one; the particular and general are equal.

This is a special portion, which is still pertinent. It deals with the spiritual force entering and correcting an ordinary person.

For the purpose of connection, a person needs both the physical force and the spiritual force, like heaven and earth. The two forces—of the Creator and of the creature—conjoin, and the human will grow out of them. This is really the purpose of our development, to connect the material substance with the human form, which is similar to the Creator.

It is not simple to make these two forces meet. Creation consists only of these two forces–the giving force, the Creator, and the receiving force, the creature, which the Creator created purposely as a replica of Himself.

The two forces have to join, so the creature becomes included in the Creator, and the Creator becomes included in the creature, where there is understanding, a connection between them. In that connection, the creature can present requests to the Creator, who understands them and bestows upon the creature through their mutual connection, through the part of the Creator that is in the creature, so the creature, too, can understand the Creator.

It is similar to relationships between people. Assume that we have no connection between us. But when we begin to tell each other about ourselves and sympathize with each other's feelings, each of us receives a part of the other. The connection between us is made through the parts we share in common.

In the material world, too, we must regulate instruments to make them work on the same wavelength, so they "understand" one another. For example, for one computer to "understand" another, there needs to be a modem with certain limitations, certain registrations, and so forth.

It is likewise with the connection between the Creator and the creature. The whole purpose of Creation is for the creature to ascend in *Dvekut* (adhesion) to the degree of the Creator. They achieve *Dvekut* according to their equivalence of form, equivalence of their qualities. In the end, the human must have the qualities of the Creator.

"The inclination in a man's heart is evil from his youth" (Genesis 8:21). We are Pharaoh; it is our nature, our "self." The first quality of the Creator that appears in us is called Abraham. This is why he is called "the father of the nation," meaning the quality of bestowal in us.

Subsequently, out of the line of Abraham, the right line, the line of *Hesed*, emerges the quality of *Gevura*, Isaac. Finally, the quality of *Tifferet*–which is Jacob–comes out.

Jacob is the beginning of the formation of the right connection between Abraham and Isaac; this is what makes him the most special of the fathers, the senior. He can combine the two forces, bestowal and reception, and arrange them within him in the middle line.

However, it is not enough. We must learn by ourselves how to implement these three lines, which come to us from above, from the Creator. The portion describes how the upper force gradually permeates us, just like water percolates into the ground to get to the place where it is dry, to Egypt.

The heart of the problem lies in Jacob's qualities, which are also in his sons. With the exclusion of Joseph, they do not understand what they must do. Joseph understands that there is a need to unite all the sons. He tells them: "You will all bow to me because I am the *Yesod*, the foundation that unites all of you." But they do not understand.

Although we contain all the qualities and begin to connect them together, we do not understand how to do it. This is why selling and buying teach us how to work with those qualities within us.

The wisdom of Kabbalah does not deal with historic events. Rather, it deals with man's correction from within. Our whole process of work is about correction. First, we absorb the quality of bestowal, love, and affinity to others. Accordingly, we draw nearer to the Creator, we change, and correct ourselves.

The portion tells us how things unfold, beginning with the selling of Joseph to Egypt. Joseph is the force of bestowal, while Egypt is our vessel of reception, the desire to receive. The desire to receive can work only as simple farmers, but Joseph is a quality that already knows how to exchange tools with others, how to sell and buy. He gives crops and receives something from the outside in return, from people who produce, such as instruments.

Through negotiation, giving and receiving, it is possible to connect, to gain wealth, and to ascend in degrees. The quality of Joseph enables it because it knows how to connect egoistic parts that cannot otherwise connect. This is what happens in the Egypt within us; this is also what happens in the physical Egypt.

We can see it throughout history. Jews who lived among the nations worked and operated in education and culture, but especially in commerce, which is a connection of all the nations. Once they developed commerce, they began to develop industry, just as it happened in Egypt, which suddenly began to thrive. Along with prosperity came a problem—the more you grow, the more you are prone to decline, to fall, to reveal the new evil.

This is where the years of abundance and the years of hunger come from. Only the force of bestowal within us can manage them. The more we advance in our correction, the more we go through the process in a good and proper manner. In this way, all the previous qualities of bestowal, the house of Jacob, move into Egypt, into the will to receive. This is enriched by them to the point that when Jacob comes with his family to Egypt, Pharaoh understands how much he gains by it.

When we begin to work with the vessels of bestowal—I help you and you help me—our egos develop. One who knows how to connect with others and exchange with them, similar to what happens within us, knows how to work with the forces of reception and bestowal together.

At first, this work is called *Lo Lishma* ("not for Her sake"), since a person is still profiting and thinks that all is going well, and therefore works with both forces. When the upper forces are included in us, we begin to discover the development of the process, which leads to the sensation of exile and the exodus from Egypt.

This happens despite the fact that, for the time being, the two forces—the force of bestowal and the force of reception—work in us in favor of the ego, and Pharaoh is gaining riches. In other words, the part of *Malchut*, the fifth part out of *Keter*, *Hochma*, *Bina*, *Zeir Anpin*, and *Malchut*, is truly being filled.

Our ego receives twenty percent of the general profit, and thus grows. It is the same for all the Egyptians, our egoistic qualities—they live and grow. The house of Jacob grows, too, multiplying by adding to itself more of the Egyptians' ego, the will to receive.

We add to the ego, growing and advancing, as preparation for the process of correction. One who studies the wisdom of Kabbalah while still in this world enjoys this world as well as the spiritual world, gaining from both. While in this world, the student comes to understand and to feel what is happening to him or her, and seemingly rises above others. Such a person gains also from the wisdom of Kabbalah, thus feeling that he or she has profited from both worlds. However, it changes after some time.

For now, however, both the house of Pharaoh and the house of Jacob are gaining riches. The profit goes to the qualities of the Creator and to the qualities of the creature; the will to receive and the desire to bestow mingle and work together. There is a great connection between them until they come across a crisis point that does not let them continue.

This is where the whole world currently stands. Until now, we have been using the force of bestowal to develop technologies, techniques, instruments, and so on. We are in a global network of industry and commerce in almost every realm. And yet, we have reached the recognition of evil—the understanding that we must be better connected in order to advance further. But our egos prevent us from connecting.

This is what the children of Israel discovered in Egypt—the point that was to push them further, to a higher level, to the land of Israel. Our world, too, will have to emerge from this crisis and into the level of the general land of Israel, for everyone.

Questions and Answers

The world is now moving into the years of hunger, yet the majority of people refuse to recognize it. Where is today's quality of Joseph, the quality that says we must collect during the good years so we have something to keep us going through the years of famine?

At the time of abundance, everything was great. Joseph was in *Malchut*, in Egypt. But when hunger begins, so does the second half of the exile in Egypt, and we are feeling the exile. This is when Joseph completes his role; he is no longer here.

The nine *Sefirot—Keter*, *Hochma*, *Bina*, *Hesed*, *Gevura*, *Tifferet*, *Netzah*, *Hod*, and *Yesod*—are the descent of abundance from above downward. Joseph is the ninth; he collects the previous eight *Sefirot* and brings them to *Malchut*. This is why he is called "Joseph" (from the Hebrew word *Osef* [collecting]). *Malchut* is our entire ego, the will to receive, the quality of the creature, us. Joseph includes all the previous qualities, the qualities of the Creator: abundance and light for all.

What does it mean that "a new king arose over Egypt, who did not know Joseph" (Exodus 1:8)?

It is the beginning of the process toward Moses. There are several stages in the process: first, the children of Israel discover that they are in Egypt. There is a difference between one's personal work and the general process in the world; they are very different.

What is happening in the world today?

The current situation in the world is that we are at a tipping point. We must understand that henceforth Pharaoh takes control, so we will experience states of hunger and states of abundance. Joseph comes and says to Pharaoh that he has no choice but to establish a new order in Egypt, where everything is under his complete control.

However, he must give them seeds and take twenty percent in taxes from them, and divide it so that Israel is poor.

In other words, our egoistic desires need to feel poor, that they have nothing other than belonging to the ego, for their mere survival, and what maintains them is the connection with Joseph. Joseph gives them seeds, sustenance, life, and receives from them the tax. This is how we, too, must feel—that only our force of connection throughout the world unites us into one and allows us to advance, live, revive our souls, and that otherwise, we are doomed.

First, we must study these things. We must go through this entire process and advance toward the revelation that we must correct ourselves, including the Pharaoh in us. We must rise above him and escape from Egypt. The whole process aims us toward escape.

The correction of Egypt entails two states: if we want to correct a certain quality in us, we must first stop working with it completely. Afterward, we can advance toward it and work with it in a new way, perhaps less than before. For example, if we are forbidden to eat salt for health reasons, we first avoid salt completely, then resume eating small amounts of it.

We must escape Egypt so we can truly and finally unite. We cannot unite while in Egypt. Within Egypt, only the children of Israel can unite, and only in a certain manner. When we are in our egos and try to build ourselves properly, to be in accord with Nature, we suddenly discover that we are building Pithom and Raamses. Everything we build is swallowed up in the ego, the will to receive, so we never gain anything. Today we are seeing how everything we have built throughout the world is under a threat of tsunamis that will leave no trace of our work, and we have no guarantee as to the future of our children and grandchildren.

Joseph gave special treatment to his family. He planned what they should say and how. This shows that he cared for them

personally. In the spiritual world, is there such a thing as being "the favored one"?

Egypt cannot exist, and the world cannot exist without the children of Israel. Likewise, we personally cannot exist without contact with the upper abundance, and we are truly about to feel it. Only by joining everyone together, including the Egyptians, meaning the entire world, will we be able to advance.

Joseph says that the children of Israel should live only outside of Egypt, in the land of Goshen. It is so because to advance, we need to separate our vessels of reception from the vessels of bestowal. Otherwise, we might find that we are working only for the ego and will never be able to come out of it.

To manage Egypt properly, the qualities of bestowal must be outside of Egypt. This is why the children of Israel, who are in the land of Goshen, outside of Egypt, work in jobs that seem undignified in the eyes of the Egyptians, such as shepherds, since with them they seemingly nurture the qualities of bestowal in the qualities of reception. The Egyptians work in such a way that all the qualities of bestowal are good to fill the qualities of reception in them, the ego. For the Jews, the work is different; their entire egos, the qualities of reception, work to develop the qualities of bestowal.

It seems as though Joseph favored his family, as though he gave them preference.

This is correct, but even Pharaoh understood that it was for his own good, until the moment when they separated. As long as they were both in the will to receive, it was worthwhile. It is a period called *Lo Lishma*. You have a part, and I have a part. You may have more, and I may have less, or the other way around, but we get along. We cannot do without each other.

This is how we advance until we reach a crisis, a barrier we must cross with effort. That transition will happen at the foot of Mt. Sinai, where the human is born.

From *The Zohar: Nefesh, Ruach, Neshama*

"Then ... approached him" is the approaching of world in a world, the approaching of the lower world, *Nukva*, *Nefesh*, Judah, to the upper world, *Yesod de* ZA, *Ruach*, Joseph, so that everything will be one. Because Judah was a king and Joseph was a king, they approached each other and united in one another.

Zohar for All, *VaYigash* (Judah Approached), item 22

There are many discernments throughout the process of Joseph, beginning with his being sold, his arrival in Egypt, the sending away of his brothers and their reacceptance. In this process, we connect within us the two qualities, that of the Creator and that of the creature.

The problem with connecting the qualities of bestowal with the qualities of reception in a person is not so simple. We see it in our friends, especially among beginners. We see how difficult it is for them to accept these spiritual qualities, which they have never felt before. They begin to feel that there is bestowal, love, and connection here, a new way of seeing the world through new "spectacles," and it is not so easy.

Terms

Crop

A "crop" is a plant that grows out of the still. It is the ability to rise from the will to receive, our egoistic desire, which is the still. If there is a seed in the still and you give it water, minerals, and the proper cultivation, a plant will grow out of it–the next degree in its evolution.

Everything emerges from the still. The will to receive is the general substance, and the forms that come out of it–vegetative, animate, and speaking–are forms of the desire to bestow together with the will to receive. The will to receive gives all the substance. If, for example, the form is vegetative, its next form will be an animal, followed by the speaking form.

Blessing

The "blessing" is the upper force that comes from *Bina*. *Bet* is *Beracha* (blessing). Without this upper force there is no growth. It is similar to water, which represents the force of *Bina* in our world.

Promise

This is the promise that Joseph was given that he would be able to come out of Egypt. The big problem is how to work with our egos and be certain that it does not "swallow" us down the line. This is why Joseph was told, "Go down to Egypt for a certain time, then return to the land of Israel with great substance."

Weeping

"Weeping" is a state of *Katnut* (smallness/infancy), when one shifts from state to state. In between, one must be "small," like an embryo, or like a newborn baby that is crying. These are signs of *Katnut*. At that stage, a person still has no *Mochin* (Light of Wisdom); one still does not understand where one is or why one exists. Such a person is in regret, in plight, in a narrow place where there are insufficient *Hassadim* (mercies), hence the crying.

Slave

A "slave" is our desire. In general, we always speak only about the desire. The whole of Creation is but one will to receive divided into 613 desires. A slave is one of those desires, which is under the complete control of below. It is below either on the side of Pharaoh or on the side of the Creator. That is, either it is a servant of the Creator or a servant of Pharaoh. It cannot be in the middle.

From *The Zohar*: Take Wagons ... for Your Little Ones

Israel were under the rule of this heifer for 210 years when they were in Egypt. ...It was only in order to scrutinize that wagon, which is *VAK* of the left, that Israel were under the *Klipa* of Egypt for several times and several years, as more than this measure, called "wagon," is forbidden to take out of Egypt.

Zohar for All, *VaYigash* (Judah Approached), item 112

Our exile was to last 400 years, like four *Behinot* (discernments), but we spent only 210 years in exile. This is the root of all the other exiles.

VaYechi

(Jacob Lived)

(Genesis, 47:28-50:26)

Portion Summary

In the portion, *VaYechi* (Jacob Lived), Jacob and his sons join Joseph in Egypt. When the time of Jacob's death draws near, he calls on Joseph and makes him swear to bury him in the land of Israel and not in Egypt. Joseph asks him to bless his two sons, Ephraim and Menashe, before he dies. Jacob blesses them and says that they will be as his sons, Reuben and Simeon. Subsequently, Jacob blesses the rest of his sons and orders them to bury him in the Cave of Machpelah in the land of Israel.

Following Jacob's death, Joseph receives special permission from Pharaoh to go and bury his father in the land of Israel. Jacob goes to Canaan with his brothers and all the elders of Egypt, arrives at the Cave of Machpelah, buries Jacob there, and then returns to Egypt.

Along the way, his brothers fear that he will take vengeance against them for selling him into slavery, but Joseph soothes their fears. He promises them that he will always remain their brother and not their enemy.

Jacob's blessing comes true and Menashe and Ephraim have many children. Toward the end of the portion, Joseph is about to die. He summons his brothers and tells them that the Creator will bring them and his sons out of Egypt, and orders them to take his bones and bury them in the land of Israel.

COMMENTARY

The Torah teaches us how to develop our souls. Initially, we have only the point in the heart. It appears when we begin to ask about the reason for, and the meaning of, life. Through this question, we begin to see that life is not meant only to live here in this world for seventy or so years. Rather, this life was given as an opportunity for us to develop the soul.

The soul develops from the evil inclination, opposite which stands the "light that reforms." In other words, if we correct the evil inclination using the light that reforms, we will thus develop the soul. This is how the evil inclination becomes the good inclination.

This correction does not relate merely to having good human relations. Rather, through the light we also begin to experience the spiritual world, Godliness, as it is written, "You will see your world in your life."*

The portion deals with the three primary forces: Abraham, Isaac, and Jacob, which are *Hesed*, *Gevura*, and *Tifferet*. These forces exist in the soul of each of us, or in the general soul called "Adam." Abraham and Isaac are two opposite lines–right and left, *Hesed* and *Gevura*–while the Jacob quality in us, the senior patriarch, includes Abraham and Isaac within it, and is the middle line, called *Tifferet*. Using the quality of Jacob, meaning the two forces that exist in it, we are directed for the first time toward the proper manner to correct the soul.

"Jacob's sons" are the qualities that emerge from the quality of Jacob, the middle quality that uses all of Nature's forces to develop

* Babylonian Talmud, *Masechet Berachot*, 17a

the soul within us, the Godly, higher part of us. The structure of the *Sefirot* ends with the quality of Joseph—the foundation that collects within us all the preceding qualities: *Hesed*, *Gevura*, *Tifferet*, *Netzah*, and *Hod*.

The righteous Joseph is called *Yesod* (foundation) because he is "righteous, the foundation of the world" (Proverbs, 10:25). The world is the structure that operates in relation to *Malchut* and the whole of Israel, toward all of our desires.

Our desires are Egypt, the ego within us. If we properly position this upper structure, which contains *Hesed*, *Gevura*, *Tifferet*, *Netzah*, *Hod*, and *Yesod*, we can act properly toward the Egypt in us, toward the Pharaoh, the evil inclination, our ego.

The portion describes the beginning of the reciprocal work with our Godly part, which includes the patriarchs up to and including Joseph. The reciprocal work includes all the qualities of Israel, which descend to the ego and operate in it. In this way, the Torah teaches us how to work with ourselves, how to find within us all the sublime qualities of the nine upper *Sefirot*, which end in *Yesod*—Joseph—bestowing upon *Malchut*, the tenth *Sefira*—Pharaoh.

Jacob is the upper part in the qualities of the Creator—Abraham, Isaac, and Jacob—which are the upper triangle: *Hesed*, *Gevura*, *Tifferet*. The qualities of *Netzah*, *Hod*, and *Yesod*, however, are the lower triangle. These are the qualities of the house of Jacob and Jacob's sons, including Joseph. When these qualities operate properly within Egypt, Egypt is granted abundance and everyone is happy and developing.

Jacob's passing marks the conclusion of the task of the upper part of the structure of the soul, which was carried out through Joseph in Egypt. Jacob is the middle line. When that quality goes down to Egypt, through Joseph, and tends to the Egyptians, Egypt is enriched and everyone, including Pharaoh, is content.

As this takes place, forces of bestowal enter Egypt and gradually develop in the egoistic will to receive, and the force of bestowal understands that it can gain from it, for example, by trading with others or by being considerate toward others. It is similar to today's international commerce, which is driven by the incentive that we can benefit through each other. This is a development of the qualities of bestowal, which still work with the qualities of reception.

In this way, the quality of Jacob goes down to *Malchut*, Egypt, to the general will to receive. This quality is like a Trojan horse entering our ego. The will to receive provides the ego with everything for its own delight. The ego enjoys the quality of bestowal working in it for its own benefit, and the sensation that everything is working smoothly. But this continues until we reach today when we are at a state where we feel that something has ended.

A similar thing happened in Egypt: Jacob passed away and the elders of Egypt, with Pharaoh's blessing, led him to the land of Canaan, to the Cave of Machpelah, where he was buried by his sons. The name, Cave of Machpelah, signifies *Hachpalah* (doubling), since there are two worlds in that cave—*Bina* and *Malchut*—joined together.

After awhile, when the sons of Jacob returned to Egypt, the narrative repeated itself with Joseph. But unlike Jacob, Joseph remained in Egypt and only after some time were his bones brought up from there.

Thus, the bone, the foundation instilled in Egypt—the qualities of bestowal that work with the egoistic will to receive—eventually brings us to a state of despair, to the seven years of famine. After all these problems, we realize that we must part from the ego. This is when the process of exiting from the ego begins.

Two forces emerge from the quality of Joseph: Ephraim and Menashe. They receive Jacob's blessing, emerge from the upper triangle into the lower one, and operate in Egypt. Prior to his demise, Joseph tells the people around him that in time they will all come out of Egypt, and that the reason they had entered it was to take from it all that could be corrected, except for the stony heart.

Everything can be brought out of Egypt except for the *Yesod* of the last evil, which we cannot correct until the end of correction. This is why it is written that they will come out with great substance (Genesis, 15:14).

Joseph passed away so we could achieve the recognition of evil. When we develop egoistically, we grow detached from anything good that the combination of the qualities of bestowal and the qualities of reception might yield. We reach a state of despair, dryness, and finally a state of "And the children of Israel sighed because of the work" (Exodus, 2:23). This is when our exodus begins.

Questions and Answers

The portion contains a repetitive element—the blessing before death. Joseph asks Jacob to bless his sons, then Joseph blesses his own sons. The conclusion of a degree means death. What is the meaning of the blessing of the sons and grandsons?

A degree that has ended becomes the next degree, which follows in its stead. The new degree is much thicker, with greater desire and greater achievements. The patriarchs were great—they excelled in their purity. We are the last ones, however, and are now doing the biggest work.

Each degree blesses the next degree, giving it all of its *Reshimot* (recollections), all of its powers, and supports it from within, from below. This is called "the burying of the bones" of the degree. Within the soul are *Moach* (marrow), *Atzamot* (bones), *Gidim* (tendons), *Bassar* (flesh), and *Or* (skin), which are five discernments. We bury the *Atzamot* of the degree, and this is how the next degree is built and continues.

The blessing is actually the light of *Hassadim* that the lower degree transmits to the upper one. In other words, it is *Ohr Hozer* (Reflected Light), *Masach* (screen), and *Ohr Hozer*. All the qualities of bestowal that we obtained in the previous degree move with us to the next. In fact, there is nothing more to take from state to state, but only the force of bestowal that has been obtained, the force of love, of relinquishing.

But this does not help with the new *Aviut* (thickness, will to receive), since the children have a much bigger *Aviut.* So how does the blessing of the father, who is on a smaller level of *Aviut,* help with the new desire?

This depends on the sons. There is much more in the father than there is in the sons, but the father cannot actualize this *Aviut*. Therefore, he gives what he has to his sons, and if they know how to work with it they will use what they received in order to advance.

The sons do not have more than the *Aviut* they received from their fathers. However, precisely because of their greater *Aviut*—their bigger will to receive, their egos—they can actualize a potential force of bestowal out of that blessing according to who they are.

How does one know that one is about to die, such as with Jacob and Joseph?

When a degree ends. In corporeality, the spiritual state affects the corporeal one. But in spirituality, there is a process in a degree called *TANTA* (*Taamim*, *Nekudot*, *Tagin*, *Otiot*). The expansion of the light and its departure are gradual. First there is the *Bitush* (battering) of inner and outer in the *Partzuf* of the soul, inside the soul.

In that state, one feels that one has stopped working due to one's inability to continue correcting oneself. To proceed with the correction, one must start anew, begin a new period, re-enter the egoistic will to receive, but more deeply and with greater force.

We all consist of four *Behinot* (discernments) of *Ohr Yashar* (Direct Light), or from the name *HaVaYaH* (*Yod-Hey-Vav-Hey*). Everything in reality divides into five discernments: root, then the four *Behinot HaVaYaH*. This is why we have to keep starting anew, why there is life and death—a process of expansion and departure of light, since we cannot make the correction all at once, in "one day," but require many actions (days) to achieve the general correction.

Is it we who perform the correction or is it the light that makes the change in us?

The light makes the correction in us, but it happens according to our request and demand. This is called "work" on our part. We haven't the strength, but we do have the power to decide and recognize, and to want it to happen.

From *The Zohar*: Behold, Your Father Is Ill

It is written, "Joseph was told, 'Behold, your father,'" belonging to the next world, ZA in *Mochin* of upper *Bina*, who is called "the next world," wanting to do good to His sons so they will come out from their exile. And if, in Your truthfulness, you will not want, meaning you will not find them worthy of it, then the Name with four, "*HaVaYaH* is one" ("The Lord is one") will correct you and Divinity will return to her place. This is so because if the sons are not worthy of redemption of their own, ZA will correct them for elevating them to the next world, which is *Bina*, and by that, the unification of One *HaVaYaH* will be established.

Zohar for All, *VaYechi* (Jacob Lived), item 37

All we need to do from the Cave of Machpelah—the connection between *Bina* and *Malchut*—is doubling. We must elevate everything that is inside the *Malchut*, sanctify it in *Bina*, i.e. the blessing, then combine the elements in such a way that *Bina* and *Malchut* are as one. This is the meaning of connecting heaven and earth. Through these acts we perform between *Bina* and *Malchut*, we correct ourselves. Finally, when all those actions are done, all the evil in us will be corrected into good.

This portion contains many entrances and exits from Egypt to Israel. Joseph entered Egypt; the brothers departed it and then

returned; Joseph went to bury Jacob in Israel, then returned to Egypt. Is this how the qualities of the upper one connect to the lower one?

Of course. Each and every moment, we are performing minuscule corrections between the nine *Sefirot*, the qualities of the Creator, and the tenth *Sefira*, *Malchut*, the quality of the creature, man, the ego. Even the most ordinary person still undergoes corrections through the passing states. This is why there is "time" in our world. However, these corrections occur without our awareness.

Because of the despair and frustration over what is happening in the world, beginning from this generation onward, we will gradually realize that we *must* make changes. In this world, these changes manifest in how we relate to one another. We must implement love of others, correct ourselves and the relations between us, and serve as an example for the world, be a light for the nations.* If we treat others well, we will thus activate the force of *Bina*, the force of Joseph, or even the force of Jacob and the patriarchs toward *Malchut*, meaning toward the rest of the world.

But the will to receive does not change, so does it always remain our "engine"?

The will to receive does not change, only how we use it changes. It always remains our engine. Using the will to receive, we can do as much good as we do harm, depending on how we use it.

But the will to receive is always motivated by the thought that a reward awaits at the end, while in the desire to bestow it is the opposite.

Bestowal is the reward. Previously, we thought we could achieve anything, that we could conquer space and make great achievements in every realm. Today, we see that we have "everything," but it is all empty. From the point of inverting our use of the desire, we find a way to

* I the Lord have called you in righteousness, and have taken hold of your hand, and kept you, and set you for a covenant of the people, for a light of the nations" (Isaiah, 42:6).

progress favorably. We simply switch the way we use our egos from the evil inclination to the good inclination using the light that reforms.

In other words, all we need is to change our values?

Correct, we only need to change our values. Then, when we all connect as one, with one heart, loving our neighbors as ourselves, we will discover the spiritual life.

It seems that there is such a process in the world today. There is calm, then a blow, then some try to revert to how it was while others are groping in the dark, wondering about the future. Is this the connection that is appearing today?

Yes, because we cannot contain all the changes at once. It happens so we can understand, grow accustomed to how it was, and then advance. Our current thinking and way of life compared to what we were like a thousand years ago are radically different. We cannot grasp how people lived then. It is not like traveling to a different part of the world; they were completely different people. This is why the process of development takes thousands of years. Although today we are developing much faster, it is still impossible to act quickly.

It is the same in mechanics; if we want to transmit large of amounts of data, we need high frequencies, many pulses. This is why it is clear that the crisis will not end at once, but will stretch on, wear us out, and return. But with each return, we will understand it more deeply.

Usually, the blows do not come as a single blow that is experienced over a long time. If it did, we would get used to it. The will to receive gets used to everything, even to constant pressure. It begins to protect itself and stops feeling the blows. Only because there are intermissions can we contemplate and understand the reason, and the next time around relate to reality in a completely different way. Each time, our recognition of our own evil deepens, and when it comes we understand it better, connect it with the cause, as well as with the possible consequence, or the desirable one, and this gives us free choice.

Terms

Death

"Death" is a state of departure of the light from the soul. This does not refer to the death of our protein body, since the Torah does not deal with the life of the physical body, but with the soul, with the filling of the light. Our desire is filled with the upper light, called "life." The departure of the light is called "death." People in our world are detached from life. This is why it is written that the wicked in their lives are called "dead."*

However, those who obtain the soul using the wisdom of Kabbalah, who draw the light that reforms, are those who achieve *Arvut* (mutual guarantee), the love of others. They have a *Kli* (vessel), a receptacle in which to discover the upper light, Godliness, which is life.

Blessing

A "blessing" is the force of bestowal that we receive through which we begin to sense the upper world. The spiritual world is all blessing, all *Bet* (the first letter in the word *Beracha* [blessing]), all *Bina*. This is why the Torah begins with the letter *Bet*, with *Beracha*.

Bed

A "bed" is a state where one ceases to work with one's *Rosh*, *Toch*, and *Sof* (head, interior, and end, respectively), meaning in an upright position, when one has lights that develop from above downward. When the *Rosh*, *Toch*, and *Sof* are on the same level and the lights *NRNHY* depart, what is left is only "a pocket of life."

The Cave of Machpelah

The connection between *Bina* and *Malchut* is called *Machpelah*. The will to receive and the desire to bestow stand together at the degree

* Jerusalem Talmud, *Masechet Berachot*, page 15b.

of *Malchut*, and there is the entrance to the upper world, the world of *Bina*. Therefore, on the one hand it is a burial, and on the other hand it is the door to eternity.

Fear (of revenge)

The fear is that if Joseph properly uses the qualities to correct Egypt, he might underestimate them and be unable to utilize their full potential. Each of Jacob's sons is a form of bestowalbut is not connected to Egypt, *Malchut*.

Only Joseph, who completes the nine *Sefirot*, can connect them all to *Malchut*. Without him they are afraid because they depend on him. Without him, it is as though they are not realizing themselves. They fear that there will not be a proper connection without Jacob, who has departed because he was the keeper of the middle line.

They also fear that Joseph will have enough power to take all the sons between him and Jacob. The upper one is Jacob, and the lower one is Joseph, and the qualities all enter man's ego, Egypt. This is how they operate.

From *The Zohar*: Egypt Is Mourning

As long as Jacob was in Egypt, the land was blessed because of him, the river Nile would flow and water the land, and hunger stopped because of Jacob. Hence, the Egyptians made mourning and it is named after them.

Zohar for All, *VaYechi* (Jacob Lived), item 816

Jacob and Joseph brought blessing to Egypt. When they passed away—when that degree ended—the recognition of evil arrived, the seven years of famine. Although there was abundance, it was unfulfilling, and all that was left was one thing: the new, higher desire, which mandated the exodus from Egypt.

Shemot

(Exodus)

(Exodus, 1:1-6:1)

PORTION SUMMARY

The portion, *Shemot* (Exodus), begins with the demise of Joseph and all of his contemporaries: "And a new king arose over Egypt, who did not know Joseph" (Exodus, 1:8). Subsequently, Moses was born in Egypt and his sister hid him in an ark. She placed the ark in the Nile and followed it. Pharaoh's daughter went down to bathe in the river, found the ark, and took the baby. Moses' sister offered to help her find a Hebrew nursing woman and brought Moses' mother in to nurse the baby.

Moses grew and lived in Pharaoh's home for forty years. One day, he saw an Egyptian man beating a Hebrew. He struck and killed the Egyptian and buried him in the sand. When he realized that one of his Hebrew brothers had seen him in the act, he feared being reported and escaped to the desert.

In the desert, he met Jethro, priest of Midian. Moses married his daughter. When he saw the burning bush, he was told that he must return to Pharaoh and to the people of Israel, and tell them it was time to get out of Egypt.

The portion ends with the children of Israel complaining to Moses about their unhappy situation. Moses turned to the Creator, who said to him, "Now you shall see what I will do to Pharaoh, for by a strong hand shall he let them go, and by a strong hand shall he drive them out of his land" (Exodus, 6:1).

Commentary

These stories deal with man's soul. The Torah tells us how to correct ourselves in order to develop the soul within us, how to open it up to the upper light, to the revelation of the Creator, and how to feel within it the upper, spiritual world.

The process begins with a special desire, called "Abraham," which awakens and asks about the meaning of our lives, leading us to open up our souls. Our developing desire must escape Babylon, the sum of our great ego.

Subsequently, that desire creates another desire, Isaac, which begets yet another desire, Jacob. These three desires form the foundation of the soul.

Jacob, which is a special desire, has twelve sons. This is a development of the third desire, which achieves equivalence with the upper force—the Creator—who is pure bestowal. The exodus from Babylon symbolizes our desire to achieve that same level of bestowal. Jacob is the first to actualize that desire through his sons, particularly through Joseph, who assembles all the qualities of bestowal from the corrections that Abraham, Isaac, Jacob, and the rest of the sons have made.

Joseph is the only one who can descend to his ego with all the corrections and begin to work with the ego, which is called "Egypt."

The whole of the house of Jacob goes down to Egypt. There, they complete their corrections and die. After awhile, a child is born in the tribe of Levi. Unlike the rest of the Hebrew children that Pharaoh put to death, this one survives. In spiritual terms, Pharaoh "swallowed" all the desires that were corrected into aiming to bestow.

He put them to death by the ego taking over all the desires. Thus, even if a person wanted to advance toward spirituality, the ego, life, and the environment would make it impossible.

In the period preceding the birth of the desire called "Moses," one could not advance toward spirituality. One had to wait until the Moses desire appeared and grew, thanks to his mother, who nursed him, and to Batia, Pharaoh's daughter, who received him afterward.

Batia is *Bat Yah* (Daughter of the Creator); she is a part of the quality of Pharaoh within us, a special part of our ego, the will to receive. This part can connect with the desire to bestow and grow.

Moses grew in Pharaoh's house as a grandson, the son of Pharaoh's daughter, Batia. He was raised as a prince who was educated in all of Egypt's wisdom until he was forty.

Age forty is the age of *Bina* (understanding). It is not an indication of a number of years, but a stage at which the desire not only grows and draws from the side of Pharaoh, the ego, but begins to correct itself, as well. The desire that reaches the age-state of forty discovers its oppositeness from Pharaoh and uses him to escape from him.

Our exodus from Egypt begins when we feel that we can no longer tolerate the struggle. It happens when there is resistance, when we feel both Pharaoh and Moses within us, and the Jews in us crave unity, but are unable to achieve it because they are Pharaoh's slaves. Here is where we discover Pharaoh's rulers. There is an inner struggle between the Jews and Pharaoh's rulers, and we perceive it as unbearable. This is when we begin to resist and must take action to correct ourselves.

The force of Moses within kills Pharaoh's men—the Egyptians—within us, and must therefore flee from Pharaoh. In fact, when Moses kills the Egyptian within him, the struggle between him and his ego only intensifies, and he has to draw very far from his ego. This is the meaning of "the escape from Egypt."

However, one cannot escape all at once because the rest of the desires, the children of Israel, are still enslaved in Egypt under the ego, working in order to receive. Only Moses grew and escaped to Midian, to Jethro, married the priest's daughter, Zipporah, and stayed there for forty years.

While in the desert, Moses understood that there was one special point, the burning bush, that could lift him up. With Jethro, he connected to it for forty years. He continued to grow there and acquire all of Jethro's wisdom, which gave him a springboard back to Egypt, to the beginning of his confrontation with Pharaoh.

The Creator said to Moses, "Let's go to Pharaoh together because 'I have hardened his heart.'" In other words, we feel two forces once again, which provide the understanding and ability to cope with what is required, with the ego. Then, we understand that "there is none else besides Him" (Deuteronomy, 4:35), that there is nothing but the singular force that, on the one hand, plays with the ego and hardens Pharaoh's heart. On the other hand, it goes with us and helps us advance above it. Thus, the Creator gradually brings us toward exiting our egos entirely as we exit Egypt.

At the same time, "the children of Israel sighed from the work" (Exodus, 2:23), building Pithom and Rameses, beautiful cities corresponding to the first and second Temples, yet were for Pharaoh. The ego continued to grow, as did the children of Israel, and all these qualities of bestowal within our forces of reception chased away the Egypt in us, our egos.

We can see the great force that exists in these qualities only as we advance. As long as they are enslaved by Pharaoh, they are cities of poverty–a state in which one desires to exit the ego and advance toward spirituality, but has no outlet by which to escape. "Cities of poverty" indicates that a person is in danger* because if he remains in his ego, he will never attain the spiritual world.

During his time with Jethro, Moses acquired the powers to cope with Pharaoh. He made a covenant and arrived in Egypt with his son, Gershon. Upon his return to Egypt, he began to struggle with

* The Hebrew word, *Miskenot*, means both *Misken* (poor) and *Mesukan* (dangerous).

Pharaoh. He reunited with his brother, Aaron, and together they collected the rest of the elders of Israel.

Put differently, we summon all the inner forces with which we believe we can rise above our egos and correct ourselves. The forces, thoughts, and intentions with which we can rise above our egos, above Egypt, are those that are in equivalence with the Creator. It is in those desires that the upper force is revealed, and we receive a glimpse of the spiritual world..

In that struggle, we can connect with the inner Aaron, the right side, and with Moses, the left side. Together, they are *Cohen* (priest) and *Levi* (Levite). Then, we summon all those inner forces and discover evidence of the Creator through "miracles," meaning forces that act on our desires. Once a bit of the spiritual force appears in us, we can sort out the desires with which we can build the *Kli* (vessel) to reveal the Creator, the "soul." These desires intend to demand of Pharaoh, "Let My people go" (Exodus, 5:1).

At that point, we feel that we are at a crossroads, and that we have the endurance. We demand that we detach ourselves from the ego and rise to the level of *Bina*, outside of Egypt. Our strength does not manifest at once. The Pharaoh within says, "No way," and "Who is the Lord that I should obey His voice?" (Exodus, 5:2).

Within us is a mighty struggle, preventing us from detaching from our nature. It resists us by pulling us toward our nature, and we try but are constantly pulled back. This is why we suffer the blows called the "Ten plagues of Egypt." These blows push us forward.

This is a tough process. The struggle resembles labor pains. Indeed, the exodus from Egypt is called "birth"—the birth of the spiritual man. In this state, we (the people of Israel) suffer from all the desires and intentions in us. We are very frustrated and need much support. It is quite difficult to go through these states without the support of the proper environment, which serves as a "midwife" in Egypt.

In that state we need those midwives in order to muster the needed strength to bring us to the necessity for the upper force, to feel that without the help of the Creator we will never rise above our Egypt.

We therefore see that there is a meaningful "game" here between the strengthening Pharaoh and the strengthening Israel. But only when we come to a state of bewilderment and helplessness does the Creator say, "Come unto Pharaoh" (Exodus 7:26) "for I have hardened his heart" (Exodus 10:1). That is, the Creator wishes to save us precisely through the hardening. By that, He shows us His greatness.

The dramatic process and difficult conditions we face are for our own sake. During the study of the wisdom of Kabbalah, as we rise above our egos and discover spirituality—the upper force—we undergo a complicated process of self-scrutiny and inner struggles between desires, forces, and intentions. We experience it so we may feel the upper force, the spiritual world, and where it is, because we can neither see nor feel it with our senses.

We must collect these supporting forces—Pharaoh, Jethro, Moses, Aaron, Israel in Egypt, and all the patriarchs—as forces that desire us to rise above the ego and discover the spiritual world. These forces face up to Pharaoh, the ego, and demand to rise above it, as it is written, "Let My people go that they may serve Me" (Exodus, 7:16). It happens so we may discover the greatness, the so-badly-needed help that one receives from above, from the Creator.

This is the only way we can acquire the power that the Creator sends us, the upper force, the force of bestowal, the love of others, through which we rise above the ego and come out of Egypt. This is our spiritual birth, and only then do we begin to feel the spiritual world. Henceforth, we will be revived.

The portion opens before us a new stage in our development. This is why the book, *Shemot* (Exodus), is the second book in the Torah. There are five books in the Pentateuch. These correspond to our five egoistic desires that we need to correct on five degrees: the worlds *Assiya*, *Yetzira*, *Beria*, *Atzilut*, and *Adam Kadmon*, until we reach the end of correction, complete redemption. Each world contains five internal degrees, which, in turn, contain another five degrees in each. Thus, altogether there are 125 degrees by which we ascend to the final and complete correction, our complete redemption.

Redemption begins after the first, preparatory stage, when we discover the true Pharaoh within, the real ego. Because we face two conflicting forces—Pharaoh and Moses—we need a third force to decide between them. That force is the Creator, the upper force, which then appears and helps us.

QUESTIONS AND ANSWERS

The portion describes the preparations for a spiritual birth. Is it similar to what is happening in the world today?

Of course. We are all in a state of scrutinizing our egos, their control over us, and the narrow boundaries that they allow us. We have yet to achieve the recognition that the ego is evil, but many people are already beginning to see that we are helpless because we don't know how to correct the crises the ego has created.

Is this the sensation of Egypt or is it not yet it?

This is already the sensation of Egypt. We are under great stress because we have not determined whether Pharaoh is our "good grandpa." Is he sitting with Moses in his lap and dispensing the joys of life (including the Jews that are in Egypt, enjoying the abundance) or is there a new stage arising here?

For thousands of years we have been progressing thanks to our growing egos, and we have enjoyed it. We thought we would thrive and prosper indefinitely. But suddenly, we have discovered that the very force we were thanking for our abundance had become a harmful force. This is Pharaoh changing his attitude toward the Jews in Egypt, becoming the bad ruler, as it is written, "Now there arose a new king over Egypt, who did not know Joseph" (Exodus, 1:8).

Over the last one hundred years, but particularly since the turn of the century, we have been involved in this self-scrutiny, and we must finish it quickly. However, everything depends on people sharing their knowledge of the situation, because no one knows what to do.

It is similar to what happens on Purim, when the city of Shushan is bewildered and people do not know who is right–Mordechai or Haman. Likewise, the story in Egypt repeats itself with the Jew who wanted to reveal how Moses killed the Egyptian.

Therefore, we must explain to everyone what is really happening, the reason for all the bad things, the crises, and how we can rise above them all. It is only our egos that have brought us into this predicament. Through the right process, as the Torah tells us, we must come to see the ego as an evil force on which we must shine the light that reforms.* In other words, the Creator that is now appearing to Moses tells him, "Come to Pharaoh because I have hardened his heart," meaning, "I caused the crisis so you would find Me, because only I can help you out of it."

We must pass this message to everyone as quickly as possible and show how we can discover the upper force that rewards us with abundance. If we relate to our crisis in the right way, we will obtain–while in this life–the spiritual world, eternity, and perfection.

What is Moses in spirituality, and what are all the stages he went through on the spiritual level?

Moses is the force that pulls us out of Egypt (our egos), raising us above this world and into the spiritual one. It is contrary to what Batia says: "I drew him out of the water" (Exodus, 2:10). Moses is the force that must now lead us from here until we enter the land of Israel.

Why is Pharaoh's daughter called Batia (the Creator's daughter)? Aren't they opposites?

Pharaoh is the posterior side of the Creator. The upper force is playing with us. It is written, "I have created the evil inclination," which is Pharaoh, "I have created for it the Torah as a spice" (*Masechet Kidushin*, 30b), because "The light in it reforms it" (Eicha,

* Midrash Rabah, *Eicha*, "Introduction," Paragraph 2.

"Introduction," Paragraph 2). In other words, He reforms Pharaoh, the evil inclination.

At the end of the process, we must take from Egypt all the *Kelim* (vessels), all the desires, and empty the Egyptians from everything, as it is written about the children of Israel that they went out with "great substance" (Genesis, 15:14). This is how we sanctify these *Kelim*, these great desires–which so far worked for our own good. We now invert them into working for the sake of others, and it is precisely in these desires that we discover our eternal life.

Why did Pharaoh refuse to let Israel leave Egypt?

When the Israelites are in Egypt, they give great substance to Pharaoh. The forces of bestowal inside the will to receive are very helpful to Pharaoh, and the will to receive knows how to trade, how to develop industry, science, and so forth.

It seems as though the Creator is waiting for Pharaoh's approval, because after Pharaoh refuses, the Creator brings them out in haste.

It is our own choice. We stand between the ego, the force of reception, and the force of bestowal. We are the ones who recognize the evil in Pharaoh, and when we see this evil gradually losing its strength by our actions, we can then leave it behind.

Terms

Moses

"Moses" is the force within us that pulls us out of this world and into the spiritual one.

Burning Bush

The "burning bush" is *Malchut* that rises to *Bina* and receives the light of *Hochma*.

Pharaoh

"Pharaoh" is the entirety of our ego. The word, Pharaoh, comes from the word, *Oref* (back of the neck), which is the posterior of our will to receive. The will to receive is the substance of Creation. That substance can aim toward its own benefit, but it can also aim toward the benefit of others, depending on how we use it.

For now we are receiving it, as it is written, "I have created the evil inclination," as Pharaoh. We must turn it into the good inclination through the spice of Torah, which is the upper light we draw through our studies. This is how we shift from hatred of others to love of others.

Nile

The Nile is all of Egypt's wisdom. It is written, "There is wisdom in the nations, believe" (Midrash Rabah, *Eicha*, Portion 2). Israel is small, the least of all the nations. It does not have the power of wisdom (*Hochma*), the great desire. It only has the force of bestowal, love. The Nile symbolizes all of Egypt's wisdom.

VaEra

(And I Appeared)

(Exodus, 6:2-9:35)

Portion Summary

In the portion, *VaEra* (And I Appeared), the Creator appears before Moses and promises to deliver the children of Israel from Egypt to the land of Canaan. Moses turns to the children of Israel, but they do not listen "out of impatience and out of hard work" (Exodus 6:9).

The Creator instructs Moses to turn to Pharaoh and ask him to let the children of Israel go out of Egypt. Moses fears that he will not succeed in his mission and asks the Creator for a sign. The Creator tells Moses that he will be as God to Pharaoh, while Aaron will be the prophet who does the actual speaking. The Creator will harden Pharaoh's heart and shower plenty of signs and tokens over Egypt. The Creator gives Moses and Aaron a staff, and when Moses casts the staff to the ground, it becomes a snake.

When Moses and Aaron come to Pharaoh, Moses is eighty years old and Aaron is eighty-three. There are many magicians and soothsayers around Pharaoh. When Moses and Aaron arrive, they

throw down the staff, and it becomes a snake. Pharaoh's magicians do the same and their staffs also turn to snakes, but Moses' snake swallows the magicians' snakes.

Despite that display, Pharaoh remains defiant and the ten plagues of Egypt begin. This portion mentions seven of the plagues: blood, frogs, lice, flies, pestilence, boils, and hail. After each plague, Pharaoh goes back on his word and refuses to let the children of Israel go.

COMMENTARY

While this depiction is graphic, it actually conveys the interior of the Torah, the true law that instructs us how to get out of the Egypt within us. The Torah does not tell us to leave one physical place in favor of another, but rather how we can free ourselves of our egos.

The portion is for those of us who work hard and discover that we are in Egypt. It also deals with our desire to not be in Egypt–the ego, the essence of evil. Therefore, we must escape from there while arguing with our egos. We cannot tolerate the ego in this situation, fearing it might bury or kill us, so we rise above it and begin to part from it.

There are two forces in us. The first is the ego, which is Pharaoh and all of Egypt. The other is a "protruding" point called "the point in the heart." All our desires that are in Egypt and are fed by it while there is a "famine in the land of Canaan" (Genesis, 42:6) create an internal struggle in us. This is the war from which we seek to escape, to rise above the ego with all our desires. In fact, only Moses, the point in the heart, escapes and rises above the ego, fleeing from Egypt to Jethro and to all that there is in Midian.

After forty years, during which we grow stronger in Midian working on enhancing the force of Moses, the Creator appears to us in the burning bush. Through our inner voice, we hear and comprehend that we must return, fight against the ego, and get out of it, or we will not be able to attain spirituality.

Spirituality is attained only by correcting our desires, by correcting our intentions from aiming to receive—the egoistic form—to aiming to give, to loving others. We have to achieve the rule, "Love your neighbor as yourself." This is the great rule of the Torah. The point in the heart, the Moses in us, feels it is time to do this. The voice of the Creator is telling us to begin working with our egoistic desires by facing up to Pharaoh.

In this state, we are completely bewildered. It is very difficult for us to stand up to our basic nature, and the world is literally showing us how impossible it is to do so. It seems that wherever we turn, we are surrounded by our egos. These are Pharaoh's soothsayers, his sages, beginning to discover how unrealistic is the spiritual path of rising above our egos and achieving love of others. Indeed, where do we find love of others in the world? Does anyone support this?

The Israel in us is a very weak force, and although it seems we can do anything through our spirituality, we can also do it—and even more "successfully"—through the forces of the ego.

Sometimes we prove to ourselves that we rise through the group we are building, through the good and right environment we are in. Just as Pharaoh agreed to let the children of Israel go, but changed his mind and captured them, we also go through ups and downs that prevent us from exiting our egos.

We experience seven blows that cleanse and correct us. These are the *ZAT* of the degree, the seven bottom *Sefirot*—*Hesed*, *Gevura*, *Tifferet*, *Netzah*, *Hod*, *Yesod*, and *Malchut*—corresponding to the seven plagues of Egypt: blood, frogs, lice, flies, pestilence, boils, and hail.

The last three plagues are like the *GAR* of the degree; the first three belong to the *Rosh* (head), not to the *Guf* (body) of the degree. Those who go through them become liberated.

In our inner work, we face tough struggles and scrutinies between the ego and the point in the heart. These draw us toward freedom, bestowal, and through what Baal HaSulam calls in the essays, *Arvut* ("Mutual Guarantee") and *Matan Torah* ("The Giving of the Torah"), "from the love of man to the love of God." This is how we emerge from our nature into the nature of the Creator.

There are only two forces in existence: the force of bestowal and the force of reception. We are immersed in the force of reception, which puts us to death, makes our lives bitter and limited, and shortens them until we have no idea what our lives are intended to be.

Spirituality provides an answer to questions regarding the suffering in our world. We come to spirituality because of the questions: "What is the meaning of my life?" "What is life for?" In spirituality, we constantly scrutinize these questions and through them emerge to the eternal and enlightened world. We do that despite the ego's grip on us that does not let go and pulls us "by our feet" back in, not letting us escape.

Kabbalah books discuss these struggles at length. This is our inner work, the reason why we study its wisdom. The light that reforms that we obtain helps us through the plagues, from one plague to the next, from below upward, toward even greater blows. The more we advance, the harder the work and the tougher the blows.

Although we feel how the evil force in us is destroying us, keeping us on the animal level, we cannot rid ourselves of it. Finally, we come to a state where we know that unless we flee now, with the help of the upper force, we will remain in the ego because we cannot escape by ourselves. The Creator deliberately makes it difficult for us, as it is written, "Come on to Pharaoh" (Exodus 7:26) "for I have hardened his heart" (Exodus 10:1).

The Creator purposely hardens Pharaoh's heart, our egos–the heart with all of our desires–so we would need His strength, so we would increasingly feel how we need Him and how we cling to Him, so He will deliver us from Egypt.

As said above, there are only two forces in reality: the bad force, Pharaoh, and the Creator's positive force, and we must choose to which of them we will cling. Through the war between the forces, we learn that we have no alternative but to achieve *Dvekut* (adhesion) through the force of the Creator. This is how we exit Egypt.

Right from the start, we see that Moses went to the people of Israel and told them that the Creator had appeared before him, and this is why he was suggesting that they come out of Egypt. But the people refused; they did not want to listen.

Their refusal may strike us as odd because it would seem reasonable that the people of Israel should want to get out of Egypt. However, we should remember that this is the people of Israel in exile, under Pharaoh's rule. Had the people of Israel been in Canaan, matters would have been quite different.

But in Canaan there were problems, too. There were quarrels and hunger because the will to receive was growing and could not be used anymore. This is why it was said that there was "hunger" there. Therefore, to use the desire, the people of Israel had to go down to Egypt, since only by adding the ego could they come out of Egypt with the qualities of Israel in them, the *Yashar El* (straight to God).

We must come out with the egoistic desire we previously had, and with which we discover the spiritual world. We have nothing but our natural essence. Following the ruin, the shattering, the sin of the Tree of Knowledge and the other sins, our nature was completely ruined. It was completely shattered, much like the world today, which is gradually discovering the crisis we are in. This was the beginning of the egoistic system that lies between us.

The children of Israel had to go down to Egypt to revive their souls. Yet, for now they are still as Joseph, as the children of Israel. They lived detached from egoistic desires until they began to mingle with the ego. It is specifically those who study the wisdom of Kabbalah—who do what is written in the essays and follow the advice of Kabbalists in order to discover the spiritual world—who feel increasingly lower, as they strive to ascend. This state is called "the children of Israel in Egypt."

The children of Israel had to be in Egypt for four hundred years, as Abraham was told. The four hundred years are four degrees from the root–one, two, three, four–or *Yod-Hey-Vav-Hey*. We also must be in exile in order to reveal the entire *Kli* (vessel) and achieve redemption with it in a corrected *Kli*. In other words, all our souls will connect and discover in that connection the upper light, the Creator. This is how the soul unites with the upper force, with the light; this is the complete redemption.

First, we must mingle with our four levels of *Aviut* (will to receive, egoism). We spent only 210 years in Egypt, so there are additional exiles after Egypt until the measure of four hundred years is full. Currently, we are standing at the conclusion of that period.

We must go down to Egypt and absorb these four hundred degrees, which are like four hundred shekels of silver, the price at which the Cave of Machpelah was sold. This is a special measure of our egos, which Pharaoh symbolizes in a broken manner in the corrected soul. In the end, we bring out these *Kelim* (vessels) from Egypt because we come out with great substance, correct them, and discover in them the land of Israel.

Questions and Answers

Why does the Creator want us out of Egypt, on the one hand, and then harden Pharaoh's heart, making it more difficult for the children of Israel to leave?

When people come to study Kabbalah, they arrive with a great desire to learn, then realize how difficult it is and do not succeed. They begin to "fall asleep." Their egos grow, they yield to it, and sink down into it. They cannot understand that what has happened to them is that they entered Egypt. We need to keep working, even when we are drowning in the ego; we must not to stay in it.

There are also those who detach themselves from corrections and from the wisdom of Kabbalah altogether. They flow with life and may even adopt new habits. But if they continue and go through the great shattering, the inner blows, until they feel they must get out of Egypt, as it is written, "And the children of Israel sighed from the work" (Exodus, 2:23), and yell for the upper force to pull them out, they will be pulled out.

The wisdom of Kabbalah deals with facts, with natural laws. Yet the children of Israel are shown tokens, such as a staff that turns into a snake. Does that symbolize something supernatural?

It is an inner state we often experience. The staff becoming a snake represents incidents where spirituality and perfection appear before us. We feel that when we truly understand and attain something of the quality of bestowal, we are ready to connect with others and be with them in mind and heart, "as one man with one heart." Then, soon afterward comes the descent, like a black cloud descending on a person. In much the same way, the staff and the snake alternate.

Can it be said that one's attitude toward spirituality is called a "staff" or a "snake"?

Yes, and we are tossed between them.

How did Egypt's magicians do the same as Moses with their staffs?

Our egos create these things to show us who is right. In the story of Ester, when they did not know who was right, they had to decide above reason. The same applies to us. We do not want to leave Egypt for our gain, but we also do not want to stay in Egypt for our gain. That is, it comes neither from the side of reception nor from the side of bestowal.

Everyone would like to connect to spirituality and attain the spiritual world and thus have everything. However, we are made to understand that in both reception and bestowal we will receive no personal gain in our egos. When we advance, like the magicians of Egypt, we advance toward the *Klipa* (shell/peel) into bestowing in order to receive, to take for ourselves the next world, too. But bestowal means that we rise above any reward whatsoever.

What does it mean that Moses' and Aaron's snake swallows the snakes of the Egyptian magicians?

It means that in the end we have to go with faith above reason. This is called a "staff," and with it our importance of bestowal increases instead of decreasing, making us descend to the vessels of reception.

Do we all experience these blows, each of us, even now?

The Torah speaks of everything that happens to those studying the wisdom of Kabbalah. The crisis that the world is in today is preparing us to understand that we have no alternatives; we must advance.

Except for the children of Israel, the world will not advance according to the steps we learn in the Torah. The world advances by joining the children of Israel, as it is written, "And the peoples shall take them, and bring them to their place; and the house of Israel shall possess them in the land of the Lord" (Isaiah, 14:2). The whole world will need to support it.

What do we need to do in order to leave Egypt now?

The Torah tells us that until as we have suffered all the blows, we will not cry out so loud that the Creator will save us. When that happens, the upper force, the light that reforms, will influence us so strongly that we will be able to detach from the ego.

From *The Zohar*: I Will Bring, I Will Deliver, I Will Redeem, I Will Take

The Creator wished to first tell them the most beautiful—the exodus from Egypt. The most beautiful of all is, "And I will take you to Me for a people, and I will be to you a God." But He told them this afterwards. At the time, there was nothing more beautiful for them than exiting because they thought that they would never come out of their slavery, since they saw that all the prisoners among them were tied by magic ties that they could never exit. This is why they were first told what they favored most.

Zohar for All, VaEra (And I Appeared), items 52-3

It is the work of the Creator. We are not the ones doing the work, and it is not the work that the Creator does when correcting us. Rather, it is the work that the Creator does "behind the scenes." It is "the back of the neck." That is, hardening Pharaoh's heart is the work that the Creator does so we will need Him.

Is this when we want to go out of Egypt?

This is when we want to go out of Egypt, and it is also when we define that exit correctly. If you ask an ordinary person, "Why are you praying?" "What is redemption?" "What or who is the Messiah?" you will hear many answers. We all have our own messiahs. But here, we are talking about a person who needs to attain a state of Messiah. This brings one into love of others, a state of "Love your neighbor as yourself," the rule that includes all of us, since we must all be mutually contained in it, in mutual guarantee.

This is why mutual guarantee is so important to us; it is as exodus from Egypt, as redemption. As long as there is no mutual guarantee, there will be no redemption. This is why we all need to work to make it happen, and to explain to everyone that the closer we come to this ideal, the greater our chances of exiting Egypt soon.

Terms

Prophet

A "prophet" is a person who speaks with the Creator, the upper force. It is one who is at a level of speaking. "Speaking" is disclosure, the emission of *Hevel* (fume, mist) from the mouth. *Hevel* of the mouth is the *Ohr Hozer* (Reflected Light) emitted from the *Partzuf*, from the soul, as the light of bestowal.

Also, there is a prophet who sees, who is at a higher level. Some prophets say, "I saw," and some prophets say, "I heard." This is a degree of a Kabbalist who is at two degrees—a degree of speaking or a degree of seeing.

Moses

"Moses" is the upper force in us, which pulls us toward bestowal, love of others, and thus to the love of the Creator. It is a force that gives us no rest. This force comes to us from the breaking of the soul as a spark of light within us. If the spark awakens in us, it is considered that we have received an invitation. It guarantees nothing, but the invitation to actually begin one's holy work has been given.

"Holy" means bestowal. "Climbing up the mountain of holiness" means that we have risen above our egos with our point of Moses, and thus actualize ourselves.

Aaron

"Aaron" is the force opposite Moses. The two forces have to work together. Following them are the priests, Levites, and Israel. There are Abraham, Isaac, and Jacob. Our work is always in the middle line.

We see the two forces, Aaron and Moses, even before the whole of the middle line emerges. These two forces work together: Aaron puts order in us, and Moses gives us direction.

Token/Sign

A "token" (or a "sign") is an illumination from a higher degree. It is an additional force by which we advance on each degree. It is a distinction in all those states that occur in us unnaturally, in a state unfamiliar to us in terms of power and intention on the current degree. That state occurs when a degree appears from above and reveals the token. The upper degree might come from the right or from the left.

The *Klipa* (shell/peel) is also in spirituality. *Klipa* and *Kedusha* (sanctity) are two lines between which we build ourselves. We take a little bit of the *Klipa*, correct it using the *Kedusha*, and in between we attain progress in the middle line, on the golden path. The same thing happens on the next degree, and the next, until we climb all 125 degrees.

From *The Zohar*: Take Your Staff

It was clear to the Creator that those magicians would make serpents. Hence, what is the importance of making serpents before Pharaoh? It is because there was the beginning of the punishments, meaning the primordial serpent that failed Adam and Eve. Pharaoh's domination begins from the beginning of the serpent, from the left side. Then, when they saw Aaron's staff turning into a snake, all the magicians were glad because so was the beginning of the wisdom of their snakes.

Zohar for All, *VaEra* (And I Appeared), items 118

Aaron's snake consumed the snakes of the magicians. There is a difference between a snake, a crocodile, and a whale. There are many appellations to the same will to receive because on the path of correction, we go through different states that we express differently in our language.

The "snake" is the primordial serpent, the evil force, the force of reception in us that fails us. We need to understand that all those failures are not really failures. Rather, when we are shown our faults, we are given a chance to ask for the light that reforms to correct them.

There are hidden opposites here: from above, we are always given something to deal with, something that is suitable for us, and for which we can ask for help. It is a state that we can correct. A person is never given a state that will fail him or her.

The magicians and the turning of the snake into a staff, and the other way around, happen so we will learn how to walk between the lines, in the middle line. We must learn how to turn the ego, our will to receive–which destroys us and grabs us by our feet until we cannot take another step forward–into a desire to bestow. It is an inner struggle, very hard internal work.

This happens so we will yell for help. Without asking for help, we will never discover the Creator. We are facing a barrier trying to discover the Creator; it is as if we are saying, "We do not need You. We are fine," because we are detached from the sensation of the Creator. This is why we need this experience; it is help made against us.

Were it not for the snake, Eve, the whole of the left side, and Pharaoh, whose heart the Creator hardens, we would not need the light that reforms. As a result, we would never move toward the Creator. Therefore, Pharaoh's help is necessary, as it is said that Pharaoh brought the children of Israel closer to their father in heaven.

Bo

(Come)

(Exodus, 10:1-13:16)

Portion Summary

In the portion, *Bo* (Come), the Creator—through Moses—tells a defiant Pharaoh that he must let the people of Israel go. The Creator casts two more plagues over Pharaoh, Locust and Darkness, and Pharaoh says to Moses, "Go away from me! Beware; do not see my face again for in the day you see my face you shall die" (Exodus, 10:28). Moses replies, "You are right; I shall never see your face again" (Exodus, 10:29). Indeed, Moses keeps his word.

The Creator tells Moses that after the final plague, Pharaoh will let the children of Israel go. The children of Israel begin to prepare for the tenth plague, the plague of the first-born, and borrow from the Egyptians silver and gold vessels, as well as garments, preparing for their release.

The Creator outlines to Moses the rules of the Passover offering that the children of Israel must follow: slaughter a lamb in the twilight, spread its blood on the doorposts (*Mezuzot*) and on crossbars, and eat the lamb that same night together with *Matzot*

(unleavened bread) and *Maror* (horse-radish). The children of Israel obey.

At midnight, when a great cry rises in Egypt at the strike of the Plague of the First-Born, Pharaoh urges the children of Israel to leave Egypt in haste. The children of Israel leave, taking the mixed multitude along with them, and flocks and cattle in great numbers.

Commentary

The exodus from Egypt described in this portion is very significant and dramatic. Each moment in our lives is a remembrance of the exodus from Egypt. This is the point at which the human in us is born, when we come out of our egos, of the will to receive.

We all begin selfish, as it is written, "I have created the evil inclination."* The evil inclination grows within us and causes us to be increasingly egoistic. Throughout human history, we have been developing in this manner until we arrived at a state where we feel that our entire nature is evil and we must exit it, and so we look for a solution. It is a process that unfolds in individuals and throughout society.

When the Pharaoh—our evil inclination—grows in us, it does not let us live. The point in the heart, Moses in us, escapes from the ego in order to gain strength, then returns in order to fight it. Only once we understand how this "game" unfolds in us do we return to battle the ego, much like Moses returns to Egypt to battle Pharaoh.

When we begin to discover the upper force, even a little bit, we discover that everything happens from above, that "there is none else besides Him" (Deuteronomy, 4:35), and that includes Pharaoh, the Creator, and Moses between them. In this struggle, our inner Moses must decide who will rule, Pharaoh or the Creator.

The Creator teaches Moses to face the ego, fight it, and rise above it. He always sends Moses to Pharaoh because "I have hardened his

* Babylonian Talmud, *Masechet Kidushin*, 30b

heart" (Exodus, 10:1). If we know, through the wisdom of Kabbalah, how to draw the "light that reforms"* and pass through the ten *Sefirot* of our evil inclination, the ten plagues, the process will not be so hard. This process is called "hastening," as opposed to the way, "in due time," which is paved with torments, wars, and other unpleasant events.

The wisdom of Kabbalah emerges in order to ease us through the "hastening." The first to experience it will be the people of Israel, followed by the rest of the world, as it is written, "They shall all know Me from the least of them to the greatest of them" (Jeremiah, 31:33), "For My house shall be called 'a house of prayer' for all the nations" (Isaiah, 56, 7). This is why everyone will face the exodus from Egypt, and the first to do it will be the people of Israel because it is our task to be "a light for the nations" (Isaiah, 42:6).

Our egos, Pharaoh, will not let us unite and achieve a state of "Love your neighbor as yourself; it is a great rule in the Torah"**—by which we must connect in *Arvut* (mutual guarantee). When we struggle against our egos, we are led to the three final and hardest plagues: the *GAR* of the degree, the first three: Locust, Darkness, and the Plague of the First Born.

During the final plague, when we feel how wicked our evil inclination is and how it detaches us from life, we detach ourselves from it. This is why Pharaoh warns Moses that if he approaches him once more he will be put to death, since this inclination truly puts us to death.

The Moses in us is ready for this plague because he knows that through it he will be born; he will come out of Egypt and rise to a level of connection among everyone, and find within him the quality of bestowal. He will attain the sensation of the next world, the sensation of eternity, perfection, and the upper force that resides in him.

When we attain perfection through this complicated process, we make a sacrifice. The Hebrew word for sacrifice is *Korban*, from

* Midrash Rabah, *Eicha*, "Introduction," Paragraph 2.

** Jerusalem Talmud, *Seder Nashim, Masechet Nedarim*, Chapter 9, p 30b.

the word *Karov* (near). When we offer a sacrifice, we draw closer to the quality of bestowal. The Passover offering expresses our efforts to reach the good inclination, which is above the quality of reception, the evil inclination. We "pass over" the ego and approach the desire to bestow. That move is done with the Passover blood, similar to the birth blood. We are born in blood, as it is written, "In your blood, live" (Ezekiel 16:6).

We advance this way until we reach the night of the exodus from Egypt. In that state we "borrow vessels from the Egyptians," taking from them desires. Instead of the intention to receive, we have only the intention to bestow. We take the desire to receive along with the desire to bestow and go out of Egypt with both. All that we leave in Egypt are the intentions to receive, which are the evil. That is, we take the inclination, but leave the evil behind.

Subsequently, we add to the inclination, the desire, the intention to bestow, thus making it a good inclination. This is why we entered Egypt to begin with–to bring out of the Egyptians the desire to receive, with which we were all born initially.

Afterward comes the Plague of the First-Born to all the Egyptians in us, to our entire evil inclination. This is the final blow, bringing with it the light that reforms and handing a final blow to the evil inclination's domination over us. This is when we rise above it and move toward connection with others.

In that connection, we begin to feel the exodus from Egypt, from the evil inclination, which was interfering with our connections and with being in the Assembly of Israel, which brings us together. Only by bonding do we discover the Creator, the upper light, the spiritual world, our perfection and eternity.

When we come out of Egypt, there is festive eating of the Passover offering with the evil. We come out with the bread, the bread of the poor, Matzot, and we are born anew when we rise above our egos, above the will to receive, and into the desire to bestow. Henceforth, we will be ready for our spiritual ascent.

The first degree we attain upon our exodus from Egypt is the spiritual birth. This is the hardest transition, in which we cast away all the habits and customs by which we perceived reality, the world, and our relationships. In this transition, we rise above all the elements that built us and through which we developed in our world. We move from there into a world that operates entirely on bestowal, on *Arvut*, on connection.

When we cross over, we begin to experience Nature in the opposite manner, following the laws of bestowal instead of those of reception. We begin to act differently, follow different rules, and reality appears different than before. We continue to develop with the same Pharaoh we had left behind; we only took the vessels from him, as it is written, "afterward they shall come out with great substance" (Genesis, 15:14).

When we are surrounded by a society, studies, and the light that reforms, we draw in the forces that pull us out of Egypt. Therefore, even in very difficult situations we need not fear standing up to our egos.

Questions and Answers

When do we feel that we have come out of Egypt?

It happens suddenly, in the dark. We feel nothing before it happens; we are dazed, disoriented, just as in birth. We come out to a new life we do not know, and take only what we need—the desires that have no intentions to receive, without the bad intentions, called the "big vessels," which we take from Egypt. The children of Israel are the ones who take them, the ones who want to be *Yashar El* (straight to God), straight toward bestowal, toward love of others.

The exodus from Egypt happens at midnight. According to the wisdom of Kabbalah, this is when the building of the *Kelim* (vessels) begins toward the dawn. In that state we feel bad because of the darkness and the disorientation and confusion. We do not understand what is happening to us. But one point in us tells us,

"Do it," and we are willing to do it, following the preparation that does not let us remain in our egos—which are really putting us to death. So we get out and escape.

From *The Zohar*: A Lamb for a Household

"Israel did not come out of Egypt until the government of all their ministers was broken above." This is called "all of the ten *Klipot* (shells/peels)," the ten plagues by which Egypt is broken. "And Israel departed their domain and came to the domain of the upper holiness," called "bestowal," "love of others, "in the Creator, and tied to Him ... that, 'I brought (them) out from the land of Egypt'; I have brought them out of the other authority and brought them into My authority."

Zohar for All, Bo (Come), item 165

The idea is to move from the intention to receive to the intention to bestow, from a state of constantly thinking of ourselves—how to profit, succeed, and exploit our world—to the opposite state. It is truly an internal revolution in one who still does not understand there is another way to live—in bestowal, love, rising above the self—though there are constant desires to receive within us.

During the forty years in the desert, the children of Israel experience events such as the golden calf and the division of the Red Sea. These events are not easier than the exodus from Egypt, but the exodus is our detachment from our egos.

Following the exit are descents and ascents, and our will to receive keeps showing more and more of itself. The children of Israel do not exit by themselves. Along with them come the mixed multitude: people who are drawn after them, who also want to reach an enlightened world, but without correcting their egos. They are willing to keep Torah and *Mitzvot*, but without correcting the ego.

What is the difference between the exodus from Egypt for those with a point in the heart, and those without the point?

There is a big difference between them. Israel is called *Li Rosh* ("I have a mind") because they do it consciously, aware of what is happening to them. We perform these actions on ourselves and experience them with the Creator. We draw the light that reforms, and this is called "working on the *Galgalta* and *Eynaim*, as it is written, "And you will be to Me a kingdom of priests and a holy nation" (Exodus, 9:6), meaning everyone in bestowal.

Conversely, those who do not need it—because they lack that type of connection to Godliness, the point in the heart—are called "the nations of the world." They do not feel they must correct the evil in them, their egos, or that they must rise and be in *Dvekut* (adhesion) with the Creator.

We are living in a very special time. The whole world is in crisis; everyone must be reborn, whether they want to or not.

True, but the rest of the world is pushed from behind through suffering. They do not, and will not, have the pull from before. The rest of the world feels the necessity to get out of their troubles, while we, Israel, feel a necessity to draw toward bestowal, love of others, and through it achieve the love of the Creator. It is a fundamental difference. We are advancing through the positive force of bestowal, the pulling force, while the rest of the world is advancing through the pushing force that prods them. It is very different, which is why they cannot advance by themselves.

We must connect to them as *Galgalta Eynaim* toward the *AHP*, and pass on the bestowal to them through us. We must be their "light for the nations." Although they will not understand what they are doing, they will connect to us, as Isaiah says, "And the peoples will take them along and bring them to their place, and the house of Israel will possess them as an inheritance in the land of the Lord" (Isaiah, 14:2). This is how they will be corrected.

What was the great cry in Egypt at the time of the Plague of the First-Born? Was it the cry of the Egyptians to the ego?

The Plague of the First-Born stands opposite the *Keter*; it was the conclusion of all the plagues. With each plague, another slice of the intention to receive was cut off from the will to receive. The intention to receive is a *Klipa* that is sorted and separated, and the will to receive remains bare and unused.

Malchut, *Yesod*, *Hod*, *Netzah*, *Tifferet*, *Gevura*, *Hesed*, *Bina*, *Hochma*, and *Keter* correspond to the ten plagues. The plague corresponding *Keter* is the hardest because it is as the *Rosh* (head) in relation to the rest of the blows, and also because its *Aviut* (thickness, will to receive) is the biggest. Of all the degrees of desire—root, one, two, three, four—*Keter* is the strongest egoistic desire.

This is how we detach from the ego and seemingly "kill" Pharaoh. Precisely in this way does the ego begin to understand that we really do exist in order to bestow, and it asks the children of Israel to bless this.

It is not simple because we still have not fully grasped all of it. In the end, "There is none else besides Him." A single force, the Creator, manages everything. Pharaoh is an angel that seems to be against us, but it, too, is in the hands of the Creator; it is how they work together. Currently, this is how our correction takes place in the right-and-left we work with, but afterward we will learn how to work with both, in three lines. We will learn it in relation to the *Masach de Hirik*, in the big corrections.

From *The Zohar*: And It Came to Pass at Midnight

Even "All the firstborn." A firstborn is considered *Hochma*, and "All the firstborn" indicates that even the higher and lower degrees were broken from their dominion. All those degrees that rule by their power of *Hochma*, which is the wisdom of Egypt, as it is written, "All the first-born in the land of Egypt."

Zohar for All, Bo (Come), item 118

Our egos suffer each blow on the highest level. Our will to receive is in us and nowhere else, not even in Egypt. Everything unfolds within because man is a small world. We are beginning to feel that the angel of death is destined to join us in bestowing, as it is written that the angel of death will be a holy angel. This is why Pharaoh asks for a blessing, as he still cannot connect by himself. And yet, he understands that a new era has begun.

Today's Egypt is also showing signs of it. There are the pyramids that the children of Israel built, and there are pyramids that the Egyptians built, and they are built completely differently.

In relation to the process within us, it seems like we are split personalities. Do we have within us the plagued Pharaoh on one side, and Moses delighting in the exodus on the other?

Yes, these two forces are within us. We usually feel them when we ascend or descend. When we are egoistic, or when we do not know what to do with our egos, we are in the dark. Conversely, when we are elated, working in order to bestow, like the Creator, the light shines for us. A beginner is like Moses returning from Jethro; he already discovered the Creator, so now he is retuning with both forces.

Do we experience both forces?

In a struggle, we experience both the force of Pharaoh and the force of Moses. We already know how to make the force of bestowal reign over the force of reception.

Is this why it was said, "Come to Pharaoh"?

Yes, and each time the Creator makes the will to receive heavier, harder. He increasingly opens up the will to receive within us, and we must overcome it and push on.

Terms

Locust

In all the plagues of Egypt, a person feels how beneficial the plagues are. The plague comes because a person is immersed in the ego, in a special situation, and the plagues help one out of that state. The plague of the locust corresponds to *Bina*.

Darkness

In each state we have darkness. However, in states of darkness, it is our personal darkness from which we can escape to another state. Here, the state of darkness comes when we are confused, not knowing anything, as it is said in the Purim story when the people did not know whether Haman or Mordechai was right. In a state of darkness, we need to obtain the light of *Hassadim* because darkness comes from the light of *Hochma*, and we come out of it through the light of *Hassadim*. We need *Hassadim*, understanding that we need the light, and because we are ready, the pillar of fire or the cloud appears.

Plague of the Firstborn

"The Plague of the First-Born" is the final, biggest blow. It is a blow that is the root because the first-born is man. It is the biggest will to receive at the level of *Keter*, after which there is nothing more to do in Egypt. It is here that Pharaoh surrenders.

Pharaoh is left without an army, without anything. Once the children of Israel leave Egypt, Pharaoh sends after them whatever he has left of his army. But afterward, the mixed multitude joins Israel, as well, and Pharaoh is left with nothing.

The Cry of Egypt

"The cry of Egypt" is the cry of our egos asking, "How will I live if I am all bare without any reception for myself, without any understanding how to exist in the world? I am not used to this situation. I have to switch to a new paradigm, to an opposite world that is all giving, connection, mutual guarantee, and love. I cannot live like that. I do not know how!"

This is the great outcry of our egoistic *Kelim*. It is a state we must go through, similar to a physical birth where the newborn baby goes through a type of trauma, too. We learn from *The Zohar* that its root is the serpent's bite of the doe. That is, *Malchut* is the source, and she is the one giving birth to the soul. It is a very dramatic and special state. If we go through that state together with unity among us, as the Torah explains, we will feel elated and alert, and we will come out of it easily.

From *The Zohar*: Praising the Exodus from Egypt

Every man who tells the story of the exodus from Egypt and delights in that story will rejoice with Divinity (which is joy from all sides) in the next world. This is a man who is delighted with his master, and the Creator is delighted with that story of His.

Zohar for All, *Bo* (Come), item 179

There are two opposites here. A person gives birth to himself by himself. On the one hand, we regret the part in us that pressures us during the labor pains until we break through and are born into the new world. On the other hand, we are delighted with that part of us that is connected to the Creator. It is similar to our joy at the birth of a child.

BeShalach

(When Pharaoh Sent)

(Exodus, 10:17-17:16)

Portion Summary

In the portion, *BeShalach* (When Pharaoh Sent), Pharaoh sends the children of Israel from Egypt following the ten plagues that he and the Egyptians suffered. The Creator does not lead the children of Israel directly to the land of Israel because it means they will have to go through the land of the Philistines. The Creator does not want the children of Israel to fear war and return to Egypt, so He sends them through the desert.

Moses takes Joseph's bones. The Creator walks before the people, lighting the way for them with a pillar of cloud during the day, and a pillar of fire during the night.

When Pharaoh learns that the children of Israel really did escape from Egypt, he changes his mind and decides to chase them. He assembles 600 chosen chariots that chase the children of Israel all the way to the Red Sea.

The children of Israel find themselves with the sea before them and Pharaoh behind them. This is when the first miracle

takes place: Moses strikes the sea with his staff, the sea is cut in two, and the children of Israel pass through dry land. When the Egyptians try to pass, the water closes on them and they all drown. In gratitude to the Creator for the miracle, the children of Israel sing the Song of the Sea (Exodus, 15).

Moses leads the children of Israel through the desert on the road to Shur. When the people grow thirsty they arrive at Marah, a place where the water is so bitter they cannot drink it. Here another miracle occurs and the water becomes sweet (fresh). Moses and the people continue to advance toward Eilam, where they discover twelve springs of water and seventy date trees. They rest there, and then continue toward the desert of Sin.

The people complain that they have run out of supplies, and the Creator performs two miracles: in the first, manna comes down from the sky. In the second, quails fly over the camp of Israel so they will have meat in the evening.

The children of Israel receive the first commandment—to observe the Sabbath. They are told that on the Sabbath, no manna will come down from the sky and that on the sixth day they must collect supplies for two days. The children of Israel continue from the desert of Sin and arrive at Rephidim. Once again there is no water and the Creator performs another miracle: Moses strikes a rock, and water gushes out of it.

Toward their arrival at Mount Sinai, Amalek appears and fights against Israel. When Moses raises his hands, Israel win; when he lowers them, Amalek wins. Finally, Israel defeats Amalek and the Creator tells Moses to write in a book of remembrance that the memory of Amalek must be blotted out from under the heaven.

Commentary

Man is born with an inherently egoistic desire to receive. However, when ascending it, our perspective changes and we no longer think only of ourselves. From the moment we are born we want to use the whole world for our own benefit. This is the Amalek in us. AMALEK is an acronym for *Al Menat LeKabel* (in order to receive). We turn the will to receive into a spiritual quality that aims toward bestowal through a process in which each of us works on the self, using the light that reforms. The light that reforms* is a force that awakens in those who study Kabbalah correctly in a group. That force awakens and we feel changes constantly happening within.

These are the changes that the Torah describes in this portion. Pharaoh really does send away the people of Israel. That is, our egos are under stress and suffering in a conflict between the forces operating on it. Finally, it "allows" us freedom and throws us away from itself.

In fact, we are only observing the unfolding of the Creator's war against Amalek (Exodus, 17:16), the Creator's war against Pharaoh, and the entire process (Exodus, 10) of hardening Pharaoh's heart, "go on to Pharaoh," and "come to Pharaoh."

When the children of Israel escape from Egypt with all the *Kelim*, meaning desires, we rise above the ego, but the egoistic intentions remain. In the process of development, we gradually rid ourselves of them during the numerous changes we undergo while exiting Pharaoh's rule and coming under the rule of the quality of the Creator–the reign of the quality of bestowal and love of others.

In the transition from love of self to love of others, we undergo various changes that make us feel as though Pharaoh is still chasing us and we are trying to escape. At times we can run and at times we cannot. This is why reality mandates a miracle, meaning the influence of the upper force on us.

The influence of the upper force on us manifests in the sensation that we are standing in front of the sea, with Pharaoh's 600 chosen chariots behind, and there is nothing we can do. Each time we arrive at a point where there is nothing ahead and all the roads seem blocked, a miracle occurs. This is how we shift from degree to degree, from state to state.

---

* Midrash Rabah, *Eicha*, "Introduction," Paragraph 2.

The difference between the degrees is that the next degree always opens *after* we have concluded the previous one. Each time, we did not know what to do and were desperate. Although we get used to this, we are surprised every time anew.

After the splitting of the Red Sea we arrive at the desert. A "desert" is a state where we cannot do anything. We have nothing with which to feed ourselves, and are in a state of emptiness, not knowing what to do. In that state, it seems that life is not life, neither in the present nor in the future.

In the next stage, the water is bitter and must be sweetened using the staff. This means that we elevate the desire to bestow and degrade the desire to receive for the sake of receiving. In this way we achieve the degree of *Bina* instead of *Malchut*, and elevate ourselves above the ego, once again breaking through to the next degree. We arrive at a place called Eilam, where there are twelve sources of water and food from seventy palm trees.

It happens every single time. Our egoistic will to receive awakens without our knowing what to do with it because we haven't the strength to cope when it yells and screams in terror. This is when the upper force saves us. Thus, repeatedly and gradually, our exodus from Egypt takes place.

In the exodus from Egypt, we correct the will to receive step by step. We rise above it continuously until we can even fight Amalek. Moses' hands, which rise and fall, symbolize the ascending force of *Bina*, and the descending MAN.

When we enter spirituality, we still have nothing with which to revive ourselves except the food from heaven. Prior to that, we were satisfying ourselves egoistically, trying to gain from everyone as much as we could. But now, in our transition to love others–altruism, bestowal–we fill ourselves with bestowal. This is why it is called "food from the sky," the "food of heaven."

This occurs when we are willing to come out into the "morning light," to be in the quality of bestowal that shines over the ego, the will to receive in which one now feels empty. When we are willing to remain in the will to receive even without fulfillment, but only in bestowal upon others, this is when the manna comes, the fulfillment from heaven.

Forty years in the desert is the period when we obtain the complete quality of bestowal. We are fed by giving to others, which is truly from heaven, as who are we to give? Do we have anything to give? Why should we fulfill ourselves by giving?

This sensation, the intention we acquire over the will to receive—the inclination toward others, the connection with others—is the degree called "that which you hate, do not do to your friend."* By connecting to others as to ourselves, we receive the filling called MAN, *Mey Nukvin* (Aramaic: Female Water), which raises our will to receive to *Bina*, the degree of bestowal.

Questions and Answers

Many miracles take place in this portion, almost all of which concern water: the crossing of the Red Sea, the bitter water, Moses striking the rock and the water gushing out. What is a miracle, and why is it so tightly connected to water specifically in this portion?

Water is the quality of bestowal, *Bina*. There is water of quarrelling (Meribah), bitter water, and sweet (fresh) water, drinking water. There is also "cold water to a faint soul" (Proverbs, 25:25), and there are other terms concerning water.

Water is life. While we develop in our mother's womb, we are immersed in water. Indeed, water is our whole life; we have evolved in water and then climbed out to land. Water is the quality of *Bina*; it emits from itself just as the oceans beget life.

This happens every time through a miracle, as we do not possess the quality of bestowal, *Bina*, love of others, the connection with others in favor of the other. For this reason, we receive it from outside

* Babylonian Talmud, *Masechet Shabbat*, 31a

in what is considered a miracle. All we do is cause that process to unfold, and when it does, it is as a miracle, as it is written, "I have labored and found."* Finding is actually the miracle, and on our way to bestowal, everything happens through miracles.

The Creator took the children of Israel for a "tour" in the desert out of fear of fighting the Philistines, so they went through Sinai. Why did He not take them straight to Israel?

The children of Israel walked in the desert for forty years, but you can actually cross the desert in a week. We have such a big will to receive: wars with the Philistines, with Amalek, sins such as the golden calf and the sin of the spies, and many other problems just to get to the entrance to the land of Israel. Additionally, there is the war to conquer the land.

It takes many wars to conquer the will to receive and turn it from an egoistic desire, Egypt, into a desire for the land of Israel. *Eretz* (land) means *Ratzon* (desire). We must aim our desire not to work in order to receive, which is Amalek, but in order to bestow, which is *Yashar El* (straight to God), *Ysrael* (Israel). It is a very long process in which miracles constantly occur.

Why do the children of Israel avoid fighting the Philistines?

Because the children of Israel are not yet strong enough. They have yet to acquire the force of bestowal that will enable them to fight and confront the Philistines. There is still no right line, the force of bestowal, so it is impossible to use the middle line and advance with it. When we have only the force of reception, the left line, we must bypass the Philistines.

From *The Zohar*: And Israel Saw the Great Hand

"And Israel saw the great hand ... and they believed in the Lord." But did they not believe in the Creator thus far? After all, it is

* Babylonian Talmud, *Masechet Megilah*, 6b.

written, "And the people believed; and when they heard." Moreover, they saw all the great deeds that the Creator did for them in Egypt. However, "And they believed" means that they believed in what he said, "And Moses said unto the people, 'Do not fear! Stand by and see the salvation of the Lord.'"

Zohar for All, BeShalach (When Pharaoh Sent), item 203

At each stage we advance by degrees. Our way, as *The Zohar* writes, is 600 chosen chariots, six days and the seventh day, Sabbath, which corresponds to the end of correction, the seventh millennium. The road from the exodus from Egypt to the end of our correction goes through 125 degrees, with each degree dividing into additional degrees. There are miracles each time, and each time we become more adhered to the upper force.

We are in between two forces: on the one hand, there is the will to receive, which is the nature we are born with, as it is written, "the inclination of a man's heart is evil from his youth" (Genesis, 8:21). On the other hand, there is the desire to bestow we must come to. On this ladder of our nature, the will to receive is at the bottom, and the Creator, the desire to bestow, is at the top, with us in the middle, as though hanging in midair. To the extent that the force of the Creator appears before us, we can rise until we achieve *Dvekut* (adhesion) with Him.

This is why we only need to reveal our need, our necessity for the Creator. It is written, "And the children of Israel cried out from the work" (Exodus, 2:23). All the crying and quarrels are disclosures of our deficiency out of the sensation that we must receive help from above.

This is how we live by the mercy of the Creator. This is also how the upper light, the light that reforms, called Torah, appears and saves us. These are the *Hassadim*, the force of bestowal that appears to us. Even today we must understand that if we reveal the right deficiency, the force that will deliver us from all the troubles will appear, and we will cross the Red Sea on dry land.

So what has faith got to do with all of this? What does it mean that they saw the miracle and believed?

Faith is the force of bestowal, of *Bina*. Through the force of bestowal, we see the world that surrounds us, the world of *Ein Sof* (infinity), the spiritual world, the degrees, and the forces. However, we still do not have the vision of bestowal, of connection with others. When we connect with others we develop new "spectacles" through which we see the entire world as circular, with only one force operating in it.

The wisdom of Kabbalah teaches us how to discover the force of the Creator that is operating in the world, the method of revealing His Godliness to His creations in this world.

It seems that the Creator continuously puts the people of Israel in predicaments, such as the bitter water, then delivers them out of it, such as turning it into fresh water. What does this process represent?

We need to realize that we can only understand things by seeing both sides, darkness as well as light, as "the advantage of the light out of darkness" (Ecclesiastes, 2:13). This is why we keep discovering that the ego is worse than we thought, and we seek a way out of it, understanding that the upper force *must* be involved.

When we become aware that we need the upper force and we cry out, the Creator appears. Each time, we have to come to such a state–revealing our deficiency, the need for His help so He may appear. This is how we build our *Kli* (vessel), and this is why we eat the manna (*MAN*) in the desert. We are never the owners or landlords; we only ask for the process to take place.

It is the same today with the process we are going through, and in the even harder processes ahead. After all, the purpose of the process is simply to bring us to a state of no control, complete helplessness and despair, which obligates the upper force to appear. Without it, we will not be able to advance. The better we understand the process, this predilection, and the better we prepare ourselves for it, the more we will be able to draw the upper force *before* we are in a desperate state. This is why the Torah was given, the interior of the Torah, the wisdom of Kabbalah, so we will know each time how to prescribe the cure before the illness.

Today it is very difficult to make people understand that they have no control. We are accustomed to thinking that through science and technology we will control Nature.

This is how it was until the outbreak of the crisis. Now we understand that we do not control anything. We do not control the education system, our families, ourselves, terror, commerce, economy or finance, and these are signs of the comprehensive crisis, the systemic breakdown in which all systems are collapsing. We are reaching a state where we will need a special revelation of Nature's collective force.

We are built in such a way that each of us pulls toward his or her side, and the rising crisis proves that we are all tied together, dependent on each other, and that only in mutual dependence will we be able to resolve the problem. However, since we cannot establish a connection of *Arvut* (mutual guarantee), we will need the help of the upper force. It will take a long time before we understand that we need the force of unity, which is the Creator making peace between us, as it is written, "He who makes peace in His heaven, He will make peace on us and on all of Israel" (from the *Kadish* prayer).

What does the process of crossing the Red Sea represent?

When *Malchut* enters *Bina*, there is upper water and lower water. Likewise, at the time of the creation of the world, there was the upper force that comes and lets the will to receive enter the sea, the water–thus connecting the will to receive with the desire to bestow. The will to receive is the force of the earth. Israel, which connects the force of the ground, reveals the ground within the sea, while the sea itself is the giving force, where there are *Gevurot*, a stormy sea.

Israel also reveals the special force, Nachshon, who jumps first into the water. It is a force within us willing to go forth with complete dedication, only to achieve the quality of bestowal, the connection with *Bina*, whatever happens. As we come out, we make the first contact with the desire to bestow. The entire escape from Egypt is an escape from ourselves out to everyone, to connect with the others.

From *The Zohar*: And Pharaoh Drew Near

Israel were nearing the sea and saw the sea before them becoming stormier, its waves straightening upward. They were afraid. They raised their eyes and saw Pharaoh and his army, and slings and arrows, and they were terrified. "And the children of Israel cried out." Who caused Israel to draw near to their father in heaven? It was Pharaoh, as it is written, "And Pharaoh drew near."

Zohar for All, *BeShalach* (When Pharaoh Sent), item 67

Each time, our egos wake up and do not let us advance. In fact, the ego does the work for us because Pharaoh (the ego) is the posterior side of the Creator, who created the will to receive. He constantly reveals it to us until we see that the will to receive, the snake, is putting us to death, so we have to escape from it.

Today we are in similar situation. We are gradually learning that our egos are not letting us connect and build proper systems, live in families, nations, and states, or build the planet and the world as circular and connected, since this is what will prompt us toward correction. This is why we are living in a special time, when we will truly have to determine that *Arvut* (mutual guarantee) is the connection between us.

Moses was instructed to write in a book that the memory of Amalek would be blotted out. What is a book in the spiritual sense?

A book is a disclosure. It is a disclosure that we have in the book of Torah, which describes the works of the Creator in relation to the creature. We act through these revelations, through the letters, which are written black over white in order to erase the intention of Amalek–to make the will to receive in order to receive become a desire to receive in order to bestow. This is called *Ratzon* (desire), *Eretz* (land), and "in order to bestow" is like the Creator, when we reach *Yashar El* (straight to God), *Ysrael* (Israel).

In other words, Amalek is the opposite of the land of Israel. Amalek is a general term, much like Haman, snake, and Pharaoh, except it also contains smaller, specific parts. We learn that each time, the people of Israel face them. Every one of us is like the people of Israel–made of the qualities of bestowal that are placed under the will to receive.

Terms

Philistines

"Philistines" are our egoistic desires. Even after we escape the rule of the will to receive, they are still connected to bestowal. It is called "bestowing in order to receive." When we give, we reach out to others. But when we begin to give, we see that we can also gain by it. Therefore, we must rise above the desires found outside the boundaries of Egypt, as well, though the correction in them is different from the one that took place in Egypt.

We could not discover these desires while in Egypt because we were "buried" under our egos. When we emerge from the ego, we see how it pulled all of us through the forty years in the desert, and even afterward, in the land of Israel, when we conquered the land.

The Song of the Sea

The "Song of the Sea" is thanksgiving. It is gratitude for crossing the border, never to return to Egypt. At times we might cry over the past, as in this portion, but there is no way back. We make the final exit from Egypt. After the escape, we begin to feel the spiritual world and not just the existence of this world, and this feeling induces an outburst of joy.

MAN

MAN is *Mey Nukvin* (Aramaic: female water). It is the will to receive wanting to rise to the level of *Bina*. When we feel that we can and must bestow in these desires, we ask that it will happen. Thus we need the help of the upper force to make it happen, and then the force will appear from above.

When we begin to use this force, it fills us with bestowal upon others, and this is called "eating manna." But in this world, we will never feel this way because in this world we are fulfilled by reception, while in the spiritual world we are fulfilled by bestowal.

From *The Zohar*: The Story of Haman

The most precious of all is the food that the friends who engage in Torah eat, food that comes from high *Hochma*, actual *Hochma*. This is because the Torah comes out of the upper *Hochma*, and those who engage in the Torah enter the essence of the roots, hence their food comes from the high and holy place.

Zohar for All, *BeShalach* (When Pharaoh Sent), item 382

Yitro

(Jethro)

(Exodus, 18:1-20:22)

Portion Summary

The portion, Jethro, starts with Jethro, priest of Midian, coming out with Zipporah and Moses' two sons to meet Moses and the people, who have come out of Egypt. Jethro gives Moses some organizational tips regarding how to judge the nation, explaining that he should divide them into ministers of thousands, ministers of hundreds, ministers of fifty, and ministers of ten.

The children of Israel arrive at the Sinai Desert on the third month of their exodus from Egypt, as it is written, "And Israel camped there, before the mountain" (Exodus, 19:2). Moses climbs Mount Sinai and the Creator tells him, "And now, if you will indeed obey My voice and keep My covenant, then you shall be to Me a *Segula* (chosen/virtue/remedy) out of all the nations, for all the earth is Mine. And you shall be to Me a kingdom of priests and a holy nation. These are the words that you shall speak to the children of Israel" (Exodus, 19:5-6).

Moses informs the elders of the words of the Creator, and they say, "All that the Lord has spoken we will do" (Exodus 19:8). The Creator commands the people through Moses to sanctify themselves for two days and be ready on the third day, for this is when the Creator will appear before the whole nation.

On the third day, the children of Israel stand at the bottom of the mountain, but they do not want to meet the Creator face to face, so Moses and Aaron climb Mount Sinai, and Moses brings down the Ten Commandments.

The children of Israel ask Moses to speak to them instead of the Creator because they are afraid to die. Moses explains to them that they need not fear because the Creator is coming down to test them. He will set the fear of Him in them so they will not sin.

The Creator instructs Moses to tell the children of Israel that because they saw Him speaking with them, they are forbidden to make gods of silver and gold. Instead, they must build an altar on the ground and make a sacrifice on it.

COMMENTARY

Jethro, priest of Midian, is not from Israel. He is from the will to receive in order to receive, a *Klipa* (shell/peel) mitigated by Moses. Jethro rises and connects to Moses through his *Nukva* (female), his daughter Zipporah, with whom Moses has two sons. This is the big and broken will to receive that the Moses in us is gradually correcting.

When Moses comes to Jethro after he has fled, a connection is made between the point in the heart, Moses, and the ego. Thus, a correction is made so that afterward it will be easier for us to make corrections on the more advanced stages.

The correction helps us begin to divide ourselves into tens, fifties, hundreds, and thousands, meaning to build the structure of the soul. The whole Torah deals with the construction of our souls, and how we can turn our egoistic desire into a desire with the aim to bestow. When the desire acquires the aim to bestow, it is called a "soul."

The force of reception is called the "self," "this world." Everything we see and feel is the force of reception. The force of bestowal is our exit from reception. When we work in order to bestow, in "Love your neighbor as yourself,"* we obtain our souls. Our inner Moses is pulling away from the quality of reception toward the quality of bestowal, bringing us out of ourselves and allowing us to see the upper world and begin to feel the Creator.

The Book of Zohar speaks about it in great detail in the portion, Jethro, but it is still not easy to grasp. It concerns the three lines, the structure of the soul, reception, bestowal, and the middle line, which is the proper combination between them. *The Zohar* describes how to divide the soul–first into ten *Sefirot*, according to the Ten Commandments, then according to the three lines, which is thirty. There is also a division into *Rosh*, *Toch*, *Sof* (head, interior, end [respectively]), and there are many other inner divisions that include the *Sefira* (singular for *Sefirot*) *Daat*.

When we relate to ourselves as coming out of Egypt, examining ourselves from the outside, we examine how we can use our egos to advance ourselves spiritually, toward the aim to bestow. We go through difficult situations, such as the escape from Egypt and the tearing of the Red Sea until we reach Mount Sinai. This is how we build ourselves on the way to correction–through Jethro's counsels, as well as through actions.

Being at the foot of Mount Sinai requires preparation. This is the "main event," when we meet the Creator. While we are in the dark, we do not understand why we need to advance and follow the point in our hearts, Moses.

In a sense, Moses helps us out of Egypt when we escape in the dark. However, we are not conscious participants in this process. At the foot of Mount Sinai is where the upper force first appears to us. This is when we begin to understand our own essence and the

* "Love your neighbor as yourself. Rabbi Akiva says, 'It is a great rule in the Torah'" (Jerusalem Talmud, *Seder Nashim*, *Masechet Nedarim*, Chapter 9, p 30b).

essence of the upper force, as well as how to relate to our situation and how we need to move forward.

In this portion, we receive our first awareness. With it awaken all of our desires on the human level. These are called "the people," or the "nation," and they are afraid. These desires still cannot connect to the Creator; they cannot see or hear Him, so they tell Moses, "You speak." This is the state at which we arrive from the exile, Egypt, our egos.

We begin to hear a little bit only by coming down from *Keter* (crown), which is the Creator. This process unfolds through *Hochma* and *Bina* when Moses and Aaron begin to bring down the great light that appears to the will to receive as laws, as the Ten Commandments. This begins with the first commandment, "I am the Lord your God, who brought you out of the land of Egypt, out of the house of slavery" (Exodus, 20:2), and ends with the final commandment.

The Ten Commandments include all 620 *Mitzvot* (commandments). There are 620 corrections, which are 613 plus seven *Mitzvot* of our sages, by which we have to correct our desires. That is, we consist of 620 desires that divide into 613+7 desires.

The 613 *Mitzvot* are divided into 248 and 365, and these comprise the structure of the soul. The soul itself consists of ten parts, ten *Sefirot*, and their correction is called "Ten Commandments," which are the primary *Mitzvot* (corrections/commandments) that were given to man. We ascend according to our position, by how we stand before the light that appears to us. Hearing is the degree of *Bina*, and seeing is the degree of *Hochma*.

When we have gone through the entire process and come out of Egypt, rising above the ego, we are willing to receive the program of bestowal, the program of connecting with the whole of humanity. Then we are ready for the revelation of Godliness in the connection between all people, as it is written, "Love your neighbor as yourself; Rabbi Akiva says, 'It is a great rule in the Torah.'"* This rule is both

* Jerusalem Talmud, *Seder Nashim, Masechet Nedarim*, Chapter 9, p 30b.

the foundation and the result of keeping the Ten Commandments, with the goal being *Keter*, achieving love, and through the love of others achieving the love of the Creator.

In our current state, part of humanity is discovering it is in Egypt, another part is discovering that it wants to come out of Egypt, and a part is discovering how to come out and advance toward Mount Sinai. We are beginning to feel we are in the dark, in a process we do not understand. Each day our need for the light, for the revelation of the Creator, is growing. We need it to bring a tiny illumination into our lives so we may understand what is happening to us.

We need to fix Jethro, the egoistic will to receive, as it is written, "If one should tell you, 'there is wisdom in the nations, believe.'"* If Moses did not connect to the desire called Jethro, he would not have received from him the knowledge of judgment and ruling, which is necessary for the reception of the Torah.

By sharing the method of correction with the nations of the world, the method of *Arvut* (mutual guarantee), and the necessity for the wisdom of Kabbalah, we are doing the work that Moses did with Jethro. For that, we will be rewarded with standing at the foot of Mount Sinai.

QUESTIONS AND ANSWERS

In the portion, Jethro, the people of Israel receive the Ten Commandments. This may be the most important portion because the Torah is correction. So why is this portion named after an "external" desire, Jethro?

Jethro is the priest of Midian, a *Klipa* that stands opposite. He is one of Pharaoh's servants, similar to other forces that stood next to the will to receive and helped Pharaoh connect and elicit as much as possible from the desire to bestow–Israel. *The Zohar* appears to be writing bad things about him, but he is help made against us. After all, everything is within us.

* Midrash Rabah, *Eicha*, Parasha 2, Paragraph 13.

What comes out of Egypt is *Kelim* (vessels), meaning desires. In the desires that come out, there is still no intention to work with the will to receive. Moses, the force of *Bina*, wants to judge the will to receive, which is detached from him. Even while standing before Pharaoh, he wanted to draw out the will to receive, though not in order to connect or to elicit anything from it, but to judge it. However, he was unsuccessful.

When we arrive at the state that exists between Moses and the nation that has come out of Egypt, there has to be a special system built according to the will to receive, according to corporeality. This systems also includes the mixed multitude and all the layers that oppose the process of bestowal and love of others. Moses cannot build it; he can only give from above, seemingly "pouring down," but it is not absorbed in the people. As it is written, Moses grows tired, and the people, who cannot find the right connection, stand next to him all day.

Because we cannot find the proper relationship between our desire upward, toward the Creator, and our egos—in the family, at work, and in the community—we need a system that will provide us with Jethro. The wisdom must come specifically from the will to receive, as it is written, "If one should tell you, 'there is wisdom in the nations, believe.'" Although it does not belong to the degree of *Bina*, it was previously included in it when Moses spent forty years with Jethro. Moses grew to the degree of *Bina* with Jethro. And now Jethro is seemingly paying back.

Does Jethro put order between Moses and the desires so that Moses can free himself for the real thing—the receiving of the Torah?

Jethro returns to Moses what he received from him when Moses was with him. Moses came to Jethro after fleeing from Pharaoh. He grew while with Jethro from the degree of *Malchut* to the degree of *Bina*, which is pure bestowal. He grew at Jethro's home and "over" Jethro, through his connection with Zipporah and their two sons, from the right and from the left, with Moses in the middle. Everything that Moses gave Jethro and instilled in him is now returning to him: Jethro, Zipporah, and the two sons. There was a mingling of *Bina* in *Malchut*, and now *Malchut* is giving back to *Bina*.

Now, Moses can build the entire system of connecting *Bina* to *Malchut*, and he is ready to receive the Torah. This is why the first encounter with the Creator is named after Jethro, since the system built earlier enables us to reach the state of being at Mount Sinai.

On the one hand, the children of Israel were afraid of turning to the Creator for fear of dying. On the other hand, it is known that the Creator receives prayers that specifically come from the heart. So where does the fear come from? Why were the children of Israel afraid?

Our will to receive is still not equipped with a *Masach* (screen) that can withstand the light, so the light still seems like darkness. What is the meaning of the exodus from Egypt in the dark? In fact, there is no dark, but it seems dark to us because we are still not corrected. The Aramaic word, *Orta* (night), is very similar to the Hebrew word, *Ohr* (light). That is, at one time it is night, and at another time it is light, depending on how we experience it.

From *The Zohar*: And Jethro Heard

They all shook and looked at Jethro, who was wise and the great appointee over all the idols of the world. When they saw him approaching and serving the Creator, saying, "Now I know that the Lord is greater than all the gods," they all veered away from their works and knew that they were futile. Then the glory of the holy Name of the Creator was glorified on all sides. This is why this portion was written in the Torah, and the beginning of the portion is with Jethro.

Zohar for All, Jethro, item 42

Jethro is the first will to receive that surrenders and accepts the sovereignty of the Creator. That is why this portion is named after him. *The Zohar* also mentions *Gematria*, why Jethro is called Jethro, why Zipporah is called Zipporah, and all the other events in the portion.

In this portion we hear that the children of Israel camped at the foot of Mount Sinai. What does it mean to camp there?

Camping is similar to what happens on Hanukah. It is clear that we cannot correct our egos at that time, but can only take advice on a way, a program, a goal that can be implemented over time according to the level of our understanding of the program. Only at the end of the desert and at the entrance to the land of Israel do the people discover everything that Moses says to them in his final words, prior to his demise.

From *The Zohar*: You Shall Not Kill; You Shall Not Commit Adultery

When that filth was removed from them, Israel remained pure bodies without any filth, and the soul inside the body was as the brightness of the firmament to receive light. So were Israel, who saw and regarded the glory of their master. This was not so on the sea because the filth was not removed from them at that time, while here in Sinai, when the filth stopped from the body, even fetuses in their mothers' intestines saw and looked at the glory of their Master. All of them, each and every one, received as befitted him.

Zohar for All, Jethro, items 572-573

Spiritual ascension can be the result of two states—an awakening from above and an awakening from below. In an awakening from above, the light shines from above and sanctifies us, giving us the force of bestowal through which we begin to look into the distance against our egos. Thus, we see the world outside ourselves, the spiritual world, and we know the upper force, the Creator. An awakening from below comes from us through extensive efforts to connect with others. When we collect awakenings from everyone, we reach the same awakening as that which can be received from above.

Naturally, our own work from below is more desirable and appreciated because if we collect the forces from our friends, and each of them does the same, and each has his or her own strength, that force becomes permanently theirs. Here, we are seemingly camping so we can take advice as to what to do. To hear the advice, we must wake up. It is similar to the exodus from Egypt through an external force from above that pushes and pulls us. But afterward, we must actualize the forces we have received during the forty years in the desert.

Something special happens at Mount Sinai—purification—a special force we receive.

The light that affects us is called "the light that reforms." It is written, "I have created the evil inclination; I have created for it the Torah as a spice"* because "the light in it reforms them."** It reforms the evil inclination and makes it good. Initially, we are all in the evil inclination, egoists, and all we need is the Torah, assuming it is the real Torah, as it is written, "If one should tell you, 'there is wisdom in the nations, believe; there is Torah in the nations, do not believe.'"***

A "person from the nations" is a desire to receive that wants to receive for itself. Israel is one that strives to achieve bestowal, love of others, and from the love of others to achieve the love of the Creator.

This is why those who are craving are called "Israel," and they learn the wisdom of Kabbalah because it brings the light that reforms. This is how we become sanctified, acquiring the force of bestowal and rising through it. The greater the force of bestowal we possess, the greater the love of others, and the holier we are considered to be.

* Babylonian Talmud, *Masechet Kidushin*, 30b.
** Midrash Rabah, *Eicha*, "Introduction," Paragraph 2.
*** Midrash Rabah, *Eicha*, Parasha 2, Paragraph 13

Terms

Jethro

"Jethro" is the will to receive that can be sanctified and join Moses, and with him make the connection between the upper system—*Keter*, *Hochma*, and *Bina*—*GAR* of the soul, and the will to receive, the people below, *ZAT* of the soul. Jethro was included in Moses when Moses lived with him; he is like the force of *Malchut* that is included in *Bina*. This is why *Bina* can connect to *Malchut* and bring to it the new system.

Mount Sinai

It is written, "I have created the evil inclination; I have created for it the Torah as a spice"* because "the light in it reforms them."** The evil inclination is Mount Sinai; it is all the hatred that appears between the nations of the world and Israel. The nations of the world are our desires to receive, and Israel is our desire to bestow. Therefore, if a gap between the desire to receive and the desire to bestow appears in us, we feel hatred, and can be said to be at the foot of Mount Sinai.

This hatred appears when we want to connect, when we are standing around the mountain and must establish mutual guarantee. This is why it is written, "He said to them, 'If you receive the Torah, good. And if you do not, there will it be your grave.'"*** That is, if you do not connect as one man with one heart, here you will be buried.

The hatred is toward unity. If we do not want to connect, we will not discover our hatred of others, we will not arrive at Mount Sinai, and we will certainly not achieve corrections. This can tell us how far we all are from Mount Sinai.

---

* Babylonian Talmud, *Masechet Kidushin*, 30b

** Midrash Rabah, *Eicha*, "Introduction," Paragraph 2

*** Babylonian Talmud, *Masechet Avoda Zara*, 2b.

Being at the foot of Mount Sinai is a great degree that comes after we have worked our whole lives in Egypt, working on the connection between people. And although we have wanted to have a connection of love of others, we could not do so until we realized that it was impossible. This is when the point that draws us out of ourselves appears, and we understand that it is possible to escape, and therefore we escape and rise above our egos.

Once we emerge from the ego, our relation toward it becomes increasingly apparent to us. What appears is the gap between the ego and the pull to be outside the ego. That gap is called "Mount Sinai." This is the state that the Moses in us is above, trying to cling to the Creator at the top of the mountain, while the entire as-yet-uncorrected ego is below, just as the people could not connect to the Creator. However, this is already the beginning of the march toward correction.

A People of *Segula* (chosen/virtuous/remedy)

Segula refers to the punctuation mark *Segol*. *Segol* is three dots [∴], representing the three lines by which we advance toward the goal, meaning right–the force of giving, and left–the force of receiving. Through them we build ourselves by joining the right to the left. It is customary to sing on the Sabbath, "Come in peace, angels of peace, angels of the upper one." Just as we walk on two legs and advance, we build the middle line by which we advance out of the two lines, two angels.

"Go out in peace" comes after we have built the middle line in four states–*Yod-Hey-Vav-Hey*–and have reached the end of correction. This is when we say, "Go out in peace."

This is how we use everything we have within to make corrections. We were given from above the right and the left–the force of bestowal, *Kedusha* (sanctity), and the force of reception, *Klipa* (shell/peel)–and it is for us to combine them. We do that in order to advance by constantly enhancing the combination between them, making it more beneficial. This is why the third line is called the "middle line." The upper force is the two lines, two forces that help us connect properly. They are called *Segula* (virtue/remedy). We live only by them; if that force does not come, we cannot do anything below.

SUMMARY

From this portion we can learn that to an extent, our connection between the desire to bestow and the will to receive must constantly exist. The wisdom of Kabbalah does not tell us to ruin our egos, but rather to use them correctly. This is why it is called *Hochmat ha Kabbalah* (the wisdom of receiving); it is the wisdom of how to use the vessels of reception.

We do not need to avoid using the vessels of reception, or to be "above" the worldly life. Rather, we need to discover that the evil inclination is detaching us from connection with the rest of the world, as it was said to Moses, "And you will be to Me a kingdom of priests and a holy nation" (Exodus, 19:6). That is, the role of the people of Israel is to offer themselves to the service of the rest of the world.

Mishpatim

(Ordinances)

(Exodus, 21:1-24:18)

Portion Summary

In the portion, *Mishpatim* (Ordinances), the Creator gives Moses a collection of laws and judgments pertaining to various topics: laws between man and man, Hebrew slaves, Hebrew maidservant, murder, theft, lending money, and others. The Creator also dictates laws concerning man and God, meat and dairy foods, the Sabbath, *Shmita* (year of omission, refraining from growing crops), etc.

Moses conveys to the children of Israel the message that the Creator will help them enter the land of Israel, and warns them about practicing idolatry. Moses reads to them from the book of covenant, and the people reply, "We will do and we will hear" (Exodus, 24:7). Moses builds an altar and offers sacrifices to the Creator, and a covenant is signed between the people and the Creator. Moses carries out the Creator's command, ascends Mount Sinai to receive the tablets of the covenant, accompanied by his servant, Joshua, and stays there for forty days and forty nights.

Commentary

In the portion, *Mishpatim* (Ordinances), Moses ascends Mount Sinai, although he had already received the laws and ordinances, and the children of Israel had already kept the Torah and laws regarding the offerings. This tells us that laws and ordinances are one thing, while the Torah is another.

The portion details all the laws of the spiritual world, everything we need to know and do. In order to be able to follow them, we must receive the Torah. The Torah was given because "I have created the evil inclination, I have created for it the Torah as a spice."* That is, one is shown to whom one is compared to be at the degree of "man," in a state of loving others and connection among everyone, a state of correction of all the egoistic desires.

This is why the laws come first. When we begin to study the wisdom of Kabbalah, we understand that first we correct ourselves, our attitude toward the group, toward people, and toward the world. There are many internal corrections of the evil inclination that we must perform. When we understand what we must do, the period of receiving the Torah arrives. We learn to receive the light that corrects us during our studies.

This is how we gradually obtain the Creator, the upper force that fills the upper world. This is why it was said, "We will do and we will hear." First we must do, and then–in the corrected *Kelim* (vessels) that we build–we will discover the Creator filling those *Kelim*.

The portion explains the structure of the soul because that is all there is. Although we are living in the soul now, too, we feel and understand this world within the soul to a very limited degree, the still (inanimate) degree. The portion tells us how to open up the soul, the *Kli* (vessel), and how to correct and expand it. This allows us to transcend the boundaries of this world.

When we correct all the levels in the soul, namely the corrupt desires, we open them up and discover within them the higher

* Babylonian Talmud, *Masechet Kidushin*, 30b.

dimension, the upper world. Thus, in addition to our perception of this world, we also feel the upper world, as it is written, "You will see your world in your life."* The Torah was given to us in order to open ourselves up to the perception of the spiritual world, so we could live in both worlds through our present perception, through our bodies.

Today, the entire world, the whole of humanity, is in a crisis. It is a stage of transitioning from only perceiving this world into perceiving the spiritual world, as well.

In conferences that discuss the future of the world, scientists and psychologists state that the whole of humanity is in transition to a new perception. We therefore see that we are shifting to new laws and a new perception of reality.

The portion, *Mishpatim*, is pertinent today, as well, as we are discovering that we do not know the rules affecting our world, making it difficult for us to cope with it. When we begin to understand the world, we will discover that to cope with it we need the Torah for our instruction, for "I have created the evil inclination; I have created for it the Torah as a spice."

We should recognize that we do not yet have the power of the light that reforms, the Torah of light, namely the wisdom of Kabbalah, by which we can correct human nature. With the corrected nature, we will see a new, expanded reality.

When Moses arrives with Joshua at Mount Sinai, he leaves him below and ascends. He stays on the mountain for "forty days and forty nights" (Genesis, 7:4) in order to receive the power of the Torah. This means that he has risen a degree.

Man is a small world. Therefore, we must come to see that the whole of reality is in us. Within us are all the laws, all the ordinances, the people of Israel, all the parts of our will to receive that we must arrange as the structure of our souls. We leave what is considered "Joshua" below, while Moses climbs to the top of the mountain. When we set up the picture correctly at the stage of our spiritual

* *Masechet Berachot*, 17a.

progress called "the portion, *Mishpatim*," we advance toward attaining the goal of Creation. In that state, we feel as one who is climbing up the mountain and is already in contact with the Creator.

Questions and Answers

The portion details many rules concerning Hebrew slaves, intake of meat and dairy foods, etc. These are divided into two parts: between man and man, and between man and God. On the one hand, we say that everything is about relations between people. On the other hand, we say that everything is about connecting to the Creator. Why do we make that division?

All the rules were intended for the correction of the soul, meaning our will to receive. All that was created is the will to receive, and each of us is immersed in it. The will to receive is divided into ten *Sefirot*: *Keter*, *Hochma*, *Bina*, *Hesed*, *Gevura*, *Tifferet*, *Netzah*, *Hod*, *Yesod*, and *Malchut*. It is also divided into three lines, into five *Behinot* (discernments), and into *Aviut* (thickness, levels of desire) *Shoresh* (root), one, two, three, and four. It contains everything.

We are living inside our will to receive, called a *Neshama* (soul), and the Creator is the general force of bestowal, love. When we are inside our will to receive, and not in bestowal and love, we cannot discover the Creator in our soul. He is hidden. We can discover Him only if we correct our will to receive so it works in order to bestow, in love of others. In that process appears the force of bestowal and love, called "the Creator."

So how do we correct it and how do we approach the correction? The whole world is mistaken when asking that question. Everyone thinks that they understand what we need to do in life; this is why there are so many religions and belief systems. But no one, with the exception of true Kabbalists, has any clear notion.

In fact, our Torah is very simple. It is even written, "It is one, easy thing."* We need to join a group that engages only in the love of

* Midrash Rabah, *Devarim*, Portion 11, item 11.

friends, and that this is its goal. If we are "as one man with one heart,"* we will receive the Torah. If we are not, here will be our burial, as it is written, "If you receive the Torah (law), good; if you do not, there will it be your burial."** That is, everything relates to connection.

There are two stages in the love of humanity. First, there is "That which you hate, do not do to your friend."*** Next, there is "Love your neighbor as yourself ... it is a great rule in the Torah."**** Both stages are to be carried out in a group, where we learn all the rules concerning man and man.

When we understand, know, and have mastered these laws, and can feel and sense them, we will understand how to advance from the love of man to the love of God, the Creator. This is when we ascend to a state of "...and you shall love the Lord your God with all your heart and with all your soul, and with all your might" (Deuteronomy, 6:5). In that state we acquire the mind, heart, understanding, and inclination toward it when we engage in love of others. This is why we go from loving people to loving the Creator.

There are rules concerning man and man, and there are rules concerning man and God. Why do we feel it is easier to observe the commandments concerning man and God?

It is easier because when we perform commandments concerning man and God we feel that we can say anything. It is enough to shove a note into a crack in the Wailing Wall in Jerusalem to calm ourselves. It is nice; we get no response; no one tells us if we are right or wrong, or if it is enough or not. However, toward friends, relatives, neighbors, the nation, state, and humanity, we need to actually reach our goal: to examine whether we love them or not.

"Love" means that one takes the desires of others and satisfies them however one can, caring for them before caring for one's own desires. This is the meaning of love. It is serving others in every way,

* RASHI, Exodus, 19b.
** Babylonian Talmud, *Masechet Avoda Zarah*, p 2b.
*** *Masechet Shabbat*, 31a.
**** Jerusalem Talmud, *Seder Nashim*, *Masechet Nedarim*, Chapter 9, p 30b.

instead of serving oneself. Today it seems impossible, so it is easier to cover it up by saying, "Don't worry, I get along with the Creator." However, this leads us very far from the true Torah.

From *The Zohar*: Administer Justice in the Morning

Why did the Creator see fit to give the judgments to Israel, meaning the portion *Mishpatim* (Ordinances), after the Ten Commandments? The Torah was given to Israel from the side of *Gevura*. For this reason, they must establish peace among them through judgments and ordinances, so that the Torah will be kept on all its sides. The world exists only on *Din*, for without the *Din* it would not exist. And for this reason, the world was created in *Din* and exists.

Zohar for All, *Mishpatim* (Ordinances), item 517

The world lives by judgment because the Creator created only the will to receive, an egoistic desire that wants to satisfy itself and feel good. There is nothing in reality but the desire to bestow, which is the upper force, and the desire to receive, which is the force of the creature. All that exists is the balance between these two forces. We can also see how it unfolds in the order of the worlds, in *Yod-Hey-Vav-Hey*, how it is rooted and hangs down to this world.

This world, too, is built on four basic principles. If they did not exist, it would not be possible to sustain the universe with all its stars, the earth, and the life upon it. These four principles exist in atoms and in the relationship between the parts of the atom.

The will to receive is the foundation. When we begin to work with that foundation in order to bestow, we permeate Creation. We have never done this before because we have only been using the laws that are in us egoistically.

Until now, we have been following the path paved for us by Nature. Now, for the first time, once we come to the wisdom of Kabbalah we begin to seemingly work against our nature. This is why this work is called "My sons defeated Me,"* because we are seemingly going against the Creator.

The Creator created the evil inclination and we can turn it into a good inclination, thus opening ourselves up to a completely new reality. Only in this new world do we feel solely our nature.

As it is written in *The Zohar*, the corrections are through the correction of *Gevura*, which is why we become *Gevarim*, from the Hebrew word *Hitgabrut* (to overcome). That is, we rise above our egos and enter the world above the ego, the other world—the world of bestowal.

The Book of Zohar is special because of the influence of the light on our correction. Never in history has there been another event where ten great Kabbalists gathered, each corresponding to a different *Sefira* at the head of the system of governance. They assembled and wrote first-hand the master plan to govern and guide the whole of reality. In fact, they were part of that source themselves.

Therefore, when reading what they wrote, we draw to ourselves that light so it may sanctify us and bring us to the level of *Bina*, which is called "holy" or "sanctified," meaning bestowal—love of others. This is when we receive our best weapon against our egos.

From *The Zohar*: The Grandfather

Many are the people in the world whose minds are confused and they do not see truthfully in the Torah. Each day, the Torah calls upon them with love for them, yet they do not wish to turn their heads back and listen to her. In the Torah, a thing comes out of its sheath, appears briefly, and promptly hides. When it appears out of the sheath and promptly hides, the Torah does it only for those who know her and are known in her.

... So is a word of Torah: it appears only to the one who loves her. The Torah knows that that wise of heart circles the gate to her house each day. What does she do? She shows her face from within

* Babylonian Talmud, *Masechet Nezikin*, *Baba Metzia*, 59b

the palace, gives him a hint, and promptly returns to her place and hides. All those from there neither know nor look, but he alone, whose guts and heart and soul follow her. This is why the Torah appears and covers, and goes to her loved one with love, to awaken the love with him.

Zohar for All, Mishpatim (Ordinances), items 97-99

When we need to reveal, we also need to conceal. And yet, it is exactly when we conceal that we reveal. This is the Torah, the *Megila of Esther* (the story of Esther). It becomes *Meguleh* (revealed) particularly in concealment. The more we conceal our egos, the more we reveal the place above the ego where the Creator appears. This is the oppositeness that people do not understand. Our senses cannot perceive it because the technique of concealment and disclosure is built on oppositeness.

What is the meaning of the commandments that the portion discusses?

All commandments are laws pertaining to the soul. Meat and dairy foods correspond to right and left, and observing the Sabbath pertains to the prohibition against touching the last part of the will to receive, which for now remains unattended to because we haven't the strength for it. Only when we complete all of our corrections and reach the seventh millennium, after six thousand years—the six days of working on our corrections, our will to receive—will we reach the Sabbath, namely rest. On Sabbath, we avoid touching desires that pertain to the seventh part.

The portion describes humanity seemingly jumping a degree; what is that jump?

When Moses and the people of Israel approach Mount Sinai, the nature they are in—which they must correct—appears to them. Today, that state of required correction is gradually appearing before humanity, and many academic and scientific conferences around the world are discussing the correction that humanity is going through.

Will new laws appear before humanity?

Yes, and people will begin to talk about it. They will understand and feel it. We are changing each day. A new awareness, new sensation, and new perception is coming to the world, making people more sensitive. Suddenly, we can perceive that there is another dimension outside of us, that we are living in our egos, inside our will to receive, and that this is where we perceive reality. We feel through our desires, and should they change, we will perceive a different reality, as it is written, "I saw an opposite world."*

What does it mean to see an opposite world?

All the laws of Torah were meant only to explain how to discover laws that are opposite from us, how to move from love of self to love of others. This is the meaning of being opposite.

TERMS

Law, or Rule

We are living under laws. The whole of Nature is a law. The Creator is a law; the creature is a law; everything is one law—the law of equivalence of form with the upper force. The upper force is the primer, the foundation, and we constantly measure ourselves and all other laws in relation to it.

The laws are particular instances of a single law—the law of equivalence of form. The whole of Creation must achieve balance, equivalence, and similarity to the force of the Creator. Each of us, at our own degree, must achieve bestowal and love.

* Babylonian Talmud, *Masechet Nezikin, Baba Batra*, 10b.

What is the difference between law and judgment?

We must accept the law of bestowal and love as superior to the ego. Hence, what controls the ego and sustains it, what gives it the form of bestowal instead of the form of reception, is the force of *Din* (judgment). Man must restrain the ego, keep it at bay, and build above it a new *Kli* (vessel).

Is this natural, coming from Nature?

No, what Nature has given us is the ego, the will to receive. In order to turn it into a desire to bestow we must have the impact of the upper light. We need an outside force to come and help us, the light that reforms, which reforms that negative force and turns it into a good one. It was a good force once; this is why it is called "reforming," turning it back to good. Now it is our task to turn the negative force into a positive one. This is our work.

Idolatry

"Idolatry" is serving the force that constantly wants only for itself. This work is alien to those of us who truly desire to keep Nature's commands, the commands of the Creator.

A Hebrew Slave and a Hebrew Maidservant

These are parts of our egoistic will to receive–which contains everything from king to slave, including women, children, men, young and old. The whole world is in it, including the animals, the sky, the earth, and the stars. All these are parts of our desires, which we see in this way–as if they were outside of us.

Murder, Theft

"Murder" refers to the egoistic desire. This is why there is a commandment that if someone comes to kill you, you must kill him first. "Theft" refers to stealing from the gentile. That is, if the will to receive is considered "a gentile," it is a commandment to steal from it, or there will not be justification. When we read the literal words, it is impossible to understand the Torah because it speaks entirely of the spiritual world, the correction of the soul, and the revelation of the Creator in it.

From *The Zohar*: Watching through the Windows

For this reason, the heart sees, the heart hears, the heart understands, and the heart knows. "And in the heart of every wise-hearted I have placed wisdom." Thus, wisdom, intelligence, and knowledge are in the heart, for in them the heaven, the earth, and the deeps were made, and in them was the tabernacle made.

Zohar for All, *Mishpatim* (Ordinances), item 424

A tabernacle is the meeting place of Godliness with the Creator.

Teruma

(Donation)

(Exodus, 25:1-27:19)

Portion Summary

The portion, *Teruma* (Donation), deals primarily with the building of the tabernacle. The Creator instructs Moses to tell the children of Israel, "And they shall take for Me a donation from every man whose heart moves him you shall take My donation" (Exodus, 25:2). The donations were intended for the building of the tabernacle and its tools—the ark of the covenant, the ark cover, the showbread table, the *Menorah* (lamp), the boards of the tabernacle, the sockets, the veil, the copper altar, and the hangings of the court. The Creator also tells Moses how to build the tabernacle. The portion is called *Teruma* (donation) because of the commandment to donate.

Commentary

All we have is the building of the tabernacle. This is where the Creator is revealed, and this is where He resides. We must build it through a donation, and raising the importance of the quality of bestowal and love of others (in Hebrew, the word *Teruma* (donation) also pertains to *Harama* (raising), as in, "raising the *Hey*"*). The more we extol the quality of bestowal and use it properly, the more we correct our *Kelim* (vessels), namely our desires, which we currently use for ourselves, as it is written, "I have created the evil inclination..."**

The building of the tabernacle explains the process of our correction from the easiest to the hardest, as we gradually build the tabernacle from our lightest to our heaviest, greatest, and most egoistic desires.

Our donation to the tabernacle must come from the heart, which contains all desires. Only those who are driven by impulse in the heart are permitted to offer a donation, and from this "investment" they will build their *Kelim*. The *Kelim* are the connections between us that establish the tabernacle. In the tabernacle appears the upper force, the Creator, according to our equivalence of form. That is, we discover the Creator to the extent of our similarity to Him.

The Creator is a hidden force, and we are not inherently born with tools to discover Him because we do not possess qualities similar to His. For example, we hear sounds because our eardrums react to certain frequencies. Likewise, we can tell different smells because we have olfactory neurons that detect them. These are our *Kelim* (in Hebrew, *Kelim* means both "vessels" and "tools"). However, we are devoid of tools to detect the upper force, the Creator, the source of energy.

Yet, everything moves and exists by this force. Its source, however, is hidden from us, as is the direction of its movement, its "vector," goal, and why it moves and operates everything.

This knowledge is revealed in the tabernacle as we correct and construct ourselves according to the influence of the upper force, in equivalence of form with it. Equivalence of form means that if

* Rabash, *The Writings of Rabash*, vol. 3, p 1806

** "I have created the evil inclination; I have created for it the Torah as a spice" (Babylonian Talmud, *Masechet Kidushin*, 30b).

He is good and does good, if He loves the bad, as well as the good,* we must also achieve the state of "Love your neighbor as yourself."** We build the tabernacle according to the gradual correction of our desires from egoism to bestowal and love.

The Torah and the Talmud teach us that the tabernacle, with all its details, symbolizes the correction of the soul. It is neither about the construction of a beautiful building in Jerusalem, nor about physical tools. Rather, it is about man's heart and his internal correction.

It is written, "I have created the evil inclination; I have created for it the Torah as a spice,"*** because "the light in it reforms."**** This is why it is written that only a person with a good heart should donate, for by that, one truly wishes to correct one's heart.

The "donation" is a gradual removal of egoistic desires that can be corrected, moving from a state of separation and hatred of others to bestowal and love of others.

This portion seemingly relates primarily to those who wish to sanctify themselves, to build themselves in such a way that that source of energy, that superior quality, appears in them. This enables them to know where life and all of our energy come from and why, as well as help them determine where they are headed.

Because of the comprehensive crisis we are in, we need information about this process. Without it, we will not know what to do. Those who study the wisdom of Kabbalah discover how they should proceed in life.

In the past, if we encountered problems, we knew how to overcome them. The world had not yet become round, global. But today, as the world has become round, global, a general law

---

* Baal HaSulam, *The Writings of Baal HaSulam*, "Introduction to the Study of the Ten Sefirot," item 90, p 789.

** Jerusalem Talmud, *Seder Nashim, Masechet Nedarim*, Chapter 9, p

*** Babylonian Talmud, *Masechet Kidushin*, 30b.

**** Midrash Rabah, *Eicha*, "Introduction," Paragraph 2.

is appearing, which we can only understand if we ourselves become round.

That is, now we are required to come out of ourselves, of our personal, individualistic mindset, and begin to connect with others. According to the common force appearing between us, namely the Creator–who appears between us as the dweller of the tabernacle–we will discover how to resolve this comprehensive crisis.

This is what makes this portion so pertinent. As soon as we begin to follow the requirement of the Torah to build a tabernacle from our hearts, even if only slightly, we will begin to understand what is required of us in order to restore balance. When we understand the Law of Balance, the general law of reality, we will know how to resolve the crisis. Today, we are bewildered over what we must do with ourselves in the future. This is why we are being shown escalating destruction that cannot be resolved, not even through war or other tragic events.

Therefore, we need to circulate the wisdom of Kabbalah to reveal the solution to all problems. This is the reason why Kabbalah is appearing here and now, so we may use the tools given to us properly. All we need is to fix them a little, and to gradually understand the Creator, reveal Him, and advance toward the correction of the crisis, toward a happy life.

QUESTIONS AND ANSWERS

It seems that the more we try to put order in the world, the more disorder we create.

This is true only if we act on our own reason instead of on the reason of the Creator.

This is the situation today; everyone is trying to put things in order because no one wants disorder.

True. Nature is drawn toward balance. We can see that if one place is hotter than another, eventually the temperatures balance out. Likewise, if there is high air pressure in one place and low air pressure in another, the wind will equalize the pressure. This is how the whole of Nature operates. Nature's movement always aims toward balance–from atoms through molecules, and to every part of Nature.

There are elements in Nature where it seems as though there is no need to add energy. Electrons, for example, endlessly rotate at a high speed. And yet, there must be energy propelling this constant movement. We have no idea where the electrons receive their energy, but that is only because the energy lies beneath the threshold of our senses.

Conversely, we know how many calories we must consume in order to function, or how much energy we have to spend in order to operate a machine. We test our energy sources, such as oil and gas, and build power plants and water drills using this energy. In truth, everything is in imbalance between those two levels, between the minus and the plus, and using the tension between them we build various things, such as batteries.

Today we are witnessing a depletion of energy sources; we are "running out of gas."

Fortunately, we will receive the energy we need from the Creator. He is wearing us out on purpose so we can switch to energy on a higher level and learn how to use it properly.

What, then, is a contemporary tabernacle? Is it the relationships between us that we must establish in this manner?

Yes, we have no choice. If we establish proper connections between us–of love, or at least of mutual guarantee–we will become responsible for one another and understand that we are parts of a single system. Then, we will discover the true power source and its program (software), and will learn how to use it properly.

We are talking about an energy that brings equilibrium to movements between negative and positive. How is this energy, which we called the "tabernacle," going to make equilibrium happen?

We do not discover the energy in the tabernacle itself. We rather discover its *source*, the Creator. The energy, the force we receive from Him, is the power of bestowal. This is the power that is missing in the world. There is plenty of matter in the world; all that is missing is the power to activate it, the power of bestowal. These days we are learning how incapable we are of working with the powers that we do have. The problem is, we have no shortage of negative energy, but we need more positive energy.

When we connect "as one man with one heart" (RASHI, Exodus, 19b), according to Moses' explanation concerning the building of the tabernacle, we will come to the place where the quality of the Creator appears, namely the upper force. This is the source of energy we call "light." Indeed, even the study of physics regards light as the highest form of energy.

When we are in balance, we are certain to succeed. Moreover, success is not only in this transient life, but also in connection to the upper force, as we flow in the current of eternal life in accord with it.

Following the tabernacle, will we receive the right kind of energy?

We will receive it in the tabernacle. The Creator is revealed in the tabernacle, which contains our corrected desires and the unknown desires we held that were previously hateful and resentful toward each other. The upper force appears when we rise above those desires.

From *The Zohar*: You Shall Make the Tabernacle with Ten Curtains

The establishing of the tabernacle is from several degrees, for it is written about it, "And the tabernacle was one," showing that all the organs of the body of the tabernacle are of a single body. It is like a person who has several high and low organs. The internal ones are inside, and the revealed ones are outside. However, all are considered one body, and it is considered one person in one bonding. So is the tabernacle: all the organs are such as above, and when they all unite as one, it is written, "And the tabernacle was one."

Zohar for All, *Teruma* (donation), items 664-665

This is how we discover the single force called "the upper force," which we must experience. Without this, we gradually lose vitality, as is evident in what we are witnessing today.

How will the new order of "feeling as one" be revealed?

Through the deficiency. First, we must understand that we are incompetent; we cannot succeed. By searching for the element by which we *can* succeed, we will discover the futility of our efforts. This, coupled with the development and circulation of the wisdom of Kabbalah through mutual guarantee, is when we will understand that we have no alternative but to gradually connect to that eternal, complete, omnipotent and omniscient power supply, which is the ultimate source of energy.

By and large, when people give a *Teruma* (donation), they want to be honored and remembered, and then the donation acquires an additional value. Is this the right direction?

It is not. *Teruma* relates to the connection of hearts. If a person attempts to use the donation in order to gain respect, notoriety, or appreciation as a great person, even if no one else knows of this ambition, it is still an egoistic fulfillment. That individual is not connecting to others, but rather, is patronizing them.

How can this change so that it truly becomes a donation for the Creator?

Helplessness makes us feel differently, and by disseminating the wisdom of Kabbalah, we are adding great power to this transformation. It may seem that we are not doing much, but our activities are inducing many revelations of the Creator in the world. For now, such revelations are on a level where people are headed toward that direction–searching, feeling that the connections between them can save them. We are seeing the riots in the world from a positive perspective, as well as from the (ostensibly) negative one. Through such rebellions, we can see that our only hope is to connect, that only connection will provide us all with the life force.

When that happens, what will the donation be?

The "donation" is the connection. If we appreciate the power of bestowal, it is called "donating." On the one hand, we extol it, and on the other, we feel how lowly and base we are. The world is round, integral, and can be saved only through unity. Yet, we are aware that we are the opposite of unity. We know we need the upper force to influence and connect us so we are in accord with Nature, with the global world.

From *The Zohar*: And They Shall Take a Donation for Me

How do we know that the Creator desires him and places His abode within him? When we see that man's will is to chase and to exert after the Creator with his heart, soul, and will, we know for certain that Divinity is present there. Then we need to buy that man for the full cost, bond with him and learn from him. We learn about that, "And buy yourself a friend." He should be bought for the full price to be rewarded with the Divinity that is in him. This is how far we must chase a righteous man and buy him.

Zohar for All, *Teruma* (donation), item 39

People who do not understand the meaning of the term, "donation," think it is about money. However, donation pertains to a *Masach* (screen) from which one projects the self, sacrificing oneself.

It is written, "Buy yourself a friend."* That is, we annul our own egos and connect to another, wanting to break down the partition between us. Our hearts inherently want to be individualistic, egoistic, and removed from others, yet we must be the exact opposite. If we want to connect to someone, we must be more humble than that someone. This is the meaning of connecting, namely the donation. This is not how we are used to thinking about it; the "donor" is one who is willing to donate oneself, one's heart and all of one's desires and capabilities. When we donate, we become included in others and thus connect.

TERMS

Donation

A "donation" is what a person can set aside, the part of the ego that one can sacrifice and correct into working in order to bestow. Each time, we must set aside more and more of our hearts for correction until they are entirely "hearts of flesh" instead of the current "stony hearts."

Atonement

The collective soul was shattered; we are all broken. "Atonement" means we must correct the intention of those broken vessels, broken desires—the 613 broken desires that are our soul.

We must bond with others and thus discover the Creator, who appears in neither of us, but rather in the unity between us. Gradually, we must all build the tabernacle, and in it attain the revelation of the Creator. It is written that the Creator tells us each time, "Do this or that work, and I will come and appear before you there, and tell you what needs to be done." The common work of people is what yields the revelation of the Creator between them, and what clarifies the next step.

* Mishnah, *Masechet Avot*, Chapter 1, item 6.

The Ark of the Covenant

This is where the upper force comes from—the place from which the Creator appears.

Menorah (the sacred lamp)

This is the disclosure of the upper force within one's *Kelim* (vessels). The *Menorah* is the revelation of the Creator, who appears as the seven *Sefirot* of *Zeir Anpin*, in seven qualities—each representing the *Menorah*.

Sockets, Veil

A "socket" or a "veil" either concerns the will to receive or the *Masach* (screen) over it, which turns it from working in order to receive to working in order to bestow. There are only three elements in the whole of reality: the substance, namely the will to receive; the quality of bestowal that may be on it, meaning the *Masach*; and the upper light, the Creator. The upper light appears as the force operating in the operated, which is us to the extent that we are open to accept that outside force.

His Heart Moves Him

The "heart" is all of man's 613 desires, which are all that we have. We want to gradually bring our hearts closer, from desires that are easier to correct to harder ones, through all 613 desires and 125 degrees, in three lines, in *Yod-Hey-Vav-Hey*. This is how we become corrected.

The correction is not done by us. We must take into account all the others who are with us in the network, and this is what we must correct. We do not correct ourselves, but our connections with others. The decisive element is how we correct ourselves, how we can connect to others. Our correction unfolds only according to others. That is, the correction is of our connections, not of ourselves.

From *The Zohar*: A Persimmon and a Sedan Chair

20) "King Solomon has made him a sedan chair from the trees of Lebanon." A sedan chair is the lower palace, *Malchut*, like the upper palace, *Bina*. The Creator called it "the Garden of Eden," and He planted it for His delight. His desire is to play in it with the souls of the righteous where they all stand and are inscribed within it. A persimmon is the upper palace, which is covered and concealed, *Bina*. The sedan chair, the lower palace, is *Malchut*, in which there is no support until it is supported by the upper palace.

Zohar for All, *Teruma* (donation), items 20-21

Supporting is the "round" quality of *Bina*, *GAR* of *Bina* and *ZAT* of *Bina*. *Malchut*—which is our entire *Kli* (vessel), namely all creations—connects to the upper force, *Bina*, the quality of bestowal. The more *Malchut* connects to *Bina*, the more she ascends to *Bina* along with other desires for correction, and the more a connection is made between the sedan chair and the persimmon.

The persimmon itself is closed. This is the upper persimmon, *GAR* of *Atzilut*. It is the entire thought of Creation, a state that will appear only at the end of correction. However, through the ascent of *Malchut* we gradually belong to it and receive from it, although it appears only in the sedan chair, *Malchut*.

Because the center is the connection between us, the tabernacle that appears between us, how do we correct ourselves?

The whole Torah speaks only of "I have created the evil inclination; I have created for it the Torah as a spice because the light in it reforms." Why does it reform? In order to reach a state of "Love your neighbor as yourself," the rule of thumb that guides us every time.

This special portion details how we correct ourselves, teaching us about the anatomy of our hearts, about our desires, their shapes, and the degree to which we can correct them.

Tetzaveh

(Command)

(Exodus, 27:20-30:10)

Portion Summary

In the portion, *Tetzaveh* (Command), the Creator provides Moses with additional details regarding the tabernacle, and commands the children of Israel to take olive oil to light the everlasting candle in the tent of meeting outside the veil, so it may burn from dusk to dawn.

The Creator instructs Moses to appoint Aaron and his sons, Nadav, Avihu, Elazar, and Itamar to be his priests. He elaborates on the commandment of preparing the holy garments "for honor and glory" (Exodus, 28: 2): the vest, fringe, coat, and the rest of the garments of the priest.

Afterward comes an explanation about the sanctification of Aaron and his sons for their roles in the tabernacle. This includes their offering of an ox and two rams on the altar, of the incense to be positioned inside the tabernacle before the veil, and how the incense is to be made. Finally, *Yom Kippur* (Day of Atonement) is mentioned, which is to take place once a year.

Commentary

The portion, *Tetzaveh* (Command), is very matter-of-fact, short, and pragmatic. The whole of the substance of Creation is the desire to receive. This is the solid basis from which we should begin. We feel the will to receive within us divided into four levels: still, vegetative, animate, and speaking. All our desires are divided in this manner, and we give them the shape of bestowal, namely to aim them toward giving. All desires must be aimed toward our connection "as one man with one heart,"* with love of others, as in "Love your neighbor as yourself."**

To the extent that we correct each one of our desires, we shape the image of man, thus becoming similar to the Creator. This is *Adam HaRishon* (the first man), who shattered and divided into myriad souls. Our purpose is to reassemble those souls into that single soul. We achieve this by annulling our egos and connecting all our desires. The connection is at the levels of still, vegetative, animate, and speaking. In these degrees we gradually reconnect everything into the new reality that the Torah has described.

First, the oil for the lamp is a special oil that must be lit in a special way. Subsequently, from the emitted light, we can prepare the priesthood garments that clothe the will to receive.

The will to receive remains the same, whether it strives to benefit others or itself. The difference lies in how we use it–for our own sake or for the sake of others. That is, do we want to use it to benefit ourselves, even if it is detrimental to others? Or do we want to benefit others? These are our two options, with myriad variations.

All this relates to "clothes" over the desire. The Torah details how to design these clothes–how to place the right intentions over our desires, meaning the degrees *Yod-Hey-Vav-Hey*, or degrees of *Aviut* (thickness, will to receive) one, two, three, and four.

* RASHI, Exodus, 19b.

** Talmud, *Seder Nashim, Masechet Nedarim,* Chapter 9, p 30b.

The corrected desires may be from the still (inanimate), such as building the tent of meeting and the ark of the covenant, or from the vegetative, such as wool or linen, or from the animate, which are the offerings themselves.

The "speaking" are people who are united in their degree, and those who wear the clothes that befit the high priest, such as a breastplate, a girdle, a miter, or a tunic. The high priest is one whose aim is entirely toward bestowal, love of others, through which this person reaches the Creator. There is a priest and a high priest. That is, there are *Katnut* (infancy) and *Gadlut* (adulthood) in this degree. These are the stages through which we must progress in order to correct our desires.

The sum of the desire that the Creator created in each of us is 613 desires, which are 613 desires that we must invert from the inclination to receive to the desire to bestow upon others. This is how we connect with one another, gathering all these desires into a single mechanism.

QUESTIONS AND ANSWERS

Can we change desires through our intentions?

Yes, we can change desires through our intentions. By wanting to give to each other, we tie our desires as a single body in a *Kli* (vessel) known as *Beit HaMikdash* (lit. The House of Holiness; trans. Temple). *Bait* (house) is a *Kli* of *Kedusha* (holiness), bestowal, love of others, the aim to give. This is the Adam that we build, our common soul, *Shechina* (Divinity), the Assembly of Israel, *Malchut* of *Atzilut*, and there the Creator appears.

This portion explains that our desires are divided, too. The writings of the ARI teach us that our souls consist of *Shoresh*, *Neshama*, *Guf*, *Levush*, *Heichal* (root, soul, body, clothing, hall, respectively). *Shoresh* is inside us. *Neshama* is our innermost part. *Guf* is the desires themselves, *and Levush* and *Heichal* are additions.

The Torah tells us that the *Levush* (clothing) consists of the five types of garments of the high priest. *Heichal* (hall) is the surroundings–the tent of meeting with all its details. Of course, none of this relates to any physical tent, person, vessels, or a lamp. Rather, the text relates to the way we develop the will to receive into working in order to bestow, as the Creator bestows upon us. Through these corrections of many degrees and parts in our desires, we achieve similarity with the Creator and *Dvekut* (adhesion) with Him.

The end of the portion also mentions *Yom Kippur* (the Day of Atonement). All the corrections we perform during the year, the preparations, corrections over the nations of the world, over the people of Israel, and over the Levites and the priests, bring us to the degree of the high priest. When we rise above those desires and bring them together to a place of general bestowal, called *Beit HaMikdash*, a place of special unity where we achieve oneness with the Creator–the point of *Dvekut*–it is called "the work of the priest in the Holy of Holies on the day of atonement."

Aaron and his sons are all in spirituality, yet we know that spirituality is not transferred by inheritance. Many Kabbalists had no children, or had children who did not become Kabbalists. And yet, here we see a very clear order of Aaron and his sons. Moreover, some researchers claim that it is possible to find genes of priests even today. What is the meaning of this order?

This is true; they can be found in both the material world and the spiritual world. There are many reasons for it, but what we understand is that a *Kli* (vessel) that is in bestowal–meaning a spiritual *Partzuf*, or *Neshama* (a soul) that is working in bestowal in order to bestow–operates in active bestowal and begets a more advanced *Partzuf*, called a "son."

Is a "son" the priest's next degree?

Yes. This is why it is impossible for a holy *Partzuf* to emerge from a *Partzuf* that is not bestowing in order to bestow, or receiving in order to bestow. In our world, we may or may not pay attention to this because in projecting to corporeality, it becomes mere customs. But in spirituality, we understand where it comes from; a *Partzuf* that has a *Masach* (screen), *Aviut* (thickness), and *Ohr Hozer* (Reflected Light), and works in holiness cannot yield an impure act. This is why priesthood is inherited from father to son.

Why do we not know what happened to Moses' sons, but do know about priests?

Moses represents contact with the Creator, in which all are included, above all the priesthood. The priests provide direction in the work of the Creator, in corrections, and Moses is the point of contact. This is not a direction, but merely a point of attachment, of *Dvekut*.

In other words, it is all in us; we are not talking about a physical Moses.

No, there is no such thing as a physical Moses; it is all within us. When we connect among us, we produce a *Kli* that yields a sensation of connection, bonding between us. First comes the love of people, as it is written, "Love your neighbor as yourself."* Afterward, the love of the Creator arrives. These are the circles we need to build in the bonding between us. The whole of humanity must achieve it—the people of Israel, as well as non-Jews who are drawn to it and can achieve real connection with the Creator.

This is why Moses did not belong to the priests, or the Levites, or Israel; he is a point *above* any definition. Although he includes them, he is still above them. The correction of the world is that all of us will unite. The more we unite and make ourselves similar to the upper light, the Creator, the more He is with us and within us.

* Jerusalem Talmud, *Seder Nashim, Masechet Nedarim*, Chapter 9, p 30b.

This portion details garments. It was said that only the "wisehearted" can prepare these garments. Who are the wisehearted?

The "wisehearted" are those whose hearts, meaning desires, are arranged according to *Hochma* (wisdom). These are not ordinary desires, but those that have been arranged by the light of *Hochma*. Therefore, the beginning of the portion talks about the general light that reforms, which illuminates all the *Kelim* (vessels). Only with this light is it possible to carry out the *Mitzvot* (commandments) described in the portion, which is why it is called *Tetzaveh* (Command). The Creator's command comes only to give us the light that reforms. The Creator tells us how to use it in order to achieve corrections, such as the garments of the high priest and the building of the tabernacle.

Is it only when we reach a certain stage of wisdom of the heart that we can wear these garments?

The heart is the tabernacle of all our desires, but only if we arrange all of our desires in the right order, using the upper light, the *Menorah* (lamp) that illuminates to that person, the light that reforms. The "right order" means in order to bestow, from easy to difficult. It is not something we need to build; it is built by itself. The commandment relates only to our willingness; we must come under the light with our *Kli*, then the *Kli* will acquire the shape of the light. The wisehearted do not know how to do everything; they only know how to prepare themselves for the light to work on them.

Why is the engagement with garments possible only from this point onward?

"Clothing" is the intention to bestow.

So what are the intentions of the wisehearted?

The wisehearted are those who prepare themselves for correction. When it comes, it brings them garments.

From *The Zohar*: And You Shall Command

When it writes, "And you," it means to include Divinity in the command and in the speech. The upper light, ZA, and the bottom light, *Nukva*, are included together in the word, "And you," since "you" is the name of the *Nukva*, and the added *Vav* ("and") is ZA, as it is written, "And You preserve them all," relating to ZA and *Nukva*.

Zohar for All, *Tetzaveh* (Command), items 1-2

Zeir Anpin is the Creator, the upper force, the light that reaches us. We who want to connect build the *Nukva*. Although she herself does not exist, this part was left after the breaking. The soul has broken and its pieces are scattered. As much as we may want to connect, we cannot. However, we have the tendency toward it, and accordingly, the light affects us and connects us. If there is an additional inclination, then additional light influences us and connects us.

This is why our work is called "day-to-day," as in "Day to day pours forth speech" (Psalms, 19:3). This is how we arrive at the end of the year, the Day of Atonement that connects us and leads us to all the corrections. This is when we atone for our iniquities.

Yet, these are not our own iniquities, but from the time of the breaking of *Adam HaRishon*, before we were created, since "the inclination in a man's heart is evil from his youth" (Genesis, 8:21). When we scrutinize these matters and want to overcome them and connect above all gaps and hatred to achieve love, we reach the foot of Mount Sinai.

Why is *Yom Kippur* (Day of Atonement) considered the holiest day?

It is the point of contact of all the desires that we have prepared to connect to everyone in a single *Kli*, to be in *Dvekut* with the Creator. That is, it is the implementation of our work in this world.

Next, we must achieve the revelation of the Creator, unity, and love of others. *Yom Kippur* symbolizes it.

Is it a specific day in the year?

No, a day is a degree. If a person performs all the corrections, the degree that one reaches is called *Yom Kippur*. It could happen on any of the days in the year because it is not a day, but a spiritual state.

What is so special about this day that only the quality known as the "high priest" makes the required correction in the Holy of Holies?

When we add all the corrections on the still, vegetative, animate, and speaking levels in their final form, we achieve *Dvekut* (adhesion). It has to be "world," "year," "soul," and "place." That is, we arrange all the desires–still, vegetative, and animate–"the clothes," which are also the cover of the tent, and all of our garments from the vegetative. The "animate" are the offerings of *Yom Kippur*. The "high priest" includes the whole of humanity, with all the corrections on the human, speaking level.

If we join them together on the special day called *Yom Kippur* (Day of Atonement) it brings us to the point of *Dvekut* with the Creator. This is the highest level we can achieve, the end of correction and the ascent to a higher dimension.

From *The Zohar*: Blow the Horn (*Shofar*) on the New Moon

Thus, "Serve the Lord with gladness," since man's joy draws another joy, the higher one. Similarly, the lower world, *Malchut*, as it is crowned, so it extends from above. This is why Israel hurry to awaken a sound in the *Shofar*, which includes fire, wind, and water, the middle line, which consists of three lines that became one and rises upwards.

Zohar for All, *Tetzaveh* (Command), item 94

The three lines describe the work of the priests—Priest, Levite, and Israel—which describes our work. There are two *Klipot* (shell/peels): the *Klipa* (singular for *Klipot*) of the right, Ishmael, and the *Klipa* of the left, Esau. Right and left are our work and our will to receive, opposite which is the desire to bestow, and the extent to which we can add these desires by removing the *Klipot* of Ishmael and Esau.

This is how we build the middle line, the line of *Dvekut*, called Adam. On this line, the more we connect all the desires among us, the higher we ascend in our connection. These include all our intentions to achieve similarity with the Creator, bestowal, and love of others, and from there to the love of the Creator. If we achieve unity in that line, we have reached the purpose of Creation.

We must understand that the current changes the world is going through, the myriad problems, the global crisis, are signs that we must begin to bond, since only by bonding will we be able to resolve the crisis.

This is the reason why the wisdom of Kabbalah is now surfacing, so that the light that reforms, the illuminating *Menorah*, can shine on those who want to sanctify themselves and arrive at the Temple, to realize their task in the world. Today, we are in the midst of the actual realization of the portion, "Command."

The Creator sounds like a forceful, domineering force, while the creature is in a state of constant sin and request for forgiveness. It is a rather complicated system.

For what should one ask forgiveness? If it is written, "I have created the evil inclination,"* then the Creator created it. Why should we ask for forgiveness? On the contrary, we should demand, "I want You to correct what You have created in me." It is called, "My sons defeated Me."** The Creator will welcome it. We misconstrue the Torah by thinking that we are sinners, while the sin is not in us. Our only sin is in not requesting correction. What

* Jerusalem Talmud, *Masechet Berachot*, 27b.
** Babylonian Talmud, *Masechet Nezikin, Baba Metzia*, 59b.

is in us did not come from us; we cannot blame ourselves for what we were born with.

We should say in regard to all our qualities, characters, and all that we are, "Go to the craftsman who made me."* We are not to blame. Our fault, our blemish, is that we do not examine ourselves and ask for correction, to become similar to the Creator—bestowing, loving others, and benevolent.

When we do not reveal and do not ask for correction, this is when we are at fault. However, we did not commit the transgression for which we demand correction. This is simply something with which to connect with the Creator, to be in constant dialogue with Him. The evil inclination is "help made against us." On the one hand, it removes us from the Creator. On the other hand, it gives us an "official" reason to connect with Him.

TERMS

Everlasting Candle

A person who wants to reach the point of contact with the Creator, called "the priest's work in the Temple," must first see to always having the light that reforms, for only with it is one sanctified—adding the aim to bestow to one's desires, thus rising closer to the Creator.

Olive Oil

In spirituality, "olive oil" is the light that reaches *Zeir Anpin*, *Malchut*.

Priest

A "priest" is man's highest degree. It comes from the left line and from the right line, and reaches pure and complete bestowal. This

* Babylonian Talmud, *Masechet Taanit*, p. 20b.

degree includes the degree of *Bina*, *ZAT* of *Bina*, and the upper degree, *GAR* of *Bina*. It is impossible to be a priest without also having Levites and Israel inside. That is, a "priest" is one who tends to the entire world, as well as to Israel, and unites with everyone.

It is hard work to achieve the degree of a priest because one must actualize the greatest and most powerful desires.

Breastplate

The "breastplate" is one of those elements of clothing that belongs to the inner part of the soul.

SUMMARY

The portion, *Tetzaveh*, is our approach to the Creator. If we want to correct ourselves, we have every possibility to do so while giving our material bodies whatever they need. The important thing in life is to reach the eternal and complete world, as it is written, "You will see your world in your life,"* here and now. It is all expressed in the connection between us: from the love of man to love of the Creator. This is how we achieve the end of correction. We can do it here and now; it is entirely up to us.

* *Masechet Berachot*, 17a

Ki Tissa

(When You Take)

(Exodus, 30:11-34:35)

Portion Summary

The portion, *Ki Tissa* (When You Take), begins with the Creator's request of each one of the children of Israel to donate half a shekel for the building of the tabernacle. The portion mentions other details about the tabernacle such as the anointing oil, the table, and the *Menorah* and its vessels. Bezalel, son of Uri Ben Hur, is appointed chief craftsman, with Ahaliav Ben Ahisemech as his assistant. The Creator also commands the children of Israel to observe the Sabbath.

Later, Moses ascends to Mount Sinai to receive the tablets of the covenant, but is delayed returning, so the children of Israel seek proof that the Creator exists. They demand that Aaron build a golden calf. Aaron agrees, takes their gold vessels, melts them, and builds the golden calf.

When Moses returns from the mountain and sees it, he breaks the tablets. The Creator wishes to destroy and ruin the entire people of Israel, and Moses pleads for their souls.

Moses speaks to the Creator "face to face," and wishes to conceal himself.

At the end of the process, the Creator agrees and makes a covenant with the people of Israel. The Creator also promises that they will enter the land of Israel, and repeats the commandment of the three Pilgrimage festivals (*Shalosh Regalim*) and the prohibition of idolatry.

Moses stays with the Creator on Mount Sinai forty days and forty nights, writes on the tablets, and comes down from the mountain. It is written, "And it came to pass when Moses came down from Mount Sinai with the two tables of the testimony in Moses' hand ... that Moses did not know that the skin of his face beamed while He talked with him" (Exodus, 34:29). It was so much so that he had to hide from the people once more because they feared speaking with him.

Commentary

Those who do not know the language of Kabbalah will find it hard to understand that the text actually discusses a person's inner development. It concerns our nature, which is the will to receive, an egoistic desire that requires correction. The Torah speaks only of the correction of the desire, as it is written, "I have created the evil inclination; I have created for it the Torah as a spice,"* for "the light in it would reform them."**

The purpose of the correction is to transform our evil (egoistic) inclination, which aims only toward self-gratification and exploitation of the entire world for itself, and turn it into love of others, as in "Love your neighbor as yourself."***

The Torah speaks of a process that is not simple, but which all of us experience. The general crisis we are in will cause us to come out to the light, to correction, similar to what initiated the exodus

* Babylonian Talmud, *Masechet Kidushin*, 30b.

** Midrash Rabah, *Eicha*, "Introduction," Paragraph 2.

*** Jerusalem Talmud, *Seder Nashim, Masechet Nedarim*, Chapter 9, p 30b.

from Egypt. Today we are all standing before Mount Sinai with huge egos, with all the *Kelim* (vessels) we have taken from Egypt. During the millennia of development, humanity has accumulated a massive ego; now we have no clue what to do with it, other than to escape it.

When we are drawn toward Mount Sinai, we discover a mountain of hatred between us. Only the point within us, called "Moses," pulls us forward toward connection with something higher, a higher human degree of similarity with the Creator.

We are all still as beasts,* operating entirely through our egos, our nature. Instead, we must be as a free nation in our country, free in its will. "Such is the way of Torah."**

To do that, if we wish to ascend to the human degree and discover the Creator and the worlds around us, we must follow the unique line known as "half a shekel," meaning neither to the right nor to the left, but at the junction of the two. The will to receive, too, takes part because it is "help made against us" (Genesis, 2:18), and against it we need the reforming light.

We have two lines: on the left is the will to receive; on the right is the light. The more we combine them, the more we correct the will to receive toward similarity with the light—working in order to bestow. It is written, "And the night will shine as the day; darkness as light" (Psalms, 139:12). This is how we advance. This is the first correction—no more and no less, but precisely half. We advance when we achieve that correction, that method of advancement.

Subsequently, the tabernacle and its vessels must be prepared, including the oil and all that comes with it. This role was given only to Bezalel. Bezalel within us is that which is *Betzel El* (in the shadow of God), under the shadow of the Creator. Bezalel replicates the qualities from the Creator, who appeared to him, and this is why he is called "wisehearted." He knows the right combination between the heart, the desire, and the wisdom, namely the intellect. Bezalel

* Psalms 49:13.
** *Zohar for All*, Pinehas, item 247.

properly combines the right with the left, and has wisdom of the heart. This is why he is the one who can establish the tabernacle.

The tabernacle is the arrangement of the soul that we build within us from our 613 desires. It is built according to the right qualities, in which all the parts are connected in synchrony with the Creator. This is how we become similar to Him.

Our evil inclination has 613 qualities we must direct in order to bestow, toward love of others. Only those who have the quality of Bezalel–copying the qualities of the Creator onto themselves and becoming as His shadow–can do it.

We achieve this by connecting to the *Shechina* (Divinity), *Malchut* of *Atzilut*, who begins to replicate these qualities from *Zeir Anpin* of *Atzilut*. *Zeir Anpin* has six *Sefirot*: *Hesed*, *Gevura*, *Tifferet*, *Netzah*, *Hod*, and *Yesod*, where *Malchut* comes last and replicates. This is why our work is to replicate these six qualities from *Zeir Anpin*–called *HaKadosh Baruch Hu* (The Holy One, Blessed Be He), or *Zeir Anpin* of *Atzilut*–in the appearance of the Creator on all the workdays.

The wisdom of Kabbalah presents our goal–the revelation of the Creator to the creatures in this world. Through our senses, when the Creator is revealed to us, we join and increasingly attach ourselves to Him.

When we conclude replicating the six qualities comes the concluding seventh quality, the Sabbath. The Sabbath concludes itself by itself from above. This is why it is considered an "awakening from above." A special light comes and sets the six qualities in the right order, and there is nothing more we need to do.

This is why the prohibition against working during Sabbath is tantamount to intervening with something that belongs to the upper light. We work for six days setting up the right and left lines, directing the will to receive and the light, the mind and the heart. Finally, we present our work, and then "The Lord will conclude for me" (Psalms, 138:8). This is when we receive the completion of the degree. This is the process we must undergo through the correction of the entire soul, week by week, until we conclude the six thousand years.

We must also consider that our souls consist of desires from the evil inclination that cannot be spotted by ordinary scrutiny. These desires require special examination that only the golden calf can make.

Although the Torah presents it this way, the golden calf does not represent a fall or a decline, nor does it blame anyone. Any person who experiences this process must go through all the descents and falls, just as it happened with Pharaoh in Egypt, and with the children of Israel in the desert after the events of Mount Sinai.

Even when we move from Mount Sinai to the forty years in the desert, we will continue to experience states that seem negative. Each time uncorrected desires surface, we "fall" into them, so we have no choice but to discover them and correct them. It is written, "There is not a righteous man on earth who does good and will not sin" (Ecclesiastes, 7:20), or "A person does not comprehend words of Torah unless he has failed in them."*

Thus, first we must fail, then scrutinize the failure and correct it. Only then we are guaranteed not to repeat it. We are guaranteed to be guarded because that desire has already been corrected into having the aim to bestow. This is how we progress toward the love of others.

When we discover that despite the work we have done, we have not revealed the Creator, it is considered that Moses did not return from Mount Sinai. That is, we are drawn back to the intention to receive, the egoistic desire called "the golden calf."

Our corrupted desires are called "mixed multitude." They ask, "Where did Moses go?" They claim we must keep going as we understand it, following our reason and intellect, instead of going above reason.

When we return to working within reason, we are delighted. It seems to us that this way we understand and feel everything. We may not be ascending to higher degrees, but at least we are in a world that suits our egos. It is a very appealing state. We can see for ourselves how difficult it is to explain to people what Nature is compelling us to do now, what is the method of correction, and how we can rise to the next level. The Creator, Nature, *Elokim* (which is

* Babylonian Talmud, *Masechet Gitin*, p 43a.

Nature in *Gematria*) presses us and wishes to raise us, and we are seemingly resisting it with a golden calf, celebrating and rejoicing.

When the point in the heart appears, it collides very powerfully with the egoistic desire that has broken out once more. That collision is the shattering of the tablets.

The collision is between the point in the heart–through which we desire to rise and cling to the upper one, to a higher degree, to discover worlds, infinity, and be in a realm of bestowal–and the revelation that we are actually at the point of being a golden calf. We cannot tolerate that contrast. This causes all the elements in which we were previously in *Kedusha* (holiness) to shatter.

Those who sinned with the calf were sentenced to death. Subsequently, Moses called, "Whoever is for the Lord, come to me!" (Exodus, 32:26). This is the correction of the desires that have now appeared, which are connected to the golden calf, and with which we cannot continue.

Following the correction of all the other desires–the three thousand discernments that Moses killed–he climbs Mount Sinai yet again. This means that that point within us rises once again, and we receive the tablets of the covenant once more. We rediscover Godliness, the Creator, and begin to descend with the second tablets.

Yet, there is a big difference between the first tablets and the second tablets: *Yom Kippur* (Day of Atonement). The first tablets and the golden calf took place on the ninth of *Av* (11th month in the Hebrew calendar). The first tablets were given from *Shavuot* to the ninth of *Av*. The second tablets take place from the ninth of *Av* to *Yom Kippur*. Forty days plus forty nights are the time frame of correction from which we can continue.

From *The Zohar*: Half a Shekel

"Half a shekel, half a hin" means half a measure. The *Vav* is the middle between the two *Heys* because the *Vav* is the middle line, called "scales," which weighs the two lights, right and left, being the two *Heys*, so the left will not be greater than the right. This is why he diminishes the left, so it will not shine from above downward but only from below upward.

Zohar for All, *Ki Tissa* (When You Take), item 4

Our big will to receive, the ego, is on the left side. The light that we can draw if we work correctly, according to the wisdom of Kabbalah, is on the right. These are the two *Yods*, as in the letter *Aleph*, with the diagonal in the middle as the *Parsa* (partition) [א]. We must join the light from above, the upper *Yod*, with the will to receive from below, namely the lower *Yod* (sometimes written as *Dalet*, which is *Behina Dalet*, the *Malchut* in us, instead of the *Yod*). The diagonal line keeps the balance between them, thus creating the line.

This is why *Aleph* is the first letter in the alphabet. The portion, *Ki Tissa* (When You Take), is the beginning of the actual Torah because it engages in the building and filling of the tabernacle. This is why we must constantly maintain that half, so the right is not more than the left or the other way around. If there is a surplus of desires to receive that we did not correct to the fullest, we are not in the desire to bestow. If we take from the will to receive more than we can correct, we are in a state of recognition of evil. It has to be a very precise operation.

Once we restrict all our desires and avoid using the desire in order to receive, but only in order to bestow, we can continue sorting out those small parts of our desire from light to heavy, and join all the corrections to the light.

This is the letter, *Vav*, with the punctuation marks, *Holam*, *Shuruk*, *Hirik*, or *Kamatz*, which is as the *Parsa*. The light must be above it because all the corrections are in ascent. In our world—our situation—we will never achieve the revelation of Godliness. There might be various psychological phenomena, but the revelation of Godliness can happen only if we rise above the *Parsa*.

Following the restriction, once we have the middle line, when we join a group and try to come out of ourselves and go above reason, above the diagonal *Vav*, from below upward, then we will receive the revelation of the spiritual world.

Questions and Answers

Beresheet **(Genesis) speaks of the creation of the world. In the desert, things take a long time to unfold, with numerous details along the way, as the portions describe. What do those details symbolize?**

The Torah cannot tell us about all that we are going through. It only explains the milestones. It is similar to driving on a road where each mile or several miles are marked by signs.

Why are various garments and a description of the altar mentioned in the desert?

It is the correction of our souls. We have received a system of 613 desires, each of which consists of all the others, and all are connected. That system is completely broken. It is as though we were given an electronic or mechanical device that is completely broken, and we have no clue how to fix it. We would look at it dumbfounded without knowing how to approach it.

This is why we are taught how to do it: "Look at this, fix that, then this, but first that." There are so many details in our souls, and all must become similar to the Creator in terms of structure and work mode. Although it is the opposite substance from the Creator, "existence from absence," the soul must come to resemble the "existence from existence."

We cannot understand how important our world is, with all its complexities and myriad connections—every atom and every cell in the universe. This is why there are so many details in the correction of the soul. When we walk this path, take part in it, and discovers it, it arouses immense excitement and a sense of harmony and fulfillment.

How do you explain that everything exists and happens simultaneously—the point in the heart is on Mount Sinai, the highest connection, while other desires in me are building a golden calf?

This is the detachment within, where the Moses in us disappears. When Moses disappears we lose contact with the Creator, as this is the only point that connects us with Him. As soon as we disconnect, we find ourselves immersed in our desires, falling into the golden calf. These are the *Kelim* (vessels) we have taken from Egypt, *Kelim* that want the light of *Hochma* (wisdom), namely pleasure for ourselves alone.

How come the desire obtains contact with the upper force and promptly afterward falls into connection with the golden calf?

There are no delays. There is either *Kedusha* (holiness) or *Klipa* (shell/peel). There are no in betweens. We must get used to constantly being in one of the two states.

Are Moses' ascents and descents on Mount Sinai the ups and downs we are talking about?

It is about alternating revelations and concealments. It is similar to the festival of Purim and the story of Esther, who is also revelation in concealment. There cannot be revelation if it is not preceded by concealment. Had Moses not ascended Mount Sinai, there would have been no golden calf. But without the golden calf we would not know what to correct. This is how we always progress, on two "legs."

TERMS

Half a Shekel

"Half a shekel" is the condition that we set for ourselves under our own scrutiny and correction, so as never to come to a state of drawing lights for ourselves from above downward, but to always receive lights from below upward, in rejection. This is how we discover *Ein Sof* (infinity).

The problem is that when we constantly draw to ourselves, we can only see the layer closest to us, known as "this world." All that stands behind this layer is worlds, *Ein Sof*, eternity, wholeness, that are hidden and cut off from us. If we perceive reality not by drawing to ourselves but by exiting ourselves, we will suddenly discover *Ein Sof*.

Is it we who determine the half shekel?

Without the half shekel, we cannot begin to work with the Torah. Each of us must give the half shekel. We must set ourselves up in such a way that from this moment on, our instrument for the revelation of Godliness will be the half shekel–balance, only giving, and in as much equivalence of form as possible.

The Golden Calf

The "golden calf" is all the *Zahav* (gold), meaning *Ze Hav* (give this). It is the whole of the immense will to receive that exists within us for all the pleasures. All our desires exist simultaneously.

Stiff-Necked People

We work with the revelation of our egoistic desires and therefore constantly return to them. The back of the neck is like Pharaoh, the posterior side of Creation. When the big will to receive appears, it actually helps us.

"Stiff-necked people" are not necessarily bad; we have huge *Kelim* with which we can attain godliness. A person with small desires does not belong to Israel; Israel must be very egoistic. The nations of the world, however, have small *Kelim*, and therefore cannot obtain Godliness. The people of Israel are called a "stiff-necked people," meaning we have something with which to progress, something to correct and work with.

Summary

The most important thing for us is to keep advancing, stick to our goal, and advance toward it. Regardless of what will happen, whether the golden calf or three thousand slain or other conditions, everything passes. And in spite of everything, we will reach our goal.

VaYakhel
(And Moses Assembled)
Pekudei
(Accounts)

(Exodus, 35:1-38:20, 38:21-40:38)

Summary of the Portions

The portion, *VaYakhel* (And Moses Assembled), begins with the commandment, "Six days shall work be done, but on the seventh day there shall be to you a holy day" (Exodus, 35:2). The portion also deals with the donation by the people of gold, silver, copper, precious fabrics, and so forth. Moses determines that Bezalel and Ahaliav will perform the holy work because they are wisehearted and will collect the donation that came from the entire nation, including the women.

Bezalel and Ahaliav tell Moses that the donations are so voluminous that there is a surplus and no need for more. Moses announces this to the people.

The portion elaborates on the building of the tabernacle by the wisehearted: the garments, boards, bolts, and Bezalel's work preparing the Ark (of the Covenant), the table, and the *Menorah.*

The portion, *Pekudei* (Accounts), mentions the names of the people who took part in building the tabernacle: Itamar, son of Aaron the priest; Bezalel, son of Uri; and Ahaliav, son of Ahisemech.

As the building of the tabernacle concludes, the children of Israel bring it to Moses, who makes sure it was done according to the Creator's commandment. The Creator tells Moses on which day to establish the tabernacle, and by which order to sanctify each of its elements. He also commands Moses to anoint Aaron and his sons as priests.

The end of the portion tells of the cloud that covers the tent of meeting. Each time the cloud rises above the tabernacle, the children of Israel travel. And each time it descends on the tabernacle, they camp.

Commentary

Both portions present a sequence of one topic. The Torah begins with "I have created the evil inclination; I have created for it the Torah as a spice."* The evil inclination is our entire nature manifesting in our hatred of one another. First we must discover it; hence, the first revelation of the evil inclination takes place with Abraham in the Tower of Babylon. Subsequently, we discover it in the hard labor in Egypt, then at the foot of Mount Sinai, where hatred prevailed between everyone, as it is written, "Hatred descended to the nations of the world."** This is the recognition of evil.

It is no simple task to know evil. It is more than discovering that one is lazy or deceitful, thieving, or exploitive. Rather, evil appears only when we want to unite with others. It happens only among

* Babylonian Talmud, *Masechet Kidushin*, 30b.

** Midrash Rabah, *Shemot* (Exodus), Portion 2, Paragraph 4.

those who are drawn to connection, to "Love your neighbor as yourself."* When we try, Nature resists, and does not let us bond.

According to the Torah, which is the upper force, if we truly wish to achieve love of others, and through it the love of the Creator (the comprehensive love) and want to discover the common, benevolent force that prevails in the world, all we need is the Torah.

Today, it may appear that the world is terrible because we are examining it through our evil inclination, through our corrupted qualities. But "All who cast fault, cast fault in his own defect."** As we correct ourselves, we become righteous and justify the Creator and His Creation. Then we begin to see the world as good. Baal HaSulam describes it in his essay, "Concealment and Revelation of the Creator's Face."***

When we begin to connect with others and love them, when we draw closer to the global and integral world–as we discover it to be each day, hence the current surfacing of the wisdom of Kabbalah–we begin to feel the evil. Then and only then do we need the Torah, the "light that reforms."****

The Torah is not about studying the text. Rather, it is about studying *in order to receive the light that corrects*, to acquire more and more love for the world. Thus, we become more and more similar to the Creator, returning to the image of man, called "Adam." The part we attain and correct over our evil inclination, the part that turns the evil inclination into a good inclination, is called a "soul."

This is why we take from Egypt the primary *Kelim* (vessels), which are valuable in the eyes of the great evil inclination. It is through these that we emerge from the period known as "Egypt" and recognize the evil inclination, building from it the golden calf. When everything appears clearly and intensely, we truly need the Torah.

---

* Jerusalem Talmud, *Seder Nashim, Masechet Nedarim*, Chapter 9, p 30b.

** Babylonian Talmud, *Masechet Kidushin*, p 70a.

*** *The Writings of Baal HaSulam*, p 766.

**** Midrash Rabah, *Eicha*, "Introduction," Paragraph 2.

For this reason, the first tablets were inappropriate for correction. Only the second tablets that Moses brought down to Israel on the Day of Atonement were suitable for correction, once the people had recognized the evil within them. We know the evil in us, and need the Torah only after we see the golden calf within us. Thus, we resist loving others, instead wanting to exploit the entire world.

The Torah explains the stages of the building of the tabernacle—we need to choose which of all the evil desires we have toward others we can correct from receiving into giving, from hate to love. This is the whole Torah, the instructions as to how to do this. Instead of being immersed in our evil inclination, seeing only the narrow reality of this world, if we correct our desires even slightly we can open ourselves to see the upper world, here and now.

As we develop in this manner, the world around us opens up and appears as the world of *Assiya*, *Yetzira*, *Beria*, *Atzilut*, and *Adam Kadmon*—the world of *Ein Sof* (infinity)—at the end of correction. First, we build a small *Neshama* (soul) common to all. This is the "tent of meeting," which includes the still, vegetative, animate, and speaking levels, that is, our quality, the *Yod-Hey-Vav-Hey*, the complete *HaVaYaH* within us. We must take from each desire and connect everything to a single, integral desire that is common to all, that will connect to everyone ready for it, building together a united, common *Kli* (vessel). This is how everyone will advance.

We must have the qualities of a priest, as Bezalel or Aaron, and certainly the qualities of Moses—the first of the priests, Levites, and Israel. The Torah explains how we can use the light that we draw in order to understand which desires we can correct now, and which we can correct later.

As Moses said in the previous portion, only half of the desires were corrected using the half shekel, the shekel of the holiness. The other half comes from above. The half is our deficiency, and the other half is the light that corrects and complements. With our efforts we build everything that depends on us, all the qualities of the soul: priests, Levites, and Israel, using silver, gold, and various precious stones.

Through the mind and heart that only the qualities of Bezalel have—as it is a replication of the Creator—we feel that we have an example by which to build our souls in accord with the Creator who appears before us. This is how we build the soul. In it, we experience the new world, the *Kli*, our corrected desires. Within those desires is the force of bestowal and love called *Boreh* (the Creator), from the words, *Bo Re'eh* (come see). This is how we come to see, discover the Creator.

The first steps alternate in appearance between cloud and fire, as the Creator ascending and descending. "Rise up, O Lord, let Your enemies be scattered, and let those who hate You flee before You" (Numbers, 10:35). In our current situation, in our world, we cannot talk about these things or about the parts we need to correct because we still have no sense of our souls. We do not find these desires in us or know how to scrutinize them or connect them in this extremely complex system.

The Torah tells us this in the form of a story that is a replica of our earthly world: rocks, trees, people, clothes, time, motion, and place. These forms are described so we may discern which parts of the soul we must correct.

Within the soul are forces that work in order to receive; these must be turned into working in order to bestow. We still cannot express these forces and name them because we do not know them, so the Torah tells us the story in its own way, and Kabbalists convey it in the "language of roots and branches."

Kabbalists tell us about the forces that operate, about the parts of the soul. *The Book of Zohar* with the *Sulam* (Ladder) commentary that Baal HaSulam wrote narrates it in the language of Kabbalah, so we can understand what is meant by the words of the Torah. We can understand that the Torah speaks only of the parts of our soul and the correction of the heart, which are our desires. In this manner, we can unravel the entire Torah, discover it in our hearts as a corrected system, and discover the upper force, the Creator, within all that.

Questions and Answers

What does it mean to gather?

"Gathering" refers to the children of Israel whom Moses assembles in order to declare the Sabbath day, the conclusion of the work. The goal must be clear from the start because "the end of an act is in the preliminary thought."* If we know why we must achieve adhesion with the Creator, why we must make ourselves similar, discover Him, and be like Him, literally "face to face," to be in Moses' degree, we must know this in advance. Even in the smallest action, there must be the same goal, the same clear line drawn out, compelling us to advance only in this direction. Whatever problems arise along the way, ascents, descents, and twists, they will all be dealt with so we can progress.

This is why in the desert that Israel traverses there is constant recognition of evil, and it is actually for the best. Additional desires keep surfacing and we must correct them in order to advance toward the land of Israel—the corrected desire where the Creator resides.

Why do we have to know all the details by which we advance, these ascents and descents?

This is how we achieve the plan of Creation, its purpose, the sensation and understanding of it. There is a difference between the will to receive that the Creator formed existence from absence in the beginning of Creation, and the will to receive at the end of Creation. At the end of Creation, that desire has a mind. It remains the same will to receive, but with a mind, comprehension, recognition, and sensation. Everything comes from the connection of mind and heart.

Will we necessarily experience all the elements described in this portion?

We will not experience them without planning to, without desiring to participate, without raising MAN and requesting to

* *Lecha Doddi*, Elkabetz, sung on Sabbath Evening.

correct. Only those of us who want, feel, and are aware of how much they hate, but want to love, will experience everything. Therefore, we must correct some of the still in us, some of the vegetative, and thus discover the reality we are in, and from it reveal the other reality.

Gradually, we become a structure that contains all the mind and heart, all the wisdom in the world. The whole of Nature is within us and we include all the worlds. There is nothing outside of us. The vast world we depict outside of us does not really exist; it is only depicted in this manner in our external *Kelim*, which must all be made internal. Hence, there is nothing but man and the Creator, who are as a single system.

From *The Zohar*: Whoever Is of a Generous Heart, Let Him Bring It

"Take from among you a donation." When a person places his will for the work of his Master, that will first rises to the heart—the persistence and the basis of the entire body. Afterward, that good will rises over all the organs of the body, the will of all the organs of the body and the will of the heart join together, pulling over them the brightness of Divinity to dwell with them. And that person is the Creator's portion, as it is written, "Take from among you a donation." "From among you" is the extension, to take upon yourselves that donation, the Divinity, so that the person will be a portion of the Creator.

Zohar for All, *VaYakhel* (And Moses Assembled), item 71

Initially, there is an egoistic desire that we correct by donation. The donation is the part of the will to receive with which we can enhance the quality of bestowal. The donation raises the part of bestowal with which we want to dominate and advance.

By donations that we set aside from the ego, namely parts we can sanctify and invert into bestowal and love, we advance toward the end of correction. At that time, we are not building a tabernacle or advancing in the tabernacle in time, place, and motion. Rather, we are reaching Mount Moriah and building the Temple.

Kabbalists attain the complete structure, the complete soul, called *Beit HaMikdash* (House of Holiness, Temple). In it are all the parts: priest, Levite, Israel, and the nations of the world. The great Kabbalist, Ramchal (Rabbi Moshe Chaim Lozzato), wrote a special essay known as "The Dwelling Place of the Most High," in which he drew in great detail what the third Temple should look like. He did not refer to the rocks in Jerusalem, but to the structure of the corrected soul, which must eventually be on the Sabbath, as was said at the beginning of the portion. We arrive at the Sabbath upon the conclusion of the six days, or six thousand years, when all the *Kelim* are corrected, and there is nothing more to do or to work with but to enjoy, in happiness and peace.

When the children of Israel bring donations, Moses says, "That's enough, you've gone too far." It sounds odd because we say that there are no limits on bestowal.

True, but each degree has its own scrutiny. The soul consists of three parts: *NHY*, *HGT*, *HBD*, or *Ibur* (conception), *Yenika* (nursing), and *Mochin* (mindfulness/adulthood), or *Nefesh*, *Ruach*, *Neshama*. *Neshama* is named after the great light that can be in it.

Hence, on the degree of Israel they give a lot, on the degree of Levites they do not give as much, and on the degree of priests they give even less. It depends on a person's degree and on who is performing the scrutiny.

It also depends on the degree to which we raise our desires. If we stay in desires of the Israel degree, whatever we bring is fine. But when the desires are at the level of Levites or priests, we haven't enough forces to be at such a high degree with all of our desires, so they are restricted. This is the meaning of the "degrees in the soul."

If the Creator gives to us and then says, "Give it back," why did He give it in the first place?

The Creator created an entire world, the world of *Ein Sof*, then broke it and gave us a broken world and a broken Adam (soul) so we might fix it. It is similar to a puzzle or LEGO bricks that we put together and learn as we advance. If we gave this game to a child without putting it together, the child would break it because children are driven by the urge to take things apart to understand them. By nature, we cannot approach a complete thing. To understand it, study it, we must break it or have it broken.

How does all that connect to donations?

We take our broken desires and raise them as high as we can toward correction, and the correction comes from above. The Creator has given us everything broken; we need only raise that corruption (recognize it), and ask Him to partake in the correction. The correction itself always comes from above through the light that reforms, as it is written, "I have created the evil inclination; I have created for it the Torah as a spice ... because the light in it reforms."*

We are in the middle. We do not belong to the evil inclination; it is not our own because in truth, the Creator has made it and given it to us. We also do not belong to the light that reforms. Our job is only to connect the two: the corrupt desire below with the light from above. All we need do is ask, demand, and pray for correction.

How do we do it properly? How should we prepare this work so that we bring it to the Creator in the right way?

Our work is to sort each desire whose time has come. First, we scrutinize it through the light, then set it up for correction through the light and ask for correction. These things can happen only by the light that shines, so without studying the wisdom of Kabbalah it is impossible to do anything, as this is what brings us the light.

---

* Babylonian Talmud, *Masechet Kidushin*, 30b; Midrash Rabah, *Eicha*, "Introduction," Paragraph 2.

Do we receive the light when we study Kabbalah?

Yes. During the study, we begin to see how everything falls into place. If we study properly, it takes some time for us to actually achieve it, but then we can study the Bible, the Pentateuch, Gemarah, and Mishnah, and they will all be a source of light to us.

From *The Zohar*: These Are the Accounts of the Tabernacle

And as the desire of all of Israel was in what they volunteered, so was their desire in that calculation. By their desire, they extended the *Mochin* of calculation, and then the whole work was done by desire. Hence, calculation is needed here in the tabernacle, since by calculation is the work done. This is why it is written, "These are the accounts of the tabernacle."

It is a calculation that faults all the calculations in the world—extension of *GAR de Hochma*—which are not of *Kedusha* (holiness), for they do not persist, but destroy the place to which they are drawn. Yet, this calculation in the tabernacle, which is *VAK de Hochma*, persists more than all the others, and by that the tabernacle persists, and not by another.

Zohar for All, *Pekudei* (Accounts), item 49

There is a big difference between *VAK* and *GAR*. *GAR* means we are drawing by ourselves; *VAK* means that we are rejecting, that everything is done in bestowal. The lights are all passing through us; we are receiving the full *Ein Sof* in order to convey it to everyone. But we are not harmed when we work only to bestow, thus making ourselves similar to the source, the Creator. He passes through Him to everyone, and likewise, when we all connect, passing from everyone to everyone, the great sphere called "the common soul of *Ein Sof*" is made.

Terms

Work

"Work" is correction of the system of the tabernacle. This is nothing more than that. There are nine works in the work of the tabernacle; the rest are neither work nor craft.

Cloud

A "cloud" indicates concealment. The Creator hides Himself, but the disclosure is in concealment, when one sees that He is hidden. There are opposites here, which is why it corrects us. The cloud leads us, and even Moses went into the cloud.

Donation

A "donation" to the Creator means that the more we increase the importance of the Creator in our eyes, the importance of the quality of love and bestowal, the more we can advance.

Tabernacle and Tent of Meeting

The soul contains a surrounding, external *Kli* (vessels). Although it contains great lights, they are surrounding lights. Also, there are the inner *Kelim* (plural of *Kli*), which are the tabernacle. Similar to our world, we have a *Shoresh*, *Neshama*, and *Guf* (root, soul, and body respectively) within us, and *Levush* and *Heichal* (clothing, hall respectively) that are the rest of the world. This is how we are built, how we perceive the *Kli* we are in. But everything is within us, even when it seems to us that everything is external.

The same is true for the tabernacle. It is an inner tabernacle, surrounded by the tent of meeting, a court, and many other details. When we begin to notice it and study it, we see that each element is truly a unique form of work.

From *The Zohar*: Beautiful Boughs, the Joy of the Whole Earth

The beauty of the world and the vision of the world were not seen in the world until the tabernacle was built and established, and the ark entered the holy place. From that time, the vision of everything, of Divinity, was seen in the world and the world was established. The worthy come into the tabernacle and the ark until they arrive at the middle point that is there, which is "Beautiful boughs, the joy of the whole ..." Once they arrive there, the ark started and said, "This is My resting place forever; here I will dwell, for I have desired it."

Zohar for All, *Pekudei* (Accounts), item 42

When we arrive at this exciting moment, there is nothing more sublime. We are in contact and *Dvekut* (adhesion) with the Creator, and discover the goal for which we have labored for so long. Henceforth, we only enhance the point of *Dvekut* through the end of correction.

Today, the world is in a crisis. It is the beginning of the inclination toward connection. More precisely, it is the beginning of the revelation of the wisdom of Kabbalah. It is written, "And they shall teach no more every man his neighbor, and every man his brother, saying, 'Know the Lord,' for they shall all know Me, from the least of them unto the greatest of them" (Jeremiah, 31:33).

In other words, everyone will know about the Creator. This is the wisdom of which it was written, "they shall all know Me," and "My house shall be called 'a house of prayer for all the nations'" (Isaiah, 56:7).

In other words, the tabernacle, the tent, the Third Temple, all the desires, everything that exists in the universe will achieve connection and correction. It is written about it, "I will bring them to the mountain of My holiness, and I will rejoice them in My house of prayer, their burnt offerings and their sacrifices shall be acceptable on My altar, for My house shall be called a house of prayer for all the nations" (Isaiah, 56:7).

VaYikra

(The Lord Called)

(Leviticus, 1:1-5:26)

Portion Summary

The portion, *VaYikra* (The Lord Called), deals with rules of sacrifice and the priests serving in the tabernacle. Some offerings are optional; some are mandatory. Some of the offerings are burnt to ashes on the altar, and some remain for the priests and the giver of the offering.

The rules of offerings speak of a "burnt offering" that one brings voluntarily from the cattle, flock, and poultry. There is also a "gift offering," which one brings voluntarily from the flora. Also, there is the "peace offering," which is an offering that one brings from the cattle, sheep, and goats. The "sin offering" is an offering brought by one who sinned by mistake. That person makes an offering to atone for the sin.

Commentary

The portion, *VaYikra* (The Lord Called), teaches us about the work of the offerings, which are also the main topic in the Talmud. We learn all the works from the works of the Temple.

When people draw near to the purpose of Creation and *Dvekut* (adhesion) with the Creator–the human level, a life in a totally blissful world–and experience all the worlds and the sensation of Nature as complete and eternal, as it was prepared for us, that nearing is called *Korban* (offering/sacrifice), from the word *Karov* (near). We are approaching it step by step by correcting our nature.

There are 613 desires in us that we must correct one at a time, each desire with all of its parts. Our desires divide into four levels: still, vegetative, animate, and speaking. The work of the offerings teaches us how to sacrifice and correct them so they are in bestowal and love. The rule in our work is to correct our nature and achieve the state, "Love your neighbor as yourself; it is a great rule in the Torah."* Thus, we become similar to the Creator and achieve *Dvekut* with Him.

The correction of the egoistic desire from receiving for myself into bestowal upon others is called an "offering." The offering may come from several sources. It may be from the still, as it is written, "On all your offerings you shall offer salt" (Leviticus, 2:13), or water or oil. It can also be from the vegetative or processed plants, such as the showbread. From the animate, only a certain kind is offered. The priests' and the Levites' daily work in the Temple is to sacrifice the flock and the cattle.

There are offerings that one must make on a daily basis, similar to our progress from day to day according to the plan of Creation, at a predetermined pace. When we do not follow suit, the negative forces push us from behind.

The offerings we cannot make–namely the desires we cannot correct into aiming to bestow upon others–become negative forces that manifest as problems. These push us from behind through suffering, and accumulate until they break out as crises, similar to the comprehensive crisis we are currently experiencing.

A crisis is not a negative state. It is the result of neglect. It occurs because we are so engrossed in materialism instead of rising above it,

* Jerusalem Talmud, *Seder Nashim, Masechet Nedarim*, Chapter 9, p 30b.

and because we are so obstinate and refuse to listen to the guidance of Kabbalists.

In fact, the crisis is a point of new birth. It points to our inability to live according to the old paradigm. Our perspective on life and our attitude toward values in our lives breaks and falls apart, as it manifests in education, family relations, and so forth.

The order of the work of the offerings is very important because it explains how we advance in life. If we follow this order, our lives will flow in order, too.

If each moment we correct more and more pieces of our egoism into altruism and love of others, into connection with humanity, with Nature, we will draw nearer to the Creator—the only force that exists in reality. In this way, we are in balance with it, and there is no better state for us than that. After all, in that state we do not need anything and reside in a world of utter bliss.

VaYikra details the order of correction of all 613 broken, egoistic desires into connection with others, and through it, our connection with the Creator. It is written, "From the Love of man to the love of God."* However, before we connect with others, we must be properly built within, and must prepare ourselves for the connection internally, as well as externally.

Assume that a person must be "married," meaning have a deficiency. A woman is a deficiency next to the man, a deficiency adapted to the ability to correct it. The feminine part of a person is like a deficiency, the left side, while the masculine part is the right side, which complements the woman. In a state of collaborative work, a person is considered "married."

The man—who is higher than the woman and wants to advance and correct the deficiency—makes an offering. The offering is also for the feminine part of the person. The same applies to the rest of the people.

---

* Rav Yehuda Ashlag (Baal HaSulam), *The Writings of Baal HaSulam*, "The Love of God and the Love of Man," p 482.

The work of the offerings is the work in the Temple, the common *Kli* of the world where we express our attitude toward the Creator. There are many details in this work: how to slaughter, burn, and discern all the parts in the offerings.

There is a part of us that enjoys, and a part that is as "smoke." The word "smoke" is an acronym for *Olam*, *Shana*, *Nefesh* (*ASHAN* [smoke]) by which we transcend the limitations of our world, thus advancing toward the purpose of Creation.

When we begin to connect and approach the Creator through our offerings, we become more suitable to the Creator. Each time, one of the 613 desires becomes more suitable to the Creator. This way, we begin to feel that the system within is becoming more similar to that of the Creator. Then, we begin to understand Him since we contain a partial sample of Him that gradually expands. The more our desires close in on a similar structure to Godliness, the more the Creator "clothes" the person. Thus, we become more similar to the Creator.

Through our internal system, where there is already a part of the Creator, we begin to understand and know Him. We can picture and imagine that system, thoughts, desires, and the approach of the Creator toward us. Thus, we can increasingly understand our own attitude toward the Creator. The model that we build within allows us to be in mutual connection with the Creator, and this is how we become man (Adam).

From the beginning of Creation through its end, we undergo a process by which we must correct ourselves and rise from our world to the world of *Ein Sof* (infinity). We must do it internally, in our inner structure, so that each time we become increasingly similar to the upper force. This is the work that this portion deals with.

The Creator is inviting us to this work, hoping that humanity will respond. The whole work is of the part of us called "Israel," and of which it was written, "And you will be to Me a kingdom of priests and a holy nation" (Exodus, 19:6). The priests are those who manage the work at the Temple, bringing the rest of the nation to this work so that all may be able to correct themselves.

All of Israel is regarded as priests, in relation to the rest of the world. *VaYikra* (The Lord Called) is first and foremost a call to Israel because Israel is obliged to teach the rest of humanity how to approach the Creator. It was written about it, "They shall all know Me, from the least of them to the greatest of them" (Jeremiah, 31:33), and "for My house shall be called 'a house of prayer' to all the nations" (Isaiah, 56:7), once it is built.

This is why *VaYikra* is a call to the entire nation of Israel to correct itself as quickly as possible, thus also correcting the global crisis, the world's problems, and abolishing anti-Semitism. Then, everyone will truly be as one nation.

Questions and Answers

We sacrifice to the Creator, but sacrifice actually means nearing between people. What is the connection between bringing people closer and sacrificing to the Creator?

There is an act and there is the intention. To perform a correction, we must draw closer to others. We cannot draw closer to others unless we have the intention to draw closer, and unless the common force of bestowal that exists in the world, namely the Creator, appears among us. With mutual nearing we can build an opportunity, a place, a space of mutual desire where the mutual force of bestowal appears, meaning the force of love, which does not exist in our world. That force does not exist in our qualities unless we exert to make it, to make room for it. The place where the force of bestowal appears is called "dweller" or "the revelation of Divinity." It requires three conditions in order to exist: you, me, and the Creator.

What is the order between them? It seems reasonable to say, "Give me this type of temple and I will sacrifice my cow there."

It is all within us. The cow, too.

It follows that we must approach the Creator so He can give us the strength to love others. Therefore, does one not reach the Creator through others, but from the Creator to others? Because the problems are between us and not with the Creator?

True, there is no other way. We begin with hating each other; we have no desire whatsoever to draw near to others. Only through troubles and problems, when we ask how and why, what is the meaning of life, what is happening in the world, do we understand that we *must* correct our nature and start looking for a solution. Our correction is from reception to bestowal, from hate to love, from understanding that the hatred is destroying the world and our lives.

Today the whole world is dealing with correcting human nature because it ruins everything, including this planet. Many scientists are warning us about these problems, which are already causing our collapse.

The problem is that we cannot restrain human nature. We are marching as sheep to the slaughter, unable to stop ourselves. Baal HaSulam wrote that the angel of death comes with a drop of poison on the tip of his sword, and you open your mouth to it because there is a last bit of pleasure in it, and then you die. You cannot see past yourself, and even if you do, you simply must have this drop."* Just so, we are advancing blindly, following our nature into wars and troubles, ruining everything along the way because it is all done without higher guidance.

We need the upper force. This need arises from the sensation of troubles and problems that are already appearing in the world, but it should come with an explanation. There must be a system that provides information that we, the children of Israel, must pass on to the rest of the world. This is the meaning of "being a kingdom of priests." The priests are those who teach the people, as it is written, "And you will be to Me a kingdom of priests and a holy nation" (Exodus, 19:6).

* Rav Yehuda Ashlag (Baal HaSulam), *The Writings of Baal HaSulam*, "Introduction to the Book, *Panim Meirot uMasbirot* (Shining and Welcoming Face)," p 149.

We must make the reason for the crisis known, as well as the means for correcting human nature, in order to bring the whole of humanity to balance with Nature, or we will not survive.

Although the conditions for it have all been prepared, we have to do our share of this work. This is why we are witnessing an increase in global anti-Semitism, which will only increase unless we make the method of correction and its use known in due time and promote its implementation the world over.

It is therefore clear that we ourselves must be connected to the Creator, study, and demand the revelation of the Creator in order to allow ourselves to advance. All we need is the sense of lack and our drive toward it, since the moment we need His strength, we will ask and receive it.

What does it mean that we sacrifice a cow, a sheep, or a goat?

The Book of Zohar explains that these are not cows, sheep, or any other kosher animal. Rather, it is a person who needs to correct, to discern the animal part within, the speaking part, which is the priest, Levite, and Israel. A person offers and sacrifices part of the animate, which is all the animate within us. Actually, sacrifice concerns the desires within us, which are divided into still, vegetative, animate, and human.

Why is it so difficult to offer the sacrifice?

We cannot perform correction without first knowing what to do, without internally distinguishing good from bad. Currently, we do not know what to correct. You might say, "Yes, sometimes I lie," but how can you tell that this is what you must correct? Anyone can say that, at least to oneself. However, even then it is not a sincere confession. So how will you know what is stopping you from approaching the goal? For this, we need the revelation of the Creator, the light that reforms, to illuminate the desires we can sacrifice.

From *The Zohar*: One Who Did Not Marry a Woman Is Flawed

"When any man of you brings an offering" means excluding one who did not marry a wife, since his offering is not an offering and there are no blessings in him, neither above nor below. This means that when it writes, "When any man of you brings an offering," he is different, not a human and not included in man. Divinity is not over him because he is flawed and called "maimed," and one who is maimed is removed from everything, all the more so from the altar, from offering sacrifices.

Zohar for All, *VaYikrah* (The Lord Called), item 63

Ask most people and they will tell you, "I'm fine with the Creator; I get along with Him." How do they know? Do they feel this way? Is this how the Creator is depicted for them?

They feel so because the Creator is hidden from them, so they are sure they are OK with Him.

If the person is OK with the Creator, why is He hidden?

We do not ask ourselves this question. We say, "I pay my taxes, I'm friendly to my neighbors, I even put the garbage in the right bins. I'm just fine."

How do you explain to people that there is a connection, that we must discover the quality of bestowal within us, that this is the Creator? How do you explain that *VaYikra* means that the Creator is calling us to approach something very different?

We determine our own situation on the scale, according to the upper force, which is benevolent, whole, in which there is no hate but only love. We measure how similar or different we are from the Unique One, from Whom everything was created and to Whom everything returns. First, we must see and feel how different or similar we are to Him. We must also engage in the wisdom of Kabbalah, or we will have no chance of approaching Him.

This is how everyone thinks, which is why it is impossible to turn to anyone in this manner. We need to measure ourselves compared to the Creator, and then it will be possible to see how obligated we are, and how the Creator has made us so. We could say, "Go to the craftsman who made me,"* since He has made me this way, and only through bringing the upper light will anything be resolved.

Our qualities have been designed since childhood by our parents, education, the environment, the Creator, genes, grandparents, and previous generations. Then there are our own additions. Over that part, which we could avoid adding to ourselves, we have a choice and can say, "This I need to correct." This is the initial scrutiny. It is a very special work, which is why we do not immediately arrive at the offerings.

During all the previous portions, we advance toward this work, discovering the Creator—the upper force—at the level we are on through the quality of Moses in us. We measure ourselves compared to his quality, and only then can we correct our qualities and know how many of them we should fix, and how. After all, we have many qualities that need no correction because they are corrected by themselves, as they are not ours.

Terms

Offering/Sacrifice

The word, *Korban* (offering/sacrifice), comes from the word, *Karov* (near), as it is written, "As Pharaoh drew near, the children of Israel looked, and behold, the Egyptians were marching after them, and they became very frightened; so the sons of Israel cried out to the Lord" (Exodus, 14:10). Pharaoh is our biggest force of advancement. In fact, everything we slaughter at the altar, all that we correct, are parts of Pharaoh, that great will to receive from which we cut slices and sacrifice. By that, we become corrected and draw closer, until the image of the Creator emerges in us from the image of Pharaoh.

* Babylonian Talmud, *Masechet Taanit*, p 20b.

Sin

"Sin" is the complete disclosure of our nature, showing how absorbed we are in self-love instead of the love of others.

Mistake

The corruption of the force of *Bina* in us is called "mistake." The corruption of the force of *Malchut* in us is called "sin" (deliberate faulty act). In our world, the sins are far greater than the mistakes. Take, for example, a person who wants to steal; the mistake is that he is jealous of another and seemingly does him no harm by being jealous.

The correction of the mistake is when a person transcends one's will to receive and does not want to use it. At that time, the person becomes detached from the mistake and later inverts the entire ego, the entire will to receive, into having the aim to bestow upon others. This is how we correct the sins.

From *The Zohar*: If His Offering Is a Burnt Offering

The burnt offering rises over the heart, meaning on the thought, which is above the heart. It is known that the one who stands over the heart is the thought, since the thought, which is *Hochma* (wisdom), is regarded as male and the heart as female–*Bina* (understanding), the heart understands–for she receives from *Hochma*. This is why a burnt offering rises up and they are all males, and this is why the writing begins with a burnt offering more than all other offerings, since the thought is the beginning of everything.

Zohar for All, *VaYikrah* (The Lord Called), item 73

It turns out that everything happens in our minds. We need not work physically. The entire world is a spiritual world, one of forces. We see by technology how we are advancing to a state where big factories and machines that produce metals are becoming redundant. When we act by thought, the world becomes much more "ethereal," spiritual. Through our thoughts, we will rise to the correct scrutiny, sacrifice offerings, and by them approach the good life.

Tzav

(Command)

(Leviticus, 6:1-8:36)

Portion Summary

The portion, *Tzav* (Command), deals with rules of sacrificing, especially those related to priests. The portion mentions the commandment to donate fertilizer, the gift offering, sin offering, guilt offering, peace offering, and the prohibition against eating animal fat.

Tzav also mentions punishments for those who eat non-kosher meat, as it is written, "The soul that eats from it shall bear iniquity (Leviticus, 7:18). One who eats fat from the offerings, "The soul that eats shall be cut off from its people" (Leviticus, 7:25), and one who eats the offerings' blood, "That soul shall be cut off from its people" (Leviticus, 7:20).

Subsequently, the portion deals with the seven days of filling and the inauguration of the tabernacle. The Creator commands Moses to assemble Aaron and his sons, the priests, and the whole congregation at the door of the tent of meeting. Moses washes Aaron and his sons and dresses them in the clothes of priesthood. Moses puts the anointing oil over the tabernacle and all that is

in it, and sanctifies Aaron and his sons, showing the priests—following the Creator's command—what to do with the various organs of the offerings.

Commentary

The *Korban* (offering/sacrifice, from the word, *Karov* [near]) is the way to draw near the Creator. There is nothing but the offerings. Today, we are in the worst state in history. There is nothing worse than this world and our current state. We must come out of that state and advance toward the *Boreh* (Creator), from the words *Bo Re'eh* (come and see). We will discover the Creator according to the changes and corrections in us because the upper force, namely the upper light, is in complete rest, and all the changes occur in us, as it is written, "I the Lord do not change" (Malachi, 3:6).

Nearing the Creator depends on our qualities. Therefore, we must all change ourselves and correct all the negative and egoistic desires in us, according to the order the Torah narrates. The Hebrew word, *Torah*, comes from the word, *Horaa* (instruction), meaning how to correct our egoistic desires, aiming them toward bestowal and love, and shifting from unfounded hatred to absolute love.

The global crisis is happening because of unfounded hatred among everyone. There is abundance in the world, but we cannot share it. We cannot establish social justice, connection, unity, and we cannot arrange ourselves and our lives better because of our character, as it is written, "The inclination of a man's heart is evil from his youth" (Genesis, 8:21). To correct the heart, which symbolizes our 613 egoistic, corrupted desires, we need the Torah.

The Torah is the "light that reforms."* One who treats the Torah properly discovers one's wickedness, as it is written, "The world was created only for the complete wicked or the complete righteous."** That is, we must discover that we are completely wicked, created with an evil inclination. Then, "I have created for it the Torah as a

* Midrash Rabah, *Eicha*, "Introduction," Paragraph 2.

** Babylonian Talmud, *Masechet Berachot*, p 61b.

spice,"* for "the light in it reforms them."** Then, we come to a state of complete righteous. This is how we must see it.

The word, *Tzav*, means "commandment." We can go through the process by suffering and taking blows, but this way is neither respectable nor desirable in the eyes of the Creator, or us. But there is another way. We can go through the process recognizing and understanding that we are being led to discover the upper force, and we are being raised to a higher dimension. The crisis and the suffering we feel in this world are intended to push us to develop to a higher level, the human one, which resembles the Creator.

There are many stages in this work. Some stages are called "the nations of the world," and in them we scrutinize our desires and slightly correct them on the level of "nations of the world" which follow seven *Mitzvot* (commandments). Only then do we reach the degree of Israel, meaning *Yashar El* (straight to the Creator), where we can already direct ourselves toward the Creator.

Keeping or observing *Mitzvot* (in Hebrew, it is described as "making") means correcting our desires. From the 613 desires that belong to the work of Israel, we achieve the degree of Levites and the degree of priests. Thus, we go through the *Yod-Hey-Vav-Hey* from below upward, from *Malchut* through *Zeir Anpin*, *Bina*, *Hochma*, and *Keter* until we achieve *Dvekut* (adhesion) with the Creator.

This is the entire order of the work that the Torah describes, and is presented in the Babylonian Talmud. The offerings are a more complicated issue–they are, in fact, our entire work. "Making an offering" means nearing the Creator through consecutive corrections of our desires. We gradually approach the Creator with corrections that begin with the easiest desires and continue through the hardest, heaviest, and most egoistic.

These are desires that we sort out within us, and then determine how to correct them. This is why the text mentions body parts, oil, time, movement, places, the force by which we correct, and in what

* Babylonian *Talmud, Masechet Kidushin*, 30b.
** Midrash Rabah, *Eicha*, "Introduction," Paragraph 2.

state. We must also keep in mind that all this concerns only our inner structure.

We are immersed in an ocean of upper light, which is the Creator, as it is written, "The upper light is in complete rest,"* and all the changes appear only to us, who are inside the light. If we do not feel that the light, the Creator, is filling the whole of reality, it means we are in a state of "double concealment." That is, we have no sensation that something is hidden from us. The first degree we reach is the sensation of concealment, the awareness that something is hidden from us.

Today, all of humanity is beginning to perceive it. Scientists and psychologists are beginning to see that the world is round. They speak of a single force that closes in on us and controls us, that there is a unified guidance and governance, and the world is tied in harmony by fixed laws.

It is written, "He has given a law that shall not be broken" (Psalms, 148:6). Like it or not, we will eventually have to approach that law, study it, replicate it, and keep it. If we want it, good. If we do not want it, we will be forced to accept it by blows, as many stories in the Torah describe.

The Torah tells us about bad things that will ostensibly happen if we do not do what we should. It is necessary to recognize evil and its disclosure. It is written, "I have created the evil inclination,"** so each time the evil inclination appears, we must correct it. We can discern the evil inclination only if we fall into it. But if we come prepared, we will not mingle with it or fall under it, but control it and correct it. This is actually why we were given the Torah.

The whole world is approaching that recognition. Many scientists already maintain that we exist in a circular system, that there is one force of Nature that is acting on us, demanding that we adapt to it in a global and integral world, in harmony and balance with Nature. They are already talking about holism and other such

* Rav Yehuda Ashlag (Baal HaSulam), *The Writings of Baal HaSulam*, p 521.

** Babylonian Talmud, *Masechet Kidushin*, 30b.

phenomena, so there is excitement and some new impressions, and nearing toward the truth.

First we must recognize that there is truly something hidden from us. This is considered "concealment," and it is good; it is the sensation of exile. When we are in exile, we feel it through our contact with the upper force that controls us and acts on us. This is so, although we do not know how it works or how it controls us, nor understand its commands or what it wants from us. In fact, even if we did, we would not know how to carry out its will. We would be incapable of improving our situation. Internally, we recognize that not knowing it would be a terrible loss. The whole world is gradually advancing toward this recognition.

Questions and Answers

When we say "Him," are we referring to a superior law, or to the Creator?

We are not referring to an image, but to a comprehensive quality that governs us–the quality of complete bestowal and love. The closer we come to it, the better we can detect it.

We draw near it by establishing good connections between us, as it is written, "From the love of man to the love of God."* If we establish groups that teach the higher nature in order to become closer and be in brotherly love, we will begin to feel the upper force according to the law of equivalence of form, namely the equivalence of qualities. Then, we will discover that we truly are in exile. This is the beginning of the process. Hence, when we read the story of Esther, we discover concealment, which is the first step.

As we approach Passover, a state where we feel we are in Egypt, exiled from the revelation of the light, the upper force, we have the "great Sabbath," which stresses the importance of the sensation of exile. It is impossible to achieve redemption

* Rav Yehuda Ashlag (Baal HaSulam), *The Writings of Baal HaSulam,* "The Love of God and the Love of Man," p 482.

without that feeling. The difference between *Galut* (exile) and *Geula* (redemption) is in the addition of the letter, *Aleph*, in *Geula*, representing the *Aluf* (Champion) of the world, in which the Creator appears. Exile is the desire to discover Him, for it is He we must attain.

When we want to discover the Creator, we bring all our desires to a state where they do not stand in the way of the upper light, as it is written, "His glory fills the world."* He fills everything with no interruption from us. When we restrict our sense of self-importance–the ego, independence, and sense of uniqueness, our entire "I"–we feel that the Creator passes through us. This is how we discover Him.

But first, we must be "transparent" and avoid being a partition, interfering with the quality of bestowal and love that prevails in the world. Then, we discover that we truly are immersed in the upper light that fills everything, and we are in it. This is the degree we should achieve. It is the first stage of redemption.

The nearing is felt within us, and we begin to sense that we are inside the upper light that fills everything and does everything, as it is written, "He did, does, and will do all the deeds."** This is our salvation from all the crises, despair, and confusion in our lives.

The offering is to the Creator. We burn it, and thus seemingly give something. Why do we not sacrifice to each other in order to draw closer? This way we could really say that through love of others, we obtain something higher.

It only seems that way because of how we use our language. Regarding how we work with offerings, we need to work with each egoistic desire that repels others, desires with which we wish to exploit others and be oblivious to them. The sacrifice is to stop that desire from hindering our approach to others.

* Part of *Tefilat Amidah* (Standing (18) Prayer).

** Said after the morning prayer (*Tefilat Shaharit*), the first of Maimonides' 13 tenets.

As we approach others, we create a system of mutual bestowal and discover the upper light that is between us, not within us individually. We draw it and discover it precisely by creating the quality of bestowal between us.

Does this nearing take place among our friends in the group?

The nearing is between people, not within us. Within us, we can only feel egoistic phenomena. This is why we currently feel only this world through our five physical senses.

How does one offer a sacrifice from the group to the Creator?

It is the same whether we correct our desires toward others or toward the Creator. We all perform the correction together, among us, to reveal the comprehensive quality of bestowal and love that prevails in the world.

The quality of bestowal is the Creator. It is a quality, the thought of Creation. We do not aim toward a certain entity. This is difficult to explain because in our world everything is very "down to earth," clothed in matter, while in the wisdom of Kabbalah there is no substance, only forces.

It is written in this portion that if the children of Israel do not make the offering properly, they will be punished. What is the punishment?

The punishment is that we will do it regardless, as it is written, "For no banished shall be cast out from Him" (Samuel 2, 14:14), and everything will return to its root.

It is written in the portion, "that soul shall be cut off from its people" (Leviticus, 7:20). What does this mean?

It means that we are cut off from our degree. If we were already on the level of "Israel" (Hebrew: *Ysrael*), meaning *Yashar El* (straight to God), and fell from it to the degree of "nations of the world," we would suffer because we had moved away from bestowal, love, revelation, understanding, and awareness. Hence, we must spend more time searching in an unpleasant way, and only then will we return. This is the punishment.

When we cannot process the information properly and quickly by working on the desire with our minds, as the Torah invites us to do, we will do the same work but it will take longer and will be unpleasant. Similarly, if children listen to what they are told and do what they are asked, they benefit. If they do not, they still do their chores because they have no choice, but they suffer.

How can we use the topic of offerings in our approach to education?

There is no difference. If we are born lazy and stubborn, can we turn to our parents and tell them, "You have made me this way; I don't want to study; I don't want to listen to you; all I want is to play, that's the way I am. Did I ask for these qualities? No, there is nothing I can do."

Is it the parents' fault or ours? What we *can* do is create an environment that will help us become smart and successful. Our environment can help us understand the purpose of Creation, how to achieve it, and how to diminish suffering. Everything depends on the environment. If we work in a proper, good, supportive environment, we will learn how to be givers and enjoy it. This is how we approach bestowal and love–it is the work of the offerings that we perform.

The portion speaks of priests, which indicate a very high degree. Can matters be attributed to education on this level, too?

We begin from zero, from the degree of "nations of the world." Everyone is destined to achieve this degree. The purpose of Creation is for everyone to come into this work, correct themselves, and reach the end of correction, called "complete redemption." In the First Temple, the people of Israel were already at the level of redemption, *Mochin* of *Haya*. In the Second Temple, we descended to the level of

Mochin of *Neshama*. Now, we must come to the Third Temple, the highest degree on the ladder of spiritual degrees, where we include the whole of humanity.

If the sacrifice means coming closer to society, do we incorporate education in it, or is it a separate matter?

You cannot be educated alone, only in a society. We are taught to connect with others in a relationship whose quality is similar to that of the Creator. We discover this quality between us because it is only between us that He is revealed. This is akin to changing something in a radio receiver so it receives the wave outside.

From *The Zohar*: *NRN* of Week Days and *NRN* of the Sabbath

A wise disciple should see himself equal to all the students of Torah. This is how he should consider himself from the perspective of the Torah, from the perspective of the noetic *NRN*. But from the perspective of the organs of the body, the perspective of the beastly *NRN*, he should regard himself equal to all the uneducated people, as it is written, "One should always see himself as though the whole world depends on him." For this reason, he should aim his mind, spirit, and soul to make those sacrifices with all the people in the world, and the Creator adds a good thought to the act. By that, "Man and beast You deliver, O Lord."

Zohar for All, *Tzav* (Command), item 71

The upper light is intended to reform everyone–those on the animate degree, and those on the human degree. This is why no one can say, "It's not for me." There must be a study of the wisdom of Kabbalah because we cannot draw the light without it. This is why the wisdom of Kabbalah is called "Torah of light," "internality of the Torah," and the light that reforms.

Is it only the light that corrects? Will we never be able to correct our relationships without it?

Never, and the world is beginning to realize it. It may take some time, but we are already approaching it and beginning to agree with it.

I feel that the world is on the verge of giving up on most everything else.

It is felt, and the world is finally going in the right direction. People already understand that the change has to happen within us, regardless of whether one is Jewish or not, secular or orthodox. The change has to be substantial and equal for all—that of beginning to correct human nature. It is fine if one follows what is called the "practical *Mitzvot*" (commandments), but it is just as fine if one does not. In relation to the inner change, we are all the same and we must all do it.

Is the direction toward which the world is heading considered a sacrifice?

Not yet. Sacrifices begin only through the light that reforms because this is what corrects us. We are all on the worst degree, though we have yet to recognize it as the worst. We are still unaware and unconscious in regard to the evil.

TERMS

Donation

"*Tarum* ("raise" but also "donate") the Creator." To advance toward the goal, we must engage in the uniqueness, importance, and greatness of the upper force. We must see that there is none else besides Him, He is the only operator in reality, we are in it, and we are totally operated upon. To the extent that we acquire His qualities, we become independent. That is, we take on ourselves the actions we can carry out correctly, and we begin to do them by ourselves until we become like Him, until we can do everything He does.

This is how we begin to recognize and understand that degree, the whole of reality, the purpose, the beginning and the end, the cause and the consequence, the whole process we are going through. Thus, we become as great, wise, strong, and united as the Creator. This is true for each of us, and for all of us together.

Once we have corrected ourselves and achieved the completion of correction, and all of us together have become completely like Him, another development awaits us. We need to correct ourselves and acquire power and wisdom to perform another, very special work after the end of correction, after the Third Temple. But for now, our perception is inadequate to comprehend the reality we will discover at that time.

The Inauguration of the Tabernacle

The "inauguration of the tabernacle" is like a housewarming. We conclude the building of a certain stage of the work, from which we can begin to correct ourselves. The tabernacle is the place of correction.

Oil

The light of *Hochma* (wisdom) is called "oil." "Oil for lighting" means that the light of *Hochma* is illuminating us. It cannot illuminate without the light of *Hassadim*, without the special *Kli* (tool/vessel) intended for it. Oil, salt, and water are forces designed to correct our desires. They ease the desires, and the right combination between them helps us bring our desires closer to correction.

Spiritual Punishment

Through punishment, we draw nearer to something good. If we know what punishment is, we learn from it. If children do not learn what is permitted and what is forbidden, they will not know how to behave properly in the world. Punishment is a boundary. We have to experience boundaries or we become disoriented. Boundaries provide a sense of grip and understanding. Without boundaries, we cannot know where we are.

Summary

Tzav (command) is an approach to Aaron and his sons through which He reaches all of man's qualities. We must understand that the Creator has set up all our work in our desires. Wherever we turn, especially in relationships, if we achieve the love of Israel we will correct everything. This is the command.

Shmini

(On the Eighth Day)

(Leviticus, 9:1-11:47)

Portion Summary

The portion, *Shmini* (On the Eighth Day), deals with the events of the eighth day after the seven days of filling.* This is the inauguration day of the tabernacle. Aaron and his sons offer special sacrifices on this day. Moses and Aaron go to bless the people, and finally, the Creator appears to the people of Israel.

Aaron's sons, Nadav and Avihu, sin by making an offering on a foreign fire, and the fire consumes them. Aaron and the remaining sons receive special instructions for conducting themselves in the situation, and among other orders, they are forbidden to mourn.

This portion tells of another misunderstanding between Moses and Aaron and his sons, concerning eating the sin offering. The portion ends with rules about forbidden food, detailing the animals, beasts, poultry, and fish we are forbidden

* "You shall not go outside the doorway of the tent of meeting for seven days, until the day that the period of your ordination is fulfilled; for he will ordain you through seven days" (Leviticus, 8:33).

to eat. Rules of *Tuma'a* (impurity) and *Taharah* (purity) are also briefly explained.

QUESTIONS AND ANSWERS

The portion mentions many details concerning the tabernacle and offering sacrifices, what is forbidden and what is permitted. How should we understand this internally?

We need to examine which of our 613 desires we need to correct, and how. It was said about Man, "I have created the evil inclination; I have created for it the Torah as a spice,"* so we may correct our evil inclination–the egoistic desires–in which we think only of ourselves and cannot perform a single act of giving and love of others.

It is written, "Love your neighbor as yourself."** This is a special force, and the Torah was given for the sole purpose of obtaining it. If we study the internality of the Torah properly–namely Kabbalah, the wisdom of light–we draw the light that reforms, which corrects us.

The desires in us are called the "evil inclination.." Initially, they are egoistic because "the inclination of a man's heart is evil from his youth" (Genesis, 8:21). Our goal is to correct it through our studies and turn it into the intention to bestow upon others, to the aim to connect and love. By correcting ourselves, we obtain the quality of bestowal, equivalence with the Creator, and *Dvekut* (adhesion) with Him in order to be like Him. This is the purpose of Man's creation–to be like the Creator.

To correct our desires and inclinations, we must follow a certain order, from easy to hard. To properly correct our nature, we must conduct ourselves according to our level of development. Like an infant who grows into a small child, then a youth, and finally an adult, each stage of our development requires more activities of greater complexity. At each stage, we draw the light that reforms. This sorts for us, according to the order of difficulty,

* Babylonian Talmud, *Masechet Kidushin*, 30b.
** Jerusalem Talmud, *Seder Nashim, Masechet Nedarim*, Chapter 9, p 30b.

the desires whose time for correction has come. This is why the Torah is called *Horaa* (instruction), as through it we advance and climb the ladder of degrees through the end of correction of all our desires.

In the portion, *Shmini*, we scrutinize which desires we can correct, how we can correct them, and which desires we cannot correct. Within us are desires that cannot be corrected, called the "stony heart." These desires are the basis of our nature. They are so intense that we cannot even *ask* for their correction.

By correcting what we must, and by regretting not being able to correct the stony heart, as well as by distinguishing what is correctable and what is beyond our ability to correct, we gain a clear perception of the difference between them. By regretting that we cannot correct, yet doing all we can with regard to these desires, they become corrected.

This is why the laws of *Kedusha* (holiness) and *Tahara* (purity) are called "laws of *Kashrut*" (the noun of the adjective, *Kosher*). We scrutinize these laws–what is kosher and what is not–in the still, vegetative, animate, and human, how we should perform them, and on which level.

The word, *Kashrut*, refers to the word, *Kosher* ("permitted," "proper," "lawful"), referring to the readiness for bestowal. A "kosher person" is one who has corrected oneself in all the desires of bestowal and love of others, at least on a certain level.

The measure of the desire is the sum of all the desires in us at the levels of still, vegetative, and animate. The more the desire mingles with emotion, reason, understanding, connection with people, and the upper force, the more we correct it. The laws of *Kashrut* tell us how to sanctify, how to bring each desire to correction, and how to use it to bestow. The Torah gives us examples from our world, like using the desire for food, which actually refers to Man's correction.

However, we are bound to fail, like children who cannot understand how a new toy works until they break it. They do not even understand that they broke it, or how, if at all, it is possible to fix it. As long as the child does not fully comprehend the making of the toy—how it was made and the role of each part—the child will not become attached to it.

Similarly, we must comprehend the foundations of Creation and touch our most basic, egoistic desires, as it is written, "There is not a righteous man on earth who does good and did not sin" (Ecclesiastes, 7:20). We must experience all the sins, fail, and then correct them. There is no other way.

We must recognize all the evil in us, as the Creator says, "I have created the evil inclination." It is we who must discover where our evil inclination resides. When we discover it, we are considered "wicked," "transgressors." We recognize the evil and regret it.

However, we do not regret the recognition of the evil within us because this is how we were made. Rather, we regret that our inclination is not to bestow, but to receive for ourselves. We demand the correcting force and receive from above the light that reforms. Thus, we shift from using each desire egoistically and looking for self-gratification, to seeking the benefit of others. This is how we correct ourselves.

The general recognition of the evil inclination occurs by the breaking of the vessels in the upper worlds. This is our root from which this world was created, prepared in the upper roots, the upper system. It is embedded in the foundation of the nation, in the acts of Nadav and Avihu, as described below. Now, we must discover it in us in this world.

Nadav and Avihu had to go through this process, and although it may appear that they committed a transgression, their deed helps us discover the foundation of "I have created the evil inclination" so we can correct it.

Nadav and Avihu wanted to reach the end of correction instantaneously. However, when they did so, they discovered the will to receive in order to receive, the evil inclination, *Sitra Achra*, *Klipa* (shell/peel), in its worst form. Nadav and Avihu drew such a powerful light to themselves that they could not receive it in order to bestow, so they received it in order to receive and therefore died.

One who advances in the degrees does so, too. Within us are forces called "Nadav" and "Avihu," in addition to the forces of "Aaron" and "Moses."

"Man is a small world,"* and whatever is told in the Torah exists in each and every one of us. We can make the same transgressions and correct them after some time. This is how we become aware of the real evil inclination, the stony heart, which cannot be touched. Through these stories, we can learn to correct the desires that can be corrected, in the right order of correction.

The laws of *Kashrut* at the end of the portion stem from all our scrutinies. They explain to us how we can correct ourselves, and how best we can bring the incense—the desires that are properly mingled, the forces of bestowal and reception within us—so they correct one another.

This is what the portion, *Shmini*, (On the Eighth Day) deals with. It is called so because *Malchut* that ascends to *Yesod* is the eighth *Malchut*, and we must know how to correct it. It is called the "Eighth" after the basic correction, to distinguish between the parts of *Malchut* that cannot be corrected and those that can be, and to know how we can draw the correcting forces. We scrutinize all that on our spiritual path, in a correction called *Shmini*.

---

* *Midrash Tanchuma*, *Pekudei*, item 3

The number 7 appears many times in this portion. Is there a special meaning to it?

It is written that there are six days of work, and the seventh is the Sabbath.* The six days are *Hesed*, *Gevura*, *Tifferet*, *Netzah*, *Hod*, and *Yesod*. "Days" are actually degrees by which we can correct our desires. The seventh day is *Malchut*, which is corrected by itself by what we have done during the six degrees, and by drawing the light. In fact, all corrections are made on the seventh day.

The Sabbath is actually not a day of rest, but a state where it is no longer possible to scrutinize or arrange anything. Instead, "One who labored on the Sabbath Eve shall eat on the Sabbath."** Only what we do during the six days enters *Malchut* and is corrected in *Malchut*, in our *Yesod* (also "foundation"), in our substance, our desires.

The eighth is the reception of the quality of Aaron, quality of *Bina*, as it is written, "Sons of *Bina*, eight days."*** *Malchut* connects to *Bina*, from which we draw the correcting force on the eighth day.

The upper system is called *Zeir Anpin*, or *HaKadosh Baruch Hu* (The Holy One Blessed Be He). It is the system that corrects us, the clothing, *Malchut*, which connects to the upper system. In other words, our souls connect to the Creator.

The soul is also called the "Assembly of Israel" because it assembles all the souls that desire correction. This is how we come to the eighth. Here, we must be careful when we encounter situations, as did Nadav and Avihu, but we will still have to experience them.

As was already mentioned, "There is not a righteous man on earth who does good and did not sin" (Ecclesiastes, 7:20). This means that we will encounter many more experiences to scrutinize

---

* "Six days shall work be done, but on the seventh day there is a sabbath of complete rest, a holy convocation. You shall not do any work; it is a sabbath to the Lord in all your dwellings" (Leviticus, 23:3)

** Babylonian Talmud, *Masechet Avodah Zarah*, p 3a.

*** As sung in the Hanukah song, *Maoz Tzur*.

as we follow our roots and follow what happened to our forefathers. After all the corrections and exiles we have been through, we will arrive at the disclosure and know how to continue. Additionally, we will have good instructions from the wisdom of Kabbalah, so when we face demanding scrutinies, we will go through them quickly and continue our journey.

Regarding the example of Nadav and Avihu, we always want our children not to make mistakes. Does this show us that mistakes are mandatory?

Without being aware of it, we constantly lead our children into mistakes. And not only children—even university students about to become PhDs learn by being presented with problems. The learning process itself actually involves solving problems. We present children with problems and want them to play and resolve them. Alternatively, we give them something to assemble or exercises in math, physics, or chemistry. We constantly challenge them with problems.

When our children become youths or young adults, we still worry that they might make mistakes. How do we raise children that will not act on their intense desires, as did Nadav and Avihu, who were burned for it?

Children learn what to do, how to do it, and if they should do it at all, only by trial and error. Similarly, we, too, learn by trial and error. We have to discover the shattering, the crisis, our nature, or we will not know how to correct it. This is why we were given the Torah, whose light shines for us and clarifies matters.

There is light for the scrutiny of the *Kelim* (vessels), and there is light for the correction of the *Kelim*. If we know how to use our *Kelim* (desires) correctly, we will go through the corrections quickly and pleasantly. If each time we encounter corruption we also know that we can fix it, and in so doing discover another portion of the spiritual world, our eternity, perfection, there is no doubt that we will be happy when that corruption appears.

In relation to education, when we see our children make mistakes and correct them, should we view this as something good?

Yes. There are customs where we act joyfully (even on the Day of Atonement [*Yom Kippur*]), as opposed to the sadness expressed by other customs. The differences stem from misunderstanding what we are discovering. In truth, there is something to be said for the expressions of all customs. In each revelation of evil there must be joy, too, since we have the means to correct it and achieve contentment. It is impossible to feel good without discovering and correcting the bad.

It is written that everyone will know the difference between the rules of *Tuma'a* (impurity) and *Tahara* (purity). It is said that at the time of the First Temple, every child from six years old knew those laws. What does it mean?

This does not refer to children in the physical sense of the word, although that was the prevailing type of education then, and children did grow with understanding, sensation, and perception of the upper force. They received upbringing that brought them to bestowal and opening of their eyes. Besides this world, which they saw through their five physical senses, they were assisted in developing a sixth sense, called *Neshama* (soul). With that sense, they experienced the upper force and therefore knew what was good and what was bad. They could distinguish between them, and thus grow.

Everything depends on the environment. The environment educated children toward corrections, and each child whose ego (will to receive) grew received the appropriate education. Education is a system of correction through the environment, with explanations and support as our desires grow. Education means teaching children that their desires are constantly growing and should be used in order to bestow, for love.

Can such education be established today, as well?

It will happen anyway because Nature is obliging us to do it. We are heading toward a state where we will have to instill this type of education throughout the world, not just for us, but for the entire world. We need to be "a light for the nations" (Isaiah, 42:6), and pass on the method, "for My house shall be called 'a house of prayer' for all the nations" (Isaiah, 56:7), so they will all be as one.

Today we are in the last exile, preceding our complete redemption. Therefore, we must first bring this education to the people of Israel, and subsequently to the rest of the world. We are in the advanced stages on this path. The crisis we are experiencing, the helplessness in education, and the collapse of the family structure were all intended to open our eyes to big changes.

Does that mean that the crisis was meant to make us ask for a solution on a higher level?

Yes. The solution already exists, and it is simple: We must understand that there is no other choice, that we have an easy and effective means to obtain bounty and happiness, especially with our children. Otherwise, what kind of world are we leaving for them?

We know that days and occasions mentioned in the Torah symbolize internal stages; what is the stage of the day of "the inauguration of the tabernacle?"

Once a person has sorted all of one's *Kelim* in mind and heart, meaning in one's desires, thoughts, and intentions, that person can work with these *Kelim* in full power. This is called "the inauguration of the tabernacle." One brings them as offerings when they are scrutinized.

The offerings are all the desires that we can turn from aiming to receive, from egoistic (evil inclination), to aiming to bestow, to the form of bestowal and love. This is the correction. By correcting more and more of our desires for bestowal and love, we draw closer to the Creator. The word, *Korban* (sacrifice/offering), comes from the word, *Karov* (near/close), and *Makriv* (bringing near/offering/sacrificing). This is Man's primary work. Thus, "the inauguration of the tabernacle" means that one has prepared the *Kelim* with which one can begin to work.

Does being in the light, in the daytime, refer to a state that is opposite from the night?

It is written (Psalms, 36:10), "By Your light we shall see light." Once we have corrected ourselves in the degree of desiring mercy—bestowing in order to bestow, the degree of Aaron—we correct those desires that are not in reception in order to bestow. We move from constantly wanting to receive for ourselves in all our desires, to a state where what is happening is clear to us. Thus, we neutralize those desires into a point where we do not want to use them for our own sake, since that would literally destroy and "burn" our soul. Preparing ourselves is "the tabernacle." Henceforth, we begin to correct these desires in order to bestow.

TERMS

Inauguration of the Tabernacle

"Inauguration of the tabernacle" is the point from which we can bring offerings, meaning correct our desires in actual fact. In that state, we can correct each desire by making it similar to bestowal, love of others, and the Creator. We become similar to the Creator in that desire, understand the wholeness and eternity of Creation. We ourselves become as the Creator, as it is written, "Return, O Israel, to the Lord your God" (Hosea, 14:2). This is what we should achieve, and these actions bring about great joy.

So it is not a coincidence that the revelation of the Creator is mentioned on the same day as the inauguration of the tabernacle. But what does revealing the Creator mean?

Upon beginning to perform the work of the tabernacle, we discover the Creator, according to the law of equivalence of form. As we perform the same acts as the Creator, the Creator "dresses" in us, and we begin to feel that our actions create our situation, our place, and our status. One who performs acts of bestowal and love, correcting one's evil inclination, becomes like the Creator. This is why such a person is called "Man" (Adam), from the word *Domeh* (similar) to the Creator.

Nadav and Avihu sacrificed with foreign fire. What does that mean?

"Foreign fire" is drawing light that comes to the will to receive in order to receive. Nadav and Avihu did not know this was impossible because they could not calculate. They intended to act with the aim to bestow; they wanted to sanctify even more, make greater corrections than was possible. This is why they failed. They ostensibly sinned, but it is not really a sin because they had no foreknowledge of it.

A "sin" is when we *know* that something is a sin, yet we do it. We have no such sins. All our sins on the spiritual path are from not knowing, and matters suddenly appear as egoistic. Next time, we avoid it. It is not like the sin of *Adam HaRishon*, of whom it is written, "I have eaten and I will eat more."* This was an actual sin.

From *The Zohar*: On the Eighth Day

On that day, there was the joy of the assembly of Israel, *Malchut*, connecting in ties of faith with all the holy ties in all the *Sefirot* of ZA. This is so because the incense connects all as one, which is why it is called "incense." Nadab and Avihu came and tied all these together to the *Sitra Achra*, and left the *Malchut* outside because they did not connect her with the *Sefirot* of ZA. They tied another thing instead of the *Malchut*, which is why he later warns the priests, as it is written, "With this shall Aaron come into the holy place," when he ties this *Malchut*, called "this."

Zohar for All, *Shmini* (On the Eighth Day), item 37

Upon reception of the light, Nadav and Avihu wanted to mingle all the desires together, to correct them and perform an act of bestowal with them, but without first performing the work of scrutiny. However, it is impossible to draw near all at once; it must be done gradually. Only through this work, which each of us experiences, do we understand how to continue in the proper order of correction.

* Midrash Rabah, *Beresheet*, Portion 19

Tazria–Metzorah

(When a Woman Delivers–The Leper)

(Leviticus, 12:1-13:59 – 14:1-15:33)

Summary of the Portions

In the portion, *Tazria* (When a Woman Delivers), we learn about laws related to a woman who has delivered. If she delivers a boy, she is considered impure for seven days. On the eighth day, the boy is circumcised and the woman begins a 33-day purification period. If the woman delivers a girl, she is considered impure for fourteen days, and the purification period lasts for 66 days.

The portion also details rules concerning afflictions. A person who is infected with something must go to the priest, who diagnoses the sore and knows the rules concerning each malady.

The portion, *Metzorah* (The Leper), is dedicated to the rules concerning leprosy, and what to do when one has been infected with it. A leper who has been healed must be examined by the priest, then bring two birds. The priest slaughters one bird and dips the other in clean water.

The end of the portion discusses the impurity of nocturnal ejaculation and the rules concerning a woman in menstruation—anyone who touches her is considered impure until the evening.

Questions and Answers

Why are the rules in the portions described in such detail?

The whole Torah is an instruction by which to correct our nature. Man was deliberately created with an egoistic desire; this is why we want everything for our own good, as it is written, "For the inclination of a man's heart is evil from his youth" (Genesis, 8:21). Creation itself is the evil inclination, the sum of our negative qualities. The inanimate nature, the vegetative, and the animate around us are completely neutral—neither good nor bad. They are managed by the laws of Nature that act instinctively on all its elements.

But Man has free choice, and therefore uses the ego to do others harm. Such is the "software" from which we are built. We constantly examine ourselves in relation to others to determine if we are worse off or better off than they are. This is how human nature constantly operates us, as we wonder, "How can I benefit myself or harm others?" One who does not see this is unaware of this law.

The Torah indicates and explains how to correct ourselves, how to transform ourselves from a form opposite that of the Creator, and into a corrected and complete form. This is why we cannot see the upper worlds, the upper force, the eternity and perfection we are in, which is hidden from us. We can only see a tiny sphere known as "this world." In this world, there is nothing but a set time during which we exist, then leave, just like animals. We incarnate from above, descend from the upper world and go back up, unaware of the rest of the stages in our development.

The Torah tells us how we can correct ourselves so we may begin to discover our eternal, complete forms. The Torah shows us how we should work in order to discover the eternal, perfect world, and how to exit our sensation that we are in exile, moving instead toward a good, enlightened world.

The two portions indicate all the corrections we must do. *Tazria* and *Metzorah* detail how we can correct the egoistic, corrupt signs we constantly discover in ourselves.

It is written in *Tazria* that birth is a good thing, a new degree. The one who can deliver is the desire that craves birth, namely to turn itself toward bestowal. When that desire can deliver from the woman the male part of her, all the surpluses of the will to receive that cannot be corrected are secreted as impure birth blood.

At that time, a person is called a "woman," though it may well be a man. It depends on whether one is in a state of reception or bestowal. If a person delivers out of oneself an act of bestowal, that person is called a "woman," who delivers a child. Then, a person is told what to do with all that did not come out in this act, called a "newborn." Thus, those desires that he or she used, but were still not corrected, come out as blood, as various secretions, just as in a physical birth. After some time, these desires return and become corrected on higher degrees.

Accordingly, after delivering a boy, we undergo seven days of *Tuma'a* (impurity), a circumcision on the eighth, and the thirty-three days of purification. After delivering a girl, we undergo sixty-six days of purification. These are special corrections. Once we have corrected these desires through a special act, called *Korban*, (sacrifice/offering), we perform an act in order to bestow. Here, we sacrifice, meaning bring ourselves closer to bestowal upon the Creator, according to the law of equivalence of form, in order to become more similar to the Creator. This is how we progress another step in the correction.

Here the corrections are in the tiny revelations of all the forms of the egoistic desire, which appears through leprosy and other problems that meet us in our homes and our animals, namely in all the degrees–desires of the still, vegetative, and animate.

The portion, *Metzorah*, details the corrections performed by the priest. We begin to discern forces in our inner structure that help us from experience–from previous corrections–to correct ourselves in all the qualities that appear as "bad."

The portion speaks of a man who brings himself or his wife to the priest. The portion details how to correct the "dresses" over the soul, called "garments." The clothing is called, *Ohr Hozer* (Reflected Light), or *Ohr Hassadim* (light of mercy), meaning an intention to bestow.

Although we are born with egoistic desires, if we "clothe" them with the aim to bestow and want to perform acts of bestowal, we will thus correct our "garments." The highest degree in this correction is to clean the clothes and show them to the priest for his examination. This is the meaning of the relation between the degrees in the upper system. In this manner, we advance in our corrected desires toward the revelation of the upper world, as it is written, "You will see your world in your life."*

We are constantly developing and discovering the world. We feel more and more included in something eternal and complete. We live in this world as animate bodies, yet discover the eternal part within called the "soul." We identify with that part because it is much greater and more powerful than the animate part. That sympathy causes us to feel that our animate part is like a domesticated animal we keep in the yard. It makes no difference whether it is dead or alive because the self, the human we have raised within, which we have built in similarity with the Creator, is as eternal and complete as He is.

All this is done through work by which we discover all that is still not "clean" in us. We clean ourselves from all the ill thoughts and intentions aimed at our own benefit and at others' detriment.

---

* Babylonian Talmud, *Masechet Berachot*, 17a.

With each correction and cleansing we become increasingly similar to the Creator.

The two portions are connected. One speaks of a quality called "woman," and the other of a leper. What is a woman? What is a leper? And what is the connection between them?

In our perception, "man is a small world."* Within us is a special force that "paints" an image in the back of our minds, in our awareness and consciousness, that there is a world before us, outside of us. But if our senses suddenly stop working, we will not perceive any world. If one of our senses disappeared, such as sight or hearing, part of our perception would disappear, as well.

The world is a product of our senses, which depict within us a certain reality. That reality has nothing to do with what is actually happening outside. If we study animals that live near us, we will find that they perceive our world very differently. A dog's world, for example, is full of scents. Dogs perceive the world through their sense of smell, and can easily discern things using that sense. Snakes perceive their world through temperature, distinguishing each element with great accuracy. Ninety-seven percent of the perception of our world depends on our vision. Thus, each one has a different picture of reality, but it is still a picture of reality.

When we attain the perception of the actual reality, a sixth sense opens in us. We begin to see the upper force, the upper world alongside this world. The upper world is present here and now, and we need not die in order to perceive it. Our death changes nothing in this case. Also, we begin to discover that the world is very different from what we previously imagined. This is why it is written about our world that it is imaginary: "I saw an upside down world."**

We attain true perception through all the corrections that appear in the portions before us, when we correct our desires into having the intention to bestow more and more. If we use our desires

* *Midrash Tanchuma, Pekudei*, item 3.

** Babylonian Talmud, *Masechet Nezikin, Baba Batra*, 10b; Babylonian Talmud, *Masechet Pesachim*, 50a.

with the aim to receive, we constantly absorb everything that our tiny, limited tools of perception depict for us. But when we come out of ourselves into the endless frequencies beyond those of our eyes and ears, whose range is very limited, we enter the sense called "in order to bestow," the "sense of giving and love." In that state, we find an unbounded reality, as though we have emerged from our skin, as it is written, "After my skin they lifted it" (Job, 19:26). Then the reality we begin to see is not limited to the five physical senses, but is the actual reality, the upper world that the Torah describes.

In that new sense, what is a woman who delivers, and what is a leper?

"A woman who delivers" is a correction of one of the senses, thus achieving new attainment, new bestowal, in which we discover another new world. Yet, we cannot use these forces for correction in order to bestow, a limitation formed by the contrast in it. We perceive everything through opposites. As creatures, we always see one thing opposite another. When we have only one color, or something without an opposite, or something for which we have no scale by which to measure or compare, we cannot see or feel it. If there is no black and white situation, we cannot see black, white, or yellow.

The revelation of our correction is always limited, and the boundary gives us a sense of orientation, that we are in something, gripping something. Otherwise, we have no idea what is permitted and what is forbidden. In that state, everything is completely amorphous and our sensations disappear.

The woman is the one who gives birth. The Creator could have created a man who can give birth; why did He create only women with the ability to give birth?

A woman is called "the will to receive." The man is called "the intention to bestow." Therefore, the man assists with the birth; it cannot happen without him. The man gives only a drop, from which the woman raises the newborn. The man begets only the will to receive through the correction he performs on himself. These corrections are called "nine months of labor."

In Baal HaSulam's book, *The Study of the Ten Sefirot*, as in all the wisdom of Kabbalah, we learn about this form in which we grow and put ourselves into a complicated situation, the upper womb–a situation from which we can grow. We are assisting our growth inside the womb. It is great work that we do in order to adapt ourselves to the degree of the Creator until we are similar to Him. Then, we are born. However, each of us has a personal reality, the stage of adulthood, opposite the stage of *Katnut* (infancy/smallness). The rest of the stages continue until we achieve the complete level.

So a woman symbolizes the will to receive and a man symbolizes the desire to bestow?

Yes.

Are matters arranged from above so that the will to receive is the only one that can deliver, while the man, who is bestowal, cannot?

The man provides the future form of bestowal. Were it not for the force of bestowal, the woman would not be able to deliver. If there is no expansion to the will to receive itself through the force of bestowal, it will not be able to give birth to anything.

The portion, *Metzorah*, deals with skin infections. Why specifically the skin? There are many other afflictions!

The skin is our place of scrutiny. Our desires consist of five degrees: *Mocha* (marrow), *Atzamot* (bones), *Gidin* (tendons), *Bassar* (flesh), and *Or* (skin). The *Or* desire contains seven layers; it is the final, crudest desire. This is why it is where we can scrutinize our egoistic intentions, our ability to correct, and how to do so.

We correct a part of the skin by writing a book of Torah on leather. There is a parchment of leather that we cut in the middle, and we write the letters of the book of Torah on the outer part. We separate the part that cannot be corrected. This part will be corrected only at the end of correction, when there are no limitations and no letters. The actual revelation of the Creator is on the last, most egoistic degree that can be corrected.

Does "leprosy" symbolize an inappropriate use of this concept?

"Leprosy" symbolizes the revelation of the boundary, the place of recognition of evil that a person corrects through the force within—the great force of bestowal called "priest."

The Torah deals with a disease that is still incurable today.

All skin diseases are hard to cure, and many of us suffer from them all our lives. It happens because the skin is the last degree of the body, so it is very difficult for us to influence it. We treat it as the ending of the body, an outer covering of our internal organs, but the skin is just like the heart, lungs, and kidneys. It is an organ in and of itself, which we have yet to comprehend.

When we weigh the skin, we find it is the heaviest organ in the body. Also, we cannot live without it.

True. We can see it with the problems that people who suffered serious burns have. It is an offshoot of spirituality, where the corrections on this degree are the hardest. It is *Malchut* at its conclusion.

Is the skin "curable" or is it a chronic disease?

Only at the end of correction, when we have corrected everything else, will we be able to correct the skin. Then, the light will shine in *Aleph* through the whole structure known as "Adam," as well as inside the skin, in the letter *Ayin*.

From *The Zohar*: Two Live Birds

"He took for the purification two live, pure birds, and a cedar tree, and scarlet, and hyssop." One who engages in the work of one's master and engages in the Torah, the Creator is over him and the *Shechina* (Divinity) connects with him. When one comes to be defiled, the *Shechina* departs from him, the Creator departs from him, and all the side of *Kedusha* (holiness) of his master departs from him. Then the spirit of *Tuma'a* (impurity) and the whole side of *Tuma'a* are on him. If he comes to be purified, he is aided. Once he has purified and repented, what has departed him returns to him, and the Creator and His *Shechina* are on him.

Zohar for All, *Metzorah* (The Leper), item 18

This concerns a person who has come to be purified. He brings two different birds, as well as part of a tree, through certain people. This is how we correct through our own forces, the desires that appear on the road to correction. Such people must discover the desires that require correction and correct them.

TERMS

A Woman in Labor

This is the will to receive that has received the power to develop and beget new acts of bestowal in every man.

Circumcision

The "circumcision" is a correction of a newly born desire. If it is a man, he must go through a special correction to stop him from using his *Sium*, *Yesod*, in order to touch the *Malchut*. Here the greatest and worst desires can be found, which can be corrected only at the end of correction. Therefore, one who wishes to be *Yashar El* (straight to God, Israel), must make a circumcision, meaning limit oneself from using the desire to bestow beyond the point of one's *Yesod*. We also recognize these signs as customs in our world.

Menstruation

"Menstruation" is the blood, the secretions we have after the scrutinies of the desires that can be corrected. We distinguish the desires that cannot be corrected and depart from them, allowing them to part from the desires intended for correction. Subsequently, there is immersion (dipping) in water, where we must bring the light of *Hassadim* by which we correct those desires.

A Bird

A "bird" is our desires at the degree of still (inanimate). It has a special meaning in the offerings. Within the still is an internal division of vegetative, animate, and human. The human is special and is on a special day. Through the special clothing on us, and the special place, one brings the special desires in a special combination for the correction called *Korban*.

We must learn all the details; each time, it has a different complexity. This is why it is called "incense," a bit like a salad. Only by combining the reasons and the right combination between them do we achieve correction. Each time, we put together an entire situation, an entire world, and this is our new degree.

Aharei Mot

(After the Death)

Kedoshim

(Holy)

(Leviticus, 16:1-18:30—19:1-20:27)

Summary of the Portions

The portions, *Aharei Mot* (After the Death) and *Kedoshim* (Holy), are connected. In the portion, *Aharei Mot*, following the death of Aaron's two sons—Nadav and Avihu—the Creator gives Moses various rules concerning the way Aaron may approach the Holy in the tabernacle: they require Aaron to offer several sacrifices. Aaron must choose between two male goats, one to be sacrificed as a sin offering, and the other to be sent to the desert as a "goat to Azazel."

The portion also describes the prohibition against slaughtering for food without bringing an offering to the tent of meeting. The

Creator instructs Moses to command the people not to follow the ways of the Egyptians and the Canaanites, and not to obey their rules. At the end of the portion, the Creator tells the people of Israel not to be defiled by all the impurities from the nations that dwelt in the land of Canaan before them. If they did become defiled, the land would repel them.

In the portion, *Kedoshim* (holy), the Creator says to the children of Israel through Moses: "You shall be holy for I the Lord your God am holy" (Leviticus, 19:2).

The portion details many different commandments between man and God, between man and man, and some that concern offering sacrifices. The portion also deals with fearing the Mother and Father, observing the Sabbath, and the prohibition against idol worship. Some of the *Mitzvot* (commandments) relate to the land of Israel, the land of Canaan, tithing, fruits of the tree, idol worship, and other laws.

The portion ends with a complete prohibition against incest and adultery, which will be punishable by death. The Creator commands the children of Israel to keep the laws when they arrive at the land of Israel, and refrain from what they did while in Egypt. They must separate pure and impure beasts, and likewise, the Creator will separate Israel from the rest of the nations. This is how Israel will be Holy to Him.

Commentary

Most people believe that the Torah speaks of this world, that it is full of physical actions and descriptions of animals, people, and objects, rules of social conduct, what is permitted, and what is forbidden. We either forget, or have never known, that this world is but a replica of the spiritual world.

In truth, the stories in the Torah narrate only the spiritual world. We perceive the spiritual forces as a replica of spirituality. They are depicted in us according to our degrees and our perceptions of the world. This is why it seems to us that we are seeing an entire world with all its details, that the Torah details exactly how we should behave–favorably or unfavorably–according to the Creator's will.

The Creator wants to do good to His creations, to raise them to His level. "Return O Israel to the Lord your God" (Hosea, 14:2) means causing them to be like Him–loving and giving. The rule, "Love your neighbor as yourself,"* is the inclusive rule of the Torah. It is the rule by which we shift from loving others to loving the Creator at the end of our correction.

We need to scrutinize the connection between slaughtering beasts and avoiding certain actions, committing other actions, and *Dvekut* (adhesion) with the Creator, love of God, love of Israel, and love of the whole world. The Torah does not speak of any other correction but the correction of the heart, as it was written that it was given to men of heart.** Hence, all the commandments written in the Torah–as Iben Ezra writes in his commentary on the Torah–were made only to correct the heart, meaning man's desire and inclination. The Torah was intended to bring us into love because our initial nature is the opposite of love: it includes the evil inclination, envy, lust, and the pursuit of honor, as we clearly see in our world.

This is why the Torah is telling us how to correct ourselves, our desires, according to our perception of this world. We cannot correct our egos instantly from aiming to receive for ourselves to aiming to bestow upon others. The numerous corrections we perform on our desires are gradual.

The two portions, *Aharei Mot* (After the Death) and *Kedoshim* (Holy), are adjacent and connected because they contain two major corrections. The first is bestowing in order to bestow, as it is written, "That which you hate, do not do to your friend" (*Masechet Shabbat*, 31a). The second is "Love your neighbor as yourself," which is a more advanced correction.

---

* Jerusalem Talmud, *Seder Nashim, Masechet Nedarim*, Chapter 9, p 30b.

** Rav Yehuda Ashlag (Baal HaSulam), *The Writings of Baal HaSulam*, p 141.

The first correction is merely avoiding harming others. When we constantly seek our own benefit, the result is always at the expense of others. The first correction was given to a proselyte, to an egoist who wants to be corrected, to rise from the ego, from the "nations of the world within, to the degree of Israel, to a state of "That which you hate, do not do to your friend." By that, we restrict our egos and avoid hurting others. The next stage is the more advanced degree, "Love your neighbor as yourself,"* which we must achieve.

Following those *Mitzvot* and corrections, we perceive the world that is depicted in each of the 613 desires that comprise us. When we correct those desires from egoism to wanting to give and to love, we see an opposite world, as it is written, "I have seen an upside down world."** We come to see a higher world running by new, completely different rules–of giving, love, and connection. Today, not only does the world appear to us as integrally connected, we ourselves are becoming integral, and we relate to the world in this way. We include everyone and see everything as one whole.

This is the reason why the two portions are conjoined. The correction in the portion, *Aharei Mot*, is the correction of emerging from the evil inclination. In the next correction, the one in the portion, *Kedoshim*, we transcend the evil inclination and raise the desires we have corrected to the next degree. First, we seemingly "brush them off," then we raise them toward giving, love, to the place of the holy ones.

First, we rise above our egoistic will to receive and shift sins into mistakes, and mistakes into *Mitzvot* (commandments/good deeds/corrections). Next, we correct the sins (that we previously turned into mistakes) into *Mitzvot*. Now, everything works for love.

By treating everyone with absolute love, we reach the love of God. This is the final result where we obtain equivalence with Him, as it is written, "Return O Israel to the Lord your God" (Hosea,

* Jerusalem Talmud, *Seder Nashim, Masechet Nedarim*, Chapter 9, p 30b.

** Babylonian Talmud, *Masechet Nezikin, Baba Batra*, 10b; Babylonian Talmud, *Masechet Pesachim*, 50a.

14:2). In other words, we obtain *Dvekut* (adhesion) with Him. This is the purpose of the corrections, the purpose of Creation, of the path we must take.

Everything begins with the shattering, with the recognition of evil. This is what Nadav and Avihu did in the previous portion, and this is why the portion is called *Aharei Mot* (After the Death). All our actions in corrections are built consecutively.

We must not forget that the real corrections are only in our desires. We correct our hearts, and our world is the inanimate world, an imaginary world in which we play like kids in the sand.

Today, the world is entering a new era, facing a global crisis that must be resolved. This is our "exercise." If we approach it correctly, as the Torah tells us, we will receive the Torah—its internality—as the Torah of truth, and we will know how to achieve redemption from exile from the sins we are in. Then, we will reach the stage of *Aharei Mot*, of *Kedoshim* (holy).

The portion tells how the people of Israel entered the land of Israel. If they chose to follow the laws of the Canaanites, the land would expel them. This portion always comes near the Israeli Day of Independence, which is odd because we have returned to our land after 2,000 years, but it appears we are not yet keeping the spiritual laws.

It also appears that we do not have a grip on the land of Israel. We are still "under a question mark" in this land. Perhaps we do not like to admit it, but we are. We are aware that we are still dependent on our neighbors and on the rest of the world. If the whole world should pressure us now, we would have no choice but to do as they say.

The words, "the whole world," refer to the Creator, the upper force that sets up the conditions by which we will truly repent and begin to actually be the people of Israel in the land of Israel. *Ysrael* (Israel) comes from *Yashar El* (straight to God), meaning to resemble the force of bestowal and love, the upper force, which demands that we be in a state of "Love your neighbor as yourself."

If we achieve brotherly love according to the laws of *Arvut* (mutual guarantee), the laws of Kabbalah, of integral education—as we circulate them—we will truly gain a grip on the land. *Eretz* (land) comes from the word, *Ratzon*, (desire); this is our innermost desire, which determines precisely how attached we are to the ground, to the land of Israel.

It all depends on us. We were given a small portion, and if we cannot live according to this part, a part of us will be cut off, then another part, and then another. It is not because the neighboring countries or the UN have decided anything; it is because we ourselves do not fit in the land of Israel.

Actually, the threat is already there because "the heart of ministers and kings is in the hand of the Lord" (Proverbs, 25:1). If we are in accord with the land of Israel, we will receive it and no one will rule over us—it all depends on our accord with the land of Israel. If we aim our desires toward holiness, as in, "You will be holy for I am holy" (Leviticus, 19:2)—holiness means bestowal and love—then there is no doubt we will receive it in this world, too, the whole of the land of Israel. No one will be able to say anything; everyone will agree that we are the ones who truly have to be here in the land. The nation that will live here will be a different one, "The people of Israel" living according to "Love your neighbor as yourself," as it was prior to the ruin.

Questions and Answers

There is a feeling that although we are officially in our land, we are still in exile.

Yes, this is why it is written that we are a gathering of exiles.

What does it mean that "the land expels the desires?"

If we do not match ourselves with the will of God, with the land of Israel, the land ejects us, rejects us. It is due to lack of equivalence of form. "Equivalence of form" is the general law of Nature that determines how suitable and connected we are to the land, to the ground. Equivalence of form exists to the extent that we connect to each other, to the extent that we achieve mutual guarantee between us, unity, and brotherly love. If we do not, we do not belong in the land of Israel.

Does this refer to today's land of Israel? After all, it says "desires," not people. So is this about desires or about the land?

We are still not in the real land of Israel because we and our desires are still corrupted and negative, as is the energy between us. Hence, we do not allow the land of Israel to be fair (beautiful). We still do not feel that our land is blooming.

From *The Zohar*: Hybrid and Mixing

When the Creator created the world, He set up each thing, each one in its side, either to the right or to the left, and appointed higher forces over them. And there is not even a tiny blade of grass in the land on which there is no higher force above in the upper worlds. All that they do in each one, and everything that each one does is all by prevailing of the upper force that is appointed over it above.

Zohar for All, *Kedoshim* (Holy), item 108

We are far behind, but we are now required to be in the degree of the "land of Israel." What can be changed here? How can we reach the degree of the land of Israel?

If we begin to examine our qualities in relation to others, we will see how immersed we are in Egypt, how our egos, our inner Pharaohs, dominate us. We disparage everyone out of envy, lust, and the pursuit of honor, and we relate to others only in order to use them. This is exile. It is not a geographical point, but an inner state. We will finally want to emerge from it by connecting to people and beginning to wonder, "When will I reach my correction, the state of 'Love your neighbor as yourself?'"

When we achieve it, we will begin to advance toward that correction. Then, we will see how incapable of it we are. This is the meaning of "the land of Israel not belonging to us." We cannot be together in brotherly love, so we must demand of the Creator that we correct it. We must shout, pray, show Him our need. Actually, everything we have been through has happened so we can recognize our dependence on Him, so we would feel that all corrections depend only on Him.

We are going through all of this on purpose; the Creator made it this way. Otherwise, we would forget about Him. When we turn to the Creator for correction, He comes and "settles in" with the quality of bestowal and love between us. We progress and discover Him between us, meaning we discover the upper world.

This is the upper system in the spiritual world between us, at which we arrive upon our correction. And because our desire was corrected due to the presence of the Creator, it is now in the land of Israel, a state of redemption called "the land of Israel." Previously, it was in Babylon, the land of Canaan, Egypt, and in a desert. "The land of Israel" is a state of connection between us, which the Creator fills.

We often speak of a spiritual connection. Are the things we talked about spiritual things, including the land of Israel?

Everything is within us and between us.

Why do we hear that the Creator does not judge the children of Israel on anything regarding this world, yet they are punished in this world?

They are judged because we must return to the spiritual degree we held prior to the ruin of the Temple.

Even though we always thought that the Creator does not "keep score" with us in this world?

The ARI begins his book, *Tree of Life*, explaining that "The upper, simple light fills the whole reality." Likewise, it is written, "I the Lord do not change" (Malachi, 3:6), and "He has given a law, and it shall not be breached" (Psalms, 148:6). There is a constant state by which we should measure ourselves. It is an absolute state of love and a tight connection among everyone, not just among the children of Israel, as it was before, but throughout the world. We are the "chosen people," the ones who must be "a kingdom of priests and a holy nation" (Exodus, 19:6). First we must achieve that state, then we must set an example to the rest of the world.

From *The Zohar*: Ah, Land of the Buzzing of Wings

"Ah, land of the buzzing of wings." When the Creator created the world and wished to reveal the depths out of the hidden and light out of darkness, they mingled in one another. Because of it, Light came out of darkness, and the deep came out and appeared out of the hidden; one came out of the other. And from the good, out came bad; from mercy, out came judgment, and all was included in one another.

Zohar for All, *Kedoshim* (Holy), item 7

Following the shattering, everything became mixed. Now, after the ruin, we must distinguish between good and bad, light and darkness, and thus build ourselves. Our view of the world and the relations between us all result from the scrutiny. The ruin is in our favor because by correcting it we build ourselves, just as children build with LEGO bricks and thus learn.

What is the degree of *Kadosh* or *Kedoshim* (holy)?

"Holy" is the highest degree, as it is written (Leviticus, 19:2), "You shall be holy for I the Lord your God am holy." This means that one transcends the ego and avoids using it, unless it is for others' benefit. "Bestowing in order to bestow" is the first stage. The second stage is "receiving in order to bestow." The first stage is as Hillel says, "That which you hate, do not do to your friend" (*Masechet Shabbat*, 31a). That is, do not harm others. This is the beginning of corrections. But once you have achieved it, you can accept others' desires and begin to serve them, fulfill them. This is called "love."

That is, *Aharei Mot* is a precondition for *Kedoshim*?

Certainly, these are two stages of the correction of *Galgalta* and *Eynaim* of the soul, and the correction of the *AHP* of the soul. There are two kinds of *Kelim* in which there are positive or negative *Mitzvot* (commandments to do something or avoid doing something) from the Torah. Each commandment is an act of rising above the ego, of benefiting others, or at least of not harming others. These are all the 613 commandment–248, and 365.

Is there a special connection between the Creator and the people of Israel? Why are they holy? Is it just because He is holy?

Man needs the upper light in order to rise above the ego and bestow upon others. We have no force of bestowal of our own because we consist purely of "reception-only" substance. We can give only if the upper light shines on us, as it is written, "I have created the evil inclination; I have created for it the Torah as a spice" because "the light in it reforms."*

Thus, the Creator illuminates that quality for us, raises us above the ego, and all we need is to want it. The actions come from above, which is why they are called "the work of God," since the Creator is the one who does the work. However, He works only at our invitation.

Terms

Kadosh (Holy)

"Holy" means using the will to receive that was previously in order to receive. It is the reverse form of the ego, and benefits only others or the Creator. When it is in favor of others, it is still at the degree of bestowing in order to bestow, the degree of Levites. But when we

* Babylonian Talmud, *Masechet Kidushin*, 30b; Midrash Rabah, *Eicha*, "Introduction," Paragraph 2.

receive in order to bestow, it is at the degree of priests, the opposite of its initial nature.

Holding a Grudge

We cannot correct ourselves if we are still "keeping score." It is an internal energy. These are very deep corrections that astonish us when they appear; we suddenly understand how deep are our calculations for our own benefit.

Prohibition against Divination

"Divination" is forbidden because it contradicts bestowal. If a person wants to bestow, it makes no difference what will happen in the future. All we need is to connect with others and to give them what they desire. In doing so, we will find a new life. If we make any calculation, it is toward the will to receive.

One who is truly advancing toward bestowal is indifferent toward the future. Pure bestowal is all that person wishes—to "be" in the other. In that state, one has no connection to divination, as there cannot be any considerations. Hence, we should make the corrections within us because in each of us is the desire to know the future or to guess it.

A Male Goat to Azazel

"A male goat to Azazel" is all the desires we still cannot correct. There are 613 desires in us, and some are still not corrected. Because there is a lack of light that shines on us, we cannot fix them. We separate these desires from us, which is why there are animals we slaughter and raise to *Kedusha* (holiness). These are the desires within us on the animate level. However, there are desires where we cannot do this. Hence, for now we are releasing them so they do not stay with us, as though we do not have them.

Emor

(Say)

(Leviticus, 21:1-24:23)

Portion Summary

The portion, *Emor* (Say), begins with rules concerning priests, forbidding them to marry a divorced woman, a widow, or a whore, and permitting them to marry only a virgin. They are also forbidden to approach the dead. Only kin are permitted to be defiled, or to approach the dead. The High Priest is forbidden to be defiled, even if his own kin have died. They are forbidden to shave their heads and beards, and they are forbidden to cast any flaws in their bodies. A *Cohen* (priest) with a blemish on his body will not be considered a priest and will not be able to serve in the Temple.

The portion also introduces laws of purity and impurity for priests, such as the prohibition against eating offerings, and the rules for a barren or divorced daughter of a priest.

The portion also mentions many rules concerning the Sabbath, Passover, the seventh of Passover, *Shavuot,* the Omer Count, and *Yom Kippur* (Day of Atonement). The end of the portion speaks of a quarrel between two men, one of whom cursed the name

of the Creator. He was punished by ejection from the camp and execution by stoning.

QUESTIONS AND ANSWERS

What is so special about this portion that elaborates so much about priests and festivals?

The correction is only a correction of the heart, which contains all 613 desires that we need to correct from using our egos to receive into using them to bestow upon others and to love others. The whole Torah deals with the correction of the heart. The first stage in the correction of the heart is when we get rid of the ego. The second stage is when we use all of our heart in favor of others.

The portion describes all the levels of correction. It is written, "And you will be to Me a kingdom of priests and a holy nation" (Exodus, 19:6). This means that everyone must reach the highest degree (a *Cohen* [priest]) following the preparation described in the portions, *Aharei Mot* (After the Death) and *Kedoshim* (Holy). The Torah constantly promotes us until we enter the land of Israel and achieve *Dvekut* (adhesion) with the Creator.

The portion starts by elaborating on the terms of the degree of priests. One must correct one's desires, as it specifies–there is a prohibition against marrying a divorcee, a widow, or a whore. A priest must also avoid shaving his face and his head. He must also maintain these prohibitions until he is corrected and sees his desires in the image of Man. It is as we learn about the perception of reality: the whole world is a reflection of our desires, an outward projection of our internality.

A priest must have natural desires that have been corrected into aiming to bestow. He must not impair his body, put any kind of paintings on it, or touch his hair. The hair is a special correction. The word, *Se'arot* (hair), comes from the word, *Se'arah* (storm). The hair is to be corrected and therefore must not be removed.

A "priest" is a state in which one can truly work with all the desires in order to bestow, with all the deficiencies, with the "stormy hair." His females, namely his desires to receive, have been corrected and are no longer on the degrees of whore, divorcee, or a widow. Rather, they are on the degree of virgins. A person arrives at a degree where he corrects his desires back to their natural state.

The priest must approach the work of God through sacrifice. He must bring his desires closer and closer to the aim to bestow, to love. Everyone must reach this degree. Those who have reached this degree are regarded as "serving in the Temple." On the degree of priests, we place all 613 desires, called "our heart," in the house of *Kedusha* (holiness) as a holy *Kli* (vessel) that is entirely in bestowal.

During festivals, we correct ourselves in stages that are seemingly external. The system changes and gives us a chance to correct our desires further in external conditions on the festivals mentioned in the Torah: *Pesach* (Passover), *Shavuot* (Feast of Weeks), and *Yom Kippur* (Day of Atonement). The Torah tells us about all the festivals, except for *Hanukah* and *Purim*.

Hanukah means *Hanu Koh* (camped here). We achieve the correction of bestowing in order to bestow when we rise above our egos and reach the degree of *Bina*, of the phrase, "That which you hate, do not do to your friend."* In this way, we detach ourselves from the egoistic will to receive and rise above it.

Purim is when a person actually achieves the end of correction. On *Yom Kippur* (*Kippur* means *Ke Purim* [as *Purim*]), we discover the evil in us and regret it. At the same time, we are happy because now we know what to correct. *Yom Kippur* is not only a day of weeping. Rather, it is a day of great joy because we are happy that a trail by which to reach *Purim* has opened up to us, and we correct all the desires into bestowal, to love. On *Purim* we kill the Haman in us, all the evil in us, and achieve the end of correction–complete equivalence with the Creator.

* *Masechet Shabbat*, 31a.

The portion, *Emor*, contains all the preparations, all the previous portions. It deals with ascending to the highest degree. The portion also deals with the Sabbath, a sabbatical year, the seventh day of Passover, the seventh day of the week, and the seventh year. It is a degree we always acquire along the way because *Zeir Anpin* contains six workdays; it is the upper *Partzuf*, from which we receive the lights.

All the lights, which correspond to *Hesed*, *Gevura*, *Tifferet*, *Netzah*, *Hod*, and *Yesod*, enter our hearts (*Malchut*) during the six days. Then comes the seventh day, when we do nothing. These qualities conclude the work, so no further efforts are required of us, except to maintain the situation so the lights will treat it and sanctify it. This is why the seventh day is considered a "day of holiness," since on it we raise all the desires to the aim to bestow.

Afterward comes the seventh day of Passover, the seventh day of *Shavuot*, as it is written, "Seven whole weeks shall there be" (Leviticus, 23:15), which are forty-nine days from Passover to *Shavuot*, and the seventh year, *Shmita* (omission). Such is the cycle of seven.

The seventh of Passover, the Omer Count, *Shavuot*–it all seems like a process. What is Passover, and what is the process between Passover and *Shavuot*?

"Passover" is our escape from the ego, from Egypt. Although we begin to detach from it, it continues to accompany us on future degrees in the form of problems that befall us, such as the golden calf, the water of strife, and spies. These are all results from Egypt.

"The desert" is a state where one detaches and cleanses from the ego up to the degree of *Bina*, the entrance to the land of Israel. That state is called "forty years in the desert" because it is the correction we receive upon our exit from the ego. It is not simple; the corrections are a recognition of our nature, the disclosing of our broken desires, and the understanding of how to correct them.

The first correction is when we emerge from the ego and rise above it. This is called the "exodus from Egypt" and the "tearing of the Red Sea." We instantaneously shift from the will to receive in order to receive, namely Egypt, and move into the desert. This is why we still do not know what to do, or what will happen to us and how it will unfold. We cannot know how to work with our nature when not for our own benefit. For this reason, we go through a period of confusion until we come to the tearing of the Red Sea and being at the foot of Mount Sinai.

Here the correction is in the same will to receive from which we have detached ourselves, and over which we transcended. Toward *Shavuot*, we begin to correct it in order to bestow, toward the reception of the Torah. Seven Sabbaths are seven times seven, which is forty-nine days for corrections. Our correction is done by the six *Sefirot* of the upper force, *Zeir Anpin*, who is called "The Blessed One Be He." This is the upper system that corrects us, containing six qualities–*Hesed*, *Gevura*, *Tifferet*, *Netzah*, *Hod*, and *Yesod*–which enter *Malchut*, our will to receive, and correct it. When these qualities correct the will to receive, we have actually corrected ourselves by counting. That is, when we seemingly count money, we pay by performing corrections each day.

During each day and night, we bless the *Sefira* (singular of *Sefirot*), a result of the passing day, from night to day, as it is written, "And there was evening, and there was morning" (Genesis, 1:5). In the previous day, we corrected in the evening, too, in the revelation of the bad, as well as during the day, in the revelation of the good. We have drawn lights that corrected the desires to receive and thus concluded the day. This is why we give thanks for having corrected the *Sefira*. We count the *Sefirot*, which is why it is called the "Omer Count." This is how all our desires are corrected.

After thirty-three days, there is a special day, *LAG baOmer*. *LAG* means thirty-three in the *Sefirot Hesed*, *Gevura*, *Tifferet*, *Netzah*, *Hod*, *Yesod*, and *Malchut*. Multiply the seven *Sefirot* by seven and you have forty-nine. We begin to search for the middle. If we receive all the lights before we reach the middle, then we are guaranteed to finish successfully. It is similar to a person not being given everything. However, if some of the forces were given and some were corrected, that person can begin to understand and advance independently toward the end–the correction of *Shavuot*. This is the state of a person on the 33rd day of the count.

We count *Hesed*, *Gevura*, *Tifferet*, and *Netzah*, which are complete *Sefirot*, the lights that must reach us. In the *Sefira Hod*, we count five *Sefirot–Hesed*, *Gevura*, *Tifferet*, *Netzah*, and *Hod*. In *Hod* of *Hod*, if we have received the lights from above up to the point of incision, we are guaranteed to continue successfully. Thirty-three symbolizes the reception of all the lights of correction; this is why we are happy and celebrate the Festival of Light by lighting fires.

Does the thirty-third *Sefira, Hod* of *Hod,* symbolize the conclusion of part of the process?

Yes. Henceforth, there is no doubt that the person will accomplish the *Shavuot*. This is why the prohibition on marrying (that begins after Passover night) is lifted on that day. Marriage means connection with *Malchut*. Other prohibitions are also lifted on that day, such as the prohibition against cutting one's hair. These corrections manifest externally, too, but the majority of corrections are inside, corrections we perform on ourselves by the light that shines on us, and through such giving we obtain the love of others.

Why is it that once you reach the degree of "priest," you are still bound by many laws and prohibitions?

It is written, "You shall be holy, for I am holy" (Leviticus, 11:44). When in *Kedusha* (holiness), we delight in these actions. They are not unwelcome, but rather desirable. Thus, if we try to take a mother away from doing half the work needed for her baby, she will not allow it. She enjoys what she does for the baby. The baby has become a source of pleasure for her. This work may seem hard to us, but when it becomes bestowal and as a result we receive the light that shines for us and fills us, we feel Nature's eternity and perfection, and rise above all the limitations of this world. Then, there is only goodness for us.

Why is marriage such a serious matter for a priest? Is marriage the connection?

His will to receive (*Malchut*) must be cleansed of any blemishes. Previously, he was seemingly "married" to a whore, a widow, or a divorcee; that is, his desires were faulty. Now, he has risen to such a degree that his desire to receive is "virginal," like the desire that the Creator created. The Creator gave us a desire to receive, but we discover it only in the final, fourth stage, *Yod-Hey-Vav-Hey*. This is how we go through all the desires until we come to the "virgin," meaning as the Creator gave it. In this way, we can work with the entire desire.

Why is it forbidden to say the name of the Creator?

"Saying" is revealing. There is an inner revelation, which is to bestow in order to bestow, and there is an external revelation, which is to receive in order to bestow. There are limitations to it, but it does not refer to saying the words *ADNI*, *HaVaYaH*, and so forth. A person makes a *Zivug de Hakaa* on the upper light that must reach the *Kelim*. In revealing, one discloses it from the lips and out to the "external ones," desires that have not been corrected. It is forbidden to disclose the name of the Creator, the upper light, to the external desires. These are outside of *Kedusha* and have not been corrected, as this would seemingly "short-circuit" the light with a *Kli* that has not been corrected with a *Masach* (screen) and *Ohr Hozer* (Reflected Light). This is why it is called the "revelation of the bad," and not the "revelation of the good."

From *The Zohar*: The Sons of Aaron

Aaron is the beginning of all the priests in the world because the Creator chose him out of everyone to make peace in the world, and because Aaron's ways rose with him to it. It is so because all of Aaron's days, he would try to increase peace in the world. And because so were his ways, the Creator lifted him to priesthood, so he would instill peace in the household of above, for by his work, he causes the *Zivug* of the Creator with His Divinity, and peace is made in all the worlds.

Zohar for All, *Emor* (Say), item 2

A priest's role is to enhance peace in the world.

A research in genetics revealed that priesthood is hereditary. The researchers sampled Jews with surnames that indicate relation to priesthood (Kahana, Katz, Cohen, etc.) from all factions of the Jewish people. They discovered the same gene among all of them. How is being a Cohen related to the corporeal world if we should all be priests?

We cannot know what genetic changes will happen when we are all corrected. Perhaps we will rise above all that is physical. We must understand that there is the first *HaVaYaH* in the world of *Ein Sof* (infinity), then a replication of the *HaVaYaH* in the four *Behinot* (discernments) of *Ohr Yashar* (Direct Light) on each degree, called "ten *Sefirot*." Every bottom degree consists of a more materialized substance than its adjacent superior, but the combination, *HaVaYaH*, remains. This is why it is written, "I the Lord do not change" (Malachi, 3:6).

The first *HaVaYaH* is the light that expands in four *Behinot* and reaches *Malchut*. That structure stays. According to this pattern, as the light descends from degree to degree, from the world of *Ein Sof* to our world, it gives us *Partzufim* (plural of *Partzuf*), worlds, *Sefirot*, and everything we learn in the upper system. This is how it is in all the worlds.

The *Neshama* (soul), called *Adam HaRishon* (the First Man), was also created by the same structure, following the same internal makeup. That pattern exists in everything.

We learn that Abraham wanted to correct all of Babylon, and that in each of us is a root by which we can reach the level of high priest. Everyone must reach it, as it is written, "They shall all know Me, from the least of them to the greatest of them" (Jeremiah, 31:33), and "My house shall be called 'a house of prayer' for all the nations" (Isaiah, 56:7).

There are desires and souls that are easier to correct, and there are those that are harder, depending on the level of the flaw. The easier ones are the children of Israel. They have to be the first to correct; hence, there are stronger sparks of light in them, which are clear and burning, and appear as Cohen, Levi, and Israel.

There are people who look at a person and know if he or she is a Cohen (descendant of a priest). It is harder to spot a Levite or Israel. Not surprisingly, we can find these things in biology and medicine because everything in our world comes from the world of *Ein Sof* and is replicated in our physical world, in our genes. This is why it must also happen in this world.

Perhaps we have not discovered all the phenomena, but it is clear that every phenomenon in the world is the same as the phenomena that exist above, except here they exist in matter, not in potential.

TERMS

Cohen (Priest)

A "priest" is the highest degree in Man's correction, where one becomes similar to the Creator in all of one's desires, in one's entire makeup, and is in a state of bestowal and love. By so doing, one matches oneself with the Creator and achieves *Dvekut* (adhesion) with Him. This is the purpose of Creation.

Tuma'a (Impurity)

Tuma'a is intention for oneself. All manner of *Tuma'a* are the same intentions under different names, such as Pharaoh, Balaam, Balak, and all the other wicked forces.

It is to the contrary with the same desires once they have been corrected to aim to bestow. The desires remain the same, but the names one receives instead are Cohen, Levi, and Israel.

Curse

A "curse" means that we discover that we cannot agree with the Creator about our desires. We discover it as Balaam, Balak, and so forth. If we discover the term of the upper force, the Creator, Nature, we must work in order to bestow, in love and giving. If we discover that our desires are opposite, working in order to receive, we curse, resist, collide with the Creator, and are opposite in form.

Divorcee, Widow

This is not the initial, great desire, but we can work with it in a more restricted manner. This is why it is not a "virgin." A virgin means that we do not touch the desire, but leave it as is. If we have touched it and performed corrections on it, it is called "divorcee," "widow," or "whore." We can work with these desires, but on the degree of a priest. In fact, we achieve the degree of priest through all the desires called by these names.

Shaving the Head and the Beard

As we learn in *The Study of the Ten Sefirot* (Part 13, *Tikkuney Dikna*), *Se'arot* (hair) is an extensive topic. The term, *Se'arot*, comes from the word *So'er* (stormy), which points to pressure. The channels of abundance that come to us from *Ein Sof* must be restricted, grow thinner, and drip to us in what is called *Mazal* (luck), from the word *Nozel* (dripping). Through the hair, the lights come very thin and in limited amounts, due to the limitations on the person. It happens this way to adjust the size of the "spoon" (the vessel) to the amount one can receive, just as with a baby. The light comes intermittently, in drops, according to the measure of time and weight.

"Shaving" refers to the hair itself. *Partzuf Se'arot* is a special *Partzuf*, a unique structure or system that creates the match between the light of *Ein Sof* and the little ones—us. We can receive only a little, which is why it is forbidden to shave or to cut the hair. A priest is forbidden because he is using this entire system precisely in order to bestow.

Ba Har

(On Mount Sinai)

(Leviticus, 25:1-26:2)

Portion Summary

The portion, *Bahar* (On Mount Sinai), deals primarily with what appears to be laws of finance. It begins with Moses being on Mount Sinai, receiving from the Creator the *Mitzva* (commandment) of *Shmita* (omission of cultivation) of the land every seventh year, and the *Mitzvot* (plural of *Mitzva*) of *Yovel* (jubilee, 50th year anniversary). The Creator gives His blessing to it so that the sixth year will be so productive that enough produce will grow to last for the next three years, to observe the *Mitzvot* (commandments) of *Shmita* and *Yovel* without worrying about sustenance.

Later, the portion details laws of selling a house or property, redemption of a house or a field from one person to another, laws of the lot of the Levites, forbidding the selling of towns or houses that belong to them, laws of selling a person from Israel into slavery, how to treat such a person, and laws prohibiting idols, pillars, and figured stones.

Commentary

The laws that this portion details are spiritual laws. *Shmita** is a profound and sacred matter. It exists only in the land of Israel, in a desire aimed toward the Creator, in order to bestow, toward love of others. A *Shmita* can occur in a desire only in the process of correcting the soul.

The soul consists of six *Sefirot*: *Hesed*, *Gevura*, *Tifferet*, *Netzah*, *Hod*, and *Yesod* (*HGT NHY*). The seventh *Sefira* is like Sabbath, *Shmita*. Also, seven times seven is 49, and the *Yovel* (jubilee, 50th year anniversary) in the Omer count. These are the degrees we climb.

We cannot correct the seventh quality, *Malchut*, only the six qualities included in it. Therefore, we leave it and avoid correction, and this is the observing of the Sabbath, similar to observing the *Shmita*. Following the corrections is a state defined as "He who labored on Sabbath Eve will eat on Sabbath," opposite "And he who did not labor on Sabbath Eve, from where will he eat on Sabbath?"**

On Sabbath, everything one has received from the corrections made during the six workdays comes true. The correction permeates the seventh day and appears in it. This is why on the Sabbath everything is twofold: the meals and the customs, as is the case with a year of *Shmita*. In that year, a person must work and live in such a way that at the end of the sixth year there will be enough crop to last for the seventh year, during which one does not work, and also enough for the eighth year, until new crops are harvested. This is why the profits on the sixth year must be threefold the normal.

When we rise in degrees as we correct the soul, we skip the three *Behinot* (discernments), one, two, three, and only *Behina Dalet* (number four) appears. It is impossible to correct *Malchut*; it is only possible to leap over it because it collects and gives us the results of what happened earlier.

---

* Omission of cultivation of land every seventh year.

** Babylonian Talmud, *Masechet Avoda Zarah*, 3a.

It is not that we do not make profits on Sabbath, *Shmita*, or *Yovel*. On the contrary, there are rules specifically for those years, making it possible to sell, buy, and make other corrections that cannot be made in other years. Specifically, in the seventh year and in its products (7x7), special conditions appear where if one has worked and gained in the previous states, the profit is received now. These are not years of empty-handedness, but rather a time to receive our reward for the labor we have given.

These rules concern the *Shmita*. Concerning buying and selling of houses, we must understand that in spirituality, a house is the "wrapping" of a person. Our inner structure consists of *Mocha* (marrow), *Atzamot* (bones), *Gidin* (tendons), *Bassar* (flesh/muscle), and *Or* (skin). Another way to put it is, *Shoresh* (root), *Neshama* (soul), *Guf* (body), *Levush* (clothing), and *Heichal* (house/hall). *Levush* is the clothing, and *Heichal* is all that is outside of us.

Specifically, during *Shmita*, it is possible to correct very large desires on these degrees, such as selling of houses, Levites, etc. It is not easy to reach these degrees, especially the laws concerning Israeli slaves: buying and selling them, freeing them from slavery and passing over, or making an idol and an image, which is a high degree.

The degrees of *Shmita* and *Yovel* belong to the degree of *Bina*. Our entire correction concerns joining *Bina* with *Malchut*. *Bina* is the quality of bestowal, known as "desiring mercy," while *Malchut* is the egoistic will to receive, which is initially corrupt. The goal is to connect the two, as it is written about Ruth and Naomi, "And the two of them went" (Ruth, 1:19).

The portion is called *BaHar* (On Mount Sinai) because specifically when we climb toward the Creator, to the degree of *Bina*, we receive the laws of the Sabbath, *Shmita*, and *Yovel*, which symbolize our egoistic will to receive with the qualities of the Creator, the qualities of *Bina*.

The symbol of Sabbath, the *Yovel*, and the *Shmita*, is the connection between *Malchut* and *Bina*, when *Malchut* is included in the degree of *Bina*, the quality of bestowal. From that bonding—the connection between the degrees of *Bina* and *Malchut*, while prohibiting touching the will to receive and correcting—emerges all the laws of the Sabbath, the prohibition against performing the 39 works, the corrections of *Malchut*.

QUESTIONS AND ANSWERS

For all the efforts of governments and economists, we cannot resolve the global crisis. We are unsuccessfully looking for a solution. What does the economy reflect today?

The economy reflects our egos. We are not working properly with our egos. If we direct them even slightly toward benefiting others, bonding, love, mutual guarantee, and sharing, we will begin to feel their benefit in every realm of life.

We must understand that the laws mentioned in this portion were given long before the modern economy was established. At that time there were no banks, investments, or multinational trade. People lived off of the land. Then, suddenly, they were told to stop tilling their lands and stop harvesting their crops.

This poses an existential question, seemingly stemming from an irrational approach to the world. It stems from the fact that we do not follow the rules of the nations, but the rules of Israel. "Israel" means *Yashar El* (straight to God). This is why we must perform corrections on *Malchut* after its connection to the degree of *Bina*, to the superior quality of bestowal, to the upper light. We must let the upper light work.

On a year of *Shmita*, we leave our desire and do not correct it. Unless we receive powers from above, we will not have the strength to correct it. Therefore, we must correct the degree in which the light gives from a higher degree, from *Bina*, and fills one up. Only then can we correct the desires in the soul using these six qualities, *HGT NHY*. Then again, we must be filled by the degree of *Bina*, receive the power from her, and subsequently become corrected.

Therefore, as was mentioned above, Sabbath comes as a result of the six days of work: "He who did not labor on Sabbath Eve, from where will he eat on Sabbath?" Moreover, it "charges" us with strength for the coming week, for the next correction, the next degree. Each week is a new degree, and the same goes for *Shmita*. The omissions do not mean that we eat what we sowed earlier. Rather, it is a summary of the former, a preparation for the next degree, the six years ahead. If we kept this in spirituality, we would be in a wonderful situation.

What practical advice can we give economists to improve the situation?

We can improve the situation only through inner work, when we have a genuine need to correct our desires and raise them to the degree of *Bina*, "desiring mercy," or at least to the attitude, "That which you hate, do not do to your friend."* That way, we could at least avoid harming or exploiting others. But ideally it should be, "Love your neighbor as yourself."**

What will the new economy look like in the near future?

Nothing can be done right now, as the economic situation in Europe, for example, is very bad. Corrections are possible, but only by educating first.

First, we need to re-educate people through Integral Education, which explains the circularity of Nature and our interconnectedness. By understanding this, we establish the first condition: *Arvut* (mutual guarantee).

We need to raise humanity's understanding in the following areas: what is happening to us, the kind of world we live in, the challenges we are facing, why they are sent to us and by Whom, why we must correct ourselves specifically in this manner, what we gain by it, and if we have free choice in the matter.

* *Masechet Shabbat*, 31a.

** Jerusalem Talmud, *Seder Nashim, Masechet Nedarim*, Chapter 9, p 30b.

How can we do this work?

We need to do it through our relations with others. We need to create the infrastructure from our corrected desires toward others, as will others, mutually, so that Godliness will appear in those desires.

So in order to solve economic problems in the new era, we must first build a social infrastructure throughout the world?

Yes, because otherwise nothing will happen. As we can see, throughout the world no one can reach any agreement. There are not even plans or fantasies of reaching one. The world does not know how to solve the situation, and exists only by accumulating debt.

How do you "translate" the laws specified in this portion into a social infrastructure?

We are talking about desires in *Shoresh*, *Neshama*, *Guf*, *Levush*, *Heichal*, or *Mocha*, *Atzamot*, *Gidin*, *Bassar*, and *Or*. Our world is only a replica of our corrupted desires over the light, similar to black and white images we see in movies. Black is the absence of white. It is we who cast shade on the light and darken it. We need to neutralize ourselves so that everything is light, and then we will be able to maintain ourselves in a complete and eternal world.

From *The Zohar*: Then the Land Shall Have a Sabbath for the Lord

Hey is rest of the upper and lower. This is why there is the upper *Hey* of *HaVaYaH*, *Bina*, and the lower *Hey* of *HaVaYaH*, *Malchut*. The upper *Hey* is rest of the upper ones, and the lower *Hey* is rest of the lower ones. The upper *Hey* is seven years seven times, the forty-nine gates of *Bina*, and the lower *Hey* is only seven years. The lower one is called *Shmita*, and the upper one is called *Yovel* (Jubilee, fifty-year anniversary).

Zohar for All, *BaHar* (On Mount Sinai), item 7

Everything stems from *Malchut* and *Bina*, between whom there are 49 degrees, as we count in the Omer Count between Passover and the festival of *Shavuot*. All our corrections are in *Malchut*, which is a collection of desires we must elevate to the degree of *Bina*, desiring mercy.

It is not the end of the process, only its middle. By making this correction, we make the correction of "desiring mercy," as Old Hillel said. "That which you hate, do not do to your friend."* However, that is only the middle of the way. The rest of it concerns elevating the degree of *Bina* to the degree of *Keter*, which is "Love your neighbor as yourself."** This is additional work, which forms a term from which onward a person will yield a crop.

How can you explain to a contemporary person that every seven years you have to stop producing?

If a person has not been reared in this direction, he or she will not be able to understand it, nor will it be possible to explain about it. Education must come first.

Education is divided into two sections: learning and education. Learning (the provision of information) entails explaining about the process humanity is going through, the system of providence and guidance, building this world in accord with the upper world, and the rules and forces that operate our world. We must learn how these forces evoke in each of us the *Reshimo* (recollection), the spiritual gene that develops us. We need to understand the direction, purpose, and goal we will reach as we develop from day to day, and from moment to moment. We need to know how we can aim our fate–as though with two reigns–to arrive in peace at the final, perfect state.

If we do not receive an explanation about the entire system, the world we are in, the physics of the world and how it functions, how it moves, we will not be able to understand it. People cannot simply be told, "Stop working."

---

* *Masechet Shabbat*, 31a.

** Jerusalem Talmud, *Seder Nashim, Masechet Nedarim*, Chapter 9, p 30b.

It is done today; we know there are foods such as bread that are made on a year that is not *Shmita*.

Indeed, but you cannot observe something to the fullest before it is kept in its spiritual root.

From *The Zohar*: The Slave and the Son

The meaning of those two degrees, son and slave, is found in the words, "And He said unto me, 'You are My servant, Israel, in whom I will be glorified.'" "And He said unto me, 'You are My servant'" is the degree of slave, left line, *Malchut*. "Israel" is the degree of son, right line, ZA. When they are included as one, it is written, "In whom I will be glorified."

Zohar for All, *BaHar* (On Mount Sinai), item 85

On the one hand, a slave of the Creator is a high degree. On the other hand, "You are the sons of the Lord your God" (Deuteronomy, 14:1) is also a high degree, and both connect in the middle line. Comparing the degrees is similar to the written Torah vs. the oral Torah, to law vs. rule, to *Zeir Anpin* vs. *Malchut*. Here, too, we must come to a state where the degree of slave and the degree of son do not conflict, but rather connect with one another, reaching the middle line, the *Masach* of *Hirik*. This is how we advance.

On the one hand, a slave is a very high degree. It was said about Moses that he was the Lord's servant. On the other hand, it is a degree of lowness. We also know that there are laws prohibiting the selling of slaves. How does it all fit together?

Man is in the middle, neither a son nor a slave, but both. Man contains both the right and the left lines. The appellations refer to a working person who advances toward the Creator, where each appellation points to a unique manner of connecting to the revelation of the Creator.

Terms

Economy

In spirituality, "economy" relates to the question, "How do I sustain my soul?" The light may enter the soul only when it is in *Dvekut* (adhesion) with the Creator. To the extent of *Dvekut* with the Creator, so is the measure of fulfillment by the Creator. This is how the Creator "sustains" the soul. It is possible to achieve this by correcting the desire. As we correct each desire from reception to bestowal, we are promptly filled with the upper light to the extent of our correction. This is called "sustaining," and this is the proper economy.

Selling of Property

When we cannot work with a desire because it is too big or because it offers such pleasure that we cannot work with it, we "sell" it. There are corrections in our desires that belong to the great desires, *Levush* and *Heichal*. We leave them out of the boundaries within which we are working, taking them out of our domain, seemingly putting them in deposit.

Shmita (Omission of Tilling of Land every Seven Years)

Shmita is connection to the degree of *Bina*, when the upper light corrects everything that happened and gives us strength for the next degree. This is why there are special rules concerning debt and the selling of items under the tutelage of *Bina*, the great quality of bestowal.

Crop (Yield/Grain)

"Crop" is the reward in the will to receive. Through it, we begin to actually work with the vessels of bestowal in order to "feed" the world.

Earth

"Earth" is desire. There are many names for "desire," depending on its degree: earth, soil, land, field. We name the desire and use it according to its degree. Our world is a depiction of the correction of our desires. Not everything really exists; rather, everything that is depicted is within us.

Slave

A "slave" is an uncorrected desire. It cannot have self-control, but it is corrected by belonging and becoming incorporated into the degree of *Bina*. It "annexes" itself to it, and thus keeps what unfolds on that degree. A slave is controlled like an embryo in its mother's womb. On the degree of spiritual embryo, we cancel ourselves and let the upper one govern.

Summary

The greatness of the degree of *Bina*—the degree of bestowal that acts on us—is that it gives us light, fills us, and grants us the strength to reach *Keter*, where "Love your neighbor as yourself" and "You shall love the Lord your God" (Deuteronomy, 6:5) exist to the fullest. The degrees, *Shmita* and *Yovel*, are the ones that elevate us higher.

BeHukotai

(In My Statutes)

(Leviticus, 26:3-27:34)

Portion Summary

The portion, *BeHukotai* (In My Statutes), deals primarily with the topic of reward and punishment for the children of Israel according to whether or not they follow the ways of the Creator. It is written, "If you walk in My statutes and keep My commandments, and do them" (Leviticus, 26:3). The portion begins with presenting the reward: "Then I shall give you rains in their season, so that the land will yield its produce and the trees of the field will bear their fruit" (Leviticus, 26:4).

Opposite that is the presentation of the punishment: "But if you do not obey Me and do not carry out all these commandments" (Leviticus, 26:14), "I will appoint terror over you: the tuberculosis and the malaria," (Leviticus, 26:16), and the worst punishment of all—exile.

If the people of Israel repent, the Creator promises to remember the covenant He has made with them and forgive them. It is written, "Yet in spite of this, when they are in the land of their

enemies, I will not reject them, nor will I so abhor them as to destroy them, breaking My covenant with them; for I am the Lord their God" (Leviticus, 26:44). The portion ends with additional laws concerning vows, ostracism, tithing, and others.

COMMENTARY

The issue of reward and punishment was not presented at the beginning of the Torah because we cannot understand it unless we have free choice. Without this ability, it is pointless for us to receive instructions on this issue. First, we must learn the laws and judgments. Then, if we keep them, we will be rewarded. And if not, we will be punished.

We cannot be punished in advance because first, we need to reach the spiritual degree of shifting from unfounded hatred to brotherly love, to "Love your neighbor as yourself,"* which is the whole Torah. This is the way we must walk: we must correct our evil inclinations and turn them into good inclinations through the light that reforms.** We achieve this by studying the wisdom of Kabbalah, the wisdom of light.

An ordinary person does not have free choice; rather, such a person is "managed" by *Reshimot* (recollections). These are desires and thoughts that awaken within without one's awareness of their origin. People simply want things without knowing the sources of their desires, living their lives with the aim to satisfy the desire that awakens within, without any ability to govern or rise above these *Reshimot*, these bits of data.

Such people cannot scrutinize and sort out their wants, as it is written, "And you will not follow after your own heart" (Numbers, 15:39). Rather, they follow their instincts as part of the process of development. This sort of work does not require reward or punishment. This is why it is written, "They are as beasts" (Psalms, 49:13).

---

* Jerusalem Talmud, *Seder Nashim, Masechet Nedarim*, Chapter 9, p 30b.

** "Through engaging in it, the light in it would reform them" (Midrash Rabah, *Eicha*, Introduction, Paragraph 2).

We begin to develop through the Torah by studying the wisdom of Kabbalah and drawing the light that reforms, thus correcting the heart. The "heart" is all the desires we must correct from aiming to receive for ourselves to aiming to bestow, to love of others, in favor of the world and in equivalence of form with the Creator, as we seek similarity with Him, to become as good as He is.

However, we do not feel this goodness because it is hidden from us. Through our egos, we feel everything as bad, as it is written, "I have created the evil inclination."* Therefore, we are required to gain extensive knowledge and experience in order to correct ourselves so we can control our inclinations and thoughts, to aim those lights, those upper forces, and connect them with the right approach in mutuality and partnership with the Creator.

By doing so, we adhere to the Creator, connect with Him, understand the purpose, the plan of Creation, everything that is happening, and the process we must undergo.

In the physical world, we teach children until they are about twenty years old. According to the Torah, at age twenty a child is ready for everything, unlike at thirteen. At twenty years of age we can control everything and be in our own right. That degree gives us the ability to withstand any correction in spirituality, to face the reward and the punishment.

We cannot tell someone who knows nothing, "Be careful or you will be punished." That person is like a little child who has no idea what is being asked. Therefore, reward and punishment requires serious preparation.

This portion comes after a person has gone through a lot—the exit from Babylon, the development leading to the exile in Egypt, the reception of the Torah, and so forth. Following the instruction in the desert, we seemingly rise a bit above the ego, and gradually reach the state of reward and punishment.

---

* Babylonian Talmud, *Masechet Kidushin*, 30b.

Today, the whole world is engaged in a process and a system that are, in fact, reward and punishment. All 613 *Mitzvot* (commandments) are to correct the evil in us toward others. We are all good to ourselves, and to an extent, mean to others. We must invert this pattern and become considerate only of others because only from the love of man do we reach the love of the Creator.

Many people doubt that if they correct their attitude toward others, as in "Love your neighbor as yourself," the great rule of Torah, all the problems and illnesses, and all the bad in the world will be corrected. Can we prevent diseases and plagues by correcting our relations? Will the climate suddenly change for the better and we will live in paradise? What is the connection between treating others well and a good life in every sense and on every level?

This is just how it works—keeping the law, "love your neighbor as yourself," corrects everything; there are no other *Mitzvot* (commandments). All 613 *Mitzvot* are the 613 desires in our soul. They appear when we begin to correct and rise above our "beasts" in the correction of the human in us, in our desire to bond with others, to give them abundance, desiring to rise above ourselves in order to discover the Creator.

As we come to know the 613 desires of the soul, we discover that they are all bad. This is why we say during the days of the *Selihot* (asking forgiveness, special days before *Yom Kippur* [Day of Atonement]) and on *Yom Kippur*, "We are to blame," "We are at fault," without understanding where all this evil came from.

As we discover our souls, we first discover that they are broken. This is how we received them because "I have created the evil inclination."* If we correct these desires, we will not need to correct anything else, and all our problems will vanish.

It is written in this portion that if we follow this instruction, we will have ample rain when needed, good health, and success in everything we do. We will be blessed in everything. It seems

* Babylonian Talmud, *Masechet Kidushin*, 30b.

perplexing that there is a connection between rain and good behavior, especially if we are talking about how we treat others. And yet, this is the solution for everyone.

According to the development of humanity, we are now beginning to take control over our fates, something we did not have before. It is surprising because we have always developed through desires that appeared from within.

Today, however, we are moving into a very special situation where the next degree is appearing to us, the degree of the "round," integral world where everyone is interconnected, and where the obligation to be "as one man with one heart"* is appearing.

For the first time in history, we must implement this law, and not only in Israel, but throughout the world. Therefore, we must tell about it and explain to everyone, learn to teach, and become the "light of the nations" (Isaiah, 42:6). We must convey the light that corrects the evil inclination, and this is how the whole world will achieve the desirable correction.

Questions and Answers

If I can see and feel the reward or punishment, there is no need to explain. If I mistakenly put my hand in the fire, I will naturally pull it out. But if I cannot see or feel the transgression, what is the point of explaining it? I cannot keep what I do not know, so what are the reward and punishment for, and for whom is the explanation?

We are not talking about putting our hands in the fire. We are talking about correcting our egoistic desires. Each desire is luring us to what appears as good so we will profit at the expense of others, consider only ourselves, and never give a thought to what happens outside of us. This is how we feel naturally, namely, that the world was created for our own pleasure. But the Torah requires

* RASHI, Exodus, 19b.

the opposite–that we rise above the ego and transform our desire into "Love your neighbor as yourself."

This is why we must establish mutual guarantee among us, which was the initial precondition for the reception of the Torah. Mutual guarantee means that we think of everyone and vouch for them. Mutual guarantee is like signing for everyone and being responsible for what every person does. It may sound unreasonable, but this is the degree and the correction we must eventually attain.

The world is advancing. Each day we are discovering that it is changing, moving toward these demands on us. The Torah explains that if we do this, things will be good, and if we do not, we will be punished. And if we are completely unworthy, we will be exiled.

"Exile" is complete detachment, a state where one is living a harsh life, detached and tormented. These torments are like the torments of Pharaoh, leading us back toward the goal, as was said about Pharaoh, who "brought the children of Israel closer to our Father in heaven."* From this point onward, we try once more to rise to the degree of choice.

It is best if we learn in advance what to do and how, and on what this rising depends. We need to learn the general law of reality using the wisdom of Kabbalah, which explains how the forces act on us, how they are set up, and how they rear us as embryos and as growing children.

As we are advancing toward that state, we must take upon ourselves the laws of this vast reality, and keep them consciously and willingly. In other words, we have to change our desires, as it is written, "Make your wish as His wish."**

The world is in a very difficult state today. If we look at where we are and at what lies ahead, we will feel obliged to make that leap of faith and spread the wisdom of Kabbalah.

* "Who caused Israel to draw near to their father in heaven? It was Pharaoh, as it is written, 'And Pharaoh drew near'" (*Zohar for All, BeShalach* (When Pharaoh Sent), item 67).

** Mishnah, *Seder Nezikin, Masechet Avot*, Chapter 2, Mishnah 4.

From *The Zohar*: If You Walk in My Statutes

"If you walk in My statutes." "In My statutes" is *Malchut*, the place upon which the sentences of the Torah depend, as it is written, "My statutes shall you keep." *Malchut* is called "law." The sentences of the Torah are included in her. "My ordinances shall you keep." An ordinance is another, high place, ZA, to which that statute, *Malchut*, grips. Thus, upper and lower conjoin. The statutes in *Malchut* are in the ordinances in ZA, and all the *Mitzvot* (commandments) in the Torah and all the sentences in the Torah and all the sanctities in the Torah are gripped to these ZA and *Malchut*, since the written Torah is ZA and the oral Torah is *Malchut*.

Zohar for All, BeHukotai (In My Statutes), item 16

Malchut is called the "Assembly of Israel" because she assembles all our souls. She is also called *Shechina* (Divinity) because the Creator *Sochen* (resides) in her. She becomes revealed by the law of equivalence of form.

The Creator is called, "The Holy One Blessed Be He," *Zeir Anpin*. Toward *Malchut*, it is her upper one, and the upper one is always considered the "emanator." Our work is only to correct *Malchut* (kingdom/kingship), as it is written, "To correct (also establish) the world in the kingdom of *Shadai* (the Lord)."*

The world is concealed, and we must reveal everything. *Shadai* means *She Dai* (enough), meaning "under limitations." When *Malchut* clings to *Zeir Anpin*, there will be a *Zivug* (coupling), a connection between them. This will connect the Creator and the *Shechina*, *Zeir Anpin* and *Malchut*, law and ordinance, the written Torah and the oral Torah.

This is not the Torah that we know as a printed book or as text on parchment. Rather, the Torah is a revelation of the Creator to us, His creatures. According to our level of revelation, we have the written Torah and the oral Torah, either at the level of *Malchut* or at the level

* *Likutey Moharan* (Assorted sermons of Rabbi Nachman of Breslev), Part 1, 17.

of *Zeir Anpin*. *The Zohar* relates to our ascent from souls scattered in the worlds *Beria*, *Yetzira*, and *Assiya*, to the collection of our souls, desires, and cravings to reveal the Creator and to rise to His degree when all of us gather in *Malchut*, the Assembly of Israel. By the force of our desire to be together, we compel *Malchut* to rise to *Zeir Anpin* and unite with him. This is how we achieve *Dvekut* with the Creator.

Do reward and punishment indicate where we are not acting according to Nature's laws, so Nature acts toward us unfavorably?

We live in the world that we have built for ourselves. Even now, we are standing right before the light of *Ein Sof* (infinity). The world is a projection of our own qualities. The Creator fills everything; we only feel the world and others as outside. That is, we feel our own qualities—still, vegetative, animate, and speaking—projecting various shades on the abstract light, which we see as the image of the world. We have no idea how truly immersed we are in that depiction, in the charade.

We build our personal worlds by ourselves. The wisdom of Kabbalah often writes about it, such as in Baal HaSulam's "Preface to the Book of Zohar," and in the ARI's *Gate to Intentions*.

Today, even science is saying that to the extent that we correct ourselves, we see an opposite world. If we change one of our qualities from bad to good, we will see a different world. This is how we correct all the desires that the light that reforms shows us. Of course, it is impossible to correct them alone, but we can ask for the correction and sympathize with it, thus achieving the corrected state.

In other words, the animate degree that humanity is currently in must pass away and rise to a higher degree, called "Adam" (human). Only then will we understand what reward and punishment truly are, and feel them.

When and how will that transformation take place?

It will happen only by disseminating the wisdom of Kabbalah, as the Kabbalists write. This is why the Kabbalists hid it until now, as Baal HaSulam writes in his essay, "Time to Act." Today, we must disseminate the wisdom and correct ourselves while working for the correction of the world, thus being a "light for the nations."

Is this the natural flow of humanity?

Of course, we have to do it. It is the future of the whole of humanity. In the near future, all of us will have to make that change. First, the people of Israel will dispel anti-Semitism and the negative attitude toward Israel that prevails in the world today.

Actually, anti-Semitism is a natural attitude that will only worsen as the ego grows in humanity and the people of Israel delay the correction. Israel will be blamed for the world not being in good condition. It is arranged this way from above. The world is feeling it subconsciously, and we are witnessing reflections of that accusation on a daily basis.

From *The Zohar*: Seven Times More for Your Sins

The Creator's sublime love for Israel is like a king who had an only son who sinned before the king. One day, he sinned before the king. The king said, "All those days I have been striking you but you did not receive. Henceforth, see what I will do to you. If I expel you from the land and take you out of the kingdom, bears might charge you in the field, or wild wolves or murderers could obliterate you from the world. What should I do? Instead, you and I will go out of the land."

"You and I will leave the land and go into exile." This is what the Creator said to Israel. "What shall I do with you? I have stricken you but you would not listen; I have brought upon you enemies at war and harm-doers to strike you, but you would not listen. If I take you out of the land alone, I fear that several bears and several wolves will rise against you and obliterate you from the world. But what shall I do with you? Thus, you and I will leave the land and go into exile, as it is written, 'And I will chastise you,' to go into exile. And if you say that I will leave you, I, too, am with you."

Zohar for All, BeHukotai (In My Statutes), item 49-50

The above text does not concern exile from the plot of land we live on and call "the land of Israel." Rather, it is exile from the *spiritual* land of Israel. The word, *Eretz* (land), comes from the word, *Ratzon* (desire). *Ysrael* (Israel) comes from the words, *Yashar El* (straight to God). We want to correct all of our 613 desires one at a time, so they all aim *Yashar El*, in order to bestow, like the Creator.

It is called "being in the complete land of Israel." As long as we want to correct our desires so they are Israel, we will be worthy of being in those desires, as well as in the physical land of Israel. Baal HaSulam writes that we have received the land of Israel and the state of Israel in advance, so we may begin the correction. However, we have not actually earned it, and if we do not carry out the correction, it will be taken away from us.

TERMS

Reward

A reward is what we all want. One cannot give others something they do not want. A "reward" is the object of our desires. It is moving toward our destination. We cannot be elsewhere because we are correcting the desire, so the move itself is the reward, as it is written, "The reward of a *Mitzva* (commandment)–*Mitzva*."* The reward of a *Mitzva* is to know the *Metzaveh* (commander). To know means to connect, as it is written, "And Adam knew his wife again" (Genesis, 4:25).

Punishment

"Punishment" is the opposite of reward. It is what no one wants or likes. It is a degree where we understand that our progress is

* Mishnah, *Seder Nezikin, Masechet Avot* (*Pirkey Avot*), Chapter 4, p 2.

rewarded, and the opposite of that is punishment. Reward and punishment are not egoistic, where a person does something and receives the reward elsewhere.

Fear

"Fear" means being afraid of failing to correct. Everything happens due to our efforts and our request of the light that reforms to come and correct us. It is possible that we did not work sufficiently in order to draw it.

Summary

This portion notes that the choice is in our hands: Either we go toward reward or toward punishment. If we learn what we need to do, and if the world learns, too, we can succeed and have both kinds of Torah, namely great lights—the written Torah and the oral Torah, the light of *Hassadim* and the light of *Hochma* that fill our souls. Thus, we will rise to the degree of eternity and perfection.

BaMidbar

(In the Desert)

(Numbers 1:1-4:20)

Portion Summary

The portion, *BaMidbar* (In the Desert), begins with the Creator commanding the children of Israel (by tribe) to bring men who had served in the army and were at least twenty years old, and appoint them as heads of tribes and as presidents. Following the nomination, Moses is asked to explain to them where each tribe should be during the journey and while stopping in the desert, how to arrange themselves by tribes and banners according to the four directions, with the tabernacle in the middle.

The portion reiterates the role of the Levites, who are to serve in the tabernacle. The tribe of Levi is special because it has no place or lot of its own; it is to serve and help everyone, especially the priests in the tabernacle. The role of the Levites is to assemble and disassemble the tabernacle at each stop during the journey of the children of Israel. They must follow strict rules that explain what to do with each part of the tabernacle, and how to keep the vessels of the tabernacle.

Commentary

The Torah is divided into two parts: external and internal. The external Torah is the one we read and know. It is the Torah that our fathers observed in the past. However, there are things to sort in it. (Actually, our fathers are ourselves in previous incarnations, since our souls reincarnate from generation to generation.)

The Torah describes the journey of the children of Israel in the desert and how they should conduct themselves there. It details how to build the tabernacle, divide into priests, Levites, and tribes, how to set up the camp, and how to continue the journey where each one moves from place to place under the tribe's banner, up to the boundaries of the land of Israel and the onset of its conquest.

The inner Torah is actually the main thing. Through it we correct and adjust ourselves internally in order to discover that upper force from which we receive the Torah in actual fact. That is, the inner Torah is about revealing the Creator to His creatures. Here, we are talking about Man as a small world, where all that is described in the Torah—priests, Levites, Israel, and the twelve tribes—is within us as replications. The inner Torah touches each of us and instructs us what we must do to discover the upper force here and now.

Until we have corrected ourselves, we are immersed in the ego, the evil inclination, as it is written, "I have created the evil inclination; I have created for it the Torah as a spice."* That state is called a "desert." The sensation of the desert is the place of the *Klipot* (shells/peels), meaning uncorrected desires. While in that feeling, we have nothing to revive us, to give us spiritual life. Even if we have material abundance, we still feel that we are in the desert.

We can see it in today's life, too, throughout our desperate world. Judging by divorce rates, drug abuse, and terrorism, more and more people are unhappy. They feel that life is no longer satisfying. We have grown and cannot settle for what we have; we aspire for more. Our sense is that this life is a desert.

* Babylonian Talmud, *Masechet Kidushin*, 30b.

If we can compare our lives to a desert, we must arrange them accordingly so we can traverse them in peace and arrive at the land of Israel. The word, *Eretz* (land), means *Ratzon* (desire), and *Ysrael* (Israel) means *Yashar El* (straight to God), so I am directed only toward the revelation of Godliness.

For that, we must use the wisdom of Kabbalah. Kabbalah is a method to reveal the Creator to the creatures in this world. "Reaching the land of Israel" means correcting our desire into a state where we discover the Creator and the spiritual world here and now, as it is written, "You will see your world in your life."*

The Torah offers us instructions, telling us that if we follow the stages described in the portion, we will traverse the desert in peace and achieve the revelation of Godliness. This is the purpose of our lives; we are built for and are intended to obtain this revelation. Hence, we should see all the rules and counsels in the portion as internal corrections we must discover and follow.

Our "twelve tribes" are our own will to receive. That is, they are our inner qualities that must be arranged according to the *Yod-Hey-Vav-Hey*, by the three lines. It is a structure of our souls–*HBD-HGT-NHY*. The priest, Levite, and Israel are *HBD*. Abraham, Isaac, and Jacob, Moses, Aaron, Joseph, and David are the structure of the qualities of the soul, and we should set ourselves up accordingly.

To the extent that we correct our desires, we gradually come to a state where we discover the stages of "walking in the desert." In that process we obtain the qualities of bestowal, *Bina*. Upon completion of the "walk," we reach Moses' state–now, we are loyal shepherds. This means that we rise to the degree of faith, bestowal, and completion. When the Moses in us dies, having concluded its work, that degree remains "on the other side of the Jordan." This is when we move to the land of Israel and begin to conquer it.

In the desert, as well as in the occupation of the land, there are *Klipot* and struggles. In the desert, we were only acquiring the new

* Babylonian Talmud, *Masechet Berachot*, 17a.

quality of bestowal over our will to receive. We rose above the will to receive. But in the land of Israel, we must conquer the land. When we enter the land of Israel, we literally invert our will to receive from reception into the desire to bestow. The occupation is managing our egos in the form of bestowal and love.

The portion explains the approach to the first great corrections we experience on our spiritual path. The whole process of our correction divides into two parts: the desert and the land of Israel. Our journey through the desert over the forty years is *Malchut* rising to *Bina*, symbolized by the letter *Mem*, which is forty in *Gematria* (numeric values given to each letter in the Hebrew alphabet).

From *Bina*, we climb to the degree of *Keter*, conquering the land and building the Temple. This is when the heart becomes a *Kli* (vessel) for reception of the light, the revelation of Godliness. This is called *Beit HaMikdash* (House of the Temple, or simply, the Temple).

Questions and Answers

Why does the portion begin with the need to appoint heads of the tribes and count everyone from twenty years of age and above?

This process represents a person having to choose which principles to follow. We are only desires to receive, but we also have a little bit of the desire to bestow from above. It is called "a portion of God from above" (Job 31:2). It is the beginning of the soul.

Using the beginning of this soul as a head, and starting to manage our overall egoistic will to receive toward bestowal, love of others, *Arvut* (mutual guarantee), "love your neighbor as yourself,"* and "that which you hate, do not do to your neighbor,"** will divide this mass of our will to receive properly. It will follow an order of tribes, thousands, and tens. This division also happens within each tribe—to priest, Levite, and Israel.

* Jerusalem Talmud, *Seder Nashim, Masechet Nedarim*, Chapter 9, p 30b.

** *Masechet Shabbat*, 31a.

The priests and the Levites who help them are detached from the tribes. They serve only our spiritual needs. This is why they are considered "the collective head." Through this internal psychology, we distinguish what is important, what is not, and gradually correct ourselves, where the secondary joins the primary and follows it.

Currently, we cannot feel this division. But as we work on ourselves, we will begin to feel that our will to receive is not merely a desire, but truly consists of twelve tribes—men, women, children, animals, the desert, and other parts—even the entire world.

We will discover that our will to receive is divided into degrees: still, vegetative, animate, and human. The still, vegetative, and animate comprise the surrounding world. The human, of course, is people. In desires that belong to the human degree, we have free choice and can manage them. This is how we should sort our desires so we can advance.

Within us, there is nothing but desires and instructions. The instructions are the Torah—the wisdom of Kabbalah as the inner Torah. We sort our desires so that each desire, which is the speaking, the *Kli* (vessel) that was taken from Egypt, is corrected into a *Kli* that belongs to the land of Israel, to the Temple, and is working entirely in order to bestow, toward love.

From *The Zohar*: The Count and the Calculation

And yet, the world was not rooted in its root until Jacob begot twelve tribes and seventy souls, and the world was planted. However, it was not completed until Israel received the Torah and the tabernacle had been established. Then the worlds persisted and were completed and the upper ones and lower ones were perfumed.

Zohar for All, *BaMidbar* (In the Desert), item 6

Abraham, Isaac, and Jacob are the three lines. The right line is Abraham, and his *Klipa* (shell/peel) is Ishmael. The left line is Isaac, and his *Klipa* is Esau. The middle line is Israel and its *Klipa* is usually referred to as "mixed multitude." We have to manage this order through the Torah, namely by proper study of the wisdom of Kabbalah, where the light is concealed, as this is the Torah of light, as it is written, "The light in it would reform them."*

If we truly want to correct ourselves and see ourselves arranged and corrected as the Torah describes, in three lines, we must study so the light will influence us. We are divided in such a way that on the left we have the ego and on the right we have the light of Torah that reforms. The more the light of Torah reforms the ego according to our labor, the middle line–which includes these two forces–accumulates and subjugates the ego to the rule of the light. Thus, a *Kli* is formed in which the power of the Creator, the upper force, appears.

We constantly add ego to the correction, using a greater light that appears. In this way, we climb up the middle line, the line of Jacob. Hence, before the arrival of Jacob, there is no match between Man and the upper force, the upper world. As soon as we put the inner Abraham, Isaac, and Jacob in the order of these three lines, we begin to match the upper force and work with it in reciprocity.

What does one need to do until these discernments develop?

We need to follow to the letter what the Kabbalists write: to study, in a group with the love of friends. Our three primary sources are *The Book of Zohar*, the writings of the ARI, and the writings of Baal HaSulam. Internally, we must follow only what is written in these books.

Why was Israel commanded to appoint men who served in the army and were twenty years of age or more?

Being twenty years of age in spirituality means that one is fit for "real estate" deals. *Ibur* (conception), *Yenika* (nursing/infancy), and *Mochin* (adulthood/maturity) are the three phases by which we grow. It is like a fetus born after nine months that proceeds to grow. The

* Midrash Rabah, *Eicha*, Introduction, Paragraph 2.

stages of spiritual growth are identical—from infancy to maturity. Spiritual infancy ends at age thirteen.

In spirituality, *Ibur* is a very high degree: we become completely annulled before the upper one, included in it as a drop of semen, while the upper one is nurturing it. For the light to influence us, we must cancel ourselves as if we do not exist. If we want to draw the light so it will raise us, we must learn with a group and be part of it; we must want the good environment and the light that comes through it to influence us. In this way we advance in stages that may last less than nine months. It all depends on our efforts.

When we are born, our will to receive is already greater than our predecessors'. We develop in awareness and understanding until we are at age thirteen, and from there continue through age twenty. At twenty, we are not merely grownups; rather, we can be owners of our land. "Land" refers to the greatest, lowest, most basic will to receive. Henceforth, we are fit for every internal correction.

Is there a connection between the spiritual degrees of Levi (Levite) and Cohen (priest), and people whose last name is so?

No, the roles of Levi and Cohen will appear according to one's spiritual level, not by one's last name. In spirituality, a person's son indicates a result of a spiritual degree because the wisdom of Kabbalah speaks only about spiritual degrees. In the physical world, we cannot know who is a priest, who is Levite, and who is Israel. All this will appear in due time.

Establishing the Temple will be possible only after we correct ourselves and restore the Temple in our hearts. Then, as with Bezalel, we will be able to build the external structure from our attainment and understanding. When we are wisehearted, and our hearts are filled with the light of *Hochma* (wisdom), the revelation of Godliness, we will know what external action to take through our feelings. In the Temple will be priests, Levites, and Israel, each according to one's degree.

This portion focuses on the tribe of Levi; what is so special about it?

It is written about Israel in relation to the nations of the world: "And you will be to Me a kingdom of priests and a holy nation" (Exodus 19:6). Generally speaking, in this world we are only required to recognize the negative, become sensitive to what is bad, and correct it into being good. To the extent that we discover that our nature is bad, we want to rid ourselves of it. But our problem is education—of ourselves and of others.

Therefore, the only role of priests and Levites is to educate the people. The priests connect to a higher degree and bring from there the light that reforms in order to pass it on to the Levites, who then pass it on to the people. Thus, each degree, each spiritual *Partzuf*, divides into three parts: *HBD*, *HGT*, *NHY*, which are Cohen (priest), Levite (Levi), and *Ysrael* (Israel).

Levites have no lot because the Creator is their lot. They are in *Dvekut* (adhesion) with a higher degree, the upper force. They have no desire to receive for themselves, which they would need to correct. They have reached a level of correction where their will to receive aims entirely to bestow. For this reason, they are attached to the upper force. Through the Levites, we—Israel, who are at a lower degree—can receive the light and the direction toward progress.

Is there a meaning to the order of the portions, and if so, does it concern our spiritual development?

Yes, it is how our world is divided. In our world, as in the spiritual world, there are terms, times in the year that are divided into portions. Everything possesses a unique force. Hence, each week has its own portion because there is a special force that acts from above accordingly. As we advance from portion to portion, we correct ourselves.

Therefore, as root and branch, this state also occurs in our world. You must not mix the portions; each must be read in its proper time. Thus, you cannot read the portion, *Bamidbar* (In the Desert), on *Rosh Hashanah* (Jewish New Year's Eve), nor can you read during the winter a portion that is to be read in the summer.

Sometimes when we read a portion, it feels as if it is no longer relevant to us.

We do not treat portions as being in the past. The Torah is the law of life. To reach the source of life, we must assume it upon ourselves. The Torah was given only for us to discover the Creator and cling to Him.

What is the meaning of the "hurly burly" concerning the tabernacle: rising, leaving, journeying, and standing around it?

It is the holy, corrected *Kli* within us. We focus all our desires, discernments, inclinations, and qualities on a state of bestowal, which is similar to the Creator, the force of bestowal, the good who does good. We try to correct and bring ourselves to a state where our nucleus, our hope, our entire being has something within that is similar to the upper force, so the upper light will come and correct us into that state.

The "tabernacle" is actually man's soul. If, out of our egoistic will to receive, we correct a part so that it aims to bestow, we feel the Creator in that part. That part is called "a soul," and what fills it is the revelation of the Creator.

The work of correction makes us a tabernacle and surrounds us in the tabernacle. We, in fact, must turn ourselves into the Temple.

What or who is the shepherd in the portion?

A "shepherd" is the degree of Moses, the loyal shepherd. We must choose this degree every moment, for at every juncture we have to choose what is leading us and where, what our lives are about, who is our shepherd, and whom we follow with our desires and thoughts.

Our correction is to walk in a way known as "the Torah, Israel, and the Creator are one." If we want to be Israel, we must follow the light that reforms. When we follow it, the light brings us to the quality of the Creator, as it is written, "Return, O Israel, to the Lord your God" (Hosea 14:2).

We must decide that we need that quality of bestowal and absolute love. This is the only reason why the Torah was given to us, and this is what we receive when we use it. It was said about it, "I have created the evil inclination; I have created for it the Torah as a spice,"* for "the light in it would reform them."**

What reforms is the Good who does good, the quality of bestowal and love we acquire. We attain that quality within, not in some image outside of us. We perceive within us the quality of bestowal and love that we call *Boreh* (Creator), from the words *Bo Re'eh* (come and see).

Will such guidance appear in our world in a more corrected state, and if so, how?

Of course the guidance will appear. Today, the world is falling into a global crisis, and we feel that we are truly in the desert. This desert will push us to advance only toward the inner land of Israel, because this is the whole purpose of the global crisis.

Terms

Tribes

"Tribes" are a part of the will to receive, which is divided into *HBD*, *HGT*, *NHY*. In all of them, there is *HaVaYaH* (*Yod-Hey-Vav-Hey*), and *HaVaYaH* times three is twelve. Our general will to receive is divided into twelve parts that, when corrected, are called "tribes."

* Babylonian Talmud, *Masechet Kidushin*, 30b.
** Midrash Rabah, *Eicha*, Introduction, Paragraph 2.

The Holy of Holies

"The Holy of Holies" is *GAR* of *Bina*, the absolute quality of bestowal.

Army

The "army" is all the desires that can join the head, faith, the shepherd.

Banner (Flag)

A "banner" is the task that I assume. Each part and each group in the twelve tribes has its own banner, which indicates how each part progresses and corrects itself. The banner is unique to each tribe, hence the division into twelve tribes remains even after they achieve the corrected desire, the land of Israel.

Tabernacle

The "tabernacle" is where I correct my will to receive into aiming to bestow. This is the best and most important place for us.

Levite

"Levites" are the assistants to the priests. Their role is to coordinate the holy part in man with the corrupt part, and to correct the corrupt part by joining it through themselves to the holy part.

Desert

The "desert" is the will to receive that must be corrected. It is a desire in which we still see serpents, scorpions, and problems. In that desire we have nothing with which to nourish our souls. Thus, we must turn the desert into the land of Israel. We move from the desert to the land of Israel, but in fact, it is Egypt that became a desert, and the desert has become the land of Israel. We always remain within our desire, which we correct further and further until the end of correction.

The Land of Israel

"The land of Israel" is the corrected desire. The desire we have corrected is entirely *Yashar El* (straight to God), fully aiming to bestow contentment upon the Creator, as He bestows upon us. We are both in *Dvekut* (adhesion), giving to each other.

Camping

As we move from stage to stage, we need to make stops, as on Hanukah. There are many stops on the journey in the desert. Camps are ascents and descents, the drawing of light of *Hassadim* opposite the light of *Hochma*.

Nasso

(Take)

(Numbers 4:21-7:89)

Portion Summary

The portion describes the children of Israel's preparations to set out on a journey from Mount Sinai to the land of Israel. The bulk of the work revolves around the tabernacle. The census in the tribe of Levi continues, and there is a description of the distribution of duties between the families of Levi, Gershon, Kohat, and Merari. The Creator gives an order to send the impure people outside the camp as preparation for the inauguration of the tabernacle.

Afterward, the portion narrates different situations in which the people need the help of the priests and the tabernacle. The incidents include negative acts, such as stealing, a person swearing in the name of the Creator in vain (for which one must offer a sacrifice), and a woman who has strayed and is suspected of committing adultery, and is therefore brought to the priest.

There are also positive incidents, such as the story of the hermit, detailing the laws that a person who makes a vow takes upon himself, and the blessing of the priests to the people.

The end of the portion discusses the gifts of the presidents and the great celebration–the inauguration of the tabernacle. The portion ends with the conclusion of the preparations, when the people of Israel can set out to the land of Israel.

Commentary

The Torah speaks only about our souls and how we should correct them. We do not correct the body because the body is an animal and acts according to its nature. We must reinstate the "portion of God from above" (Job 31:2); this is the soul.

We do it as it is written, "I have created the evil inclination; I have created for it the Torah as a spice,"* for "the light in it reforms."** When we begin to connect to others under the condition, "Love your neighbor as yourself,"*** we find this act repellent. We do not want to *see* anyone if we cannot use them for our own benefit.

This is our nature, as the Creator said, "I have created the evil inclination." However, the more we study and try to draw closer to each other, the more we discover how utterly impossible it is and the more we feel our nature as bad, as ill will, as the evil inclination. Then, we need a means to correct it, and this is the light that reforms.

When we study the wisdom of Kabbalah in the right group, with people who want to acquire the good inclination, the revelation of the Creator, who want to change and improve, then we discover within us a whole world of layers, degrees, and other parts. Indeed, the priests, Levites, Israel, and the entire world with its still, vegetative, animate, and speaking are all in our desires, in the evil inclination.

The Torah tells us by which context and with which order we can begin to transform the evil inclination into a good inclination. This is what we need to do in this world. The Torah teaches us how to use the light that reforms, which parts of the evil inclination should be treated first, and which ones later.

* Babylonian Talmud, *Masechet Kidushin*, 30b.
** Midrash Rabah, *Eicha*, Introduction, Paragraph 2.
*** Jerusalem Talmud, *Seder Nashim, Masechet Nedarim*, Chapter 9, p 30b.

This process is like a doctor telling a patient, "First, we will take care of one thing, then the other. If a patient has a heart problem, it is the most urgent issue, even if the patient says, "But my sore leg hurts more." Here the doctor has to say, "Wait, we'll get to it, but it is not your most urgent problem." The same goes for us.

The Torah instructs us how to scrutinize each detail, how to correct it, how to tie all the corrected parts together, and how to temporarily part from desires that still cannot be corrected because they are too big, so we must put them aside for now. We advance toward connection with others in order to discover the *Kli* (vessel) of the soul, where we discover the upper light, *Boreh* (Creator), called *Bo Re'eh* (come and see). We discover Him gradually, one at a time, through cause and effect.

The previous portion talked about dividing our desires into tribes, priests, Levites, and Israel. Who are the priests and what is their role among the people? How should the people divide into twelve tribes? Why is it specifically twelve, three lines and *HaVaYaH*, three times *HaVaYaH*, which are four letters, making up twelve parts of the will to receive?

Now, we are talking about the next stage in the correction of the soul of one who wants to correct and nurture it, since it is a "portion of God from above." The Creator is utterly good and does good, so those who want to work with the good inclination, instead of with the bad one, do it by acquiring the good inclination, the form of the Creator. This is why it is called "come and see."

The portion describes how this is done. The tabernacle is mysterious and unknown, a special place in our will to receive. There is nothing but the will to receive; the whole of Creation is desire to receive, and within our desire is a special place where we are connected with the upper light. We bring our desires there the same way we go to a doctor. It is called "a healer for the brokenhearted,"* and they are corrected there. The tabernacle is the primary place where our desires are corrected.

* *The Book of Zohar, Chayei Sarah* (The Life of Sarah).

Questions and Answers

Does each of us connect to the Creator separately?

Yes, each one must do it. This is why our work is mainly the work of sacrifices. Prior to that, we make all the scrutinies: what is kosher (fit/proper/legitimate), how it can be done, and what within us is a Levite, a priest, Israel, nations of the world, *Klipot* (shells/peels), still, vegetative, animate, or speaking. We need to learn how to sort and arrange our desires. At the end of all the scrutinies, we bring an offering. The word, *Korban* (offering/sacrifice), comes from the word *Karov* (near/close). When we correct our will to receive in the tabernacle, we are at the point of nearing the Creator.

It is truly holy work because the priests are the pure quality of bestowal in us. The high priest is *GAR*, meaning the "head" of this quality in us. This is the force within us that is called "priest." This is also what can correct all the layers of the will to receive that are below it. This is why there is such elaboration on what to do with parts of the will to receive such as an uncorrected woman or man, or other problems that arise in the process of correction.

Our whole progress on the path of correction is similar to being in the desert. We discover our evil inclination and learn that it is an entirely egoistic desire, and we cannot draw any vitality from it. This is why we feel as though we are in the desert. Hence, we are all nourished by the light from above, called "manna from heaven"; this is how we advance.

The desert is a short phase in the process. Why did we stay in it for so long? It is written that we could have traversed it in three days, yet it took us forty years. Why?

The "three days" are what it takes to obtain three lines. "Forty years" is the participation of *Malchut* in *Bina*, which is called the "degree of forty." It is not forty years; the Torah does not refer to years the way we do. Rather, it is a degree. A person who attains a degree in the will to receive that is called *Bina* ascends to the degree of the quality of bestowal, and is entirely immersed in the desire to bestow. Although the will to receive that has not yet been corrected burns within just as before, that person "freezes" it and restricts it, holding the burning inside. It is as if there were a box about to erupt like a volcano, and one puts the lid on top and remains above it. Such a person controls all the egoistic desires, and this is called "ascending to the degree of *Bina* and being ready to enter the land of Israel."

"Rising above the volcano" means rising above the great desires, over all the big *Kelim* (vessels) that we took from Egypt. Each time we discovered the bad in the desert, it is considered that we sinned in the desert. Throughout this process of erring and sinning, time and again, Moses and Aaron were attending to these matters.

In other words, we discover all the corrupt thoughts and desires in the mind and in the heart, and are constantly looking for actions and efforts to connect to the environment, to the group we are in, to the upper light, the Creator. This is done in order to find how we connect to external elements, bring them closer, and are sanctified through them.

We keep saying that the only thing we need to correct is our connections; however, all that is described here seems to be internal. If we say that the preparations are over and we can begin, is this about something that we did alone?

We completed the preparations with all the desires, arranged and sorted them in order. We have already been equipped with our arms. Now we can set out and discover the new desires that will indicate how to proceed in the desert.

With whom do we proceed?

We proceeds with our own desires, which are already prepared for this process, including the priests, Levites, Israel, tribes, and the divisions made in the previous portion. After tending to every desire, we set out with them. In other words, we are now ready to advance toward the land of Israel, *Bina*, with all the desires that have been "paused." Now we proceed with all those desires–the women, children, and all the men.

Even the animals are taken, meaning all the desires, our entire inner world. From here, we advance entirely toward bestowal, to the quality of *Elokim*, called *Bina*.

What is the measure of dependence? For example, if a friend is already there but I am not, does that mean that I am holding my friend back?

This has nothing to do with friends; it is one's own inner work. Our friends can only help from the outside, evoke the importance of reaching the land of Israel and being in the state of *Yashar El* (straight to the Creator), where all the desires aim to bestow. Friends can help us increase our desire to correct the entire evil inclination into a good inclination, and they can increase the importance of the goal, thus indirectly helping us wake up and muster our strength.

Are some of the scrutinies we make done with friends?

All scrutinies are internal. It is inner work, and others should not know the work we are doing.

What are "impure people," or a woman who strayed?

We all have such desires, hence we discover them. The Torah speaks of what exists within us. This opens up our own interior and explains what we can find inside: desires, qualities, and thoughts. It also explains how we should work with the "self." We need to bring out all these qualities and desires to identify with the Creator, as it is written, "Return, O Israel to the Lord your God" (Hosea 14:2). It is not referring to us rising "above the moon," but about spiritual ascension, our inner elevation from our own qualities.

My thoughts are also sent to me; is it the Creator who sends them?

Everything is sent to us. The Creator says, "I have created the evil inclination." We have nothing to worry about; it is "His problem." All we need to do is *ask* that the light that reforms will come and turn our evil inclination into a good inclination. This is our entire work; our entire lives are for that purpose.

If, for example, I discover within me the quality called a "woman who strayed," what does it mean that I bring it to a priest? What does the priest do?

It refers to what we sanctify. In this case, we sanctify a desire called "a woman who strayed." "A woman who strayed" is a desire to receive that does not want to work in order to bestow, but only to receive. It is a desire that wants to draw the light of *Hochma* (wisdom) from above downward, instead of from below upward. In other words, it does not want to work in bestowal and love of others, but for itself. It is an egoistic desire at the degree of a woman.

There is a husband, a wife, and nations of the world. These are all inside of us. Our desire suddenly appears as one that wants only for itself, as having no intention of ever being close to the Creator, to others, or to bestowal. When we discover we are like that, and that this is what delays our progress, we discover it as "a woman who strayed."

In response to those who say, "What about women who commit adultery," one might say that there are male adulterers, too. Moreover, today adultery is very prevalent.

The men and the women in this case are our own desires. You cannot say that men or women are doing something wrong. Everything is in our inner world—the men and women are all our own desires.

A woman carries with her a greater deficiency, while a man is more prone toward *Masachim* (screens), toward the power to overcome. But in fact, when a person discovers these discernments within, it does not pose a problem as it does in this world. After all, it is about one's own desires, and it makes no difference what they are called, "woman," "man," "priest," "Levite," "Israel," or "nations of the world." All of them must be arranged by levels and qualities to see what should be done according to the Torah, called *Hora'a* (instruction), meaning what should be corrected within me next.

Is there any connection between that and our relationships in everyday life?

No connection whatsoever. You might meet a person on the street who seems wicked or foolish, or someone who seems smart, or someone who is completely righteous, but you cannot really tell about that person's insides. It could be nothing but an act.

From *The Zohar*: A Woman Who Strayed

Why should a man bring his wife to a priest and not to a judge? The judge is the best man of the queen, correcting the *Malchut* for a *Zivug* with ZA. Hence, the correction of the flaw of the straying woman, which reaches *Malchut*, belongs to him. ...Only the priest is fit for it. It is the quality of *Bina*, the strong quality of bestowal. Priests have a special character. It is such a powerful and strong desire, and so corrected in order to bestow, that it can add to itself all the small, corrupted desires and correct them ... because he is the queen's best man. Also, all the women in the world are blessed by the Assembly of Israel ... while the priest is poised to correct the words of the queen, *Malchut*, and look into all that she needs. This is why only the priest is worthy of it, and none other.

Zohar for All, *Nasso* (Take), item 61

We talked about the strength of the priest, but this portion also mentions hermits and even rules about them. What is a hermit?

A "hermit" is anyone who limits himself or herself. If a person who weighs 300lb (136 kg) stops eating something, does that make him or her a hermit? Likewise, when we see that we cannot work with the revelation of the Creator, with the great pleasures being revealed, and we take everything for ourselves and become egoists once more, we limit ourselves and do not draw these pleasures. In the wisdom of Kabbalah, it is considered "not drawing light of *Hochma*." Such a person does not touch grapes or grape products, such as wine. This is called "being a hermit." However, it is not so for a priest, who is permitted to have some of it.

These are forms of correction that everyone will have to experience in some of their desires. Through them, we correct the desire and move on. In that state, we already know how to use the light of *Hochma* from below upward and receive it. Everything that was forbidden was only for lack of strength to use it with the aim to bestow.

Assume that a person offers us a box of great chocolates, and we love sweets. Although we could give it to others, we say, "Don't give it to me." This is called "being a hermit." Afterward, we acquire a bigger *Masach* (screen), and acquire a measure of love for someone, and that measure is greater than the love we have for the chocolate. Now we say, "Give it to me" because we are now ready to make an act of bestowal, to pass this light, this pleasure, to another.

In our world, Kabbalists talk about having to enjoy life, marry, and lead a normal life. That is, we can do anything as long as we bring these pleasures to a spiritual level and not lose them on the corporeal one. After all, on the corporeal level we cannot enjoy everything in life.

The Torah teaches us how to rise to such a level of pleasure that it will flow through us to others and return, going back and forth. This is called "spiritual life"—endless, whole, and to which we are being elevated. When we grab for ourselves everything we think we deserve, it immediately stops the flow and leaves us with nothing in its stead until we die. However, if we enter the circle of energy, flow, knowledge, and sensation of endless pleasures—because it passes among everyone—we are regarded as leading a spiritual life.

What is a blessing in spirituality?

A "blessing in spirituality" is a force that exists on the level of *Bina*, influencing lower desires and blessing them, leading them to the level of *Bina*, too. A blessing is the degree of bestowal, *Bina*; it is the ability to bestow, to give.

Terms

Mount Sinai

"Mount Sinai" is a mountain of *Sina'a* (hate). If we discover all the evil within, it is considered being at the foot of Mount Sinai. However, it is possible to discover it only if the point within, called Moses, climbs up that mountain. There, in the chasm between the bottom of the mountain and its peak, under that condition we acquire the Torah. This happens because we feel that we simply must correct, but do not know what to do. Such people are worthy of receiving the light that reforms, called "Torah."

Family

A "family" is a whole person consisting of a man, woman, children, a house, and the entire world. It is a complete *Kli*.

Impure

One who is "impure" is fraught with self-interest. Such a person defiles everything he or she touches because anything that person wants is only for self-gratification, instead of giving to others. Conversely, giving, or bestowal upon others, is called *Kedusha* (holiness), purity.

Camp, or Being Outside the Camp

A "camp" is the part of the will to receive that we can define and say, "in this part, we are advancing only with the intention to bestow." That is, a "camp" is our corrected desires.

Tabernacle and the Inauguration of the Tabernacle

"Inauguration" is when we establish the tabernacle. It is when we have reached the point of establishing that state.

Gift

To the extent that we can relinquish the will to receive for ourselves, it is as though we are giving a gift to the priest, to our own form of bestowal, to the quality of bestowal. When we relate to the degree of a priest, to that desire to bestow, it is considered that we have received a blessing for this in return, and that we have sanctified that desire.

Blessing

A "blessing" means that the light that reforms pours down into the will to receive and corrects it into having the aim to bestow. This is the correction.

Blessing of the Priests

The "blessing of the priests" is the light that comes from the degree of *Bina* to the degree of *Malchut* and corrects it, when *Malchut* begins to relate itself to the degree of *Bina*. A "priest" is the degree of *Bina*.

This is not only the correction of the will to receive; it relates to bestowal and comes closer to the degree of the Creator. A "priest" is the degree of *Elokim*, *Bina*, desiring mercy and bestowal. Priests have no lot; they are at the degree of desiring mercy, entirely in bestowal. Hence, if *Malchut* can join it, she receives a blessing, a correction, the blessing of the priests.

False Oath

A "false oath" occurs when we connect to the degree of *Bina* and receive its strength, then deliberately use that blessing with the intent to receive, meaning to bestow in order to receive. That is, we are willing to give, but we intend to receive a benefit for ourselves as a result.

From *The Zohar*: Why Have I Come and There Is No One

How loved are Israel by the Creator? Wherever they are, the Creator is with them because He does not remove His love from them, as it was said, "And let them make Me a Temple, that I may dwell among them" (Exodus 25:8).

Zohar for All, *Nasso* (Take), item 105

"And let them make Me a Temple, that I may dwell among them" means that if one makes one's will to receive as a Temple, there is where one finds the Creator.

BeHa'alotcha

(When You Raise the Candles)

(Numbers 8:1-12:16)

Portion Summary

The portion, *BeHa'alotcha* (When You Raise the Candles), takes place a year after the reception of the Torah. The people of Israel are getting ready to journey, and hold a special ceremony for the inauguration of the altar. The portion details the laws concerning making the offering of the Second Passover for those who could not take part in the first Passover.

The portion speaks of the tabernacle, over which there was constantly a cloud. It is an indication to the children of Israel as to when they must rise and journey, and when they must settle down. The portion also tells of the two silver trumpets that were used to assemble the people at times of war, when making offerings, on Sabbaths, festivals, and special occasions.

Toward the end of the portion, several events take place that point to the heightening of the ego. The wicked in the nation complain about Moses and the Creator, and a consuming fire is sent to the wicked at the camp's edge. The rabble, a group of proselytes that joined the children of Israel during their exit from Egypt, complains about their condition, and in return, the Creator showers quails on the camp. Anyone who jumps on the quails is put to death. This is why the place is called "the graves of craving."

The end of the portion talks about Miriam—Moses' and Aaron's sister—slandering Moses. She says to Aaron, "The Creator appeared to me, as well as to you, so why is Moses the leader? Why are we listening only to him?" She is punished for it with leprosy. Moses asks the Creator to forgive her and He commands her to isolation for seven days. The nation, which was to travel, waits for seven days until she returns.

COMMENTARY

All the events are spiritual states within us. We need to correct ourselves and achieve equivalence of form with the Creator, as it is written, "Return, O Israel, to the Lord your God" (Hosea 14:2). The text speaks only about correction. It is not about having to cross the desert and reach the Jordan River, cross it, and reach the land of Israel. Rather, it is about ascending, as in *BeHaalotcha* (When You Raise).

"Ascending" refers to building the soul. Each of us builds our own soul, and does it gradually. The soul is called "a portion of God from above" (Job 31:2). One begins the spiritual work, wanting to build oneself and achieve bestowal and love of others, connection with everyone, because this is how we become similar to the Creator, as it is written, "From the love of man to the love of God,"* from loving people to loving the Creator.

* Rav Yehuda Ashlag (Baal HaSulam), *The Writings of Baal HaSulam*, "The Love of God and the Love of Man," p 482.

We achieve the love in stages, although we hate it because we are its complete opposite. These are the stages described in all the portions. At first, the Torah speaks only about when we receive the spark called the "point in the heart." With that spark we begin to correct ourselves. The Torah describes this process until the end of correction, through what is called "before the eyes of all Israel" (Deuteronomy 34:12), through the end of the Torah (Pentateuch).

Therefore, when we begin to work and correct ourselves, we immediately find all kinds of problems within us. It is written in the portion that a year after all the preparations, when the children of Israel begin to move, problems began to arise in the camp. People began to find these problems after all the preparations had been made, when it seemed they were ready for the spiritual ascent. They began to encounter many obstructions such as thoughts and desires that went against spiritual ascents.

The obstructions that appeared were actually revelations of the desires and the thoughts, the mind and the heart that needed correction. It is precisely by correcting them that we ascend. Hence, we need not see these as obstructions, but as a means for ascent, a springboard. We can see in ourselves and in groups in Israel and elsewhere that problems begin the moment everything is organized and everyone is ready and eager to begin to correct the connections. This is when trouble starts, but it is the right way, the only way to ascend.

The problems that appear reveal different desires and layers of desire in us. Our general desire is divided into many layers, so it is no surprise that "people" suddenly appear, meaning those desires within us. The whole of Israel is called "Adam." He includes everything, even the nations of the world within us. However, "Israel" are the desires with which we can advance for the time being, while the nations of the world are kept "frozen" so as to not deal with them.

When we want to go only with desires with which we can rise to spirituality, we discover that even with these, it is not easy. There are desires that have not sanctified themselves, which is the purpose of the Second Passover. All those who did not accomplish this during the exodus from Egypt can now have them corrected, so now we sanctify them. "Sanctifying" means that we bring the desires to the quality of bestowal, *Kodesh* (holiness, from the same root as the word, *Kedusha*), bestowal, or love of others.

We should learn how to sort the desires that are ready to be corrected in us from those that are not ready. The same goes for thoughts, working in the tent of meeting, and in the tabernacle. These are works of scrutiny and correction.

The work of the sacrifices, or the *Mitzvot* (commandments) connected to the offerings, is the most important because it entails instructions on how to separate each desire from the rest of them, how to process and understand them, know what they are, and how possible or impossible it is to advance with each desire.

Our only way to advance is by turning our egoistic desires into desires of bestowal and love. There are always problems in this process, such as leprosy or plagues, as described about Miriam or those who wanted to eat meat. It happens because our desire is divided into still, vegetative, animate, and speaking. "Speaking" refers to different kinds of people that the Torah mentions: priest, Levite, and Israel. Yet, we find that there are also strangers, proselytes, mixed multitudes, and others that seemingly do not belong to Israel, yet joined it.

The sorting and the scrutiny are not done immediately upon the exodus from Egypt, but later, when it turns out there is more to correct. We need to separate the sanctified part from the rest of our desires, which we temporarily "put on hold." Some of these desires can be corrected, and through them it is possible to be sanctified and advance. It is possible to bestow with them, to ascend on the ladder. But with some desires it is impossible to do so.

The parts that can already be in bestowal and receive in order to bestow have already awakened. The light shines in them, as it is written, "When you raise the candles" (Numbers 8:2). There are clear signs in the scrutinies, which indicate when to take certain actions. If we are under a cloud, sitting, it is preparation. If the cloud wakes up, the heaviness and scrutinies awaken in us and we can start moving. The entire Torah is about how to correct the will to receive, which parts of it, and how we can scrutinize them.

Questions and Answers

What is the Second Passover? Do desires we have not brought out suddenly make a higher discernment and discover that they, too, deserve to come out?

It is not a higher discernment, but a more accurate, finer one. We discover that desires with which we thought we could leave Egypt and continue toward the reception of the Torah and the land of Israel do not really support bestowal. *Eretz* (land) means *Ratzon* (desire), and *Ysrael* (Israel) means *Yashar El* (straight to God). After taking a few steps forward, we discover some "uncleanness" within us that we previously overlooked. Only now that we have advanced can we discern desires with which we cannot advance, so we sort and correct them.

We sort and correct our desires in stages. It is possible to ruin the desires, kill them, separate them, or somehow mend them, as with the work of the offerings. We divide our desires into still, vegetative, animate, and speaking, and we sort the desires at the level of speaking into priest, Levite, and Israel. We should also remember the mixed multitude, the proselytes, and the nations of the world—the various gentiles that awaken within us.

There are primary desires on the animate level because the soul consists of *Shoresh* (root), *Neshama* (soul), *Guf* (body), *Levush* (clothing), and *Heichal* (house/hall), or *Moach* (marrow), *Atzamot* (bones), *Gidin* (tendons), *Bassar* (flesh), and *Or* (skin), depending on how we divide them. When referring to *Moach*, *Atzamot*, *Gidin*, *Bassar*, and *Or*, we cannot correct the *Or*. The correction of the *Or* is making parchment out of it, on which the Torah is written. The *Or* is divided into two–the outside, and the *Duchsustus* (inner part). This is how it achieves correction.

Before that, we correct a *Kli* (vessel) of *Bassar* on the animate degree. This is our main work at the altar. While there are salt, water, and other elements at the altar, the main one is the flesh. This is the *Kli* by which we correct our will to receive, which is the most important. The flesh is red; its structure is the great will to receive; hence, the work of the offerings, as the Torah describes, is primarily in the *Kli* (vessel) of *Bassar* (flesh).

Before that, we do not know or think that there is a need to perform these corrections. We understand it only as we advance at each stage, park at the stops, prepare all the camps, each with its own banner, and each in its place in the division. If we take the entire population of Israel divided into camps, tribes, according to location and form, we either advance or stand still. Instead of finding the tent of meeting, all the desires stand around the tent. The Levites, the priests, and the whole camp only describe the structure of the soul.

Bigger problems surface each time in the camp–whether it is external thoughts and desires that want to join the ranks, tribes along the way that attack them, or people in the desert who have not corrected themselves from their desires into a desire that is entirely *Yashar El*, which is the land that is full of milk and honey. That is, there are light of *Hassadim* and light of *Hochma*, while in the desert everything is dry; there is no water, no light of *Hassadim*; hence everything is only scrutinies.

There are many "physical" descriptions, such as the cloud going in front of the camp, and when the children of Israel rest, it rests, too.

This is concealment: we only see our measure of concealment from the revelation of the Creator. If the cloud, meaning concealment, departs from us, we advance. If the concealment descends on us, we lower our heads, sit, and scrutinize. Indeed, most of the forty years in the desert were spent sitting and scrutinizing, only to move a little forward and stop again for scrutiny.

Why is it written that the cloud is going before the camp?

We follow the concealment because we want to accept it, since according to the concealment we discover the process by which we are going.

What is the concealment in relation to us?

"Concealment" is when we receive it from the will to receive, when we want to be in it, as it is written, "wisdom is with the humble" (Proverbs 11:2), or *Safra de Tzniuta* (*Book of Humbleness*, part of *The Zohar*), meaning disclosures. *Safra* means book (in Aramaic), and a book is disclosure, a *Megillah* (scroll), from the word *Gilui* (disclosure). When we hide ourselves, agreeing to receive concealment from the Creator, this is when we advance.

True, it contradicts common sense, since what does it mean to "walk in bestowal?" This is when we *do not* want any disclosure and are seemingly rejecting it. We advance with *Ohr Hozer* (Reflected Light) because we are in the forty years in the desert.

What does it give us?

This is how *Malchut* rises to *Bina*. We acquire *Bina's* qualities of bestowal in our *Kli* of *Malchut*. With the qualities of bestowal, we walk with our eyes shut because we are following the concealment, the cloud, until we reach the entrance to the land of Israel. Upon entering the land of Israel, the light of *Hochma* begins to appear through the light of *Bina*, which is acquired during the forty years in the desert. This is when we begin to see.

The land of Israel is a land where the Creator is present, a desire filled by the Creator, when we have already discovered Him. But before that, when *Malchut* only rises to *Bina*, we acquire the concealment and consent to work only in bestowal without anything in return.

From where does the strength to walk in such concealment come?

The strength is given from above. It is the strength of the light received when receiving the quality of bestowal. The whole problem is that spirituality is not like corporeality, where everything is in our hands, in our vessels of reception, and this is how we advance. It is not hard to advance this way, since we remain in the ego.

In spirituality, we do not advance egoistically. Rather, we have to receive additional strength from above, an additional desire called "a new land," "a new heaven." Everything is new. "Through the desert" means that we cannot find any answers in our will to receive, and cannot find any fulfillment in it.

So what motivates us? Why do we advance?

The motivation comes from beginning to feel that we are following the upper force. It is good to feel it, but only if we are willing to follow the cloud, the concealment, with our eyes shut.

What does it mean to walk "with our eyes shut"?

"Walking with our eyes shut" means that we do not receive any justification to advance in bestowal, neither in our minds nor in our hearts. Our hands, namely our corporeal, egoistic *Kelim* (vessels), are where we feel in the heart and understand in the mind. Here we do not feel or understand anything. All we want is the chance to go above these worldly *Kelim* and rise to another, higher dimension. We exist there in completely different *Kelim* from the ones we understand and feel.

How do we know that we are even making any progress there?

The cloud, the concealment, is showing us the way, but only to the extent that we are willing to make constant sacrifices. That is, we sacrifice parts of the flesh of the various desires. If we sacrifice and do not want to engage in them, and are also willing to leave them with no rhyme or reason, we will draw closer. *Korban* (sacrifice/

offering) comes from the word, *Karov* (near/close). In this way, we draw closer to the quality of the Creator, to pure bestowal, *Bina*.

What is the meaning of what happens to Miriam the prophetess? She makes a just complaint regarding Moses' leadership. If a person wants to lead, then why only Moses?

Moses' quality of *Bina* is perfect, complete, GAR of *Bina*. It is not so with any other desire.

How does the Creator speak to Moses, and how did Moses speak to Him?

This is the revelation. In spirituality, we have no sight, hearing, taste, smell, or touch. Rather, we are invited to "Taste and see that the Lord is good" (Psalms 34:9). We do not taste in the mouth, but in the new *Kelim* that appear.

Does a person taste beyond the five physical senses?

There are *Hochma*, *Bina*, *Zeir Anpin*, and *Malchut*, *Yod-Hey-Vav-Hey*. *Hochma* is vision, *Bina* is hearing. Some prophets said, "I saw," and some said, "I heard." The Creator spoke to Moses, at the degree of *Bina*, GAR of *Bina*, pure, faithful *Bina*. He was faithful, meaning at the degree of faith. He heard, meaning he was primarily at the degree of hearing, which is the degree of *Bina*. This is how the Creator appeared to him.

Did Miriam not know this? What is the punishment she got? We know that there are no punishments, so how come after the leprosy she understood?

All punishments are corrections. When Miriam is made ill and sits for seven days outside the camp, the whole camp waits for her return, and only then do they advance in the desert. "As they walked" speaks of corrections. The *Nukva* (female) is a deficiency that stands opposite Moses. She does not speak at the degree of GAR of *Bina*, as does Moses, but from the degree of VAK of *Bina*. That is, the whole degree is connected to that hearing. The Creator speaks to everyone, but Moses also *knows* because he is in the part of *Bina* where the light of *Hochma* (wisdom) dresses, in GAR of *Bina*.

Are Aaron and Miriam not in *GAR* of *Bina*?

No; this is why Moses is considered the Creator's house trustee, as it is written, "He is faithful in all My house" (Numbers 12:7).

Miriam is a woman, and almost everywhere in the Torah it is men who lead.

Not quite. Women exist in every stage and every action, but they are not mentioned. For example, Abraham begot Isaac, but he also had daughters.

Where it writes *Et* (the) in the Torah, does that refer to a female?

Yes, of course. The woman is the primary part of the Torah; she carries the deficiency that the man corrects. The reason we talk more about men than women is that the male part is the *Masach* (screen) that brings *Ohr Hozer* (Reflected Light) that discloses the *Zivug de Hakaa* (coupling) on the deficiency of the woman. In this portion, it is quite clear that without Prophetess Miriam, we could not draw near. In other words, she is at the degree of *Bina*, the degree of revealing the Creator.

Terms

Menorah (Lamp)

The "*Menorah*" symbolizes the soul. It symbolizes the seven *Sefirot* of the soul that we need to know how to light, in which way, and in which order.

Korban (Sacrifice/Offering)

A *Korban* is the will to receive that we correct, and through it become more *Karov* (near/close) to the Creator.

Second Passover

The "Second Passover" relates to desires that we find either unnecessary or impossible to sanctify. These are desires that we do not recognize. However, they can be corrected later, at a more advanced stage in the process.

Impurity

"Impurity" is a force that works in order to receive, the egoistic force that appears in us.

Cloud

A "cloud" is concealment that comes either from the Creator, who hides Himself from us, or from us, who hide ourselves from Him. The latter is called "clouds of glory."

A Guide

A "guide" is the pure quality of bestowal that we want to follow and cling to, thus reaching our goal.

Trumpets of Silver

The two forces that we discover, and by which we advance, are called "trumpets of silver." These forces pull us forward from the right and from the left.

Silver

"Silver" is the degree of *Bina*; gold is the degree of *Hochma*.

Proselyte

A "proselyte" is a desire to receive that has converted and is willing to be corrected and join Israel.

Rabble

The "rabble" is a type of desire to receive that we need to discover, and find it "infected" with an intention to receive.

Quail

"Quails" are fine (thin) desires, a type of desire on the animate degree from which we can make an offering.

Leprosy

"Leprosy" is a disease in Man's desire, in the intention to receive, which appears on the last and worst degree of the skin.

Mouth to Mouth

A *Zivug* (coupling) "mouth to mouth" means spirit with spirit, when two souls, or the Creator and a soul, are in that sort of connection.

Punishment

A "punishment" is a correction. The punishment is given when we feel unable to use the desire in order to bestow. It is not an inability to receive. Rather, the punishment is inability to bestow. However, the punishment leads one to correction because we already know what to correct in that desire, and have reached a *Mitzva* (commandment/correction). A *Mitzva* is an act of bestowal, an act of love.

Miriam

"Miriam" is a type of will to receive in us that stands opposite Moses. Moses, too, discovered that part in himself. In other words, the degree in us that is called "Moses" discovered a certain touch by the *Nukva* (female), Miriam, which still required correction. Moses also rises each time along with the people; he is a discernment in the soul, hence, with each discernment, the discernment of the degree of Moses is corrected, too.

Each term and each stage, our egoistic will to receive grows and swells, and we correct it with the intention to bestow, to serve others and the Creator.

The Creator within us is what punishes us?

Everything is within us. Man is a small world that needs to achieve the complete correction.

From *The Zohar*: And the Waters Were Made Sweet

In those secrets that will be revealed through you, "The waters were made sweet." Like the salt that makes the meat sweet, they will be sweetened by the secrets that will be revealed through you. All those questions and the dispute of the bitter water in the oral Torah will return to being the sweet waters of the Torah. And your agonies will be sweet to you through these secrets that will be revealed by you. And all your troubles will come back to you like fleeting dreams. A dream (in Hebrew) has the letters of the word "salt," reversed. As salt sweetens the meat, so agony sweetens.

Zohar for All, *BeHaalotcha* (When You Mount the Candles), item 86

Summary

The portion, *BeHaalotcha* (When You Mount the Candles), deals with lighting the candles, with seeing all of Man's desire. Man divides into many parts, and we need to see them as a *Menorah*. The *Menorah* is the symbol of the soul. We need to light up all of its seven qualities, shining with the upper light, with bestowal upon others, with love.

Shlach Lecha

(Send Forth)

(Numbers 13:1-15:41)

Portion Summary

The portion begins with Moses sending the twelve heads of the tribes to spy in the land of Israel, to examine it, and to prepare to enter it. The spies return and describe a land flowing with milk and honey, but occupied by giants that will make it impossible to enter, conquer, and rule the land. Their words spread fear in the people, except for Joshua Ben Nun, and Caleb Ben Yephunneh. This angers the Creator and He wants to destroy the entire people. Moses prays and asks for mercy on the people. As a result, only the ten spies who slandered the land die in a plague. The other two, Joshua Ben Nun and Caleb Ben Yephunneh, continue to accompany the people.

Later in the portion, the children of Israel blunder once more and seek to run back to Egypt. In the end they repent and abort their decision. Afterward, Israel make another mistake: they try to fight and conquer the land without instructions to do so, and therefore fail.

The portion ends with the instruction to wander another forty years in the desert until the entire generation of the spies passes away, except for Joshua Ben Nun, who is to lead the people into the land of Israel.

Commentary

We have to develop from our will to receive, from our egos, into a state in which we come to be "the people of Israel," when we are all *Yashar El* (straight to God), having the quality of the Creator: bestowal and love. We will all be in "Love your neighbor as yourself,"* in love of others, because we have no other choice.

We must not go by our own reason, which alternates between dictations to advance and to retreat. Rather, we must fight while examining if we are doing what is right, and if the way is right. The portion explains that we cannot know what to do or even where to start. It is a problem because we are accustomed to work by the mode, "A judge has only what his eyes see."** It appears we must advance by following our essence, according to our *Kelim* (vessels/tools), using our minds and hearts.

The Creator demands that we develop and do something. But how can we do something if we cannot tell between right and wrong, if we do not know whether to move forward into war or run back to Egypt? We can see that there are giants in the land of Israel. And while there are also fruits there, we cannot tell who rules there, which desires exist, and how big they are.

Hence, the portion, *Shlach Lecha* (Send Forth) explains how we should advance correctly. There is a demand by which we must check the road with our reason and see how to advance in spiritual development. The Torah speaks of spiritual development, such as how we can move from a state of egoism into one of love of others, as in, "Love your neighbor as yourself; it is a great rule in the

---

* Jerusalem Talmud, *Seder Nashim, Masechet Nedarim*, Chapter 9, p 30b.

** Babylonian Talmud, *Masechet Baba Batra*, 131a; *Masechet Sanhedrin*, 6b.

Torah."* This is why we must go by what our eyes see, and examine our egos, our ill will, so we can see how we hate others, repel them, think only of ourselves, and learn how isolated we are from others, that we cannot even think of them.

Instead, we should picture what love is, if and how much we love others, how much we can think of others and unite with them (as the global crisis demands we do these days). We feel that we are facing this great assignment, which is why the wisdom of Kabbalah is appearing, so we may ask for help to rise to the degree of connection and unity, of real love of others, since without it we will not survive in this developing world.

The time has come for us to begin to actualize the Torah. This is why we have come to the land of Israel and settled here after the exile, after all the preparations we have experienced all through history. Today, we must be as spies, scrutinizing the meaning of "being a spy" and the meaning of "Love your neighbor as yourself" to see if we can do it or not, and what we must do in order to achieve it.

When we consider our current state, compared to the ideal state we must achieve, we see it is impossible. This is the problem of the spies, who were not told that they had to do anything other than to check and see that it was impossible. Yet, they want it so much that we feel we have to achieve love of others because this is the Creator's will. This is how our entire development should be.

We must reach one of two pressure points: the first is that we cannot achieve love of others, and the second is that we must achieve it because without it we have no life. We have to come to a great cry with faith above reason, and then the light that reforms will come, as it is written, "I have created the evil inclination; I have created for it the Torah as a spice,"** for "the light in it reforms."*** The light embedded in the Torah–in the proper study of it, in the internality of the Torah, namely the wisdom of Kabbalah–comes and corrects us.

---

* Jerusalem Talmud, *Seder Nashim, Masechet Nedarim*, Chapter 9, p 30b.

** Babylonian Talmud, *Masechet Kidushin*, 30b.

*** Midrash Rabah, *Eicha*, Introduction, Paragraph 2.

Therefore, there is no need to run back to Egypt or cry that we cannot do it because "It is not for us to complete the work, neither are we free to idle away from it."* Rather, all we need is to act, as it is written, "Whatever your hand finds to do by your strength, that do" (Ecclesiastes 9:10). And the minute we come to a point of complete shattering, then "The Lord will fight for you" (Exodus 14:14).

Therefore, we need not go to war and think that we will win by our own strength. Who are we, after all? On the one hand, before us is the massive, bursting ego that is stopping us, as the giants living in the land of Israel portray."** In truth, they are our own desires facing us, and we cannot fight them. However, we must confront them, although we know we cannot overcome them. On the other hand, we must rise to faith, to a great power of demand until the light comes and corrects these desires from hostile ones into desires of the land of Israel.

Indeed, it is a dilemma that we face prior to entering a new degree for which we must prepare.

It happens every time. The inner war is against our desires and qualities because "the inclination of a man's heart is evil from his youth" (Genesis 8:21). We are all born with an ego that keeps developing. If we advance toward spiritual ascent, it develops even more, as it is written, "He who is greater than his friend, his inclination is bigger than him."*** This is why we cannot fight the ever-growing ego.

However, if we are in the right environment and annul ourselves before it, regarding the people around us as the greatest in the generation, we begin to absorb from them the importance of the goal. Our friends give us the sensation that it is possible, that we can erupt in such a way that will lead to a genuine prayer, to the "gate of tears."

On the one hand, we are aware that we cannot undergo that correction in us; on the other hand, we know that the light, the

---

* Mishnah, *Seder Nezikin, Masechet Avot* (*Pirkey Avot*), Chapter 2, Mishnah 16.

** Deuteronomy 1:28.

*** Babylonian Talmud, *Masechet Sukkah*, 52a.

Creator, can make it happen in us, if we only ask, if the goal is more important to us than anything. This is why our work is in a group, in the right environment, because this is the only way we can muster the strength to advance on the right path.

QUESTIONS AND ANSWERS

It takes time before one can adopt a new environment.

True, there are many inner struggles and things to overcome, but it does not always feel like that. That is, we experience different situations. Some are good, some are not so good, and some are frightening. It depends on the pace of progress and the time we dedicate to it.

What are the spies? Whom are we fooling?

The spies are within, and when we want to know how to advance despite everything, we need to examine the road ahead. After we examine it, we must not continue with the spies, favor them, or listen to them, since we examine the road with only our five egoistic senses.

In other words, should we not believe what we think and feel?

Of course not. Assume that we are at a certain degree and need to rise to a higher one. The gap between the degrees is an entirely different life, and different mind and heart. How can we rise from degree to degree when we do not know what the next degree is like because it is in a different, spiritual dimension? In that dimension, the qualities and thoughts are different, the perception of reality is different, and so is the world view.

When do we understand that we have risen a degree?

We understand it only once we are there. The question is, "How can we reach it?" The desires and the fruits in the land of Israel are so huge; everything is big. From the point where we stand, we cannot ascend by ourselves because only the upper light that created the ego can correct it. This is why it is written, "I have created the evil inclination; I have created for it the Torah as a spice," for "the light in it reforms." That is, only through the light are we reformed. And once we are corrected, we rise to a higher degree.

What does it mean that ten spies say one thing and two of them say something else? It is very confusing.

They are qualities within us. "Man is a small world."* All the portions in the Torah deal with the development of man's soul. This portion describes the spies, with ten thinking one way and two thinking another. However, this is a good situation, when the soul advances properly; this is why ten are against and two are in favor.

How do we know to whom we should listen?

It is a problem. We have to make mistakes. It is written, "A person cannot understand words of Torah unless he has failed in them,"** and also, "There is not a righteous man on earth who does good and will not sin" (Ecclesiastes 7:20). At each step, we sin, fall into wickedness, and taste our own evil. Our lack of progress is caused only by us. We see how we make our own lives bitter, as though retreating farther from our initial point.

This is actually a sign that we are advancing correctly, and we must move on. That is, we must go through everything that is happening in the Torah, all the mistakes, problems, and everything that is coming to us.

Is there nothing we can do?

We cannot avoid doing. We must examine our evil inclination to the fullest and ask for help each time we are stuck. If we do not taste the bitter, we also will not demand the light that will come and correct our evil. Then the light enters the evil, corrects it, and we

* *Midrash Tanchuma, Pekudei,* item 3.

** Babylonian Talmud, *Masechet Gitin,* 43a.

receive a soul. The evil, along with the light that corrected it and filled, it is called a "soul." This is the only way to obtain a soul. Prior to that, we have none.

Is this what "a land flowing with milk and honey" means?

Yes. *Eretz* (land) means *Ratzon* (desire), a desire that is all milk and honey. That is, it is the degree of *Bina*, the light of *Hassadim*, the desire to bestow, with the light of *Hochma* inside, meaning attainment, closeness to the Creator.

The spies point out the nations that live in the land; why is it important?

These are desires within us that we need to correct in three lines. We need to correct them in the twelve tribes—*Yod-Hey-Vav-Hey* in three lines, to make it *Yod-Hey-Vav-Hey* times three.

The land is also called "the land of Canaan." Did Moses not lead them to the land of Israel?

Before it was called "the land of Israel," it was called "the land of Canaan." Before it was the land of Canaan, it was Egypt, and then a desert. It is the same desire; there is only one land, but it is given different names each time according to its corruption or correction.

Is Canaan a desire that is scrutinized before it becomes Israel?

Before one conquers the desire in the proper manner, it is called "the land of Canaan."

What are the giant fruits?

The fruits are what we receive as a result of our work. It is the flavor of the intention to bestow that we perform and feel in the will to receive. These are truly huge fruits, 620 times bigger. We taste pleasures because we develop and understand what bestowal means, what the Creator feels like in a corrected desire.

The children of Israel are still in the will to receive, yet they are told about fruits that exist in the desire to bestow. How can they grasp what it is about or know it is good?

When we stand before the next degree to which we will ascend, it is possible to see that degree "from afar," similar to Moses, who saw the land of Israel from Mount Nevo.

What does it mean that we taste the good, which is then taken from us so we may climb another step?

We can take these fruits, carry them on our backs, and possess them, but not taste them. There is still no *Kli* (vessel) in which to fill ourselves with all the attainments, pleasures, and fulfillments that exist in the desire to receive in order to bestow in a corrected soul.

It sounds like a great promise; why would anyone want to run from it?

It requires substantial, difficult corrections, which are impossible to make. The reward for making them is wonderful, but this requires fighting huge desires—all the nations that dwell in the land of Israel.

But it is not a war that one fights alone; rather, the light does it. It is not easy to attain it, to grasp that we do not correct the desire. The children of Israel want to advance, which is a mistake. Alternatively, they want to run back to Egypt or go to the land of Israel by themselves, both of which would be mistakes, as well.

So what do you do?

Cry out and demand help.

Where does one find the strength to endure not being able to fight or run? Is it the group that gives strength?

Yes, we gain strength from *Arvut* (mutual guarantee). The Creator broke the single soul that He created into myriad pieces.

He created nothing else. And He did this so we may feel that we are independent in our own shares, and be able to acquire the rest of the parts, thus becoming similar to Him. Each of us acquires that great soul; each one becomes as great as the Creator and is in *Dvekut* (adhesion) with Him.

Our whole purpose is to keep acquiring parts of our soul, which seems to us as though it is not ours, but belongs to others. The means to do this is the group, as it is written, "Either friendship or death."* When we connect to a group, to people who want the same goal, we create unity among us, which elevates the importance of our goal until we are ready to demand it. Then the light comes and reforms.

The Creator wanted to destroy the people of Israel and Moses prayed for them. What kind of a solution is that?

It is a struggle within. Moses is the point that pulls us forward, the point of *Bina*. He is the faithful shepherd. We constantly advance with faith, with the power of bestowal. The term, "faith," does not refer to blind faith, as we normally define it, where we do what we are told. Rather, faith is the quality of bestowal. It is when one is willing to give to everyone, as it is written, "That which you hate, do not do to your friend,"** and "Love your neighbor as yourself," meaning give everything we have. This is the goal we must achieve.

Moses is that point within each of us, the spiritual gene that pulls us toward that quality. It gradually develops in us, and through it we can reach the land of Israel.

Why did the ten spies die?

There is no life and death in the sense we think of it. Their death means that their role has ended because they could not advance in their current form. These are all qualities within us. It is possible to advance with the qualities known as Joshua and Caleb, but not with the rest of the qualities. Joshua and Caleb are two lines, *Gematrias*, qualities.

---

* Babylonian Talmud, *Masechet Taanit*, 23a.

** *Masechet Shabbat*, 31a.

From *The Zohar*: The Spies

However, do not rebel against the Creator. We must not rebel against the Torah because the Torah does not require wealth or vessels of silver and gold. And you, do not fear the people of the land, for if a broken body engages in the Torah, it will find healing for everything. It is written, "And health to all their flesh." All the slanderers over a person turn into his helpers and declare, "Make way for so and so, the King's servant!" In other words, let no one stop him from coming to the King to serve Him.

Zohar for All, *Shlach Lecha* (Send Forth), item 67

It is impossible to advance to the next degree, the land of Israel, until we see it as a great, sublime degree, the degree of *Bina*. When entering the degree of the land of Israel when we acquire it, it becomes *Keter* (crown), meaning "the world of *Ein Sof* (infinity)." When we see what fruits grow there and how incapable we are of getting them, we enter the desert.

We cannot go around the desert or avoid walking through it. Forty years is the distance between *Malchut* and *Bina*, the distance of the ascent to that level. After forty years, we are ready to reacquire the quality of bestowal, to reenter the ego and begin to correct it into the intention to receive in order to bestow, namely the degree of the land of Israel.

Following the desert, we enter the land of Israel, where wars over the conquest of the land take place. There, we turn the will to receive into the desire to bestow. In all forty years of the desert, we only had the intention to bestow in order to bestow. That is, we corrected ourselves only to the point of not harming others. But once we enter the land of Israel, we do good to others.

Why did the Creator not let the people win? After all, they awakened with a certain desire and He seemingly prevented it from them.

The Creator did not prevent it; He only showed how unprepared they were to enter the land of Israel. However, by seeing that they were unprepared, they understood which *Kelim* they had to acquire. These are the forty years in the desert, the great corrections we have to undergo.

Terms

The Land of Canaan

We are immersed in desire. All we have is a desire that must be corrected from harming others into doing good to them. The "land of Canaan" is that desire when it is still uncorrected, but is about to be corrected.

Forty Days

"Forty" is the degree of *Bina*. The gap between *Malchut* and *Bina* is called "forty." It is the gap between the will to receive, the ego, and the degree of faith, *Bina*, the level of bestowal.

Flowing with Milk and Honey

"Milk and honey" represent the abundance we receive in the corrected desire.

Amalek

"Amalek" is the foundation of all evil. It is the intention to receive in order to receive, which exists within our nature.

Joshua Ben Nun

Nun is fifty, the fiftieth degree, fifty gates of *Bina*. Joshua, like Moses, pulls. Joshua saves the children of Israel by bringing them to the fiftieth degree, the gates of *Bina*. Moses completed the degree of forty because he passed away at the entrance to the land of Israel, and Joshua succeeded him.

Spies, the Quality of Spying

The "quality of spying" is our egoistic desires to receive that constantly seek to steal for ourselves instead of to give, bestow, and rise above reception.

The Generation of the Desert

The "generation of the desert" is our own desires, which must all die with their intentions to receive. The intention to receive must die, and only the desires with intentions to bestow enter the land of Israel. This is why the whole generation of the desert had to die in the desert.

Plague

"Plagues" are the biggest and best corrections we can experience. All of a sudden, we can correct many desires and qualities at once, which are inverted into having the aim to bestow. By that, we feel closer to the Creator. This is how we gradually approach Israel.

Conquering the Land

"Conquering the land" follows this portion, when the spies went to spy. The word, *Eretz* (land), comes from the word, *Ratzon* (desire). We take the egoistic will to receive that we corrected in the desert into having the intention to bestow, and now that desire has become bestowal. In other words, now we receive from others only because we want to bestow, to give. In this way, others enjoy, and we enjoy, too; we all enjoy giving to one another. Having this sort of relationship with the Creator means being in *Dvekut* (adhesion) with Him, in the world of *Ein Sof* (infinity). But even if it is the world of *Ein Sof*, we must all attain Him here in this world while we are still alive.

Grapes, Vine

"Wine" and "vine" are the degree of *Hochma*. It is the same light, attainment, and sensation of the Creator that dresses in the light of bestowal, the light of *Hassadim*.

From *The Zohar*: Flying Letters

When the letters fly, a person sees writing in the air, made of big letters, which are *Bina*, for the time being. "In the beginning God created the heaven and the earth." These words are from *Bina*, big letters. Afterward, small letters struck them, *Malchut* ascended and struck *Bina*, which diminished her. This is the *Yod* that entered the light, creating *Avir* (air). They fly, and the verse, "And God said, 'Let there be light,' and there was light. And God saw the light that it was good," appears from them.

Afterward, the small letters strike the big letters once again, meaning that *Malchut* rises to *Bina* once again and diminishes her. Then the words, "And God said, 'Let there be a firmament,'" appear in them, as well as the whole work of creation. The works of these letters are great wonders and joy to the poor. Happy are the people who await all that.

Zohar for All, Shlach Lecha (Send Forth), item 153

Summary

Man needs to make every effort, and only then does he reach the "land of Israel." This is the purpose of Creation, truly a land flowing with milk and honey.

Korah

(Numbers, 16:1-18:32)

Portion Summary

The portion begins with the story of Dothan and Abiram, and 250 of the presidents of the congregation who rebelled against Moses and Aaron with what seemed like a just argument: Since the entire nation is holy, Moses and Aaron should have the same status as the rest of the people. The reply they received was that although they are all equal, Moses and Aaron are the only leaders who can be in contact with the Creator. Following the mutiny, the ground swallowed the 250 presidents of the congregation, as well as Korah and his company, and the people suffered from a plague until Moses asked the Creator to end it.

The end of the portion debates the question of leadership in the nation. A test was held between all the staffs (rods) of all the leaders, and the only one that blossomed was Aaron's staff, which signaled his unequivocal leadership.

Commentary

We can interpret the explanation of the Torah (Pentateuch) on two levels—the level of this world and the level of the hidden, spiritual world. On the level of our world, the story of Korah is very relevant even today.

For thousands of years, our world has been developing through our egos. 3,800 years ago we lived in what is now known as Ancient Babylon. This is when Abraham—the quality of *Hesed* (mercy)—rose, as well as the priests who followed him, who are also from the quality of *Bina*, *Hassadim*.

Abraham discovered that the whole world must develop and achieve a state of unity and connection, and shared his revelation with the Babylonians. While many followed him, they were only a handful compared to the majority who rejected his ideas. Abraham had to flee from Babylon, chased by Nimrod, the king of Babylon.

Abraham established a method for correcting human nature. Today we call that method, "the wisdom of Kabbalah," whose purpose is to elevate man from the depths of egoism to the level of bestowal and love.

This ascent is, in fact, the goal of our development—to rise from the level of this world to the level of the spiritual world. Spirituality is bestowal and the love of others by which we acquire eternity and wholeness. This is the meaning of the text in this portion, as well as in *The Book of Zohar*, which talks about freedom from the Angel of Death.

According to the wisdom of Kabbalah, initially everyone in Babylon was united as one nation speaking the same language. But then the ego "plague" broke out, and people started hating each other, eventually alienating themselves from one another. Because the Babylonians didn't take upon themselves Abraham's method of correction (but rather that of Nimrod), humanity dispersed throughout the globe.

Kabbalah explains that from the moment people chose between the methods, it became necessary to reunite them. That unity will come because we are compelled to achieve it. Had we corrected ourselves then, we would have achieved unity back in Babylon and would have reached the purpose of Creation—being "as one man with one heart." We would have achieved the revelation of Godliness and would have concluded the correction. But since the Babylonians chose a different path, we are now compelled to follow through with the correction process.

We went down to Egypt and came out of it, ascending in spirituality to the degree of the First Temple, followed by the Second Temple. We went through destructions, exiles, redemptions, and today we are at the end of the last exile—beginning to rise toward the last, complete redemption.

Today, we are in a very similar situation to the one that formed in Babylon. The difference is that today we have nowhere to disperse, since we have already covered the globe. While there can be many "Nimrods" today, they cannot say anything because we have already recognized our negativity. We are already aware that our egos are destroying human society. Reality shows that unless we unite, we will disappear from the face of the earth. The worst-case scenario is that we will finish ourselves off, or that ecology and the rest of Nature will finish us off, since we're living opposite to Nature, which is God.

In *Gematria*, *Hateva* (Nature) is *Elokim* (God). We must achieve balance with Nature, and this is achieved by uniting "as one man with one heart." Unity pertains not only to the small number of people who fled from Babylon, stood at the foot of Mt. Sinai, received the Torah, and became a nation. Rather, it pertains to *everyone*.

Jews must be "a light for the nations," explaining to them Abraham's method by which we can all unite, as it is written in the Torah, "They shall all know Me, from the least of them to the greatest of them," and "For My house shall be called a house of prayer for all the peoples," and also, "And all the nations shall flow unto Him."

We are faced with a huge, crucial challenge: to finally achieve the purpose of Creation. We will succeed in it only through unity among all people.

That unity can take place after great pains, which the wisdom of Kabbalah and prophets have prophesied concerning the days of the Messiah. Or, we can take the method of Kabbalah, which is intended to draw the light that reforms.

Kabbalists warn us that unless we use the wisdom of Kabbalah, a third and even a fourth world war will break out, that only a handful will survive, and they will still have to implement the purpose of Creation. Hence, we have no choice but to do it. We can do it in a favorable manner, which is short, pleasant, and easy, through *The Book of Zohar*, the writings of the ARI (Rav Isaac Luria), and the writings of Baal HaSulam (Rav Yehuda Ashlag). We can use them to unite us through the light that will affect us. Kabbalah is called "the interior of the Torah," "the true Torah (teaching/instruction)," due to the light within it. For this reason, today we must explain to everyone the need to disclose and utilize this method.

The story of Korah is a perfect example of these words. Korah came from the tribe of Levy. Dothan, Abiram, and 250 representatives from the entire nation, all the tribes, apparently objected to the unity. They rejected the hierarchy, but there was no other choice. There had to be a leader, Moses, connecting the Creator to the priests, followed by his priest brother, Aaron, the right line, the quality of mercy that they taught to the people. Those who actualized the entire work, besides the priests, were the Levites, followed by the rest of the tribes, which were arranged according to the structure of the common soul.

The Creator created one soul, one desire. The people of Israel are arranged by that structure, and the rest of humanity should be connected around it. When people suddenly rise up and say, "No! We want a different order; we don't want to be so tightly connected," it goes against the purpose of Creation, against unity itself.

"Love your neighbor as yourself" is the rule that induces the connection between us. It is the great *Klal* ("rule" but also "collective") of the Torah. It is a *Klal* that is a common *Kli* (vessel) that we build and in which the light—the Creator—appears. Our only means to be "as one man with one heart," in mutual guarantee, is unity, connection, just as when we received the Torah. This is how we, the creatures, achieve the revelation of the Creator.

This is why there is nothing worse than what Korah did. It is called "a dispute not for the sake of the Creator," which is unlike other disputes, such as the one between the house of Shammai and the house of Hillel. Those were "disputes for the sake of the Creator," where matters are discussed and scrutinized.

There is right, and there is left. Each time we acquire a little more spirituality, a bigger ego—left line—appears in us. When we acquire a little more spirituality—the right line, Aaron—*Dinim* (judgments) reappear. This is how we rise, as though walking on two legs, climbing from one step to the next, as though on a ladder.

The right and left lines appear alternately, one by one. The left line gives the substance, and the right line corrects it into having the intention to bestow. On the one hand, there is an egoistic desire; on the other hand, there is the right line that comes and corrects it to being in order to bestow upon others.

This is how we advance, and this is why the wisdom of Kabbalah encourages the increase of the desire, hence its name, "the wisdom of *Kabbalah* (reception)." It teaches us how to receive everything—all the light—to achieve the goal in its entirety. Kabbalah is intended specifically for the most egoistic of people, but who also know how to correct their egos.

This is Abraham's method, which differs from all the other methods that originated in Babylon. Abraham taught other nations, too, such as the children of the mistresses that he had, whom he sent eastward. He taught them the opposite method, since if you don't correct the ego using the wisdom of Kabbalah—by drawing the light that reforms—it's best to keep the ego in check and not let it grow.

For that purpose, he gave them methods, religions, and faiths that encourage decreasing desires and cravings and treating others kindly, diminishing the will to receive as much as possible. He did that because if we don't know how to correct a desire, it is best to have a small ego rather than a large one, thus causing less harm to ourselves and to others.

But when we use the wisdom of Kabbalah, we use the biggest ego. And when it grows, we're even happier because "He who is greater than his friend, his inclination is greater than him," except that that inclination is corrected.

This is why Korah wanted to divide, to tear the connection. What he really wanted was to break that ladder. He wanted the people of Israel to not be connected, to not be under that hierarchy, according to the proper structure of the tribes.

The tribes are *Yod-Hey-Vav-Hey*. When multiplying the four letters by the three lines included in each of them, you get the twelve tribes. Korah wanted to break the structure, but this is impossible because without that structure, we cannot reach our goal. This is why his sin is so grave, and it is called "a dispute not for the sake of the Creator," not in the direction of the progress.

The argument of Korah and his company was seemingly right. All they asked for was equality. They didn't say they did not want to unite, at least not openly. They only asked why Moses and Aaron were of higher status, and asked for proof of their superiority.

It is impossible to break the correction process midway. You don't show a fool a job half done. Korah was right in saying that we will all reach equality, "as one man with one heart," one desire. However, this is the *end* of the process, which will happen at the end of correction, not in the middle, in the stage of the desert.

The desert is an intermediary stage that we go through in order to acquire the quality of *Bina*, the intention to bestow in order to bestow. Only afterward comes the entrance to the land of Israel, where we turn the will to receive into complete bestowal—an intention to receive in order to bestow. In the desert, we are still only conquering our own ego, not letting it burst out in order to receive for itself and against others. This is a degree called *Hafetz Hesed* (desiring mercy).

On these degrees, it is impossible to do what Korah says. On the one hand, he's right, but on the other hand, his timing is wrong. There will come a time when that desire is fulfilled, but it isn't now. The desires and claims of people, whether good or bad, become fully satisfied only at the end of correction.

The solution is in the *Mateh* (staff/rod). *Mateh* means that we know where to go and how to get there. We receive a sign that we cannot advance the way we are going, unless by using the light of faith, following Aaron's staff and Moses' staff.

Questions and Answers

How does patronizing eventually becomes positive?

The Torah explains our internality, our qualities, our thoughts, emotions, and our desires. The struggles we have are not only between us, but also *within* us. We want to advance egoistically, but we know that it's wrong and that we have to overcome it and follow a path of bestowal and love of others. After all, it's written so. This is the purpose and the quality of the Creator—bestowal and love—and we are opposite from the quality of the Creator.

These calculations always work within us and toss us from side to side. Each of us has an inner Pharaoh, an inner Korah, Haman, Moses, and Aaron. We are "small worlds" made of all the forces. As we advance along the spiritual path, these forces grow and become contradictory, and we find ourselves fighting mighty inner battles.

This is why people are correct, when viewed from their own subjective perspective. These are Nature's forces, which the Creator created, and there's a good reason why we think one way or the other. After all, all these forces—from worst to best—exist in Nature.

The question is how a person uses them. We mustn't erase anything that exists within us. In the end, we correct even the Korah within us. We will cut out the beast within, burn it, and spill the rest of its blood.

For now, when we perform such physical actions, we have no idea what internal actions they represent. At most, we only "freeze" the desire. But that, too, is a correction, to be used later.

Why does Korah see it as patronizing?

There is always a struggle between the forces within us. We put ourselves on the scales and must make sure that one force doesn't override the other, that the right line isn't much lower than the left. We must constantly keep the right higher than the left. It is called "walking on the right line." The commandment is to always be on the right, although the left line will grow accordingly, and will balance us so we will still advance on the right.

That sensation of internal struggle is a very good feeling. Each time, we feel how much we are immersed in these changes. It's like a wheel, where the top moves forward and the bottom appears to move backwards, yet the wheel is constantly moving forward.

What is the Correction of Being "Swallowed" in the Ground?

"The earth" is the general will to receive, the force that we currently cannot use correctly, with the aim to bestow. Its correction is similar to the one we make with a dead body—we bury it.

A "deceased" desire is one that we cannot use with the aim to bestow, and which appeared in us with the aim to receive. That aim to receive is Korah. The desire itself is neither good nor bad; what matters is the *intention*—whether we use this desire for ourselves or for the sake of others. The Torah instructs us how to accurately examine our intentions, whether for ourselves or for others, and we must turn the intention to receive for ourselves to the benefit of others, to bestow.

We can either "bury" the intention to receive in the ground, or burn it. That is, either the ground swallows it, or it is offered as a burnt offering (Hebrew: *Korban*, from the word *Karov*–near) in order to bring us closer. When we correct that aim from reception to bestowal, we bring ourselves closer to the Creator, hence the name, *Korban*.

These corrections have nothing to do with flesh and blood people, or such tragic events as being swallowed in the ground, burned, or dying by a plague, although these things do occur in our world. Rather, these descriptions relate to corrections that occur *within us*. This is why it is said that man is a "small world."

We need to check and find Korah, Abiram, Dothan, and the 250 presidents within us, what it means to be equal or unequal, and discover the purpose of Creation. This is why we need to sort out our desires and our intentions.

Also, we should learn about Aaron's staff, Moses' staff, and what their blossoming means within us–that along the way we open the vessel for reception of the upper light, and thus advance.

From *The Zohar*: And Korah Took

"Korah went by way of dispute, which is removing and repelling above and below. And one who wishes to repel the correction of the world is lost from all the worlds. A dispute is removing and repelling of the peace. And one who disagrees with peace disagrees with His Holy Name, since His Holy Name is called Peace."

Zohar for All, Korah, item 5

Shalom (peace) refers to *Shlemut* (wholeness), a state we achieve when the left and right lines complement one another. Our nature and the nature of the Creator equalize and reach connection and *Dvekut* (adhesion). This is the desirable outcome that yields peace, so we will never be opposite, detached, or distanced, but rather so connected that it will be impossible to tell us apart.

We must achieve *Dvekut* with Godliness, when He and we become one. As unrealistic as it may seem, it is our goal, and we must move toward it. The more we advance by ourselves, the more we will spare ourselves suffering.

Why is the spiritual path filled with so many doubts?

The reason we are constantly filled with questions and uncertainties is that we must grow and develop. When we encounter serious doubts, we might come to a state where we ask for the ground to "open up and swallow us whole." We may seem as if we are the operators, but it's actually the Creator who operates. We only observe the events happening before us, as though a movie is playing within us.

Gradually, we develop an inner vision that detects qualities such as Moses, Aaron, Korah, Dothan, Abiram, tribes, staff, and the earth within us. We sort out these elements in our qualities and see the situation as a picture within us. This illuminates how we advance while examining the network of connections between the elements.

Within that inner network of qualities–the 613 egoistic desires that aim to receive–we redirect our desires so they will work in order to bestow. This is called "observing the 613 *Mitzvot* (commandments)." The light that comes and corrects the intention to receive into an intention to bestow is called "performing a *Mitzva* (correction/good deed)."

As we perform the *Mitzvot*, we discover our inner world, and in that world we see how we connect to others. This is how we discover our souls and learn how to fulfill them. These are the scrutinies, struggles, and connections that we undergo, and the fulfillments we receive. It is how we discover the work of the Creator. This is the real work of God that we perform.

In this way, we come to a state where we understand the purpose of Creation, the correction of Creation, and how to carry it out. In the end, we come to a state where we understand everything. It is called "And they shall all know Me, from the least of them to the greatest of them." We obtain a complete *Kli* (vessel) that is called "a house," "For My house shall be called a house of prayer for all the peoples" (Isaiah

56:7). It is the house of all our desires; they are all there, and in all of them we actually feel Godliness in our entire soul.

TERMS:

President

A "president" is the quality that currently controls all the other qualities.

Counters' Envy

This is the desire to count how much we have gained, how much we receive, how much we give, and how much we advance in spirituality. We advance specifically through envy; it is good envy. Our envy of our environment prompts us to be more spiritual.

Korah

"Korah" is the will to receive that appears opposite (in contrast to) the quality of Moses. It is through this dispute that we advance.

Plague

A "plague" is a manner of correction. The correction detaches and sets our intentions to receive in order—it corrects them to be in order to bestow, either on the degree of *Bina*, or on the degree of *Keter*.

Fire from Heaven

"Fire" is *Gevurot* that appear on the left line, without *Hassadim*. There can be mitigated *Gevurot* and good *Gevurot*. It is a correcting force that comes from the left.

Holy

This is the degree of *Bina*, bestowal.

Atonement

The light that comes and gives us the strength to atone for our iniquities, to turn them from reception to bestowal. All our iniquities, our ego, everything that was in us, has now become bestowal.

Staff (rod)

The "staff" is the middle line by which one achieves the goal. If we properly connect to it all the qualities, all the discernments, it blossoms.

Blossoming

"Blossoming" is the middle line that shows us we are being filled with light.

What Is 'Peace, Peace, to Him That Is Far and to Him That Is Near,' in the Work?

"What is a dispute? It is removal and rejection above and below ... removal and rejection of the peace ... the peace of above—the middle line, which is called Torah, making peace between right and left—and of below, of Moses. ...A dispute is wherever there are two opposites ... A dispute is necessary ... because it is impossible to correct anything unless you know the fault. Therefore, when we know the dispute between the desires, we can make peace between them."

Rav Baruch Ashlag, *The Writings of Rabash*, vol. 2, p 1361

We must respect disputes but make them constructive, as it is written, "A contradiction of elders builds" (*Babylonian Talmud, Nedarim*, 40a), and by that we reach the goal.

Hukat

(The Statute)

(Numbers, 19:1-22:1)

Portion Summary

The portion, *Hukat* (The Statute), deals with Israel's continuing journey, with the *Mitzva* (commandment) of the red cow (heifer), the laws of impurity of the dead, and the episode known as *Mei Meriva* (waters of Meribah [Heb: quarrelling]). In this episode, the children of Israel complain about the lack of water and the Creator commands Moses to speak to the rock. However, instead of speaking, he strikes the rock. Moses and Aaron are punished for this act by being banned from entering the land of Israel. The people of Israel reach the land of Edom, and the king of Edom forbids them to pass through his territory.

Aaron dies, and Elazar, his son, succeeds him as the high priest. The people of Israel continue to complain about the difficulties along the way, and the Creator sends snakes to bite them. Moses makes a copper snake and shows it to his people, and anyone who sees the copper snake is healed.

The people of Israel reach the boundary of the land of Moab and sing "the song of the well." The people fight Sihon, King

of the Amorites, and Og, King of the Bashan. Israel wins and inherits their land.

Commentary

This story details the primary correction in the corrections of the souls. Because our souls are initially the desire to receive and to enjoy, in order to correct them, we must invert the intention of that desire toward bestowal. We must correct our souls to have the aim to bestow, to love others, by which we will resemble the Creator. This will endow *Dvekut* (adhesion) with the Creator, the purpose of Creation, for each and every one in the nation. This is why we need to mingle and become integrated with the force of bestowal, called *Bina*, and with the force of reception, called *Malchut*.

Connecting the two forces—the two *Sefirot* just mentioned—results in four options: *Malchut* in *Malchut*, *Malchut* in *Bina*, *Bina* in *Bina*, and *Bina* in *Malchut*. When *Bina* is inside *Malchut*, it is the evil force because *Malchut* governs *Bina*, and when that happens, all the evil forces emerge.

While these forces may occasionally appear as good, they appear so only to lure and entice us, leading us toward evil. It is a special *Klipa* (shell/peel), cunning and shrewd, which is in *Malchut*. This is how *Malchut* acquires *Bina* and uses it. This is also why it was said that evil can exist in the world only if it initially appears as good.

At first, the only forces that exist in Man are the still, vegetative, and animate, meaning *Malchut* at the degree of still, vegetative, and animate. This is a straightforward will to receive. Those who possess the power of *Bina* within the will to receive become very clever and very shrewd. Such people know how to appear as giving to others and serving them, while they are actually taking from others and using them as much as possible. This is how the negative forces operate when the force of bestowal is "taken captive" by the force of reception.

Conversely, when we raise *Malchut* to *Bina* and become included in it—when we want to permeate *Bina* and be there as servants, as an embryo inside its mother's womb–*Bina* is called "upper *Ima* (mother)." At that time, we want to develop only by integration, by being dominated by the power of bestowal under the "protection" of the power of the Creator. These are the good forces, which gradually take bits of the egoistic desire and correct them.

The portion, *Hukat*, begins with the red cow, which corrects some of the desires and corrupts others. It is that pendulum between *Bina* and *Malchut* that purifies the impure and defiles the pure. That topic is scrutinized all through the portion on different levels, such as the ashes of the cow, the well, and the pit.

The pit is dry, absorbing everything but remaining completely empty. On the other hand, a well is full of water. This compares to *Bina* in *Malchut* and *Malchut* in *Bina*. If the well is empty, it is *Malchut*. If there is water in the well, it is the right kind of integration. And when *Malchut* ascends to *Bina*, *Malchut's* deficiency rises to *Bina*, to heaven, and brings down water from heaven, which is the rain.

Afterward, the serpent is mentioned. The serpent isn't just the will to receive; it is a person in whom there is integration of *Bina*, opposite which there is the copper serpent.

In the story of the waters of quarrelling (Meribah), there is the rock, the ground. If we are integrated in *Malchut* and speak with it at the level of the desert (the level of *Bina*), we elicit water from it. Conversely, those who strike the rock elicit waters of quarrelling. This water is called "waters of *Gevurot*," which is dominated by *Malchut*. Hurricanes, floods, and tsunamis share the same root as the forces dominated by *Malchut*.

QUESTIONS AND ANSWERS

What is the meaning of the red cow?

The word, *Adumah* ("red," in feminine form) comes from the word, *Edom*, meaning connected to the *Adamah* (earth). The cow symbolizes the power of *Bina*, giving milk, which is one of the symbols of the festival of *Shavuot* on which we eat dairy products. It is a symbol of the power of giving.

However, when connected to *Malchut*, which is *Edom*, she has the powers of the mingling with *Malchut* opposite the power of *Bina*. When the force of bestowal and the force of reception–*Bina* and *Malchut*–are together, everything depends on the individual. If we wish to be corrected, to achieve bestowal, combining these forces in a combination known as "red cow" allows us to elicit the force of bestowal and become purified.

Conversely, if we are pure, the mingling of *Bina* and *Malchut* has the opposite effect. We need to understand that this opposite form is only our discovery that we are on a good degree. That is, we discover an additional desire with which we cannot work.

What is the meaning of the acts of purification?

These are rituals, a sort of idol-worship. It is not that simple to find a red cow, burn it, and then deal with its ashes. The red cow doesn't exist in our world, but we are still looking.

It is said that in the past, there was indeed a red cow at the time of the Temple, when the whole nation was on a spiritual degree using the wisdom of Kabbalah. It is written, "They checked from Dan to Beer Sheba and no ignoramus (uncorrected person) was found from Gevat to Antipris, and no boy or girl, man or woman was found who was not thoroughly versed in the laws of purity and impurity (corrections according to Moses' law)."*

That is, the laws of impurity and purity (*Tuma'a* and *Taharah*, respectively) explain precisely what it means to work in order to receive, and what it means to work in order to bestow, with all the desires, all the problems, and all the communications with everyone and with Godliness.

In the past, the majority of people achieved complete attainment except for a few, as we know from history about the quarrels that

* Babylonian Talmud, *Masechet Sanhedrin*, p 94b.

took place as far back as the time of the First Temple. Those who attained a spiritual degree knew the laws of impurity and purity; they were at the level of connection of *Bina* and *Malchut*, a level known as the "red cow (heifer)."

The Torah details an order of correction and instructions as to how to correct the soul. These people lived by it and corrected themselves from the state of "Egypt" to the state of "reception of the Torah," going through the "desert" and into the "land of Israel," names that represent spiritual degrees.

If Edom is *Bina*, why did the king of Edom not let Israel through?

The red cow is *Bina*. The land of Edom is the connection between *Bina* and *Malchut*, as it should be according to the degrees. The king of Edom is a desire that sits within us. Even though the people of Israel wish to go through the land of Edom, they must first enter through the *Klipa* (shell/peel) that is in Edom–the king of Edom. They must go through the mingling of *Malchut* and *Bina* on the degree of Edom. That *Klipa* does not let them through. The passage depends on correction–either they go around Edom, or they fight and go through it.

Is that a desire we simply cannot work with?

It is our own desire. The King of Edom resides within us.

Moses, the greatest of the prophets, leads the nation. He is man's most sublime quality, and it seems as if he is not doing what the Creator told him to do.

In fact, it is not that he disobeys the Creator. Rather, there is the nation, meaning individual desires, there is Moses, and there is a possibility to absorb "waters of *Bina*" by raising *Malchut* (the will to receive) to *Bina*. Given the state of the people at the time, Moses could not muster the strength to draw all of his desires, which are called "people" or "nation," to the level of *Bina*. Thus, instead of climbing a degree and speaking and acting there, he acts on the degree of performing actions. This was his transgression.

Why does it seem as though he was punished?

All the punishments in the Torah are corrections. Although it is clear that one must attain the level of speaking–a level of connection between *Malchut* and *Bina* that is simpler, shorter, and more correct–we cannot find another manner of correction, but perform it in actual fact. It is similar to Moses using his staff.

Is it like an experiment, where we are given the tools to carry out a task, yet we must fail?

Indeed we have to fail. Although it seems as though we are punished in our corrections, in truth, there are no punishments.

But when Moses wished to enter the land of Israel, he was refused.

Of course he was refused. The land of Israel is not the degree of Moses. Moses is "the faithful shepherd," whose highest degree is *Bina*. There must be an upgrade here, which must be performed by his followers, those who are not from the generation of the desert, such as Joshua.

From *The Zohar*: They Journeyed from Mountain to Mountain

"And Israel journeyed ... and they went after the slant-serpent that was ruling in the land of Edom."

Zohar for All, *New Zohar*, *Hukat* (The Statute), item 3

"Slant" means that it keeps twisting and walking ahead of a person, so it is impossible to discern what is good about it and what is bad.

They seemingly "detoured" the mountain. In truth, they could not climb the mountain because of the thoughts along the way, the doubts in the faith and in the attainment of mutual bestowal and unity. And because they were unable to attain, they "went around" that situation. On the one hand, it is not the right way. On the other hand, if they do not circumvent the mountain, they cannot go above it. For now, this is the way–by the hardening of the heart. The correction is always done on an egoistic desire that is very hard to cope with, but after which one obtains abundance.

From *The Zohar*: They Journeyed from Mountain to Mountain

"They complained about everything–about the oral Torah, the written Torah ... for there is no bread, oral Torah, and no water, written Torah, and the words of the oral Torah were trivial in their eyes."

Zohar for All, *New Zohar*, *Hukat* (The Statute), item 3

"Trivial" means that the oral Torah was not very important. This was the problem, since the oral Torah comes to us from above, from the degree of *Zeir Anpin*, while the written Torah is in *Malchut*. This creates a disconnect between *Zeir Anpin* and *Bina* for reception, to receive the quality of bestowal. Also, it is clear that they did not have the strength, and therefore went around Mount Horeb.

Concerning the serpents, we know the story of the serpent and Adam, and the story from *The Book of Zohar* about the snake that bites the doe and retreats. However, the portion before us presents another aspect: a copper serpent that heals anyone who sees it.

We cure the flaws in us, our egos, according to the way we connect to the serpent, by how we look at it and take from it the strength we want. It is the will to receive that we can extract for our *Kelim* (vessels), and the desire to bestow for our intentions, by which we are corrected.

Our advancement is according to our egos, through forms of serpents–a slant serpent or a copper serpent–that turn all those desires that currently hide within us and are initially cruel and cunning, in order to receive–from Adam's first serpent–into desires with the aim to bestow.

Now, as then, there is nothing worse than the snake, the venom, the destructive force. We must turn the power of the serpent into a healing force, just as in the symbol of medicine, because healing comes from the same place. It is all a question of approach: if we know how to use that force correctly, it is a healing force; if we do not know how to use it correctly, it is a potion of death.

Is the serpent a messenger of the Creator?

The serpent is our will to receive, which comes from the Creator. The Torah, which is called "the potion of life" and "the potion of death," also comes from the Creator. In our desires, intentions, in every thing and in every detail, there is good as well as bad, and we can use them for better or for worse.

It is written that everyone loved Aaron even more than they loved Moses. What is the quality of Aaron within us, and what does it mean that something dies?

Priests are on the degree of action; they are the power within us that actually performs the corrections. Moses is the only force that connects to the upper one, to the next degree, to Godliness, while Aaron prepares the actions and carries them out. This is why his whole work is the Temple.

What about his son, who was appointed after him? Is this work hereditary?

These are two degrees, just as in our world there is a custom that the son inherits everything from the father. It is likewise in kingship, and even in biology, in genes.

It seems as though the story repeats itself: there is a will to receive that needs correction, and needs to receive light and turn from reception to bestowal. Why, then, are there all these

subtle differences, as though each portion is a different story altogether?

Indeed, the only thing that was created is the will to receive. That desire is used egoistically, and the Torah depicts its process of correction. The will to receive contains 613 "sub-desires," all of which must be shifted from being used egoistically into being used altruistically—for the sake of others, for the love of others. This is called "observing 613 *Mitzvot* (commandments)." The whole Torah consists of instructions by which we can receive light in these corrected desires, a light called "Torah," or "the revelation of Godliness."

Therefore, these are not subtle differences, but consecutive degrees appearing one at a time in a manner of cause and consequence. At each stage, we correct all 613 desires from "In the beginning" to "In the eyes of all Israel," the final words in the Pentateuch. Only when we achieve it do we actually become Israel—*Yashar El* (straight to God).

TERMS

Place

A "place" is a desire. Each desire is a place in which something appears, whether good or bad.

Purity

This is the power of bestowal.

Impurity

This is the power of reception.

Death

"Death" is the inability to work in order to bestow.

Water

"Water" is a force that revives the will to receive and turns its intention from reception to bestowal.

A Rock

A "rock" is a will to receive that needs to be corrected so it can be used in order to bestow, meaning that one can use the water that comes out of it in the act of bestowal. There are two modes of action to perform an act of bestowal: 1) striking the rock, which are waters of Meribah (quarreling) or waters of *Gevurot*, 2) speaking, which are waters of *Hassadim* (mercy), waters of bestowal, the water of life.

A Boundary

A "boundary" is a place where one must stop one's act of bestowal for lack of strength to aim in order to bestow. It is a point where one must restrict oneself and refrain from using one's desire any further.

A Serpent

The egoistic will to receive that destroys a person and consumes him is the "serpent." The serpent exists at the core of the will to receive existing in every person.

Healing

"Healing" is a correction. If we use that same serpent correctly, in favor of people's lives, it becomes a good force. It is written, "I have created the evil inclination, I have created for it the Torah as a spice," because "the light in it reforms him," meaning reforms the serpent. That is, the evil inclination becomes a good inclination.

Inheritance

"Inheritance" is what we receive from a higher degree, from the father or the grandfather. In spirituality, too, there are degrees. We receive strength from a higher degree, a force that lets us ascend; it is called "inheritance."

This Is the Statute of the Law

"The creatures were created with a nature of being receivers ... Since it is impossible to go against Nature, He has given us the advice that through Torah and *Mitzvot* we will be able to turn the nature within us."* This is why the laws of the Torah are considered laws only when the evil inclination asks ... and then one needs to take upon himself everything as a statute, which is *Hassadim*, bestowal, where everything is only above reason, which is called "faith."

* Rav Baruch Ashlag, *The Writings of Rabash*, vol. 3, "This Is the Statute of the Law, no. 2" p 1825.

Balak

(Numbers, 22:2-25:9)

Portion Summary

The portion, Balak, begins with the people of Israel conquering the land of the Amorites. Balak, king of Moab, understands that the children of Israel are nearing him, and prepares to face the nation that came out of Egypt. He sends messengers to Balaam, son of Beor, who was famous for his great wisdom and the power of his curses–and asks him to curse the people of Israel.

Balaam leaves for the land of Moab, having accepted the harsh stipulation to say only what the Creator will permit. Along the way his mare stops. Balaam beats her, but the mare won't move. Balaam cannot see the angel stopping the mare. The mare opens her mouth and speaks to him, and instead of cursing Israel, Balaam blesses them.

Balak is furious with Balaam. As compensation, Balaam reveals that Israel has a weak spot: the daughters of Moab. Balak sends the daughters of Moab, and the people of Israel fornicate with them so much that even Zimri, son of Salu, one of the presidents of the tribe of Shimon, takes a Midianite woman.

This situation leaves Pinhas, son of Elazar, with no choice. He takes a spear and stabs Zimri and the woman to death, thus

stopping the plague that has spread in the nation claiming twenty-four-thousand lives.

COMMENTARY

This story does not happen on the corporeal level. It is not about a process unfolding between two nations, but rather an internal correction process that one experiences. The story itself shows us how to correct the evil inclination. It is not a tale about children or grownups, nor is it a story about nations, countries, wars, prostitutes, or mares. All it describes is the correction of the evil inclination. It is the only thing that the Torah (Pentateuch) describes from the very beginning, from Adam—who began the correction—to the end.

The text speaks of one who went through this path as *Adam HaRishon* (Adam), as Abraham, and as Moses, and who went through the whole process in Egypt and in the desert. During the gradual correction of the desire, one gradually nears the land of Israel until one is faced with the "conquest" of the land.

The "desert" is a desire that we still cannot use correctly, and therefore cannot see the fruits of our work with it. These corrections precede the ones known as the "land of Israel."

The spies discovered that the land of Israel was a desire that, if aimed entirely at the Creator, yielded beautiful fruit (Israel means *Yashar El* [straight to God]). Those who approach that correction initially acquire the land of the Amorites, then the land of Moab, which is a higher degree. Man's egoistic desire, known as "the king of Moab," Balak, begins to seemingly rebel against him because it did not want the corrections.

All our desires are initially evil inclinations, as it is written, "I have created the evil inclination." This is why the desire called Balak seeks out a way to resist. It is resistance to one who is trying to correct one desire at a time, degree by degree, until all the desires are *Yashar El*, straight to the Creator, aiming to bestow upon the Creator.

The desire called "Balak" cannot do anything by itself. A desire is just that–a desire–devoid of any strength. The power is found in the *intention* that directs the desire and works with it. The desire is called "Balak," and the intention is called "Balaam." The intention of working in bestowal in order to receive is called a "curse." In this manner, the evil inclination operates in its fullest form.

This is why Balak invites Balaam and tells him, "Come, let's work together." In the meantime, a conflict breaks out between the substance (mare) and the angel (human) who is walking straight to the Creator and aiming himself toward success. On the one hand, within Man is the next degree, Moab, the will to receive in Moab, which is Balak. On the other hand, a person intends to control the desire in order to receive, which is Balaam, who is awarded the real egoistic benefit from it.

The inner substance in that degree, the mare, cannot advance because it detects the resistance, the angel standing before it not letting the substance advance, which is help from above. However, the man cannot detect it because he is on the degree of Balak and Balaam. In other words, we cannot advance in the intention, but the evil inclination can no longer fail us with the intention because the previous degree, the Amorite, has been corrected, and there is no reason why we should fall now.

We are in a position in which we do not make mistakes in our intentions or desires. The people of Israel stood before the next degree, but could not advance further. On the one hand, they were blocked by Balaam and Balak. On the other hand, there was no other way to advance.

After his blessing, Balaam did not let Israel advance because the blessing had nothing on which to rely. The blessing must "ride" over the will to receive of the next degree in order for advancement to occur. "I have created the evil inclination; I have created for it the Torah as a spice," because "the light in it reforms him." This is how we advance with a bigger desire, a desire that is corrected in order to bestow, and we continue degree by degree.

This is why there is nothing we can do in the next degree. We advance by failing, but that failing is not because of our corrupted intention. Rather, it is because of the heightened will to receive on the left line.

This is why Balaam advises Balak to make the people fail by increasing the evil inclination, the "women" in them. The deficiencies begin with hardening the hearts of the children of Israel with a desire that is more egoistic, more centered toward oneself. This desire is called a "fornicating woman." A woman has two "directions": either righteous or a whore, meaning in order to bestow or in order to receive. This is why it is possible to make a person trip and fall because in truth, it is impossible to advance without falling.

The Torah tells us about the degrees we must all experience. All the actions and names in the Torah are holy. When we kiss a word in a book of Torah during a service, we pay no attention to the word we are kissing. It might very well be Balak or Balaam, yet we kiss it and make the blessing of the Torah.

The stages of the progress all aim toward our correction. However, there are steps along the way called Balaam, Balak, countries, Midianites, their wives, and we reach a state where we correct them.

When we kill the desires to receive with the intention to receive, we are actually killing the *intention*. Along with those desires, we should kill the connection between Israel and Midian, which is a degree of twenty-four thousand, twelve and twelve, corresponding to the tribes, in Direct Light and in Reflected Light. The "thousand" is the height of the high degree of twelve-twelve on the level of *Zeir Anpin*. When rising to the high degree of *Arich Anpin*, it is called "one thousand."

QUESTIONS AND ANSWERS

What is the difference between a blessing and a curse?

A "blessing" is an act that a person can do, an act that aims to bestow. A "curse," however, is an act in order to receive. We should note that an act in order to receive is necessary because without it, we would never discover the evil inclination. On each degree, there is a process of disclosing the evil and correcting it through the Torah. This is how we are reformed, and rise to the next degree, as it is written, "I have created the evil inclination, I have created for it the Torah as a spice."

Once on the degree, the left-right-middle "ritual" repeats itself, meaning a curse from which one is corrected and ascends. Correction is impossible without curses, without the evil inclination. Without Hell, it is impossible to rise to the degree of Heaven.

Who is Pinhas, Son of Elazar the Priest—the power or the light?

Pinhas, son of Elazar, is the highest degree that appears. The light is what makes the correction using the *Kli* (vessel). Everything happens in the *Kelim* (plural of *Kli*). Even when we speak of "lights," we actually refer to an impression of the *Kelim*, an impression we call "light."

Similarly, we cannot sense the electricity that runs through a lamp, but we experience its manifestation. In other words, we can only sense manifestations, not the forces themselves. The forces must "express themselves" through a substance.

In our case, Pinhas, son of Elazar, was from the priests from whom we have all the corrections.

Can a person curse another person, cast an evil eye on another?

If we are talking about our world, regardless of this Torah portion, then, of course. All our desires have an impact, even the smallest ones. People are connected; our thoughts are connected. We are living in a global and integrally connected network.

We can prove for a fact that there are instances when people think of something on one end of the world, and people on the other end of it think of the same thing at the same time. It was said that this concept was also proven in monkeys. The book, *The Hundredth Monkey*, reports a study of macaque monkeys on an island near Japan in 1952. The scientists observed that some of the monkeys learned to wash sweet potatoes, a behavior that spread through the pack. Once it spread among a critical number of monkeys—the so-called hundredth monkey—this behavior instantly spread to monkeys on nearby islands.

From *The Zohar*: Fear Not, My Servant Jacob

"That wicked one, Balak, was wise in all the degrees of above, in those who tie ties by which to perform witchcraft and magic, in all those degrees above them by which they would force the lower degrees. ...Balak and Balaam said to him, 'All through that time, we witches, magicians, and soothsayers have certain degrees and certain angels that are known to witches and magicians. But henceforth, you should look elsewhere, higher.'"

Zohar for All, *New Zohar*, Balak, items 60-61

A person knows only about one's own degree, which is the degree of Balak. Here Balak rules over the piece called "Moab." The will to receive in order to receive that operates in a person from one degree to the next, with the aim to receive, is called "Moab."

Does a person know of the limitation, that there is another, higher place?

Yes, this is why we need to draw a bigger force and not let the correction happen.

Will we be able to see Moab as we advance in our studies and scrutinize within?

Even without reading the weekly Torah portion, we would discover the Torah within us. This is also how Kabbalists discovered and wrote—by sensing it within. The Torah comes out of the will to receive that is gradually corrected.

When a person discovers the portion Balak within, does one also discover a speaking mare?

He or she will speak just as it is written in the Torah, and at the same time know the details in their true sense.

What does it mean that a mare speaks in a person?

It is the will to receive. The mare is the female of the donkey. That is, out of *Malchut's* ten *Sefirot*, nine are the donkey and the tenth is the mare.

Is it specifically the will to receive that senses the angel?

Yes.

Is the will to receive unable to see? Is it blind?

It is specifically the will to receive that will perform the act, that will sense—either in order to receive or in order to bestow. It is there that all the operations of the forces take place. This is why all the forces of correction or corruption aim toward it.

Is this why it is said that the Messiah will come riding a white donkey?

A "white donkey" means that a person needs to make the donkey white. Only then will one feel it.

What does the whitening mean?

It means that a person completely "whitens" the substance, making it entirely in order to bestow, which is called "white."

There is a strange process happening here. Balaam is the will to receive in order to receive, or even the will to bestow in order to receive. Balaam undergoes a process: in the beginning, he wants to curse, but then he swears that he will act only by the command of the Creator, and finally he blesses. Balaam acts with the intention to bestow.

Was he corrected?

No, he cannot do it on the next degree. In fact, Balaam performs no actions here; nor does Balak, or the Creator. Only Israel acts. That is, if we want to rise to the next degree, the blessing is before us and we can advance, except we do not have the strength.

We need to discover that we cannot advance using Balaam, Balak, the Creator, the mare, or any other factor until we stand bewildered, not knowing how to advance to the next degree, or how to acquire this desire called "Moab." The children of Israel must conquer Moab, something needs to appear, and it appears only by connecting to the women of Moab.

We need to take the females from there, the deficiencies of that degree. When taking those deficiencies, there is plenty of substance to move ahead. Once we connect to all of the substance, a correction appears that is known as "the killing of the intention to receive." We correct the will to receive into aiming to bestow. This act is called "the conquering of Moab."

There is a sexual element here. On the one hand, the sexual desire is very natural, but on the other hand, it seems to be a bad example because they took Midianite women.

We are not dealing with morals here, or with ethics. In our world, sexuality is animalistic, meaning it exists in animals.

But in this portion, sexuality is presented as an obstruction, with the president bringing a Midianite woman into the tent.

True, it appears negative. However, all the measures discussed here are necessary steps along the way. We cannot succeed without them. It is written, "There is not a righteous man on earth who does good and does not sin." That is, we *must* go through the sin; we have no choice, even if we do not want it.

The order of degrees is such that a person falls and then rises. But the fall is not of one's own volition, though it is how one builds the ascent.

Therefore, Israel did not seek to mingle with the Midianites; they simply had no choice because one must mingle with all the females of the next degree. To "mingle" means to be at the degree of the female, *Malchut* of the next degree, the fornicating woman, entirely immersed in her intention to receive, and subsequently correct it.

When rising from one degree to the next, we need to seemingly despair, then ask for help. Clearly, there is a force that opens it before us and helps, but we forget it from one degree to the next.

Why do we forget it? Why does it seem to become more difficult? After all, if we got the idea once, it should have been easier. The thing is that we got it in the previous sin that we corrected. In the current sin, we perceive nothing. Everything we had is in the past, and it is as though we have forgotten everything because we are rising from below upward. It is not that we really forgot, but the old ways simply do not work on the new degree.

In the correction of "killing the Midianite," the president of the tribe of Shimon is killed, as well. Why is this so? After all, he was part of Israel and was supposed to be corrected?

He belongs to the previous degree.

So he could not cope with the new degree?

He could not cope with it because he connected to her, and they are both in the intention to receive. Both need to correct. It is not only the evil inclination that is corrected; it is also the force that comes down to the evil inclination and connects with it. They both rise together.

One who descends, descends entirely into the intention to receive, down to the *Klipa* (shell/peel) with all the previous success. Afterward, the light takes effect and saves them both. This is considered that along the way it "kills" them because they are aiming to receive.

Terms

King

The force that governs a degree is a "king."

Messengers

The forces by which actions are performed on a certain degree, a certain state of a person. A person's state is called a "degree." The one who governs each degree is called the "king of the degree," which is usually the *Sefira* (singular of *Sefirot*) we call *Keter* (crown). The messengers are forces acting within that degree. By and large, it is the eight *Sefirot* from *Hochma* to *Yesod.*

Curse

The egoistic force that works in order to receive, which governs us, and for whom it acts as a curse.

Mare

The mare is our substance, the donkey's female. It is the actual will to receive that feels and distinguishes between the forces within us.

Angel

An angel is the force that acts in a degree and is directed by the ruler, the *Keter*, the king.

Blocked Road

It is the way by which one is going to correct one's will to receive, with the intention to reach the next degree, greater *Dvekut* (adhesion), greater clarity of vision in spirituality, but which he cannot reach. That is, in this manner, it is impossible to advance. One finds that to reach the next degree, a new substance is needed..

Deviating from the Way

"Deviation" happens when we advance on the path toward bestowal when suddenly something goes awry and we discover we have strayed from the path. However, this discovery is already a correction in itself.

How is the discovery of the deviation a correction?

By discovering the deviation, we know how to continue. Our effort toward the goal is like a guided missile. The missile must constantly detect its deviations and correct them. If it moves in a straight line, it cannot hit its target. It is the same for us: we cannot move in one straight line toward our goal. Rather, we must constantly examine our deviations, as only through them do we advance toward the goal.

Oath

An "oath" is when the will to receive, *Malchut*, connects to *Keter* on a single axis and is ready to follow *Keter's* will above reason.

From *The Zohar*: The Creator Plays with the Righteous in the Garden of Eden

"Once the Creator smelled and played with them, and with all their secrets of wisdom, He appears before them and they see that pleasantness of the Creator. Then they all rejoice in great joy until their brightness and light spread. From that spreading, their brightness and light of their joy bear fruit and buds in the world, which are the souls, and those fruits come under the wings of Divinity until the proper time."

Zohar for All, *New Zohar*, Balak, item 6

We are the broken souls in the worlds of *Beria*, *Yetzira*, and *Assiya* in this world. We must rise to the state of *Malchut* of *Atzilut*, to that Divinity—that correction—by connecting our souls in unity, in mutual guarantee. Along the way, we will conquer the Sinai Desert and the Land of Israel.

Pinhas

(Numbers, 25:10-30:1)

Portion Summary

In the beginning of the portion, the Creator thanks Pinhas for stopping the plague and gives him a "covenant of peace" and a "covenant of an everlasting priesthood" to him and to his descendants. All the while, the children of Israel are preparing to fight the Midianites.

Following the instructions of the Creator, Moses divides the land into lots, following censuses held in the people by tribes and by families. At the conclusion of the censuses, the daughters of Zelophehad, from the tribe of Menashe, complain to Moses that their father died, and as women they did not receive their lot. Moses looks into the matter and the Creator rules that to do justice, the daughters of Zelophehad will be given a lot in the land, which will be named after their father.

The Creator commands Moses to climb up the Mountain of Avarim to see the land of Israel, which Moses will not enter, and to appoint Joshua, son of Nun, as his successor.

At the end of the portion, there is a detailed description of the offerings that needed to be sacrificed each day and on different occasions during the year.

Commentary

According to *The Book of Zohar*, the portion, Pinhas, is profound and evokes many questions. The story tells of people such as Pinhas, who are seemingly greater than Moses. The Creator blesses and praises him, saying that he is as great as Joshua, that he is replacing Moses, who is climbing down from center stage. There is also the issue of women's rights, some of whom can be as the men, receiving a lot.

As we know, the Torah does not speak of corporeal events or physical bodies, but of souls. The souls are what is important, the eternal part in each of us. This is why we need to understand that the text describes the "human *within* us," which must experience all the portions of the Torah along our spiritual development.

This portion speaks of a very special point that awakens in us, a special desire called "Pinhas." Only this point, this desire, achieves the "covenant of peace"–peace and wholeness with the Creator. The desire known as "Pinhas" unites in *Dvekut* (adhesion) with the Creator, in a covenant of complete and eternal connection that lasts forever and does not wane. This is the first of the stages of correction and connection that the soul goes through. In that correction, it becomes attached to the highest degree in its correction and development.

The second stage comes after all the successes of the children of Israel. Now, all the forces within us are called "Israel," *Yashar El* (straight to God), having received the previous corrections. We begin with an egoistic will to receive that has come out of Egypt in its entirety. In that stage, we have hardly escaped our egos and want to avoid using those qualities. In that stage we have nothing. It is as though we are standing in the desert with nothing to eat.

"Eating" is an attainment of spirituality that fills the soul until it is completely satiated with Godliness, with the revelation of the Creator. "Return, oh Israel, unto the Lord your God," consciously, with understanding, fulfillment, and a sensation of the attainment of the Creator. These are the stages of the correction of the soul, from the entrance to the desert through the wars, and up to that point, Midian.

Once we have a grip on a high degree, a part of the common soul, then we are all part of a single soul, "as one man with one heart." We are all in mutual guarantee, in that covenant that we agreed on for the first time when we received the Torah.

The children of Israel constantly strengthen the covenant. Each day, we pass through the "desert" in our empty lives, not knowing what to do, immersed in struggles and corrections. Each transgression and mistake that the children of Israel make is because the evil inclination is surfacing. However, it is a descent in order to ascend.

We discover that we are broken and cannot bestow, so we cry out and demand the light that reforms. The light, meaning the Creator, comes and corrects, and guides us how to act against the will to receive. It is called "punishing the ego," so the Man in us ascends.

This is the process we go through. It is a stage of deep egoistic discernments in us that we can correct. These discernments are called "Midian."

This is how Moses—who emerged from Pharaoh's house—grows. His wife comes from the house of Midian because Jethro was the priest of Midian.

Moses nurtures Pinhas, who is actually Moses on a higher degree, and in this progression it is a complementation of the degree.

On that stage, all the forces, all the elements within us are ready to wage war on Midian. A "war" is a reawakening of all the corrupted desires in us that seemed to have calmed down, but which have yet to be corrected. We must reawaken them and mend them. It is a time to calculate, to find the number of Israel, who is on the camp, who is outside the camp, and it is a time for counting the heads of the tribes.

Calculating means reaching a degree in which the light of *Hochma* (wisdom) dresses in light of *Hassadim* (mercy). Seeing a calculation (accounting) is the light of vision, the light of *Hochma*. On that degree, we can already count what is in it and what is not. It is not a degree of *VAK*, the degree of the desert. Rather, it is already the *GAR* of the degree.

On a complete degree, there is light of *Hassadim* and light of *Hochma*. We use our desires both in bestowal and in the intention to receive in order to bestow. These are acts of *Gadlut* (adulthood) of the degree, with which we correct our souls on a very high level.

This is a profound correction of part of the will to receive, of the deficiency in our souls. This is why women come and say, "We need the correction and we cannot receive it. How do we do it?" It is the point of deficiency in a man, the profound will to receive that is corrected into working in order to bestow. This is also the reason for Moses' reply to the daughters of Zelophehad.

For this reason, when the biggest desires appear, the desires called "a woman's desires," it is possible to correct them, as with those of a man. With the men, it is an intention to bestow in order to bestow, while with the women, it is an intention to receive in order to bestow—bigger desires and deeper corrections.

The portion, Pinhas, narrates a stage in the advancement toward the end of correction. The portion details very deep corrections in the soul in the corrected part of the soul. Our souls are the entire desire that the Creator created. They appear as broken in us, as our egos that must be corrected.

We should be happy when a piece of ego appears because it is written, "I have created the evil inclination," which is the appearance, "I have created for it the Torah as a spice," because "the light in it reforms." That is, after the revelation of the evil inclination in us, once we have learned that we have no idea how to work with it, we discover the spice of Torah. Through the Torah we can correct the evil inclination.

The spice is the hidden light that is called *Zohar* (brightness), or *Ziharah Ilaa* (Aramaic: upper brightness). This is the light that corrects and reforms, and this is the process we must undergo.

Afterward, the portion speaks of Moses climbing Mount Avarim and watching the land of Israel from there. This is the conclusion of the degree of Moses, who is the "faithful shepherd," entirely adhered to *Bina*, bestowal, the aim to bestow in order to bestow. That state does not allow him to enter the will to receive called "the land of Israel," in which the correction is to work in order to bestow.

The Hebrew word, *Eretz* (land), comes from the word, *Ratzon* (desire). The word, *Ysrael* (Israel), comes from the words, *Yashar El* (straight to God), meaning straight toward bestowal. This is why that stage was given to Joshua, and not to Moses.

The Creator said to Moses that his place was given to Joshua, that Joshua is the one who will enter the land of Israel, while Moses will stay outside, on Moses' degree. The next degree is the next stage, which Joshua, son of Nun, must correct. Joshua is an extension of Moses' degree, just as Pinhas is an extension of the same soul.

The quality called "Moses" in each of us develops into the quality called Pinhas, then advances to the next quality, Joshua. Moses, the observer, brings the light of *Hochma*, the light of seeing. He brings that degree to all of Israel. However, the one who carries out this action is the corrected part in the soul—Joshua, son of Nun.

The portion also speaks of the offerings (sacrifices). When we discover that our nature is bad, we want to rid ourselves of it and escape it. We are willing to sacrifice, burn, kill, slaughter, and do anything to rid ourselves of the evil inside. In sacrificing, we do not slaughter something outside of us, only the beast *within*. We slaughter the vegetative and even the still (inanimate) within, using water and salt, as it is written, "On all your offerings you shall offer salt" (Leviticus, 2:13).

We "process" the desires below the human degree—on the degrees of still, vegetative, and animate—through the human degree within us. We turn desires that were with the aim to receive, egoistic desires with the evil inclination, into those that will work with the aim to bestow. We "sacrifice" them. In Hebrew, *Makriv* means both "sacrificing" and "bringing closer." Thus, we bring the desires closer to correction, and through it we draw closer to the Creator and become like Him.

This is called the "work of the sacrifices," "holy work," "work of the priests," the "Levites" that exist within us. Israel is the part that brings the offerings. The part of Israel within us brings the part in the desires on the levels of still, vegetative, and animate to the Levites and the priests. In this way, we take all the desires within and raise them to correction through the work of the sacrifices.

From *The Zohar*: Keeping the Covenant

"It is written in Pinhas, 'I give to him My covenant of peace,' meaning peace from the angel of death, who never controls him and in whose judgments he is not judged. Should you say that he did not die, he died but he certainly did not die as do the rest of the people. He lived longer than all his contemporaries because he clung to that upper covenant. When he passed away from the world, in sublime passion and in comely *Dvekut* (adhesion), he departed from the rest of the people in the world."

Zohar for All, Pinhas, item 22

Each time we correct our corrupted desires and add them to the structure of the soul within us. The corrupted desires are called "desires that comprise the soul, the "*Kli* (vessel) of the soul," the "body of the soul." The desires are corrected to work in order to bestow for the sake of others, and from the love of others to the love of the Creator.

The soul has a body: it is the desires outside us that work for the sake of others. These are desires that act out of the evil inclination in favor of ourselves, but receive the form of the good inclination, working in order to bestow and in love, as it is written, "Love your neighbor as yourself," this is the great rule of the Torah. To the extent that we act within those desires, performing acts of bestowal and true giving, we feel the "clothing of the Creator," the "clothing of the upper light."

This is why it was said that Pinhas did not die like others. Rather, it is a stage within us that only grows. It is that corrected degree of attainment of Godliness within the corrected *Kli* with the light that fills it.

QUESTIONS AND ANSWERS

Can spirituality be passed on by inheritance?

There is an unbreakable law here: it is all one man. There aren't many people in the world; there is only one. In other words, the Torah is written for a single person who includes the entire world within. It is written that "Man is a small world" (*Midrash Tanchuma, Pekudei*, item 3). Everything is included within us; we perceive the whole of the outer reality within us.

We have no idea whether anything exists outside of us. All we know is that we feel it within. For example, when we touch something, we cannot tell whether we are actually touching it, but we *can* feel it as solid, liquid, warm, or cold.

We *feel* that it exists and that we are touching it. But in the end, all we feel is ourselves. We see ourselves existing in some reality, but that reality is depicted within us, in the back of our minds. The people and the objects around us are not really there; they are within us.

The reality we perceive is divided into still, vegetative, animate, and human. We are the ones who sense all of them in this way because this is how our will to receive is built. It is divided into four stages—1, 2, 3, and 4—where it perceives sensations and impressions.

As far as the history of the Jews is concerned, it is as though the Torah is describing a play, but these are all things that happen within us. If we want to read the Torah as it truly is, we should ascribe everything that is written there to ourselves. We should read every word in the Torah as an explanation of what exists within us: Pinhas, Joshua, Midian, a Priest, a Levite, Israel, the tribes, and everything else.

A priest, for example, is a degree of a person. It arrives when the will to receive is entirely corrected into working in order to bestow. This is why priests have no lots.

When the degree of Moses ends and the degree of Pinhas begins, Moses climbs Mount Avarim and looks at the land of Israel. This is a certain degree called "seeing." Through it, he makes a correction for the entire nation. What is the correction of seeing?

Moses performs a great correction. There is a correction in potential, and there is a correction in actuality, *de facto*. A "correction in potential" is when there are still no *Kelim* (vessels) that are large enough to fit the correction. Moses is a degree in which one does not work with vessels of reception with the intention to bestow. This is why he did not enter the land of Israel—the desire that must be turned into *Yashar El* (straight to God), Israel.

His following degree, Joshua, son of Nun, will do it, as it is a more practical degree. Joshua is an extension, a degree that is annulled before the degree of Moses. This is why Joshua was Moses' assistant, always supporting and always by his side, and he was chosen to succeed him.

The relationship between them was such that Joshua would set up the benches at Moses' seminary. However, Moses, too, made great spiritual corrections. He belonged to the degree of *Bina*. But because *Bina* is detached from *Malchut*, Joshua was the one who implemented the corrections.

Terms

Covenant

A "covenant" is the connection between the Creator and the creature. When people oppose one another, they are considered distant. The more alike they are, the closer they become. When they are similar in only one way, it is as though two circles begin to overlap. If they are completely equal, they are in a covenant, in unity. A covenant is unity. It is a match between the qualities of the creature and the qualities of the Creator. Achieving such a state makes one similar to the Creator, and then that person is called Adam (man) from the word, *Domeh* (similar).

Everlasting Covenant

An "everlasting covenant" is the one that the Creator had with Pinhas. It is a degree in which the quality that a person has acquired never disappears and never becomes corrupted.

Lot

A "lot" is the will to receive that has been corrected into working in order to bestow on a degree that neither disappears nor needs to be reacquired.

Family, the Family of Zelophehad, the Family of the Gershonites

The creature is only a single desire that was created, called "one soul." That soul is divided into many interconnected parts, like cells in our bodies. Some cells are similar, close, helping and supporting one another, existing in wholeness and working in mutuality, in a special connection. These are called "family."

These "cells" are parts of one soul that work among themselves in a special mutual way that is at the same time independent, like our children. We come from different areas and no one chooses anything, but things happen according to the hierarchy by which we hang down through the worlds from above downward.

Changing

This is the next degree. Today we can be one way and tomorrow we are different. It is as though we change ourselves.

Leader

Each degree comprises ten *Sefirot*. *Keter* is the leader, the one who illuminates to all the degrees through *Malchut*, where the execution actually occurs. *Keter* has heads of tribes, hundreds, thousands, and so on, and in the end, the execution is in the people.

Matot

(Tribes)

(Numbers, 30:2-32:42)

Portion Summary

In this portion, Moses alerts the heads of the tribes about the commandments connected to the making and untying of vows. The portion also speaks of Pinhas, who leads Israel into a war with Midian and emerges triumphant. Following the war, the text details the division of the spoils (some of which are dedicated to the Creator), as well as the commandments to make the *Kelim* Kosher by dipping and immersing them in boiling water.

At the end of the portion, the tribes of Gad and Reuben ask to stay on the Eastern bank of the Jordan River because of its good soil for their voluminous cattle herds. They infuriate Moses because he thinks they are seeking to avoid the war for the conquest of the land. In the end, they commit to participating in the war, and Moses grants their wish for a lot outside the land of Israel.

Commentary

Kabbalists attain the forces and discernments of the spiritual world. These are the forces that operate and manage our world, including the still, vegetative, animate, and human, each of which has a force that runs it. This is why it is impossible to ask anything of people who are not Kabbalists, as they have no free choice, as it is written, "They are all as beasts (animals)." When we read a story in the Torah that seems to be happening in this world, we need to understand that its roots are in the spiritual world, in the network of forces that governs the world.

Today, we already feel and understand that we are approaching the network of the forces of the integral nature. They close in on us and compel us to behave accordingly. This is the appearance of Godliness, which is gradually nearing us.

We see that we can no longer manage the world, as each day we are feeling more and more clearly that nothing in the world depends on us. We are losing our ability to manage the world because we can no longer act in life using our egos.

Kabbalists discovered the upper network and told us how it manifests on the upper level. They did so using words and stories of this world, our world, because everything that exists in the upper one descends to the lower one.

During the forty years in the desert, and even before, Moses wrote his five books, the Pentateuch. Through his attainment, Moses wrote part of the Pentateuch about the times preceding his own. He wrote it in the language of the branches, in the connections between upper and lower. Moses wrote about everything that takes place in the upper world and how the forces are managed. He spoke of them as results, as "marionettes" that move about our world and change.

This is why it is pointless trying to deal with this world; it is utterly governed and there is nothing in it of its own. To know everything, we need to rise to the upper degree, the place where decisions are made, where forces operate and influence our world.

We cannot change anything in this world, and we are well aware of it. Yet, there is one way by which we can change. If that happens, we can be in bestowal and love according to our nearing to the forces in our nature. In this way, we can change our fate here in this world.

In fact, only by changing ourselves can we achieve "I have created the evil inclination, I have created for it the Torah as a spice," because "The light in it reforms them." Only through the light that we draw from the study of the wisdom of Kabbalah can we change ourselves and rise to the upper degree. From that upper degree, we can influence the decisions and the mechanisms that operate our world. This is why Moses turned to the heads of the tribes and explained to them about untying the vows, going against Midian, and more.

We need to imagine Man as a small world, and everything that happens in the world as happening within. Indeed, within us are Moses and the entire structure called "the people of Israel," with its priests, Levites, and Israel being the three lines that comprise our souls. There are also the nations of the world within us, the Midianites, Pharaoh, and everything else that the Torah narrates.

When we discover ourselves and detect within us all those forces and qualities, we recognize the Torah as an instruction. Accordingly, we act to change, and adapt ourselves from being in this world to rising to a higher, spiritual human, aware of the spiritual world at the spiritual degree known as *Matot* (tribes).

This is a very high degree, working out of *Hesed*, the highest *Sefira* (singular of *Sefirot*) of the structure of the soul. Out of the ten *Sefirot*, *Keter*, *Hochma*, and *Bina* are the top *Sefirot*. They are above our attainment and are the ones that manage us. We approach them through our inner qualities, through arranging them properly as *Hesed*, *Gevura*, *Tifferet*, *Netzah*, *Hod*, *Yesod*, and *Malchut*, which are the seven remaining *Sefirot*.

We correct these seven *Sefirot* repeatedly on each degree, and they are called "the seven days of the week." *Hesed*, *Gevura*, *Tifferet*, *Netzah*, *Hod*, and *Yesod* correspond to the weekdays, and *Malchut* corresponds to the Sabbath. By correcting them, we go through the weeks in a circle that eventually brings us to *Keter*, *Hochma* and *Bina*, the top three *Sefirot*, meaning to the end of correction.

Each week in the year has its Torah portion or portions. These are degrees by which we gradually elevate ourselves to the top degree by opening up to our interior. As we do that, we find the forces within us and act alongside them.

The quality of Moses in us turns to the heads of the tribes in us, according to the division of the soul into twelve tribes. These were the tribes he arranged correctly while working with the growing ego, from a state called "reception of the Torah" to a state called "entrance to the land of Israel." The process we undergo between the states is called "the forty years in the desert." The desert represents our need to sort out the desires within us and correct them from reception for ourselves into the altruistic form of bestowal, to the right approach toward others, which can be summed up in the maxim, "That which you hate, do not do to your friend." On the degree of "tribes," we scrutinize our qualities and learn how to work with the will to receive.

At first, we can scrutinize the vows. "Vows" are states and conditions by which we attain a higher degree. The vows indicate the limitations we can take upon ourselves without failing. However, when we cannot persist with them, we can rid ourselves of them, much like the untying of vows before *Yom Kippur* (Day of Atonement).

There are fundamental laws in spirituality that concern Man and the scrutiny that takes place within, such as to what extent we can ask for correction for ourselves and work with the force that corrects. Following these preparations, we become aware of our ability to work with our egos on the level of Midian. Thus, we work with the force known as Pinhas, which is the next stage of the force of Moses.

This is when we can truly go to war. We go against our egos in order to conquer them and work with part of it in order to bestow. We ascend to a spiritual degree by correcting the evil inclination into a good inclination. There is no other substance but our own will to receive.

First, it comes with only the intention to receive. At that point, it is called "the evil inclination" because it prevents itself from participating with others. When it turns into the good inclination, it connects to everyone. This means that we have succeeded in the war and have conquered the ego.

Once we have done so, we give spoils to the tribes, the priest, the Levite, Israel, the women, and the children. We give spoils from everything we can take from the still, vegetative, animate, and the speaking (human) degrees. The Torah details what we must do with the masculine part, which is the right side of the *Klipa* (shell/peel), and what we need to do with the feminine part, the left side of the *Klipa*.

Questions and Answers

On *Yom Kippur*, there is a custom to untie vows. Why, then, is there a need for vows in the first place?

We cannot grow without a vow. When approaching a higher degree, we have to annul ourselves before the upper one because we have not yet reached that degree and therefore cannot accurately evaluate it. As we study, we constantly correct and "upgrade" ourselves."

There are also complementary actions, such as the Second Passover, where if we did not prepare ourselves for the correction known as "Passover," where we "pass over" the ego, we can arrive at it a month later.

This sounds like a negotiation. We make vows so we can complete the work later, so if we do something, we will receive so and so.

No, there is no such thing. This is not how spirituality works. We do everything honestly until we discover that it is impossible to keep moving forward, or that the conditions have changed. We are in a system of interconnected souls that supports us when we fall. We learn about our being in an integral system from Moses, who did nothing wrong except for striking the rock, yet the whole nation suffered because of it.

There was only one Moses, but we are just beginners.

There is nothing we can say about this world. Here, we are nothing more than outcomes of the spiritual world. If we can influence the spiritual world through the study of Kabbalah, we will change this world, as well. If we do not, we will change nothing.

In fact, we can impact the spiritual world just by *aspiring* to ascend to spirituality, and this will impact this world favorably. If we have no ability or desire to change our spiritual situation, even if we can, our world will still advance, but it will advance on a path of suffering.

How can we change our world if it is only a world of results and we are being operated on without any free choice?

As soon as we begin to ascend toward the spiritual world, we begin to change this world. Nothing in this world changes it except the forces that influence it from above. Therefore, our only choice in this world is to rise above it.

Is this done by connecting and uniting with others?

Yes, through unity with others.

Will we improve our financial situation, too, by studying Kabbalah?

Everything will change. All the outcomes in this world depend only on the connections between us. There is nothing truly worth doing but securing our sustenance, and dedicating the rest of the time to spiritual ascension. This, in turn, will change everything.

Is the correction personal, or does it affect everyone?

The correction is both personal and general, but today it is primarily general.

Why is it so hard to understand it, even though it sounds so simple?

We are built according to our individualistic egos. We view the world egoistically. And precisely because of this, today's systems of economy and education are becoming dysfunctional. We cannot succeed anymore because everything is broken and scattered. Throughout history, we have become used to advancing by using our egos and trying to profit and benefit ourselves the most. But today, these egotistical, linear systems have stopped functioning. We are moving into systems that are round, integral, connected.

Is the reciprocal impact sensed immediately?

Yes, people will feel more important, more successful, and even stronger than the government. Governments act egoistically, like a linear arrow. Conversely, the connections between people are circular. Today, we are in a global mechanism, in a nature that is integral and global. As a result, we cannot continue to advance egoistically or linearly, as before. Now we *have* to learn how to ascend, how to increase the aim to connect "as one man with one heart," because only through unity can we change the way things are.

From *The Zohar*: *Matot* (Tribes)

"'And you who cleave unto the Lord your God are alive every one of you this day.' What is the reason? It is because the soul of Israel comes from the spirit of the living God. 'For the spirit before Me will enwrap.' 'Before Me,' meaning before Divinity, from ZA, the living God."

Zohar for All, *Matot* (Tribes), item 5

What is the spoil?

The "spoil" is a result of man's work with the evil inclination. In this war, we turn the evil inclination into a good inclination, using the light that reforms. As a result, we receive light through that inclination. The light that fills us—the attainment, that sublime sensation—is a great possession. This is the spoil.

The division of the spoil refers to how one divides the light among all of one's parts, all of one's desires and qualities. It denotes how one operates that division mechanism, who receives more, and who receives less.

This portion seems to discuss the root of the conduct of making utensils kosher.

The root of the matter is in our *Kelim* (vessels), the will to receive. This is where we receive the light. The light may appear in our desires on the condition that they are not working only in order to receive, but also in order to bestow so they can be shared with others. When we connect ourselves to others in this way, the light appears in us. It follows that all our corrections are really qualifications of our *Kelim*, making them kosher.

Put differently, we need to qualify our will to receive so it aims to bestow, so it is connected to others. The water, which represents *Hesed*, qualifies the *Kelim*. If we need to correct a metal *Kli* (singular of *Kelim*), meaning make it kosher, it requires a deeper correction. It has to be passed through fire, representing *Gevura*. A metal *Kli* represents a desire that was used egoistically, which must be corrected and cleaned more powerfully through "whitening" (heating to the point where the metal becomes white), *Mikveh Kelim* (a tub used for ritual immersion of utensils), and *Hagaalah* (dipping in boiling water).

Correcting our *Kelim* is all that we have in the wisdom of Kabbalah. The correction of the *Kelim* takes place once we have acquired them and have shifted them from the aim to receive to the aim to bestow, having conquered our desires. This is not only about correcting *Kelim* in the sense of utensils, or dishes, but about correcting the *Kelim* when we make offerings.

The offering is a *Kli* on the animate level. We "kill" our will to receive, meaning the manner in which the will to receive was used before, egoistically. We bring it as an offering (*Korban*), from the word *Hitkarvut* (nearing), toward bestowal, in favor of others. Only then can we bestow love upon others, using that same will to receive that now becomes holy.

This is not the only Torah portion where there are wars and struggles.

We are always at war, always struggling, until we reach the end of correction.

If we have already attained a certain degree and enjoy the light in it, why should we relinquish it?

Because we would want to pass it on to others.

But what if that person still has no desire to pass the light to others.

Wanting to pass it on is a precondition for receiving the light.

You mean, in order to receive the light, you first need to want to give it away?

Of course. We already want to receive it because we hear it is good. But we will not receive it until we desire to share it with others. Our world mandates that we become connected because we are approaching the end of the correction process.

Once one has experienced the light, what would stop him from wanting it all the time?

We advance "on two legs." One receives *Kelim*, corrects them, fills them with light, shares them with everyone, and thus does a very good deed, a *Mitzva* (good deed/commandment). Using the will to receive in favor of others is called a *Mitzva*. Once a *Mitzva* is done, another part of the person's ego that was hidden inside rises and appears.

Eventually, the entire "Egypt" of a person appears, and one is now immersed in an ego that is spreading over the good. The bad suddenly becomes dominant over the good. When that happens, a person becomes wicked and the struggle begins anew: the previous degree disappears inside, "drowning" in the bad.

When Israel enters Canaan and conquers it, there is the eastern side of the Jordan River. Gad and Reuben wanted that lot. Why did Moses object to their dwelling on the eastern bank of the Jordan?

Our will to receive is in the three worlds, *Beria*, *Yetzira*, and *Assiya*. There is also the Temple, Jerusalem, Mount Moriah, and the rest of the degrees: the land of Israel, around which are Jordan, Lebanon, Syria, and Babylon. Additionally, there are the rest of the lands in the world, but they are not regarded as spiritually significant.

The Eastern bank of the Jordan is the first boundary outside the land of Israel, and therefore does not have the same level of sanctity as the land of Israel itself. This is why Moses, the force that manages all the corrections within us, opposes the children of Israel's presence there. All the children of Israel must first be inside the land of Israel, and only afterward are there the conquests of David, which include Lebanon, Syria, and Babylon, from the Nile to the Euphrates.

TERMS

Tribe

A "tribe" is a group. Just as the body has systems such as the lymph system, the cardiovascular system, the nervous systems, etc., a tribe is one of the twelve systems that comprise the soul. The soul divides into twelve systems known as *HBD*, *HGT*, *NHY*. In each *Yod-Hey-Vav-Hey* there are three lines, which add up to twelve.

Vows

We cannot advance without them; they are a type of consideration toward the next degree. Although we do not know what it is, we still go for it. In spirituality, it is considered that one makes a vow to correct oneself, and only afterward checks to see if this is at all possible.

Spoil

The "spoil" is the light received in the corrected *Kelim* in spirituality, the light of *Hochma* (wisdom) that dresses in light of *Hassadim* (mercy).

Hagaalah of *Kelim* (dipping utensils in boiling water)

Hagaalah is one of the forms of correcting our spiritual *Kelim*. We have *Kelim* on the still, vegetative, animate, and human levels. The desires divide into four degrees according to their *Aviut* (thickness). The *Kelim* that are similar to our *Kelim* are corrected through what is called *Hagaalah*.

A Kosher *Kli*

A "Kosher *Kli*" is a desire to receive that has acquired the intention to bestow. Conversely, a desire to receive that has the intention to receive is "non-kosher."

Eastern Side of the Jordan

This is the part that still belongs to the land of Israel, but is in *Tifferet* of the world of *Beria*. It is written about it in the writings of the ARI and in *The Study of the Ten Sefirot*.

Anger

This is the increasing of the *Gevurot* in *Malchut* because they cannot receive for lack of *Hassadim* (mercy). In our world, a person becomes angry for lack of light of *Hassadim* inside the *Kli*.

From *The Zohar*: *Matot* (Tribes)

"'I said, 'Let a world of mercy be built.'' *Hesed* (mercy) is one of the upper *Sefirot* of the king, a higher *Sefira* than the seven bottom *Sefirot*. The Creator named the soul of Israel *Hesed* on the condition that the *Hesed* will be built, and the *Hesed* will not be blotted out from the world."

Zohar for All, *Matot* (Tribes), item 6

Hesed is the highest of the seven *Sefirot*, *Hesed*, *Gevura*, *Tifferet*, *Netzah*, *Hod*, *Yesod*, and *Malchut*. This is why *Hesed* is the top *Sefira* of the structure of the soul. It is in charge, drawing and managing our entire process of correction. In this way, *Hesed* truly acts as *Hesed* (mercy).

Masaei

(Journeys)

(Numbers, 33:1-36:13)

Portion Summary

The portion, *Masaei* (Journeys), describes the journeys of the children of Israel, the stops where they parked in the desert, and their final preparations to enter the land of Israel. The portion details several commandments, such as the obliteration of idol worship, cities of refuge, rules regarding involuntary manslaughter, appointing presidents to the tribes under the leadership of Joshua, son of Nun and Elazar the Priest, dedicating cities for the people of the tribe of Levi, and a description of the boundaries of the land.

The portion ends with the continuation of the story of the daughters of Zelophehad, the fear of the tribe of Menashe that their women would marry men from other tribes, thus causing the tribe to lose its lots. In consequence, Moses issues a warrant prohibiting the daughters of Zelophehad from marrying men of other tribes, as well as other prohibitions that concern marriages of people from different tribes.

Commentary

The portion is a preparation to enter the land of Israel. At this stage, we begin the inner work, rising to a degree where our will to receive connects with the upper force. Here we discover the upper force because we are living inside that desire.

It is written that the land of Israel is the land where the Creator is present from the beginning of the year to its end. That is, He is always in the land of Israel—in a desire aiming entirely to bestow, *Yashar El* (straight to God). We discover the upper force within that desire and are in *Dvekut* (adhesion) with it. This is the intention of the land of Israel.

From this, we can learn to what extent we are *not* in the spiritual land of Israel, but in the corporeal one. Kabbalists tell us that we have been given the opportunity to return to the corporeal (physical) land of Israel so we can rise to the spiritual one. For this purpose, we must all be together, united as a family, "as one man with one heart," as in, "All of Israel are friends" and as in, "Love your neighbor as yourself." We have connected on the stipulation of mutual guarantee, for only if we meet this criterion will we enter the land of Israel.

All the conditions and laws we have adopted thus far—and have attempted to keep when coping with the problems that arose within us as unfavorable desires that should be corrected—have been corrected in the previous portion, *Matot* (Tribes). In *Matot*, we arranged the *Kelim* (vessels) as a summary of what we went through during our period in the desert, when we rose to the state of wanting to bestow in order to bestow. Now we are facing the entrance to the land of Israel, the will to receive in order to bestow.

For this reason, before us is a summary of the previous matters and a last examination of the conditions. We are coordinated in our corrected state, a state called "the land of Israel." On the one hand, we must be connected with all the tribes, all the others, our brothers. We must be in a state of "all of Israel are friends," "as one man with one heart," seeking everybody's favor, and we must be in equivalence between us.

On the other hand, we need to see the other aspects of the people: to detect the twelve tribes and to adhere to the prohibition against intermarriage. That prohibition means that we must match the right desire to the right act. This is called, "matching a woman to a man" so they are in congruence and can achieve the proper, good results, and are not confused by one another. To obtain something, we must work with the desires with which we were born, and not confuse others about achievements on the earthly level.

The same is true for the cities of refuge, the division of the land, and the boundaries of the land. The word, *Eretz* (land), comes from the word, *Ratzon* (desire). By knowing one's own desire and the people's general desire, we must all, like cells in an organism, work as cogwheels in a uniform manner to achieve the state of "the people of Israel in the land of Israel." Then, according to the level of congruence between us, the favorable integration and the right connection, we will feel that the upper force is present among us. That state will protect us against every trouble and plight, from the smallest to the biggest.

If we all arrive, even if just a little, at a state that resembles that desire, a state of mutual bestowal, mutual love, mutual connection, like the true definition of the land of Israel, we are guaranteed to be rewarded with the upper force. We will be rewarded with the strongest possible spiritual "roof," under which we will thrive and chase our enemies away.

Questions and Answers

The people of Israel returned to the land of Israel sixty-four years ago, but still seek the real meaning of being "in the land of Israel." What does it truly mean to be in Israel?

Man comprises the whole of the will to receive (which is the heart) and the thought (which is the mind). These are the two primary elements that exist in us, that distinguish humans from animals, from beasts. Man's body is an organism that is part of the animal kingdom, but we are distinguished from that kingdom by our desires and thoughts. For this reason, it is only our thoughts and desires that we must correct.

Our desires are divided into "bodily desires" for food, reproduction, and family, and "social desires" for money, respect, power, and knowledge. We may want many things, but all our wishes basically fit into those seven primary wants. We want to fulfill all our wishes, both on the physical-corporeal level of food, reproduction (sex), and family, and on the social level of money, respect, power, and knowledge. All of these desires exist in everyone but in different combinations in each of us.

There are other desires that arise in our day-to-day lives of which we are unaware, such as desires between people. These desires are turned toward others, such as one who gives of oneself to others, not seeking to obtain any benefit for oneself. These desires are the 613 desires between man and man.

When we connect to others without the aim to exploit or gain, but truly come out of ourselves for the sake of others, we discover those 613 desires. We first discover them in their egotistical form, but if we shift them into working for the sake of others, this is a correction, the performance of a *Mitzva* (good deed/commandment).

We perform the *Mitzvot* (plural of *Mitzva*) through the light that comes to us when we study the wisdom of Kabbalah correctly. It is called "the light in it reforms." The wisdom of Kabbalah is called "Torah," "The Torah of light," "the internality of the Torah," or "the true law (Torah)," since by studying it we draw to ourselves the light that corrects the desires between us.

Correcting the 613 desires in the relations between man and man leads one into the corrected desire that includes the 613 desires of love, bestowal, friendship, unity, connection, and mutual guarantee. This desire is called "the land of Israel," where all the desires are *Yashar El* (straight to God, the Creator). They are *Yashar El* not only because of our approach to others, toward the friends, toward the people of Israel, but because this is a desire to bestow, the same desire as the Creator's—a desire to do good to all.

Hence, when we reach the land of Israel, the desire straight to others, we can also live in the physical land of Israel. That, however, must be with the condition that we have a reciprocal connection, called "the spiritual land of Israel," a state of "all of Israel are friends."

This is why Kabbalists such as Baal HaSulam (Rav Yehuda Ashlag) and the Rav Kook wrote that today we have been given an opportunity to return to the corporeal land of Israel. However, we have yet to merit it, so we may achieve correction—connection—in the short time we have been given. Kabbalists explain that if we do not contemplate this and move in that direction, we will not merit staying here and will be exiled.

Why is there such a strict division into twelve tribes with a prohibition against intermarriage?

"Connecting" means to marry. The different organs in our bodies work very differently from one another. You cannot connect the kidneys to the lungs or the liver to the heart because each organ works within its own system. It is like an engine in which one piston is working in one direction, and the other is working in another. You cannot connect these opposites without the proper adjustment. It has to follow an overall plan.

Is the end result a single system?

The result is one system: the people of Israel in the land of Israel.

What are the parts?

The parts are like pistons, like parts of an engine, moving in opposite directions but according to the same vector.

So is an individual person like a piston?

The individual is part of the whole. Each part must actualize its desire in the right manner. If we all realize ourselves with the qualities we were born with, we will reach the end of our correction on the personal level, our personal fulfillment. In this way, we will not confuse one another.

Is this equality vs. difference?

Precisely.

How does one do that equalizing?

Initially, we are not equal; we are different. There is no reason to deny it. Imagine a person having a unique talent for something, such as music, and we tell him, "No, you have to be a mechanic." Can you force a musician to be a mechanic?

How does one know one's role?

These days, we get "scattered" in every direction. This is why we are told, "Don't marry, don't look at others, find out for yourself where you belong." If we are born to a certain tribe and possesses certain qualities in the common soul called "the people of Israel," we must find our destiny and actualize it. This is when we will be happy.

With children, it is easy to see how each is special. Yet, this leads to competition.

There cannot be competition if one is a mechanic, another is a musician, a third is a physician, a fourth is an author, and a fifth is an engineer. The only competition that *is* possible is in how much each of us *contributes* to society.

Assume that two mechanics are born into a tribe of mechanics. One of them is smarter than the other and can invent special machines. The smarter one should be a team leader in a big factory that develop engines, while the less astute should be working at a small garage or for a garage owner.

Why does today's society appreciates the smarter mechanic far more than the simple one?

The problem is that our society is not uniform and does not appreciate people according to their relative efforts. In a family, we admire a baby who does the silliest thing as though it were the greatest achievement. But to an uninvolved observer, it would seem like nothing to cheer about.

The point is that if we treat each other with love, we will feel that when one contributes to society from the bottom of the heart, that person should be appreciated far more than one who is simply talented and to whom the contribution is effortless.

Today, we have no regard for those who contribute to society, but we idolize the rich and famous.

This is the problem. We are not actualizing the goal for which we received the land of Israel. This is why our situation is so bleak.

Is this the "idol worship" that the portion mentions?

Yes, it is idol worship when we admire famous people and social icons and so forth.

How can we change that? Is it not part of the human mechanism?

The only way to change it is through education, explaining it to people on a daily basis over a period of time until they see the situation as it truly is and change. Today, the world is pressing upon us, and we will not be able to keep doing as we please. We cannot isolate ourselves from the declining world.

To enter the land of Israel, idol worship must be abolished. Is this a feasible task?

Any act that does not unite the nation in equality and love, or places the concept of unity above all other values, leads to idolatry.

How can we recognize the borders of the desire called "the land of Israel" before we enter it?

Our desire contains within it the whole of reality. From that, we can single out all the desire that is on earth. Out of the desire that is on earth, we can single out the additional desire called "the land of Israel," which is a very small country if we look on the map.

It can hardly be seen.

This gives us an idea of what we correct. First, we must correct this desire. Once we correct it, we can move on to correct the general desire, the rest of the continents, and the entire world. This is the meaning of being "a light for the nations." The text does not mention it, but the entrance to the land of Israel must be by one's transcending one's egotistical desire and being ready to begin to correct one's desires into love of others.

How does one find the boundaries of this land?

When we work on our connections with others, we begin to see with which, out of our 613 desires, we can relate to others. These are the boundaries. Within us are many more desires, called "desires of the nations of the world." These are very powerful, like the size of the world compared to the size of the land of Israel, but we correct them later.

These are the stages. Anyone who engages in the wisdom of Kabbalah reaches both types of desires.

In the Torah, we read about far wider borders than the dot we see on the map today. Is this something we will ever reach?

Without a doubt.

Physically?

We will reach it physically, but they will not be borders anymore. That is, there will be no borders whatsoever because we will be in the state of complete redemption.

Are there borders in spirituality, as well?

No, which is why all of us, the entire world, will be as "one man with one heart." The children of Israel will be the ones to begin the correction, but later, as "a light for the nations," they will join the entire world in the correction, as it is written, "For My house shall be called a house of prayer for all the nations" (Isaiah 56:7). What was previously limited will become boundless.

Another issue is the cities of refuge where, if one person murders another, the murderer can escape to a city of refuge and be protected there.

This occurs when we are still not working with all of our desires. If we make a mistake or fail in something, it is not because we are no longer worthy of being in the land of Israel, but because there are various scrutinies and problems in it, too. Clearly, we enter the desire so it will be directed toward brotherly love, love for all. This was impossible in the desert, except through the law, "That which you hate, do not do to your friend." When entering the land of Israel, the law, "Love your neighbor as yourself" applies, the law of love.

Is it possible to make mistakes here?

Of course. There are new desires, new corrections, and there is the conquering of the land. In all these desires, we need to face up to our egotistical desires and truly exploit, defeat, break, and expel them. We need to do all the work that the people of Israel do in the land of Israel in the story. Here, however, it pertains to an internal story concerning the desires within us, and here we can err. This is why we were given the Torah. Just as Israel repeatedly made mistakes in the desert and then corrected themselves, the same applies to the conquering of the land. We make mistakes and then correct them.

What does it mean to make mistakes if we say that there is no one else besides Him?

It means we must discover those desires.

Where do I truly begin to correct?

Each time we succeed, we immediately fall into a mistake, a transgression.

Is it because we attribute the success to ourselves?

No. The mistake, the transgression, is not even ours. We are being introduced to a new, corrupted desire where we see ourselves as sinful, like the sin of the spies, the sin of the water, the sin of the serpents, and many other sins. The people of Israel seem never to listen to what they are being told.

However, this happens only because they *do* succeed. They are introduced to more and more of their corrupted desires in order to correct them. We all come from the breaking, from Pharaoh. This is why Pharaoh gradually appears as cruel, broken, and egotistical, and we need to correct him.

Therefore, we need not attribute our egotism to ourselves because "he who is greater than his friend, his desire is greater than him." On the contrary, all that is revealed to us in the Torah is our own broken soul, which we correct. And it is not even we who do it; it has been done before us. The Creator tells us, "I have created the evil inclination," and "I have hardened Pharaoh's heart" (Exodus 10:1).

Does "obliteration" relate to idol worship?

Our work is to correct. This is why we constantly reveal the evil and correct it.

But it seems endless.

It is not endless. We are already living in the land of Israel, and we are building in it a house of sanctity. There is already light of *Hochma* being filled with light of *Hassadim*, and it is filling our souls, so we are already beginning to discover the eternal, perfect world.

Is the land of Israel a state of "no errors," a perfect state?

It is the perfect state. Today we need to come to a state where the land of Israel spreads throughout every country and every continent. It is called "the land of the gazelle" because the desire with the aim to bestow, to love others, must eventually encompass the whole of reality.

We have the method that explains how to do it, and we must explain it to the rest of humanity. The work of disseminating the wisdom of Kabbalah is called "the Messiah's *Shofar*." It is our duty to carry it out because otherwise humanity will still achieve the complete correction, but after great torment, while doing it our way means that humanity can achieve correction quickly, using the light that reforms.

TERMS

Stops

"Stops" are degrees through which we advance toward correction. There is the preparation period and then the states where we come into correction, to the desire to bestow in order to bestow, a state of "That which you hate, do not do to your friend." We must be neutral, as though neutralizing our egos. This is called "obtaining the degree of *Bina*," or keeping the *Mitzvot* (commandments) of 248 organs. In spirituality, it is called *Galgalta ve Eynaim* (skull and eyes). These degrees are called "the degrees of the desert."

Afterward, we enter the degrees called "land of Israel," *Yashar El* (straight to God), where we reach "Love your neighbor as yourself." In those degrees, we have the correction of the desires called "365." There are 248 organs in the degrees of the desert, and 365 tendons in the degrees of the land of Israel, and all of them are parts of the soul.

Idol Worship

"Idol worship" is when we do not want to work in bestowal toward others, but only for ourselves. We treat ourselves as gods and bow to ourselves.

The Borders of the Land

The "borders of the land" are the borders by which our big will to receive marks how far we can reach, with which desires we can bestow, and which desires we must restrict and refrain from using.

City of Refuge

"Cities of refuge" are desires that we "freeze." Sometimes we are immersed in such thoughts, desires, and predilections that we cannot work on correcting them. We therefore put those desires "on hold." This is a state where we are powerless, devoid of a *Masach* (screen) with which to work in bestowal upon others. However, we *can* be in a "place" where we correct ourselves, and after some time we will go outside and return to the world.

The Complete Land of Israel

"The complete land of Israel" is perfection. It is called *Shalom* (peace), from the word *Shlemut* (wholeness/perfection). It means that everything is corrected into love of others, as it is written, "Love your neighbor as yourself; it is a great rule..."

There is nothing more than that. This is why the complete land of Israel is a desire that is fully corrected into being *Yashar El*, toward bonding with others. The point of this portion is to discover the Godliness in it through connection, in *Dvekut* (adhesion).

Devarim

(These Are the Words)

(Deuteronomy, 1:1-3:22)

Portion Summary

The portion, *Devarim* (These Are the Words), begins with a long speech that Moses makes before the people of Israel just before his death. The portion contains a historic review of the forty years in the desert, which Moses describes to the people of Israel.

The portion also deals with appointing the presidents of the tribes and the judges, the sin of the spies and their punishment, the relationships between Israel and Edom, Israel and Moab, and Israel and Amon, as well as the wars with Sihon and Og. Moses supports Joshua, son of Nun, as the next leader of the people of Israel, who will lead them into the land of Israel.

Commentary

From the cascading of the spiritual degrees and what we have learned about the perception of reality, we know there is no world outside of us. All that exists are the spiritual states we go through, states depicted within us. Everything is within us, as it is said, "Man is a small world."

We move from state to state. Each state emerges out of its predecessor and is included in it. This is called a *Partzuf* (face). Each state contains what exists in the previous one, the *Reshimot* (recollections), impressions, and memories from which it was born, and which it must now implement. Nothing comes out of thin air; everything relies on what precedes it.

These are the stages by which we ascend from the degree of the desert to the degree of the land of Israel. The degree of the land of Israel contains all the previous degrees, from *Adam HaRishon* (the first man, Adam), with whom the Torah begins. This is why we find that the Torah always repeats states described in previous books, and extends them to the next, higher degree.

We use the same pattern in our daily lives at school, repeating the same material, but each time on a higher level. That is, we study the same laws but in greater detail. When we study Newton's laws on a college level, we reencounter what we already learned several times at school. The difference is that more formulas are added. This pattern repeats itself in various areas of life.

In this portion, we ascend to a very high degree. "The land of Israel" comprises all of Man's desires that are processed and corrected into having the aim to bestow, meaning they are completely corrected.

All we need is to correct what is in us from the state in which we were born, and from which we evolved. We need to turn it from aiming to use our traits egotistically into using them for the sake of others, as in "Love your neighbor as yourself; it is a great rule in the Torah." Actually, it is the whole Torah that explains to us how to correct the heart, meaning of all our desires, which are called "heart."

Today, we do not know where we are. We want to discover the meaning of our lives, the reason for life. These and similar questions awaken specifically in our generation and often lead to depression and drug and alcohol abuse, as we have no idea what to do with them.

A little less than a century ago, we thought that the more we had, the happier we would be. We believed that over- consumption was better than balanced consumption until we found ourselves in a state of crisis, specifically because we received too much and did needless things only to satisfy ourselves. We acted out of the assumptions, "the more we sell, the happier we will be," and "the more we buy, the happier we will be." We created the monstrous advertising industry to promote redundant products and to make us think that they were actually essential.

In the last hundred years or so, humanity has progressed in this manner until we have come to a situation where we are not only unhappy, but also becoming increasingly poor. We are experiencing repeated instances of scarcity, emptiness, and helplessness.

And yet, we have to learn all that by first hand experience. It is the first stage in our development, the "preparation period."

From the current stage, we will advance to the next one in which spirituality develops. We will understand that if we continue living as we have been, we will ruin ourselves completely. We have become machines that consume and dispose, but in the end, the world will be depleted of raw materials and we will have nothing with which to sustain ourselves.

This brings us back to the old questions: "How are we to survive?" "How can we have a happy life, and live in a society that is balanced, just, and equal?" "What are the values we should follow in order to have a good life in which we have what we need and deserve?"

The heart of the problem is that part of society receives without any restraints while others suffer. To mend that, we begin with the questions we just mentioned as we enter the next stage—the stage of correction, when we must correct ourselves. That stage begins at the foot of Mount Sinai, when we realize that we must establish a just and equal society, with spiritual happiness for everyone. This will spread through unity and mutual guarantee. If we agree to it, we will take upon ourselves the correction method.

The wisdom of Kabbalah is the correction method. It explains how we go through the first stages of our correction. The first stage after the preparation period is called "forty years in the desert." In that stage we must have a leader who understands what must be done, who moves ahead, and whom everyone follows toward the desert.

A "desert" is a place where we do not know how to survive or sustain ourselves–our children and women, as well as the cattle–without food and water. We pass through the desert, whether an entire nation or an individual, in whom there are desires and thoughts that we must gradually correct.

In the desert, we correct all our desires to the degree of "desiring mercy." On that degree, we consume what is necessary for living, and give the rest to society. "The rest" is everything that we can produce or do in favor of others. We dedicate everything to society, for this is the correction of desiring mercy. Moses, who is in that correction, is the force that pulls us from the ego into bestowal upon others. He is the one who takes us through various individual corrections.

Within that process is a disclosure of man's egotistical desires, called "the sin of the spies," "waters of quarreling," and wars with certain nations–Amon, Moab, and Edom–some of which should be "slaughtered." These are desires we must refrain from using for the time being because they are so intense that we cannot correct them, but can only restrict them.

Under special conditions, we can correct some of our egotistical desires, such as "women." We can also correct desires that were not used egotistically, but still belong to the ego.

For example, the spoils are some of those desires, some of the *Kelim* (vessels), the abilities that we can correct. This is how we advance through the desert, where each portion is a stage as we pass through stops and camps where we advance and correct ourselves toward a stage of "desiring mercy."

This is why the children of Israel, with all their tribes, count who is and who is not advancing toward the state of desiring mercy. It is work for the sake of the public to ensure that each person has what he or she needs for normal sustenance. This is called "just division." The rest, one gives to the public.

It is not that we should all have the same. Rather, it is that each of us should have what is suitable for our relative consumption. In other words, since everyone is born different and unequal, the meaning of equality is interpreted differently for every person.

Questions and Answers

Moses' speech prepares the people for the next degree. The next degree is not one to which Moses belongs, but is the degree where Joshua continues. How can Moses prepare the people for the future challenges in the land of Israel—with just division and equality among them—when they conquer the land, encountering desires they have never used, but must now cope with? How can Moses prepare them for this degree?

The children of Israel have used the desires that they corrected and that they will now correct on a deeper level. In total, there are 613 degrees within us. First, we correct them only on the level of the desert, meaning use them only on the degree of *Bina*, the degree of desiring mercy. Subsequently, on the level of "the land of Israel," one turns these desires into those with the aim to bestow.

These are the same desires; there are no others. Within us is a kind of package of desires, all of which are egotistical with respect to others. They are called the "evil inclination." We correct these desires in two stages—the "desert" stage and the "land of Israel" stage. However, we *always* work with the same desires.

In the "desert" stage, we correct the desire using the special upper force—the Creator. However, the means to do that is Moses, our connection to the upper force. Within us is a quality named "Moses." By using it and connecting to it, we connect to the upper force. This is why Moses is called a "leader," one who can help us connect to the upper force. The leader understands and knows all the processes we must go through, or we would have no need for him. He is the highest quality within us, recognizes the Creator, and is similar to Him. With this ability, the leader connects to the upper force.

We set ourselves in a special, direct line where all of our desires connect to Moses, and through Moses to the Creator. For now, this is how we discover the Creator–partially, from time to time. He "speaks" to Moses openly and through signs to others, as much as those desires in a person can discover the Creator.

In the next stage, when we enter the land of Israel, the quality of Moses in us can no longer accompany us. There needs to be a more advanced quality toward the other corrections, a quality called "Joshua," son of Nun. In fact, it is still the quality of Moses, but with a higher role and more responsibility. Although Moses seemingly gives him this role during their forty years in the desert together, Joshua is actually Moses having ascended to the degree of the land of Israel.

The degree of Moses passes away on Mount Nevo, on the other side of the Jordan River. The desires are divided within us into the land of Israel, Jordan, beyond the Jordan River, Lebanon, Syria, and so forth.

Afterward, Moses begins the next degree, called Joshua, son of Nun. We all begin our corrections on the degree of the land of Israel. That is, all the desires at the level of the desert climb up to the level of the land of Israel, becoming fully in favor of others.

First, those who live in Israel today must become aware that they are not yet in the "land of Israel." Can it be said that they have hardly reached the desert?

According to the wisdom of Kabbalah, we are in total exile, not even in the desert.

What about leadership? Do we have it?

We have no leadership because we do not want a leader. If we wanted spiritual leadership, we would discover the leader internally, as well as externally.

How will there be leadership if we are entering uncharted territory?

Indeed, the leaders themselves have no idea what to do.

Where is Moses?

If we want him, we will have him.

Does this require inner work?

It requires inner work. If we want to correct ourselves, we will discover him on the outside, too. All of a sudden, a new leader will appear whom we did not see or know before. And we will know that it is truly him.

The children of Israel also did not wish to accept Moses' leadership. Several times during the period of the desert, they tried to bring him down. On each degree, we must scrutinize whether or not this is truly the force that we are following, since its power constantly increases.

It is not a nation or cattle that one takes with them. Everything is obtained by educating the people. Only with education do people begin to see where to go and who can be the leader. The people will see it very clearly, which is why everything must be done by education. All the slogans that people write must first be explained: "What is equality," "What is justice?"

Indeed, what is equality? After all, we are different and we have different needs.

True, everyone should receive different degrees of both quantity and quality. It cannot be any other way.

But someone might say, "My ego requires ten million dollars a year."

This is why we first need an education system that will teach us Nature's laws, the laws of Creation that are appearing before us now. First, we must all learn about them, open our eyes, and see the world we live in. Perhaps we are unaware of what the world is truly like; perhaps we are demanding things that harm us, as babies sometimes do.

Those who are suffering might listen, but right now not everyone is suffering.

We all think we are suffering, and we all think we deserve more. Therefore, according to the wisdom of Kabbalah, we must begin to balance out society, and at the same time begin to educate, teach, and oblige everyone to study Nature's laws. We send our children to approximately twenty years of school and university to prepare them for life. Now we are all as school children in regard to the world appearing before us, and we must all go to school.

The wisdom of Kabbalah explains what we are facing. This is precisely why it is appearing. If we do not learn, we will continue on our path, just like obstinate children who do not listen to their parents and put themselves at risk.

We need a preparatory stage. At the moment, many people are out on streets yelling with pain. First, they need to be given something to calm them down so they may listen.

It has to be in tandem, or it will lead to terrible destruction.

You mean you cannot settle for just one of them, but must establish both?

Yes.

The ruin of the Temple occurred due to unfounded hatred. How can we avoid unfounded hatred today?

This hatred is the result of our heightened egos, the sin of the spies. We do not want to go to the land of Israel, and it seems to us that it is hard, forbidden, not for us, that it is dangerous. We are made to think that Kabbalah can make us mad, that it is mysticism. In short, we are repelling our own correction any way we can.

The spies tell us, "We must correct ourselves; we must come to a state where we are all friends, brothers, in mutual guarantee and equality." But what equality are they talking about? Do they want equality? These are nothing more than slogans. Everyone is saying, "Give me what I deserve!" But do they deserve what they demand?

For people to listen, there must be a terrible decline.

True, but we can prevent it. To do that, we need to make our real situation known. We are currently in a new generation, in a completely different place. Our reality is different. We have yet to find the proper name for it, but social ties are different, and so are our international connections.

When people are in pain, they begin to hate those who are not like them. And yet, we are now witnessing a process of fusion. How do we keep from disintegrating due to unfounded hatred?

This is a process of coalescing, whose purpose is to break, not to build. This is the biggest problem—that all these forces are now uniting in order to break. Therefore, we should explain as much as we can that there is something very risky here, that we *must* deliberate, that we must set up roundtable discussions and conduct them everywhere and all the time.

What is social justice? Is there such a thing as objective, absolute justice?

Yes, there is, when each receives only what is needed to survive in a reasonable manner.

Who would monitor it?

According to the overall budget, it would be monitored as much as possible. First, it would be tested in percents, how much each one would need overall. Similar to Social Security, everyone would receive the same amount, just as the poor and the rich receive the same allowance from Social Security.

This is an economic calculation that in the end must be balanced out. The important thing is to let the world and the nation know where we are and why we are the way we are. Now, we are required to understand what is a state (country), what is that system, how it works, and how to determine rules. Each of us must partake in this outreach, giving something of ourselves.

What is the condition for success?

The condition for success is that we sit down and learn about the new world, just as children are prepared for twenty years before they become productive citizens. We have yet to reach that level–being citizens of the integral world we live in. There are new laws that have surfaced, and no leader or government knows what do with them. Answers can come only by studying the new foundations, which the wisdom of Kabbalah reveals to us.

TERMS

What does it mean that nations must be destroyed, such as Amon, Moab, and Edom, which are desires within us?

Destroying them means that we temporarily avoid using them. We cannot, and should not, destroy these desires. On the contrary, we must freeze them within us until we can correct them and use them properly.

What is a speech or a dialog? It seems as though one desire is "talking" to another.

It is an internal scrutiny.

Speech

Man is his own psychologist.

Does he analyze himself?

Yes, we analyze which desire to use and which not to use, and whether a desire should be used one way or another.

But once we have made a scrutiny, where will we find the strength to carry it out?

This requires two lights—one for scrutiny and one for correction. This is why it is written, "I have created the evil inclination, I have created for it the Torah as a spice," for "The light in it reforms them." That is, only through the light does one go through all those stages. During the study, the wisdom of Kabbalah brings us inner light with which we see how things are. We begin to see our own internal system and how we partake in the overall system of the world.

Leader

A "leader" is one's highest quality, whereby after scrutinizing it, we advance.

Equality

Everyone is distinctively equal. Put differently, we need to take into account that we are not born equal in our qualities or desires. Therefore, each of us should receive differently.

Does that apply to both this world and to spirituality?

Yes, but for spirituality, we need to know people's internal state. Otherwise, we will not distribute justly. Today's society cannot resolve these problems until we learn the laws of Nature. Society must come to know the internality of the world, so eventually we will have no choice but to study the wisdom of Kabbalah.

Unfounded Hatred

These are forces of rejection that we discover within, when we want to draw closer to people. However, this is appropriate only if one truly wishes to unite with others. We discover that these forces exist without expecting to find them–they are things that we received at birth, deliberately, from above.

New World

We have now entered a new, circular, global system of Nature that is closing us together in a sphere. We are interdependent and cannot break apart or manage ourselves independently, either within the factions of the nation or throughout the world.

The formulas for this are found in the wisdom of Kabbalah. If we study them, we will be able to manage the world beautifully.

From *The Zohar*: Then Moses Sang

"Should you say, 'Since they are tied in the bundle of life and delight in the upper pleasure, why should the Creator bring them down to earth?' When all those spirits and souls that were in the highest degree were born and came out to the world, the Creator brought them down to earth below. It is all the more so now, since the Creator wishes to straighten what is crooked by showing them the signs and wonders that He will do for Israel."

Zohar for All, *BeShalach* (When Pharaoh Sent), item 218

VaEtchanan

(And I Besought)

(Deuteronomy, 3:23-7:11)

Portion Summary

The portion, *VaEtchanan* (And I Besought), repeats what Moses was prohibited—to enter the land of Israel—and that Joshua was to succeed him and lead the people to the land of Israel. The portion deals with the commandment to keep the Torah and remember the standing at the foot of Mount Sinai, as well as with the concept of repentance, which appears here for the first time. Here appears the known text of *Shema Ysrael* (Hear, O Israel).

Moses makes another speech, where he repeats the Ten Commandments. He also distinguishes three cities of refuge on the eastern side of the Jordan River, warns of idol worship in the land of Israel, and instructs how to destroy the statues. He also reminds the people that it was the Creator who led them into the land of Israel, the good land that they are destined to inherit.

Commentary

The portion, *VaEtchanan* (And I Besought), contains all the conditions for the dwelling of the people of Israel in the land of Israel. The people of Israel began their history with Abraham, who established a group in Babylon. That group distinguished itself from the rest of the Babylonians, who did not wish to unite "as one man with one heart," meaning to be in the quality of *Hesed* (mercy), which is Abraham's quality.

That group of people agreed to live in *Arvut* (mutual guarantee), and actually began the formation process of the people of Israel. Following the exodus from Egypt, the group took upon itself the commitment to be as one nation, despite the problems and the egos of the people.

The formation of a single nation was conditioned upon a successful "passage" of the ordeal at the foot of Mount Sinai, a mountain of *Sinaa* (hatred). On Mount Sinai, the people assumed the preparatory stipulation for climbing over that mountain—being "as one man with one heart." Only by adhering to this condition is it possible to receive the Torah, the upper force that can unite everyone. That condition is met through the "point in the heart" of each person, a point named "Moses," which draws people onward into the desert and subsequently to the land of Israel. This is the point where everyone must unite.

The stipulation that held the people together was *Arvut* (mutual guarantee). Even today, to be a nation we must meet the condition of caring for one another on the material level, too. This is the scrutiny that we are facing in Israel today—having everyone see that no one lacks basic sustenance on the material level.

When we come together, we enter the land of Israel through the correction called "forty years in the desert." This is a state in which all become a nation and are willing to live together in a global and integral manner, as is appearing in the world today, and as Nature requires.

Today, some have much more than they need, while others barely meet their most basic needs. The only way we can acquire what we need is by being responsible for one another. Only through unity will we be able to create a special force that will help us overcome the difficulties and properly divide our produce and profits, just like a family.

"As one man with one heart" really means "as a family." In a family we divide what we have to each one based on each one's needs. We sit at a round table and talk. We take every argument and problem into consideration, weigh each one's priorities, and decide how to divide what we have gained among us. We reinforce the weak and support them.

If we manage the people and the country in this way, we will find that the nation is connected, and that the Creator–the force of bestowal and love–is among us. We will feel how we resolve all the problems and rise above all the obstructions. When we take upon ourselves the good, we immediately produce new powers among us, and then, "This day you have become a people" (Deuteronomy, 27:9).

The condition of unity between us allows us to resolve all the problems, as it is written toward the end of the portion, that adhering to that condition leads us to being as one: "Hear, O Israel, the Lord our God, the Lord is One" (Deuteronomy, 6:4). When the force of love is between us–the force of unity, the necessity to be together, the *Arvut* (mutual guarantee)–we sustain and keep one another. That force is leading us, the people of Israel, to the land of Israel–to the desire, *Yashar El* (straight to God), straight to the quality of love and bestowal.

Only if one produces the force called *Elokim* (God), which is the overall love, the *Arvut*, does the force, "The Lord your God," which one has created, walks ahead when one enters the land of Israel. That force helps us cope with the difficulties there, and fight the seven nations there, which are stronger than us.

In many ways, it is similar to Israel's current situation, being surrounded by nations that wish to destroy it. It is only by that force that we truly "defeat" everyone. In the end, we bring not only ourselves into unity and connection, but the entire world. We become "a light for the nations" by showing how we can all be united in our world, which requires a global-integral connection among everyone. It is just as Nature, the Creator,* appears to us as one, and closes us in such a way that compels us to be like it, as one, in *Dvekut* (adhesion) with it.

When we produce the force of love between us by bonding, we become similar to the Creator—the overall force in Nature. In that state, we are in harmony with Nature and we balance the ecology, technology, economy, and every realm of life. Everything falls into place only by the force of unity, though it may not seem that way, and it may not be clear what the force of unity has to do with resolving any of these problems.

We have yet to understand that we are part of Nature and that we are in it. The network we are in is integrally managed, with all its parts interconnected. If we, too, connect in synchrony with Nature, we will be rewarded with the fruits of the land of Israel, as the spies saw them but thought they would not be able to enjoy them because the fruits were so great, and the people that dwelled in the land were so mighty. Here lies the solution: if we unite, that force will march before us and will shatter all the enemies.

As long as we produce between us the force of *Arvut*, it will resolve everything. Whatever happens, through the force of unity we can all be under the umbrella of *Arvut*, the umbrella of love, through which the world will truly be corrected.

QUESTIONS AND ANSWERS

Following Moses, Joshua had to lead the nation into the next stage, the next degree. How does one lead the people while keeping everyone united despite the challenges?

The Torah does not tell us what happened after the entrance to the land of Israel, or how to break the idols, which are our evil

* In *Gematria* (Hebrew numbering of letters), *Hateva* (The Nature) is tantamount to *Elokim* (God).

inclination. When idol worshipping, we place before us statues such as money, power, respect, envy, and hatred. The Torah does not tell us precisely how to break them within us. Nothing is said about the construction of the Temple and the conduct within it.

We basically have two ways to go. We can take the short, good way, where we achieve our own correction and the correction of the world, or we can take the hard way, if we do not keep the condition of *Arvut*.

Now we are going through difficult times, through troubles ...

We need not regard it as trouble, but as an opportunity. The conditions we are in are an opportunity, and in them we must become corrected. Without difficult times, how will we overcome the evil inclination? How will we know it?

Assume we all establish *Arvut*, we all take care of each other, and people go along with it because it solves their problems. What is the next step?

There is nothing but maintaining the *Arvut*.

What about the love we have to reach?

It is *Arvut*. The first stage in *Arvut* is "That which you hate, do not do to your friend," meaning at the very least avoid harming others. The next stage is "Love your neighbor as yourself," which is the overall rule of the Torah. There is nothing more than that. There are two conditions we must follow: avoid harming others, and then, above it, treat them with love.

Lately, we have seen many people openly admitting that what they really need is love.

People need to understand the true meaning of *Arvut*. We need to sit together at a roundtable and discuss things, explain the definitions of each word until we actually *feel* what we are talking about.

Arvut means that we are *all* responsible for one another, in everything in life. When one has the right relationship with others, there is no need to think of oneself. While you think about others, others think about you.

It is just like a family. In a family, you do not care about yourself, but rather about the entire family: your children, your parents, the sick, and the weak. We divide the family income and everything else we have according to everyone's needs.

How do we make decisions in a roundtable format on a countrywide level?

Imagine what it will be like when we need to make this type of decision on a worldwide level! We need to aspire to have all factions around the table. We need to find factions whose representatives have not come to the table, perhaps because they are too weak or have despaired. We need to help them raise their questions.

Also, the roundtable must be an ongoing operation. We must set an example of a nation that is discussing with love, with everyone seated together around the same table: left, right, and middle, even enemies and foes. The common point that connects us is that we all belong to one nation, as it is written, "love covers all transgressions" (Proverbs, 10:12). The transgression is the hate that we feel for each other. In other words, it is fine that we are hateful, but there is one rule: we must all live like a family.

Will that make the hatred subside?

No, it will not subside. The principle in the wisdom of Kabbalah is that "love covers all transgressions." In other words, the transgression of hate remains. It points to disagreements and to the difference in qualities that we all have. Disagreements between us are good because above them we build a *Masach* (screen), an umbrella that covers those transgressions.

We unite despite our disputes because the principle of love must be above everything else. That principle "uses" those disputes as a lever to raise us above Mount Sinai, above the mountain of hate. We all sit around the table and build above us the concept of "Moses on Mount Sinai," and Moses pulls us up. When we achieve the quality of love that connects us, we become a nation. Before that, we are not considered a nation.

Is this true for the rest of the world, as well?

First, about us here, in Israel: We have had the spiritual gene since the time we were a nation. Today, we are not a nation but a collection of exiles. If we implement the principle of *Arvut* and use the differences between us to *add* to the concept of *Arvut*, we will truly feel that we are in the land of Israel.

If we are united, no one will be able to harm us. It will not be because we will be strong, but because the force of Nature will be in us, in sync with the global, integral Nature, as it was written that the Creator walks before us and fights all our wars,* just as He shatters man's hatred toward others.

There is no doubt that our neighbors will gladly join us, and then we will see that the hatred was there only in order to unite us. No other country in the world is in a similar situation. Our unity calms our neighbors because there is only one force that operates in Nature, and its purpose is to lead us all to unity, connection, harmony, and balance with the global Nature.

Do the Ten Commandments detail how to achieve *Arvut*, or do they detail what we find once we achieve it?

The Ten Commandments are a condition. The system of unity between us consists of ten parts, called "Ten *Sefirot*." We should interpret each of them. We need to set those ten parts—our connections to others—in order. If we put our relations toward

* "The Lord your God who goes before you, He shall fight for you" (Deuteronomy, 30:1).

others in order, in ten distinct approaches, we will put our entire attitude toward others in order.

Do these ten *Sefirot* appear once we achieve *Arvut*?

It is also about how to achieve *Arvut* because this is the goal. In discovering the *Arvut*, you discover your own higher state, where you have risen above troubles. All of a sudden you discover that Nature is already producing everything you need. You discover the sources of energy, vitality, health, and love that exist in the world, and the close relations that exist between all parts of Nature, and which we have suppressed.

This sounds like a miracle.

If you speak to people who live in the wild, such as in the woods, they often say that Nature actually radiates love to them. The unity, the holism in it radiates an attitude of love.

Will we enter a new realm of reality through our desire to achieve *Arvut*?

Yes, we will discover internal forces that are currently hidden from us because we constantly view others through our egos. When we begin to give as Nature gives, we will begin to perceive a completely different wavelength, much like a radio receiver.

How do we begin? What is the first step toward *Arvut*?

We have to sit at the roundtable, scrutinize those concepts, and see how we can achieve unity. *Arvut* is the condition that made us a nation in the past. Afterward, we lost it with the ruin of the Temple. We have been in exile, and now we need to re-create ourselves as a nation.

A nation is like a family. We must see ourselves as one big family. We need to relate to all the problems, and we will find that it is good that they are appearing now. The problems give us something to talk about, a need to feel each other. These days, people's primary need is connection with others; they even riot and go on protests just to feel connected.

From *The Zohar*: You Have Begun to Show

"Come and see, the Creator has given all the nations in the world to appointed ministers who rule over them," meaning the different forces of Nature. "But Israel, the Creator holds them as His lot and His share, to actually unite with them." We see what is happening with us throughout history. We are a special people and there is no way to avoid it. "And He gave them the holy Torah to unite in His name. Therefore, 'You who cling to the Lord,' and not to any other appointee, such as the rest of the nations."

Zohar for All, *VaEtchanan*, item 17

What is the holy Torah? It is "love your neighbor as yourself, this is a great rule in the Torah." There is nothing but the love between man and man; this is the whole Torah, and there is nothing else. We think that these are different actions and means, but these are customs, superficial actions whose purpose is to sustain the people as long as they do not understand what is required of them, meaning while they are still in exile. It is only when we come to the global situation that Nature demands of us, that *Elokim* demands that we unite.

What Nature are we talking about? What is this law? What do you mean by "Nature"?

"Nature" is the common force that runs the entire universe according to a purpose and a plan. We see that all of Nature's parts are connected. That connection includes us, except we are detached from the rest of Nature. This is why we must first unite in a manner of "Love your neighbor as yourself," become global, integral, connected like the rest of Nature.

When we achieve that, we will begin to feel the common force that operates and has operated throughout evolution. We will unite with that force and be aware of the path that we have taken. In that state, we will discover the reasons for everything that happened along the way, the reason for and the meaning of life, and the goal to which we are drawn.

TERMS

Observing (Keeping) the Torah

"Observing" is the constant keeping of our attitude toward others. The Torah means "love your neighbor as yourself." It is love that must always be before our eyes.

Repentance

"Repentance" is returning from the ego, from the negative attitude toward others, and into a good attitude to others.

The Ten Commandments

We must distinguish ten parts that are all egotistical, cruel, aiming to exploit others, and which are then corrected from aiming to receive into aiming to bestow.

Annihilation of Idol Worship

The idols are money, gold, beautiful cars, and whatever we want that is not necessary for our sustenance. With them, it is as though we steal from others. It is written that without flour, there is no Torah. That is, one must care of one's necessities and also care for the needs of others.

Shema Israel (Hear, O Israel)

This pertains to unity. "Hear, O Israel, the Lord our God, the Lord is One." "The Lord our God" means pure love and bestowal. It is about a bond between us that consists of love and bestowal, and which discloses to us the force of Nature with which we are in *Dvekut* (adhesion).

Remembering

We should constantly remember, and remind others, about mutual guarantee (*Arvut*). We must all remind each other that we are obliged to treat each other favorably, above the bad relations between us. We need to love others as we love our children: at times we may be unhappy with our children's character, but we love them nonetheless.

Do we have to become as one family?

Yes, and we must always remember it.

So *Arvut* is the umbrella that should cover all the gaps between us, all the conflicts. In fact, we need not change at all, just place the *Arvut* above us.

Precisely, and then we will reach abundance. This is what lies ahead.

Ekev

(Because)

(Deuteronomy, 7:12-11:25)

Portion Summary

In the portion, *Ekev* (Because), Moses continues his speech to the people of Israel. He reiterates that if Israel keeps the laws and the ordinances that the Creator commanded them, the people will be awarded happiness, health, and triumph over their enemies. But if they do not, the Creator will not keep them and they will be lost among the nations.

The portion also describes the virtues of the land of Israel, the seven species. Finally, the people are commanded to teach these things to their children and to carve the *Mezuzah on their doorsteps.**

Commentary

Moses warns the people to keep the laws of Nature because the Creator is *Elokim* (God), and in *Gematria* (numeric values ascribed to Hebrew letters), this is "The Nature."

* *Mezuzah* (doorpost): Texts from Deuteronomy inscribed on parchment and rolled up in a case that is attached to the doorframe.

The Creator gave us the Torah (Pentateuch), the laws of the world. The Torah is like a physics book except that the laws in it are absolute and precise. Only Israel received them. If we act according to these laws, we will be above everything. We received a promise in advance, and this is truly what is happening. If we keep the laws before us, we will receive anything we want—happiness, respect, security, health, eternity, wholeness, this world and the next world.

These laws come down to one: “Love your neighbor as yourself; it is a great rule in the Torah.” All we need is to keep that law—love of others. The whole Torah speaks of nothing but that.

The problems begin with keeping that law. We cannot do it alone. It is only possible in an environment that sustains us, along with all the members of that environment. Only through mutual support can we truly keep that law. Baal HaSulam (Rav Yehuda Ashlag) mentioned in that regard a story about two friends sailing in a boat. When one of them began to drill under him, his friend asked, “What are you doing?” The other replied, “It is none of your concern, I am drilling only under me.”

We are living in special times. We all feel that we are in a single boat, and this is the proper situation to finally begin to follow the general law of love of others, the common law of Nature: mutuality. The global and integral crisis has placed us against our will in a single boat where we are all drilling under us without regard for anyone else.

Now we must all begin to reorganize and connect with one another in mutual guarantee. Everyone must guarantee that everyone else will not break the law, and everyone will care for everyone else in the same manner. We muster the courage and power not to harm others and not to drill a hole. If we approach the general law of Nature in this manner, we will truly feel that we are lacking nothing because there is nothing better than when we are in congruence with Nature.

It is like the spies: we begin to see the fruits of the land of Israel, the sun, and the light, as it is written that the Creator is present from the beginning of the year to the end of the year, meaning happiness, health, and safety. No one will be able to approach our borders and say that the land is not ours, because we will be in congruence with the laws dictated from above. These are the same laws that are actually only one: "Love your neighbor as yourself." It is the same mutual guarantee that helps us care for one another.

Therefore, if we keep this law, which is the essence of the Torah, we will have abundance. If we do not, we will find out with increasing clarity, as is happening now, that we are dependent upon everyone. We have no idea what is happening with our country's defense, and even when we do understand, and know in advance what might happen, things still happen. If we refrain from keeping the clear condition, we arrive at where we are, and who knows where we might end up.

We are dependent on the World Bank and the Common Market. In fact, the whole world is interdependent without understanding why it is so. We were given excellent starting conditions, a book that explains the laws of the world, and the wisdom of Kabbalah, which explains how to rise above these laws, and shows us that we can rise above our nature. If the Creator promises us security, happiness, and health, it is all we need. These three parameters are all that demonstrators throughout the world are asking. They, too, need nothing more than safety, happiness, and health.

Security is a fundamental element that defines our attitude toward life. Happiness defines our independence with regard to the rest of the world, without anyone being able to bring us down or up. The same goes for our health; it all depends on us. All we need to do is keep within our nation the condition, "Love your neighbor as yourself." It is easy to keep that condition in mutual guarantee. If we understand it and support each other, in a short period of time we will rise to such a level that no one will be able to harm us, not on the economic level, not on the level of health, and not on the level of defense.

It is time that, through explanations, we will achieve the feeling of mutual guarantee and mutual love in the nation, and everything that is written in the portion will come true.

Questions and Answers

If we are in a state of mutual guarantee, will we not have to be considerate of the entire world? Will we be happy even if other things are happening elsewhere, or will we suddenly understand how dependent we are on everything that happens in the world?

It is not written anywhere in Kabbalah that we must take into consideration what is happening in the world. The world is governed from above. All the leaders, whoever they are, are managed from above. Our world is a world of results, the lowest world.

The common force, the light, comes from *Ein Sof* (infinity) through all the worlds, which are concealments of the light. Through them it influences our world, us, and all the nations of the world. We can only react to it and adjust ourselves to the upper world through our actions.

The bonding between us indicates that we are in congruence with the upper world, which is entirely as one. Our soul above is called Adam, and it is one, just as the upper force is one. Adam's soul divided into many souls, but if we collect them all together, all our desires, our inclinations, we will adjust ourselves to the upper force, the common force of Nature. *Elokim* (God) in *Gematria* is "The Nature."

Will the world not influence us then?

Not only will the world not influence us, but by elevating our desires, we become the ones who influence the upper world. Then, the upper world will influence our world and all the nations of the world. Prophet Isaiah wrote that the nations of the world will take the children of Israel on their shoulders and bring them to Jerusalem to build the Temple. It is an allegorical way of saying that the whole world will understand that there is only one place for the land of Israel.

Will all the people have to achieve that mutual guarantee, understanding, and *Dvekut* (adhesion)?

Yes, mutual guarantee and mutual love. We have to keep the law, "Love your neighbor as yourself." However, we need not think about when it will happen because as soon as we keep this law and move toward it, even by a fraction of an inch, we will no longer be opposite from Nature, but in congruence with it. The *tendency*, the *intention* is in the making, just as when a disobedient and troublesome child suddenly begins to behave well. We immediately begin to treat him differently. As we do these things, we will immediately see that we are on the right track because suddenly we will feel empowered and that our actions are blessed.

We hear that everyone wants love. When we begin to talk about mutual guarantee and mutual connection, people feel satisfaction, a sensation of love. No budget can cover all the problems and troubles that exist in the nation. No one will agree to be the last to receive a piece of the pie; each will pull in one's own direction, and there will never be an end to it.

We must sit at a roundtable like a family, and first and foremost, treat each other with love, and bring everyone under the umbrella of mutual guarantee, where we are all one. We must make our decisions like a family: one needs housing, another needs some money, another's health is poor, another is old, and so on. As in a family, after the conversation at the roundtable, everyone will understand what we need to do in order to change the situation. Everyone will also feel satisfaction in being the one who made concessions and was big-hearted.

We are assuming that in a family, people care about each other.

This is the point that we are missing. Without it, we will never reach a solution. We will have more and more committees, but nothing will help. People will not even go to those committees, and if they do, it will only show that they are useless. Our world is global, round, and if we cannot find a solution or a process that agrees with the laws of the world, we will lose. This will be a big loss because the next eruption could be much worse. We need to think about it in advance, so we will not say afterward, "We tried but it didn't work out." The damage that will be done to the people will be very big and will invoke such bitterness and pain that we cannot tell where it will lead.

What does it mean that today the world is global? How did it suddenly become global?

There is nothing new about the laws of the world; only *we* have changed through history. It is written in the wisdom of Kabbalah that from the end of the twentieth century and the beginning of the twenty-first–as Baal HaSulam, the Vilna Gaon, and others said–our world will move into a state of being global.

"Being global" means that the primary law appearing in the world is the law of the circle: we are all connected and dependent on each other. And if we are dependent and connected, it is impossible to start fighting. We must come to some settlement, something sensitive, considerate, in mutual guarantee. We are quickly approaching that state around the world.

We will soon find that not only do we feel the need for a solution, but that there is no other solution other than mutuality. Once we arrive at a solution after having sat with everyone, we will feel satisfied. We will be respected for having made concessions for others, and we will feel warmth because we were considerate of others. We will feel safer because we will not be alone anymore; we will be together with everyone.

In this way, we discover the power in unity that acts in accord with the upper force. Everyone must feel that power, the entire nation, all nations. In the wisdom of Kabbalah, the force appears immediately to those who become connected to society. Now, the world is about to discover it. The unrest throughout the world is only the beginning of this surfacing because what people really need, even when they cannot express it, is love.

It is written that we should teach our children and write on the *Mezuzah*.* Does this concern internal states?

The sons are us. In previous portions, the sons were our own future states. The current state is called a "father," and the next state is considered a "son," the result of the first state..

Is it not clear that we are moving from state to state? Is there something we must do in order to move to it?

Of course. We must constantly move toward it when ascending to the level of keeping that law, as well as in the new conditions in which we nevertheless maintain the law of unity, the law of love.

Does that mean that a greater measure of connection between us is our sons?

Yes. In fact, the whole portion is a result of *Shema Ysrael* (Hear, O Israel) from the previous portion, which is why it is written so. It is also written on the *Mezuzahs*. A person going out of one's state or returning to one's state refers to the exit and the entrance to the house.

The "house" is one's *Kli* (vessel), one's heart, and all of one's desires. When we connect the new desires and correct them, when we enter and exit, the light is always with us. This is the correction called *Mezuzah*. It is a special light with which we must be equipped in order to embark on new corrections.

* "You shall teach them diligently to your sons and shall talk of them when you sit in your house and when you walk by the way and when you lie down and when you rise up. You shall bind them as a sign on your hand and they shall be as frontals on your forehead. You shall write them on the doorposts of your house and on your gates" (Deuteronomy, 6:7-9).

In total, our souls consist of 613 desires. We need to correct those desires one at a time, from light to heavy, so they have the aim to bestow upon others, and through others to the Creator.

A state of *Arvut* (mutual guarantee) is when we all care for one another. Today, when people are feeling bad, they will agree to unite. But what will keep them together a day after the trouble is over?

Mutual guarantee. This is why it is not enough to decide to love each other now. The question is "How can we keep the love over time?" The answer is that only through mutual guarantee is it possible to connect us in such a way that if one falls, everyone falls, and so everyone sustains everyone else.

If I had nothing before and suddenly have something, thanks to mutual guarantee, of course I will be happy about it. What about those who had plenty and gave it up?

This is why, when we speak of implementing mutual guarantee, we are speaking of a round-table around which we will all sit together, even a hundred people. Each of us will raise his or her concerns and request what he or she needs. But first, we must unite among us. Only through our unity in mutual guarantee, as one nation in a small country, will we resolve our problems. There is no other way to work them out, as we have no other resources, and no way to divide the pie in a way that fills our deficits. We will be only hurting ourselves this way, and it is clear that nothing will come out of it.

We have only one alternative: a deliberation that leads to bonding and love. If we begin to organize the entire nation around the table and begin to act through the media, on reality shows, on TV, on the internet, in theatres, in music, and in cooperation with different artists, we can educate people to appreciate the concept of "mutual guarantee," and then we will see how everyone is connected. It will not be long before we see a different side to people.

We will feel it when we drive our cars, and we will feel it in children being less violent toward each other. We will feel it everywhere. We will begin to influence the entire world with this force because it will be us giving to the entire world, though it may not seem that way right now. As soon as we have the good force, it will spread to the entire world.

We cannot bring security to the country unless we muster the power of *Arvut*. Today it is impossible to govern in the traditional way, however we may try.

There is only one thing we need to add to the efforts to keep us safe: we must implement the law, "Love your neighbor as yourself," as it is promised here. This is called "Torah" (law) and not other symbols, as others think about the Torah, and the meaning of the *Mitzvot* (commandments) of the Torah.

The Torah means, "I have created the evil inclination, I have created for it the Torah as a spice," because "the light in it reforms them." We need to come to a state of love. If we come to it, there will be happiness, health, and security.

When Abraham established the nation, he explained to everyone who came to his tent in Babylon about the meaning of *Arvut*. He described the quality of *Hesed* (mercy), which is Abraham's quality, and said that this is how we should relate to one another. This is how he established the nation, and this is how thousands of people followed him. It all depends on whether or not we can connect today. This is not merely an idea; we have no other choice; it is the only possible solution, and we must listen before the troubles come.

TERMS

Benevolent (the Good Who Does Good)

The light comes from the Creator, who is benevolent. However, because of our disparity from the light, we feel it as the opposite. It is like a mother who loves her child, but the child sees her behavior as bad. Inside, her heart is good and open, but on the outside she must behave differently with her child in order to "straighten" him out. It is the same with us. Everything works according to the promise that is written in this portion.

Laws and Ordinances, Opposite the One Law

The "One Law" is the light that stands opposite all of our desires, which are the 613 desires. If we arrange all of them in bestowal and love, in congruence with the light, we will be in a state of benevolence (the Good who does good).

Enemy and Triumph

The "enemy" is our ego. Triumph is when we can rise above it, as it is written, "Love covers all transgressions" (Proverbs, 10:12). The ego is under an "umbrella" in mutual guarantee, and the character of everyone remains inside. It is burning, and this is very good, but we are above it, united.

Fear

"Fear" is one's first contact with the ever-growing will to receive. The fear comes when we cannot rise above the ego. There are always such states, but once we rise above the ego, fear no longer exists.

Re'eh

(Behold)

(Deuteronomy, 11:26-16:17)

Portion Summary

The portion, *Re'eh* (Behold), begins with Moses' words to the people to come and see the blessing and the curse, which the Creator commands them. If the people adhere to the Creator's commandments, they will be blessed. Otherwise, they will be cursed.

Afterward, Moses surveys with the people the preparations to enter the land of Israel, the duties and the prohibitions that accompany the entrance, the work of the Creator, specifically in the Temple, and the prohibition against listening to false prophets that deflect the people from serving the Creator. The portion also cites the laws of *Kashrut, tithing, *Shmita* (remission), and the three festivals on which it is customary to make an *Aliya la Regel* (pilgrimage) to Jerusalem.**

* Laws of *Kashrut* define what is kosher, meaning permitted for eating or for preparing food, wearing, and other areas of human conduct.

Commentary

The Torah speaks only about the inner meaning of all the matters just mentioned. It is written, "Behold," referring to the reception of light of *Hochma*, which is seeing. "Seeing" is the highest of the five senses, and marks the highest level of attainment. When a person truly sees whether what is happening is a blessing or a curse, he is standing right before the entrance to the land of Israel.

Eretz Ysrael: *Eretz* means *Ratzon* (desire), and *Ysrael* (Israel) means *Yashar El* (straight to God). In other words, *Eretz Ysrael* is a desire aimed entirely toward bestowal, toward mutual guarantee, connection between everyone "as one man with one heart." At the foot of Mount Sinai, we accepted the condition, "Love your neighbor as yourself," to be "as one man with one heart." Forty years later, we complete the correction and are ready to enter the land of Israel, where all desires are connected in true mutual bestowal. This is why it is called *Yashar El* (straight to God). The Creator, whose quality of bestowal and love exists in the world, governs the whole of reality.

After the forty years of correction—forty degrees from *Bina* to *Malchut* and from *Malchut* to *Bina*—we must obtain the general correction of our will to receive so it is entirely in bestowal upon others. This is the degree of *Bina*, the degree of *Hesed* (mercy), the degree of Abraham. Afterward, there are the 613 *Mitzvot* (commandments) by which one corrects all 613 desires into having the aim to bestow upon others, because "Love your neighbor as yourself" is a great rule in the Torah, a rule that includes everything within it.

All we need is to correct our egotistical desires into bestowal, love, and mutual guarantee. This is, in fact, the condition for our receiving the Torah. The Torah is an instruction how we can correct ourselves. The light that reforms is really the power of the Torah, the power of the light that corrects us.

It is written, "I have created the evil inclination, I have created for it the Torah as a spice," because "the light in it reforms them."

One who discovers the evil inclination within, the egotistical desires, the hatred, repulsion, the inner Mount Sinai (mountain of *Sina'a* [hate]), deserves to receive the correction method called Torah, or "the wisdom of Kabbalah," because this is where the light is hidden. This is why Kabbalah is called "the internality of the Torah," and "The Torah (law) of truth."

This is how we advance toward the entrance to the land of Israel. Henceforth, we must be able to "see" how to distinguish our corrected desires toward others from uncorrected ones. Have we truly become a nation now, with our common desire, which was previously the land of Canaan, then Egypt, and then a desert?

These are degrees of our common desire, in which we passed through stages in our relationships. Now, we are entering a relationship called *Yashar El*, which is solely toward mutual bestowal. We are becoming similar to the *Shechina* (Divinity), to the Assembly of Israel, with all of our desires aimed straight at the Creator (*Yashar El*), directly toward bestowal and mutual love, where we are discovering the common quality of bestowal called "the revelation of the Creator to the creatures."

It is written that the Creator appears only in the land of Israel, in a desire that is directed only by equivalence of form. When we are in a state of love and bestowal upon each other, we discover that common force in Nature and it appears to us.

The common force that appears within us is called "the conquering of the land" because at that time we can enter our egos with the quality of bestowal and begin to conquer all of our desires. We can begin to place them under the governance of mutual bestowal and mutual love. We gradually fight all the nations, meaning our own thoughts and desires that rebel against bonding and mutual guarantee, against the unity between us. Once we sort out those desires, we separate them from the *Kedusha* (holiness).

This is the portion's main theme. Within us are several kinds of desires, called "still," "vegetative," "animate," and "speaking."

We correct them from "easy" to "difficult." The list of laws before us tells us how to tell them apart and how to perform scrutinies and corrections. These are the rules concerning *Kashrut* in the still, vegetative, and animate, and show us how to distinguish the relations between humans.

The preparation for this process has already been made by the light of *Hochma*. We did it in the desert, meaning in the state of the "desert" within us, through the light of *Hassadim*. Now we are correcting ourselves through the light of *Hochma*. We shift from the degree of *Hafetz Hesed* (desiring mercy), which is "That which you hate, do not do to your friend," and enter *Eretz Ysrael*, a degree of "Love your neighbor as yourself." These are the two stages leading to correction.

We test all our desires to see whether they are a blessing or a curse. If a person is in self-love in those desires, these are a curse because nothing good will come from them to that person. However, if one corrects them, there is the promise that one will always be in equivalence of form in those desires, in closeness to the upper force, the common force, and that no harm will come to that person.

Even today, if we wish to live in Israel safely and prosperously, with just division, we can achieve these only by correcting our egotistical desires, only through mutual love. If we begin to connect, we will immediately feel that there is a force among us that is putting things in order. No one understands how to do this, but we have the Torah and we can make that connection and be an example to the rest of the world.

We need to understand it and make these corrections. These are the corrections of the three years of *Orlah* (uncircumcised) fruit, the seven years of *Shmita* (remission), and the *Yovel* (jubilee, fifty years' anniversary), as well as the rules of *Kashrut* on different levels—prophets and priests. All of these explain to us how we should arrange things within us to destroy the idol worship that we see all around us and within us when we bow to other goals besides the love of others and the establishment of our Temple.

Bringing an offering is also related to the correction. The word *Korban* (offering/sacrifice) comes from the word, *Karov* (near), meaning to draw near to the quality of bestowal, to the Creator. The *Ketoret* (incense), from the word, *Maktir* (crowning), brings us closer to *Kedusha* (holiness), to bestowal upon others. We need to understand that *Kedusha* and *Tuma'a* (impurity) are the love of others and its opposite.

Questions and Answers

What are the blessing and the curse of our generation?

This has not changed through the ages. The Torah is eternal, since the time of the creation of the world, since the creation of the entire reality, since the world of *Ein Sof* (infinity), through all the worlds down to the cascading of our reality today. Today we must relive history and climb back to the world of *Ein Sof*, not with our physical bodies, but in our minds, in our awareness.

This can happen only by correcting our egotistical desire that was created this way to begin with, as it is written, "I have created the evil inclination." Correction means achieving love of others through the upper light, the upper force. In fact, it is the whole of the work of *Kedusha* (holiness), the work of the offerings, that brings one closer to it, always knowing where one is still not corrected.

When we read the Torah, we see that we are constantly making mistakes, such as in the desert and in other places. Almost every portion repeats the story of the children of Israel falling time and time again. However, we fall only to discover the desires that are still uncorrected, and to bring them to *Kedusha*, to correction. Through the corrupt desires, we achieve correction, bonding between us.

So why are we falling now? What have we fallen into in our time?

Our generation is special. We have reached the final realization, the complete correction of the world because the whole world is discovering that it is in a vague and unclear situation. All our systems are corrupted; we cannot find our way in this world because we are incongruent with the laws of Nature.

The nature that is now appearing to us is appearing from within. It is a nature of bestowal, a nature of love of others, a global world. Although we are still relating to the manifestation of this reality egotistically—not getting along with it, declining to connect or to unite with others—the reality that is appearing compels us to do so. It is emerging from within, out of the network of connections between us that forms a global-integral world that we do not match.

It is precisely when we discover that we cannot find our way in the world that the wisdom of Kabbalah appears. Without it, we will be lost because we will not understand what is happening to us. The wisdom of Kabbalah explains that we must reach mutual guarantee, the law that was given to us at the foot of Mount Sinai, which we must keep. That law states that the more we feel reality as opposite from us, as one we cannot get along with, the more we and the world must be corrected.

The corrections are in unity, in moving toward reciprocity, in communicating, in congruence with Nature, which we will feel as good, helping, supporting, and not as resisting or threatening, as we currently feel it. Although all our systems are currently on the verge of collapse, we feel primarily the economic and financial systems because all our life systems depend on them, especially the food that we need in order to survive.

The wisdom of Kabbalah reveals to us the short, good, and easy way. All we need is to listen and life will suddenly run smoother. If we engage in it, we will see how much light there is before us, which we will follow safely and enjoy life.

It is especially true here in Israel. We have a method. If we unite, we will form a focal point for the rest of the world. All of life's events happen specifically to disclose to us the problem we must solve in order to be saved. We will truly have to correct ourselves in unity and truly become the people of Israel—connected, bonded, and liberated from all the troubles. By doing that, we will become "a light for the nations."

Is it against human nature to ask people to love everyone?

For now, we must begin superficially. We need to understand that solving our problems and truly arriving at the land of Israel, in prosperity, safety, and abundance, is possible only if we unite.

"Uniting" means being in mutual guarantee. This is the condition we took upon ourselves when we received the Torah at the foot of Mount Sinai, and it is where Nature is pushing us, because it is the law of the comprehensive integral system that is appearing before us today. We can learn this law from science, too. It tells us we have no other choice; if we are tied together in this way, we must arrange our systems accordingly.

It is especially true for us, and subsequently for the rest of the world. This is why charity is pointless, and the same goes for thinking that we can succeed through the work of this or that committee, by raising taxes or by paying this or that sum.

Even if we divide the common pie, we will not succeed because the law of Nature—which determines that we have to be connected "as one man with one heart"—is against us.

How do we do it?

We need to learn how to do it. We go by trial and error, but we see that it can be done, and actually quite easily. The only obstacle is a psychological barrier that we must leap over. When we do, it will happen easily. We only need to turn a tiny "knob," like a child who presses a button and switches on a huge machine. Indeed, this is who we are.

It will happen quickly, but only if we comprehend that unity is the solution to all our problems. If we do not, we will suffer more and more blows. From them, we will still learn what to do. However, this is a long and painful road.

But there are problems all over the world.

Yes, and in the end the whole world will come to us.

Pointing the finger at us?

Yes, they will subconsciously, and even consciously, feel it. They are even saying that we are to blame for all the troubles in the world. They will demand practical solutions from us. So before it happens, we must make the wisdom of Kabbalah known throughout the world and show everyone what it means to be "a light for the nations."

From *The Zohar*: And the Lord Said to Abram after Lot Was Separated

"Only the Creator governs over the land of Israel. When Israel sinned and were offering incense to other gods inside the land, Divinity was seemingly rejected from her place because they were anointing and burning incense for other gods to connect with Divinity, and then they were given governance. The incense makes a tie so as to connect. Hence, they were sucking from Divinity and received the governance from her, and then the rest of the nations ruled, the prophets were cancelled, and all those high degrees did not rule over the land."

Zohar for All, Lech Lecha (Go Forth), item 185

In truth, everything depends on whether a person "invites" the upper force to be next to him. The upper force is a force of bestowal and love that is above our egos. This is why it is called "upper"; it is a nature above our own. We must bring it a little closer to us, draw it according to the equivalence of form so it will be in us, and then we will fear nothing.

What are the laws mentioned here, such as *kashrut* and tithing?

They are all corrections of the will to receive.

Can following these laws only on the physical, material level award me those corrections?

No, following on the corporeal level will not help. It is as if we want to share our income through our own calculations. This will not work because it is our *hearts* that need correction, not acting with our hands and legs.

However, we need not avoid physical actions because they sustain the framework of the nation. It is a certain approach that should persist in the nation, but the important thing is the correction of the heart. Baal HaSulam wrote that the Torah was given to men of heart,* meaning to correct the heart, as it is written, "Write them on the tablet of your heart" (Proverbs, 3:3). The whole Torah was written only to correct the heart.

Correcting the heart is inner work.

Inner work is all that is required of us, correcting the desire. Our bodies are flesh, and there are different things we can do with them. The flesh can smile at others while in truth we want to kill them. We have no need for this bogus smile, this superficial attitude toward things. We need the heart, the connection of the hearts. If we do not do it, we will be in big trouble, so let us hope that it will become more prevalent in the nation and we will advance favorably.

From *The Zohar*: For who is God, besides the Lord? And who is a rock, besides our God?

"For who is God, save the Lord?" Everything is in the permission of the Creator. It is not as it seems in the stars and fortunes, which

* "Introduction to the book, Panim Meirot UMasbirot."

show something and the Creator changes it into another way. "And who is a Rock, save our God?" means that there is no such painter as the Creator. He is the perfect painter, who makes and paints a form within a form, a fetus in its mother's insides, and completes that picture in all its corrections, and instills a high soul within it, which is similar to the upper correction.

Zohar for All, *Lech Lecha* (Go Forth), item 328

All that we need to do is to want the correction. That force that is over us, the overall desire to bestow, is called the "Creator." It is that which depicts in us the right images. The connections between us are called "its forms," and in the end, according to our requests, it connects us and is found within us. It is called "the dweller clothing in the *Shechina* (Divinity)."

We are the *Shechina*, the Assembly of Israel. When we are united, the quality of bestowal is in us.

When we truly achieve this mutual guarantee between us, will we discover the *Kashrut*, the tithing, and all these laws between us?

When we begin to come closer, we will experience *everything* that is written in the Torah.

What is the work of the Creator, the Temple?

Man's heart is called "a house." All of man's desires are called "man's house" or "man's heart." When everyone intends toward bestowal, toward bonding with others, it is called "holiness."

Is it a certain state of mind, in which one does the work of the Creator?

It is not a state of mind; it is one's attitude, one's intention with regard to others.

Can it be anytime and anywhere?

Yes, of course. It makes no difference where you are physically.

The portion mentions the three *Regalim* (pilgrimage festivals), which in our world appear as festivals of *Pesach* (Passover), *Shavuot* (Feast of Weeks), and *Sukkot* (Feast of the Tabernacles).

These are degrees. The more we correct ourselves, the more we advance on the 125 degrees. And the more we advance, the more breaks there are between the degrees, such as days of the week, the Sabbath, beginnings of months, the three pilgrimage festivals, then the *Shmita*, *Yovel*, and so forth.

The three pilgrimage festivals, Passover, *Shavuot*, and *Sukkot*, are special degrees. In the ARI's *Gate of Intentions*, he mentions them quite often as "great" and "sublime." These are measures of our connection. If we work and work, and connect between us, and suddenly something closes, it is called a *Regel* (leg), meaning a step forward. And as we connect and correct our relations, making them closer, we reach another stage.

The three stages are *NHY*, *HGT*, and *HBD*, or *Ibur-Yenika-Mochin* (conception-nursing-adulthood). We learn about them in the wisdom of Kabbalah. This is how we advance until we build between us a complete *Partzuf* (face), called "Adam" (man) who is *Domeh* (similar) to the complete quality of bestowal, which is the Creator.

Is the state of *Eretz Ysrael* an absolute, or is there still more work in it?

According to this portion, we are now moving into the land of Israel and must correct all our desires through the light of *Hochma*. Working in the land of Israel is not simple. It does not happen all at once, but is rather a long process.

Can we understand from the *Regalim* that we are working on bonding, but see no results until a new state suddenly appears, and this is the next step forward?

Yes.

Is this a *Regel*?

A *Regel* is the end of all the previous stages. It is when a person stops, as though parking, and continues from it toward the next period.

How does tithing connect to all of that?

"Tithing" means a tenth of *Malchut*. *Malchut* is the tenth *Sefira* (singular of *Sefirot*) in our entire structure. We have desires called *Keter*, *Hochma*, *Bina*, *Hesed*, *Gevura*, *Tifferet*, *Netzah*, *Hod*, *Yesod*, and *Malchut*. *Malchut* is the tenth, but since we cannot correct it, we pass it on by giving a tithing (ten percent), and this is its correction.

To whom do we give it?

To the people, to the Temple. The house is more than just man's heart. *Beit ha Mikdash* (The Temple House) is entirely outside of us. It is in our connections with others, in our desires toward others, and we dedicate *Malchut* to that.

Terms

Blessing

If we want to reach the quality of bestowal, the light affects us and builds that quality in us.

Curse

The opposite of a blessing. If a person wishes to have the intention to receive, to exploit others, to receive from them, that person suffers blows that teach him that he should be the opposite. It always works that way.

A Must, as Opposed to a Prohibition

Correction as opposed to corruption. It is forbidden to be in the egotistical will to receive. Rather, it is "a must" to correct it into a desire with the aim to bestow.

Place

A "place" is a desire. There are no actual places; the world we are in is called an "imaginary place." It seems to us that we are in a place in space, in a universe, but the truth is that it is a desire of the Creator, where we perceive certain phenomena.

Temple

A *Mikdash* (Temple) comes from the word *Kadosh* (holy). This means blessing, bestowal, love of others, anything that is outside a person is called Temple. Within us is only a point. When we connect to others, our attitude toward them builds in them a Temple. A person should come to the Temple and enter it.

A "Temple" is all the desires of others toward which we are in bestowal. We bring them contributions or tithing; we come there with all our gifts, with the "holy ones." We can bestow upon others anything we want. We bring offerings and do this work. The offerings are very important because by giving to others, we bring ourselves closer to bestowal.

Prophecy

This is a special degree that the Ramchal (Rabbi Moshe Chaim Lozzatto) wrote about in his beautiful style in the book, *The Way of the Lord*. He elaborates there all the ways to achieve the degrees of bestowal, one of which is prophecy.

Is this something that exists in every person along the way?

It exists in everyone and anyone can achieve it.

Kashrut

With each of our desires that were corrupted, we make various scrutinies. We cut and arrange them in such a way that we can use them with the aim to bestow. This is considered making them *Kosher*.

Shmita (Remission)

Shmita is like the Sabbath. After a certain number of degrees, a person takes a break at a stop, performs a correction, and moves on after seven years.

Three *Regalim* (Pilgrimages)

The three *Regalim* are *NHY*, *HGT*, *HBD* that we go through *Ibur-Yenika-Mochin* (conception-nursing-adulthood) in our connections. We go through these three stops, corrections, and then reach the end of correction.

SUMMARY

All we need to do is to connect. In the bonding between us, we will discover the whole Torah, we will resolve all our troubles and problems, and we will be given the great respect that the people of Israel deserve.

Shoftim

(Judges)

(Deuteronomy, 16:18-21:9)

Portion Summary

The portion, *Shoftim* (Judges), continues to explain the *Mitzvot* (commandments) connected to the entrance to the land of Israel. The portion begins with appointing judges to make the laws and officers to enforce them so there will be true justice in Israel.

The portion describes the laws of the king, who must be chosen from among the people. The portion also deals with the prohibition against engaging in witchcraft, and turns the people to the true prophets. Finally, the portion teaches the people how they should conduct themselves in a time of war.

Commentary

The Torah was given to every person for self-correction, as it is written, "I have created the evil inclination, I have created for it the Torah as a spice." Every person, whether or not demanding social justice, should first discover that one is filled with the evil inclination. We must discover that we are completely egotistical in order to perform our correction. Put differently, we need to discover that we are living as criminals.

During the High Holidays* we say, "We are at fault; we have betrayed." It is written about these words, "Keep far from a false word" (Exodus 23:7). We need to discover that it is we who have committed those transgressions. If we think what is written is overstated and is not a true depiction of who we are, it is a sign that we have not yet come to know who we really are, and that we still need to discover the entirety of our evil inclination.

This is when the Torah comes to us, because "the light in it reforms them." That is, the Torah instructs us how to elicit from it the light that will reform us, so we may achieve love and bonding with others.

There is much work for us to do: We walk in the darkness, in the desert, in cries, in scrutinies, in raising *MAN*, in various transgressions, such as with the spies, and the waters of quarreling, until we reach the boundaries of the land of Israel. We correct ourselves until we can use our desires in order to bestow.

However, it is more than a mere restriction of our desire; it is actually using the desire in favor of others. The same desires we discovered within us—which worked only in our own favor to cheat, lie, steal, and manipulate—have now come to a point of correction and cleansing through the forty years in the desert up to the entrance to the land of Israel. This is when we approach the stage of the inner work on the ego, the point where we turn the use of the ego into bestowal, in favor of others. Here, it is considered that the angel of death has become a holy angel.

It is a very different type of work. In this work, a person needs judges and officers. The judges are the decisions that a person makes in advance, from the *Rosh* (head) of the spiritual *Partzuf* (face), the *Rosh* of the *Neshama* (soul). "Judges" are the premeditation concerning precisely how to work with one's ego, how to manipulate

* The ten days beginning on *Rosh Hashanah* and ending on *Yom Kippur*. Known also as the "Ten Days of Repentance."

it, and how to set it up so that it gives its fullest power and turns all of its negativity toward the favor of others.

Afterward, one needs to establish officers over oneself so as not to suddenly deviate from the way, since even if the decision is initially correct, one cannot tell the future. This is called the *Guf* (body) of the *Partzuf*, of the *Neshama*. The *Neshama* are those egotistical desires that one turns into the intention to bestow.

If we use the desires according to the form of the ego, we have no *Rosh*, nor do we need one because we are being pushed. However, if we want to begin to use our desires in favor of others, we must first restrict them and then act according to scrutinies and decisions we have made before, through the light that reforms. When we use our egos favorably, it is considered "repentance." In that state, we use those desires only in favor of others, without any favors returning to ourselves.

The premeditation is called "judges," and the execution is called "officers." These are two qualities of bestowal: one that plans the action (judges) and the other that executes them (officers). These are the same terrible desires that were in us before, and which we used only to harm others and to benefit ourselves. These desires now become *Yashar El* (straight to God), *Ysrael* (Israel). They are called *Eretz Ysrael*, where *Eretz* means *Ratzon* (desire), and *Ysrael* means *Yashar El* (straight to God). This is how we advance, when our desire is aimed entirely toward bestowal upon the upper force, the Creator, through bestowal upon others.

This is why we need the two forces—officers and judges—keeping us and tending to us, performing the right scrutinies. Previously, we had only the scrutiny of bitter and sweet. "Sweet" means what we wanted, and "bitter" means what we did not want. Here, however, it refers to another scrutiny concerning bitter and sweet—a scrutiny of true or false.

"Truth" means bestowal upon the upper force, nearing him, connection with others and actualization of the quality of bestowal.

This is why humanity was given it, so we may carry out the connection and work on ourselves, as it is written, "Through the love of man to the love of God."

Correcting the desires means changing them from caring for ourselves, from reception, into using them in favor of others. It is a correction from falsehood into truth, so it will not be bitter to us, but sweet. "Truth" means using the desire in favor of others, even if it tastes bitter. It is called "making a *Mitzva*" (singular of *Mitzvot*).

Man is made of a desire to receive pleasure. There are 613 *Mitzvot*, which are the 613 desires in us, our 613 egotistical drives with which we exploit others. We should turn them into being in favor of others.

There are two degrees here: one is called the "desert," through which a person reaches the degree of *Bina*, bestowal, and the other is called *Eretz Ysrael* (land of Israel), the desire to bestow, when a person actually acquires, meaning corrects the use of all the desires with the intention to bestow. This is how we become Kabbalists—receiving the revelation of Godliness, which is our goal. It is the same for each person and for the whole of humanity.

In truth, we are already in our final correction, in complete redemption. We transcend the egotistical use of our desires and qualities and elevate them into altruistic use in favor of everyone and in favor of the upper force, the Creator. This leads us to the general correction of our desires, connecting us together so that each of us achieves the revelation of the Holy Divinity, the Assembly of Israel, through our correction in relation to others.

Questions and Answers

When we discover that all our desires are to use and exploit others, we ask for correction. But does that mean that we actually desire to harm others?

Of course we do not feel or understand if we should imagine ourselves as harming others, or perhaps agree that it is so, even if we do not feel this way.

We tend to judge people by their actions. However, the majority of the transgressions discussed here are in the intention, and not in the action.

We are unaware of them in our actions, too. We begin to see that we are committing these sins when we begin to move toward others. Mistakes and sins are only in relation to others. When we truly begin to act toward bonding, we discover how incapable we are, how we reject, forget, and oppose it, and how we are fooling ourselves all the time, even subconsciously.

All of a sudden, we discover that we have totally forgotten that the Torah behooves us to achieve bonding, love, "All of Israel are friends," etc. It is a process that happens to everyone; we cannot achieve spirituality and observe the Torah unless we follow the path of bonding between us.

What is a judge?

"Judges" are thoughts and desires that appear to us out of many others that are still buried in us. We more or less know our qualities; we can judge the state they are in, and we can turn their aim in favor of others, or at least see how much we have no desire to give to others, and what felons we are. This, in itself, is a high degree.

The wicked people in the Torah are not ordinary people. This is a high degree. The Torah was actually written for the wicked, as it is written, "I have created the evil inclination." The Torah is *intended* for those with an evil inclination. If we do not feel that we are selfish, criminals, we do not need the Torah, and it is not meant for us.

By which law does the judge sentence? By which law is one declared a transgressor?

The judge is the individual. Once directed toward connection with others, we begin to judge ourselves: "Do I really want to connect with others?" We scrutinize why we want to connect: "What is the basis upon which I should observe that law? Is it clear what should be done? Has anyone told me that I should do it? Do I want the next world or this world? Am I hoping to gain something out of it? Or, do I really want to do it for the Creator without any self-gratification?"

Each step along the way contains many degrees on which we discover that we are evil. If we do not push ourselves toward bonding with others, we will not discover how opposed to unity we are. There is a lot of work before we reach the state of "I have created the evil inclination." In that work we discover that the Creator has created the evil inclination in us, and without it, we have nothing.

We do not understand the nature of Creation. Creation is the evil inclination. We are unaware of the extent to which we seek only our own good, and not the good of others. Moreover, the more others suffer, the more superior we feel, which gives us pleasure and fulfillment.

It is very misleading. An ordinary person in a law-abiding society does not feel like a criminal if he or she did not do anything unlawful.

True, but you describe the corporeal, earthly life. Here we are talking about something else. If you want to discover the Creator, you need to turn your intention to bestowal, to loving others.

What if we stated what you just said to a person without knowledge in Kabbalah?

We would be ridiculed, no doubt.

It makes no sense, and it is completely untrendy.

True, which is why we need to explain that today, we must use the true Torah. The wisdom of Kabbalah is called the "true Torah"; it is the internality of the Torah because the light in it reforms. In other words, it is a method for the correction of the soul. We are in exile from the spiritual world, and we must therefore correct ourselves and discover spirituality, discover the

Creator. This is the purpose, and the Torah was given to us so we would come to "know the God of your father and serve Him" (1 Chronicles, 28:9).

In a corrected state, will there be no judges and officers, no laws?

No. Here, in this world, we have to live according to what humanity determines, according to what the people and the government decide. We should respect these laws because they were made by a hidden Providence.

In this world we have to be like everyone else, "I dwell among my own people" (2 Kings, 4:13). However, within us we need to come to know Him, to rise to the level where we somewhat resemble Him if we wish to open our eyes in the Torah, if we want to discover Godliness and the upper laws, and to feel and come to know the Creator. We attain the revelation of the Creator to the extent of our *Dvekut* (adhesion), the measure of our equivalence of form.

Can there be a match between the corporeal laws and the spiritual one?

Yes, at the final and complete correction.

And before that?

Before that, certainly not, because we determine corporeal laws according to our egos. The more we begin to keep these laws in spirituality together, we will also want to project them onto the corporeal world. We cannot do this separately. Prior to the ruin of the Temple, when the people of Israel kept these laws, we kept them and also lived by them.

Are there any officers in society today?

No. Today, officers and judges work by laws that people determined. It has no connection to spirituality. We also cannot establish spiritual laws between us because we cannot keep them. All spiritual laws deal with the love of others. These are laws of the general, global system, which is appearing today and is beginning to require us to keep it.

But the current situation is to the contrary. People want justice, but do not know how to implement it.

The network of connections between us is appearing all over the world. We are all connected through it, and we are all dependent on one another. This is why people sense the need for change, that they must do something. We all feel uncomfortable because nothing that we try succeeds. We are in crises in our families, at work, in the education system, in culture, and basically everywhere.

But this is something deeper. We often feel we're in crisis regardless of what is happening outside.

It makes no difference; what matters is what we feel. On the outside, things can be beautiful. On the whole, people are not starving, yet many are going out to the streets and raise a cry. They are unaware that behind their demands for social justice lies a cry from the lack of connection. This is the truth that is appearing in the world today.

The world is manifesting itself as integral, global, as entirely interconnected. Yet, people feel disconnected by the lack of unity, and this is what awakens them to riot.

The portion speaks of a king who must be chosen from among the people. If a king is an all-powerful ruler, how can we speak of kingship in that state? It is as if today the people were to democratically appoint a leader as king; it sounds completely unrealistic.

When all the thoughts and desires work toward the land of Israel, to the desire for the Creator, the desire for comprehensive, mutual, and complete bestowal, a person chooses the foundation with which one influences everything. With that foundation, one reaches the *Keter* (crown), meaning similarity to the Creator in every way.

We creatures are in *Malchut* (kingship), which is our big will to receive. The upper force that created us, on the other hand, is in *Keter*. We need to connect all our desires from the "people." Out of the unity of everyone, we choose our most basic foundation, and call it a "king," like King David, Messiah son of David, who is *Malchut* that reaches *Keter*. A "king" in Israel is not as a king in other nations, the way romantic novels picture it. Being a king in Israel is the hardest work there is.

Is it about a person?

The "king" is the supreme judge. He is the person to whom people come to ask questions, and he cannot turn away those who come to him.

Does he also pass judgment?

Yes. Maimonides and other sources write about that work, which is hard work indeed.

Is it realistic to have a king in Israel today?

The king is not one who sits on the throne. He is the supreme judge. The king is the one who knows how to arrange, bring together, and correct the most crucial decisions with the aim to bestow. He is responsible for the entire nation, for collecting all the people's desires within him, and raising them up to the *Keter*.

There is either a king in each of us or a general king between us, raising us to the Creator and leading us toward correction. Messiah, son of David, is the one who pulls the whole of *Malchut* to the degree of *Keter*.

Today, people have no faith in the government; they want to take charge and make decisions. Is this a new phase emerging that will

lead to the conclusion that people need a representative to speak for them?

No. The people need to demand help from the government to receive education toward mutual guarantee. This is the obligation we received on Mount Sinai, when we were asked if we are responsible for one another, and if we want to be as one man with one heart.

This is our correction—"That which you hate, do not do to your friend." This is the stage of the desert. "Love your neighbor as yourself" is the stage called "land of Israel," mutual guarantee, to be "as one man with one heart." We must provide the education of mutual guarantee by ourselves to all the people. The government can help because it has the instruments, resources, and the media, but it is the people who must demand it.

What about the judicial system? Will we need officers and judges to keep the mutual guarantee?

We will have to rebuild the system so it is an educating system, with people who advocate, like officers and judges, a sort of renewed Sanhedrin.

The portion mentions witchcraft and divination. Why were they forbidden? Wouldn't people change for the better if they knew where the world was headed?

We are forbidden to rely on miracles or tell the future. The only permitted actions are those in which we serve as our own judges and officers to promote our progress. The wisdom of the Torah, meaning Kabbalah, objects to any witchcraft and blessing. It objects to notes and pleas from the Rabbi, to red strings, holy water, and horoscopes of any kind. All of it is considered "idol worship."

It is similar to what is said about Abram before he became Abraham, the father of the nation. He was engaged in selling idols, a preliminary degree that exists in each of us, in anyone who has not yet been corrected through a genuine disclosure of the evil inclination, because then one demands the actual spice for the Torah.

The people of Israel learn about conducts during war. What is war?

It is a struggle against the evil inclination. Man's enemies are those who dwell with him in his home, those in his heart, meaning all the desires, thoughts, sins, and mistakes that he should turn into *Mitzvot*, into acts of bestowal. An act of bestowal is called a *Mitzva* (singular of *Mitzvot*). There is an endless war here—the Creator's war with Amalek, which lasts for generations.

But as a result, we built an army with an ethics code and values.

We had no other choice. In the past, too, we had an army. So did King David, and so did all the others. As long as people have not been corrected, there has to be an army. If we were to change ourselves even a little toward mutual guarantee, we would immediately come and see that our neighbors all leave us in peace.

After all, we are not doing anything that is fundamentally wrong. The minute we direct ourselves correctly toward love of others between us and within Israel, and begin to connect as before, in brotherly love, we will tilt the direction toward the positive, the mutual, and we will witness peace and quiet throughout the country, health, education, and the end of external or internal struggles.

Terms

Judge

A "judge" is the one who decides.

Officer

Officers, as well judges, tend to the good influence on people.

Judgment and Justice

"Judgment" is a state in which one works above one's great will to receive. "Justice" is a state in which one works only in favor of others, without any thought of self-gratification.

King

This is a state where a person has the strength to do what is required according to the *Keter* (crown), according to the Creator, upper force that appears.

Witchcraft

Any action by which one wishes to obtain benefit without honest work, meaning that he is working for his ego.

Future

The result of an act of bestowal.

War

The only war is the one against the will to receive, against the ego. All other wars, including those in our world, result from the fact that we are not fighting against our egos. If we succeeded in that just a little, even our worst enemies will leave us.

Law

Nature around us is a law. It is similar to the law that appears and points to our interconnectedness, but detrimentally. The right, and beneficial connection, is called the "upper law."

Transgressor

One who uses one's will to receive for one's own favor and against the good of others.

Mutual Guarantee

The realization that we are interdependent and should be in favorable mutuality toward each other.

From *The Zohar*: Great Sanhedrin, Small Sanhedrin

The subsequent *Mitzva* is to assume the great courthouse, *Bina*, which–from the side of *Hesed*–is called *Elokim*, *Bina*, "the great court." Great is *Hesed*. It is great in its *Dinim*, left, and great in its merits, right. When the left of *Bina* is included in the right, *Hesed*, they are both called "great," as it is written, in the *Mitzva*, "You shall surely set a king over you." "Set" means above, in *Bina*, and "Set" below, in *Malchut*. This is how he should assume the great court from the side of *Bina*, although he already assumed the small court from the side of *Malchut*.

Zohar for All, *Shoftim* (Judges), item 21

Ki Tetze

(When You Go)

(Deuteronomy, 21:10-25:19)

Portion Summary

The portion, *Ki Tetze* (When You Go), details special and infrequent *Mitzvot* (commandments), such as the attitude toward a rebellious son, a firstborn son of a loved one or the hated one, and the commandment to send a bird from the nest and not harm it when taking the bird's eggs or nestlings.

The portion also details many *Mitzvot* that deal with everyday life, ethics, and social order, such as returning a loss, divorce, and the obligation to be considerate of others in vulnerable situations, such as poor, proselytes, orphans, and widows. Additionally, the portion mentions the importance of a just sentence. The last *Mitzva* (singular of *Mitzvot*) is to always remember what Amalek did to Israel when they came out of Egypt, when it jumped them when they were unprepared, and to blot out the memory of Amalek.

Commentary

The portion marks a stage in the spiritual development after the reception of the ego, the reception of the evil inclination from

Egypt. First, the evil inclination in us should appear, as it is written, "I have created the evil inclination." That appearance happens when we try to achieve love of others, to come out of ourselves. When we attempt to do it, we discover how much we are actually immersed in self-love and hatred of others. At that time we determine that our hatred of others and our love for ourselves are what is called the "evil inclination."

That revelation is profound inner work. It is no small task. There is a very good reason why it is written, "I have created the evil inclination." "I have created" means that the Creator created. The recognition of the evil inclination in us—hatred of others and love of ourselves—is precisely what brings us into contact with the Creator. From that recognition, we march on a path of hard work, trying to be good to others, as it is written, "Love your neighbor as yourself." Then we discover great internal obstacles, which actually come from above, from the Creator. This is Man's first contact with the Creator.

Following the initial contact with the Creator, we begin to move along with Him in partnership. This is when there is, "I have created the Torah as a spice," and we have someone to turn to, someone to help us correct ourselves.

It is precisely through the evil inclination that we make contact with the Creator. The evil inclination is the mediator, the connector between man and the Creator. This is the only reason why we would need it. We might lead an entire life without needing anything until we try to nurture love of others, and then we see how impossible it is.

Some people recognize the merit of love of others from their own feelings. It is a drive for something spiritual, to discover the meaning of life, its purpose, and its essence. Others achieve love of others through suffering, hopelessness about life, or an overall crisis, as we are now seeing the world over. These people search for a way out of the plight they are in, and discover that the world has become global, integral, and that the only choice they have is to connect to others in a reciprocal manner, or they might be left hungry the next day.

This fact is becoming increasingly evident. Some people discover it through an inner drive, and some are pushed to it by suffering. But sooner or later, all of us will have to connect to others in mutual guarantee, even just to obtain our sustenance.

We are discovering that connection is impossible because our nature is preventing us from connecting to others, as if it is failing us. We are beginning to recognize that there is a higher governance here, that the Creator, the upper force, is not letting us do anything. At that time, the three of us—we , our evil inclination, and the Creator—begin to work together, like Moses in Egypt.

It is written, "Come unto Pharaoh; for I have hardened his heart" (Exodus 10:1). Moses, the Creator, and Pharaoh all work together in us. It is how we advance. We discern the evil inclination, the help made against us, and we have no choice because with its help, we turn to the Creator. Were it not for the evil inclination, we would never turn to the Creator, we would never discover Him, and we would never need Him.

We advance through corrections made on our evil inclination while increasingly connecting through it with the Creator. The more attached we become to the overall force of bestowal and love that governs the world, even if hidden, the more we become exposed to it and attribute it to ourselves. We learn to use our evil inclination and eventually, gladly relinquish it because it was created in order for us to obliterate it.

In this portion we are reaching a greater level of *Aviut* (thickness) of the evil inclinatio, expressed in the aforementioned special *Mitzvot*. A *Mitzva* is a correction of the evil inclination. Our evil inclination is divided into 613 egotistical desires that we must correct into having the aim to bestow upon others, into love of others. In this portion, we are dealing with the biggest, meanest, and heaviest desires. Although it seems that we meet these desires only rarely, once we have made many lighter corrections, we come to meet the evil inclination in us that requires this type of correction.

It follows that the *Mitzva* concerning a rebellious son, the sending of the bird, and the blotting out of Amalek are the toughest *Mitzvot*. It is truly our stony heart, the foundation of all the evil. This forms our final contact in our eternal connection with the Creator, as Man and the Creator connect together: "Israel, the Torah, and the Creator are one" (*The Book of Zohar*, *Beresheet* (Genesis), item 85). This is expressed in absolute love toward others; as it comes from the Creator, so it comes from the creature. This is the goal.

QUESTIONS AND ANSWERS

What does it mean, a rebellious son?

Ben (son) comes from the word, *Mevin* (understanding). We do things without recognizing, understanding, or feeling them. We must correct our egos–the will to receive that is expressed precisely between us and others–absentmindedly, without quite knowing the nature of that correction. We do not know what it means to bestow or to not bestow, and we only notice that we do not have good connections with others, and that hatred and rejection are arresting our progress in spirituality and corporeality.

We see that our lives are quite miserable, and we have no idea what might happen tomorrow, which brings us to the need to correct our relationships with others. When we correct the relationships between us, we do something that is above our reason, even against it, because by Nature, we have no desire for it: We ask for correction against our will.

We are willing to love others, even though we feel no need for it. This work is called "work above reason," where we do not understand what we are doing or what is happening. When we work against our will, it is considered achieving understanding because once we correct, a new reality truly opens to us, where we see and feel in all our senses, in our minds, and in our hearts. That degree is called *Ben* (son), *Mevin* (understanding), because then we understand the situation, feel it, and control it.

So what does a "rebellious" son mean?

It is a situation in which we do not want to know our next degree, and do not want to correct ourselves. It happens when there is something within that resists the correction so fiercely that we cannot overcome that rejection. Sometimes there are sons who are obstinate, whatever we do. On the one hand, he is your son. On the other hand, there is nothing you can do with him. In that state, the son needs to be brought into correction the way the Torah describes.

These are corrections we need to do because everything is within. To an extent, they happen in each state, called "The pain of raising sons."

Today, it is very difficult for parents and children to communicate, and the same is true for teachers and students. There is a big gap between them.

Yes, especially today because we are approaching the generation of correction. We are beginning to discover our true nature, which is truly an evil inclination. We see it within us as we discover how cruel and inconsiderate we are. We hardly get along with ourselves, let alone with our partners, our children, and in general.

This is who we are today. However, it is not our fault; it is our nature, which appears in this way. We feel it in our children, too. But it is precisely these conditions that bring us to correction. This is called "Pharaoh bringing the children of Israel closer to the Creator." Our evil inclination helps us recognize that it is no longer possible to continue without putting things in the proper order.

This portion mentions divorce. Today, the number of divorces is nearing the number of marriages.

It has surpassed it. In Europe, fifty-seven percent of the people are divorced, and it is also spreading in the U.S.

Can we do spiritual work with a spouse?

We cannot correct the world without correcting ourselves. If we ever want to marry and have a truly good, solid family, we need to see to the correction of couples. But first, we ourselves must be corrected.

Today, it is almost hopeless. It is impossible to commit to marriage because it is a contract where the groom commits before the bride, and today it is very hard to commit. These days, men can commit only if they are under the social pressure of certain circles in society.

It seems that with a spouse, it is easier to correct because people are hesitant to leave their families. Is this truly a good place to work?

We have built many systems that help us get along without a family. We have Social Security, health insurance, old-age homes, etc. Money buys everything, and people can do without the family warmth because they can seemingly buy it.

Today, we are moving into a world that is far more complicated, where the money will not help us. We are in an economic crisis that demands that we connect in a friendly way with the environment, with friends, with family, with children and with parents. We do not have all that, and this is the revelation of the evil that will help push us toward correcting our relationships, correcting human nature. We will eventually come to a state where we will feel lost without a family, and even now, we have no family because we have lost the *concept* of the family along the way.

What is divorce, in spirituality?

"Divorce" means that we can no longer correct our *Malchut*, the will to receive, and therefore we do not sign a contract with that desire because, as a man, we cannot place ourselves over the woman, over the desire that must be corrected. Therefore, we divorce it.

But we know that a greater desire will follow it, so what is the point of the divorce?

This is why it is written that divorce is the worst option, and that Divinity cries every time we divorce. We are all parts of Divinity, and if we cannot correct it, it is as though we are delaying the correction, and this is very bad. That said, sometimes people have that feeling, that understanding, that additional corrections are required here.

If a man quarrels with his wife and feels that he hates her, and then turns to the Creator and asks for a correction to love her, is this the way to be corrected?

It happens in spirituality. Indeed, we need to cope with our will to receive. He is wrong and she is wrong, too. But when we know that we have no choice and we must become corrected, we do it. All those *Mitzvot* (commandments) are about the inner man and wife; it is a person's desire to bestow. The strength to overcome is called "man," and the deficiency that one must correct, that corrupt desire one has found, is called "woman." In the connection between them, we correct the relationship.

We receive a desire for correction from the inner woman, and the strength to correct from the inner man, who is connected to the Creator. It is written, "A man and a woman, if they are rewarded, Divinity is between them" (*Masecht Suttah*, 17a). Through those three, we correct that relationship into the right one. If we correct it, we have performed a *Mitzva*, and so we continue to the next woman (deficiency), and the next man, and the next deficiency, and again, "A man and a woman, if they are rewarded, Divinity is between them." Then, once again, we correct them and perform a *Mitzva*. A will to receive with a *Masach* (screen) and *Ohr Hozer* (Reflected Light) performs a *Zivug de Hakaa* (coupling of striking), and the revelation of the Creator arrives within the connection called a "son," meaning one acquires understanding, sensation, *Dvekut* (adhesion).

From *The Zohar*: Giving a Bad Name

"A man should speak with his wife before coupling with her because she might have been replaced with another. The thing about a woman is that she is from the side of the tree of knowledge of good and evil." In other words, she can be good, and she can be bad, and who knows from which side you should now speak with the will to receive, meaning examine it, how to connect to it and how to correct it. "Her marrow tends to change. However, if she is from the *Shechina* (Divinity), there are no changes in her." The *Shechina* is called *Malchut* of *Atzilut*, the corrected state, when she is ready for correction. "This is the meaning of, 'I the Lord do not change.' I am the *Shechina*, who is not afraid of all the other sides, the *Klipot*, as it is written, 'All the nations are as nothing compared to Him.'"

The quotes are from *Zohar for All*, *Ki Tetze* (When You Go), item 8

Can it be said that the "me" in spirituality is really the will to receive, with the addition of the point in the heart, and we only try to balance them out?

The self of a person is the husband and the wife within. We need to know how to work with both of them together, so that the self will be similar to the Creator.

What is the *Mitzva* of sending from the nest?

It is a very complicated *Mitzva*. It is quite cruel to drive a bird from the nest and take her eggs. Many books have been written about it, and it is also mentioned in *The Book of Zohar*, and in the writings of the ARI.

We are the *Malchut*, the will to receive that must be promoted and adjusted to *Bina*. The "mother" is *Bina*. The mother of the sons is the "mother" of the understandings, the attainments.

We need to take the eggs from the mother, the future nestlings, and rear them. We do it by connecting to the nest and performing the *Mitzva* of sending from the nest. It is considered a *Mitzva* (commandment–correction, good deed) because once we reach this degree, it is a *Mitzva* for that person.

"Sending the mother away" is actually detaching oneself from *Bina*, and working with the ZAT of *Bina*, a part of her that belongs to the person. That person then takes her and turns the desires of ZAT of *Bina*, correcting the part of *Malchut* through them. This is the connection of *Bina* with *Malchut* in *Tzimtzum Bet* (Second Restriction). It is a very big *Mitzva*. When a person ascends, when *Malchut* ascends to *Bina*, *Malchut* becomes detached from her, and corrects herself.

In other words, here, too, as there is a son, there are nestlings, which are the continuation of that quality.

Yes, but it is only when one becomes detached from *Bina*, when one can use part of her to correct oneself.

There is the issue that Amalek "jumps" on a person when one is unprepared.

Amalek is a big problem. It is essentially the same evil inclination that is in our will to receive. Amalek is really an acronym of *Al Menat LeKabel* (in order to receive). *The Book of Zohar* also writes that it is *Am* and *Lek*, where *Am* is from Balaam and *Lek* is from Balak.

From *The Zohar*: Blotting Out the Remembrance of Amalek

"He asks, 'Who is the root of Amalek above, in spirituality, for we see that Balaam and Balak are from there, from Amalek of above?' They were their souls, which is why they hated Israel more than any other nation or language. This is why Amalek is written in the names, meaning *Am* of Balaam, and *Lek* of Balak. Also, the Amaleks are male and female."

Zohar for All, Ki Tetze (When You Go), item 110

When Balaam and Balak conjoin, they build the name, Amalek. Amalek is their common root, and this is how they work within us, connected between them. The foundation of the evil in us is Amalek–Balaam and Balak.

But this is how we were created.

True, it is not from us. From the beginning, the Creator said, "I have created the evil inclination," so Amalek is from Him. Balaam, Balak, Pharaoh, Hitler–they are all from Him.

So who is supposed to blot out the memory of Amalek?

It is for Man to correct, and to correct so thoroughly that no trace of it will remain. In other words, the whole of the will to receive will come to aim to bestow through the last element, because if anything is left of it, it grows again.

Why does Amalek jump them?

Amalek emerged from one root, one incident. It is known, even according to what is said in the Torah, that if anything is left of it, it grows within us once again. In other words, until we blot it out completely, the problems will not end.

Amalek is presented as shrewd.

Yes, this is why we constantly focus our corrections on Amalek, parts of the will to receive, which are all from it. And yet, it is not considered one of those parts because the first nine, our evil inclination, also consist of the ten *Sefirot*, the ten *Sefirot* of *Tuma'a* (impurity), while we *can* correct the first nine *Sefirot*. This is why we do not call them "Amalek," but "evil inclination."

And yet, the essence of the evil inclination, the "Egypt," the extract of the evil inclination, since *Mitzraim* (Egypt) comes from *Mitz Ra* (evil extract), is Pharaoh, and Amalek is a result. Balaam and Balak, however, are its representatives from the sides of male and female. It is still this way today.

Is there a distinct expression to the term, "Amalek," in the desires of our generation?

"Amalek" is when a person bears such vehement hatred toward the people of Israel, toward bestowal, toward love, that he or she cannot accept them in any way, even after all the corrections. Naturally, none of us wants them, but once we correct everything, almost to the end, then Amalek appears. It does not appear prior to it.

It is written about it that after all the *Mitzvot*, after the whole desert, after all that we corrected in ourselves in connection with the upper light—the Creator—we have reached the very special, rare

Mitzvot in our portion. Only then, in the end, do we arrive at the blotting out of Amalek.

But we are talking about blotting out the memory of Amalek.

Yes, because we have reached the end of the correction.

Does that mean the worst is still ahead?

No. When we enter the land of Israel, there is no longer any evil. Here we are trying to turn it into good. Of course, we still discover it, but in a different way, in scrutinizing how to connect to others, not in how to detach ourselves from the evil in us, but how to connect to others.

Terms

Son

A "son" is the next degree, or *Ben* (son), from the word *Mevin* (understanding). We can never understand what we are doing–both in corporeality and in spirituality–until after we act. It is written about it, "By Your actions we know You" (Prayer Book, The Song of Unification on Sabbath). Through actions, we begin to understand. It is like children playing without understanding anything, but all of a sudden they grow smarter.

The same is true for us. This is why *Ben*, *Mevin*, is a degree that comes to us as a result of actions. It is also why it is written, "By Your actions we know You" (*Megillah*, 6b). Make an effort, act, and you will understand and see.

Beloved Woman and Hated Woman

A "beloved woman" is the will to receive with which a person can work in order to bestow. A "hated woman" is the will to receive with which one cannot work with the aim to bestow, which does not support us because we are weak. This is why there are prohibitions against separating them and treating each of them differently.

It is the same with the sons—the firstborn sons from the loved woman and from the hated woman. This has to do with our desires, and depends on how we relate to them, how we can or cannot lift the will to receive toward correction.

Loss

In spirituality, a "loss" means that we lose the ability to remain at a degree that we had already acquired. In other words, if we lose something, it deliberately comes from above as a kind of help to us, and we need to search for it. This is the root of the commandment to return a loss that has been found to its owner.

Just Sentence

"Justice" means that we properly connect judgment and mercy, the right line and the left line, so that we correct our will to receive to have the aim to bestow upon others in the optimal measure. In other words, under any circumstances, we do the utmost act of bestowal.

From *The Zohar*: Giving a Bad Name

"The Creator is not called a 'King' until He is riding His horse, which is the Assembly of Israel, meaning *Malchut*, as it is written, 'To me, my darling, you are like my mare among the chariots of Pharaoh,' which is all good, without any bad at all. When the Creator is out of His place, He is not a king. When He returns to His place, 'And the Lord shall be king.' And this is what is said about Israel, 'All of Israel are sons of kings.' Like the father, so the sons are not sons of kings until they return to the land of Israel."

Zohar for All, *Ki Tetze* (When You Go), item 5

Let us hope that we will soon return to the real land of Israel, first the inner, spiritual one, the *Yashar El* (straight to God), that we will all be in united and bonded as brothers.

Ki Tavo

(When You Come)

(Deuteronomy, 26:1-29:8)

Portion Summary

The portion, *Ki Tavo* (When You Come), begins with the last part of Moses' speech before the people prior to his death. Upon the entrance to the land of Israel, Moses orders the people to write the words on big, whitewashed stones and to build from them an altar for the Creator.

Moses describes the blessing that will come to Israel if they keep the *Mitzvot* (commandments), and the curses that will come to them if they do not. He describes the state of the blessing and the curse on Mount Eival, and on Mount Gerizim: who will stand on each side, what are curses and what are blessings, and how they should be spoken.

The portion also deals with the *Mitzvot* of the first fruit and the tithing laws. At the end of the portion, Moses summarizes the events through which the people went, the Creator's help at every step, and the people's commitment to keep the *Mitzvot*.

COMMENTARY

Our souls consist of 613 *Mitzvot* (commandments). Initially, they are all as the evil inclination, meaning aiming to benefit ourselves. In each of our desires appears—in the best case scenario—concern for ourselves. In the worst case scenario appears how we lie, steal, and use others for our own benefit.

Even if we do not use others, we still feel that the worse off they are, the better off we are. By Nature, we are built to compare ourselves to others.

And yet, there is no one to complain to about it because the Creator admits, "I have created the evil inclination." It is a process that began in Egypt, where we received the big evil inclination, the will to receive.

We discovered it at Mount Sinai, where we agreed to be "as one man with one heart," to bond. Although we were by a mountain of hate, we united around the mountain and expressed our willingness to unite. Although we were unable to actualize it, we were prepared to go for it. That was enough to receive the force of correction called "Torah," whose light reforms.

During the process known as "forty years in the desert," the majority of the Torah—which narrates primarily what happened in the desert—we prepared ourselves, corrected ourselves, and discovered our nature each time anew. We discovered how wicked we are, we ran into trouble, committed sins, and were repeatedly punished for them.

The process we went through in the desert qualified us for the correction of our *Kelim*, the correction of our desires from reception to bestowal, from intentions to benefit ourselves to intentions to benefit others. The correction takes place through suffering from above, or through our own understanding of how to correct ourselves. In this way, we achieve a state called "the land of Israel," in which we are more or less ready to turn our desires from benefiting ourselves into benefiting others.

In the beginning of the desert, by Mount Sinai, we corrected all of our 613 desires from which our corrupted souls consist, having been created that way, as it is written, "I have created the evil inclination." We reached a state where we did not wish to harm others, which is called "passing the desert." Now, right before the entrance to the land of Israel, we must correct our desires so that with them we will do good to others.

The work of the desert is "That which you hate, do not do to your neighbor." The intention to *favor* others is called "Love your neighbor as yourself." This is the next stage, the conquest of the land and the work in the land of Israel. This is our work, our correction, to aim our desires from ourselves to others.

This is why we were given the Torah, as it is written, "I have created the evil inclination, I have created for it the Torah as a spice." If one takes on this work, it is called "studying Torah," "serving the Creator." This is how we perform our correction. If we do this here and now, in our lives in this world, carrying out these two stages in the work, these two degrees, we will traverse the desert, reach the land of Israel, and achieve the end of correction.

The more we advance through the desert toward the entrance to the land of Israel, the more we can see how our demand for correction becomes better focused, more concrete, more practical, and clearer. Thus, it can be explained in practical terms to any person who advances and corrects oneself into love of others.

This is why the portion speaks of stones, the building of *Malchut* and *Bina*, and the connection between those two degrees–the blessing and the curse. The uncorrected *Malchut* is the curse, and the corrected degree of *Bina*, to which *Malchut* joins, is the blessing. They stand as two mountains before a person who uses them, and the person stands between the blessing and the curse. Thus, we stand between those two lines, building ourselves as the middle line, and this is the structure of the corrected soul.

The portion speaks of stones, of building the altar. The word, *Even* (stone), comes from the word, *Havanah* (understanding). A stone is the degree of *Bina*. We need to go above reason, above our understanding. We rise above it and acquire a truly Godly mind and heart, above our nature. Out of the awareness in this new attainment, we write on the stones, on *Malchut*, which is a stone, our stony heart. Although the heart does not wish to be corrected, we gradually bring it to corrections and build with it the altar.

The portion speaks of the tithing, the tenth part, which is *Malchut* herself, the tenth *Sefira* that builds herself according to the amount she receives, or does not receive. The portion also deals with the matter of circumcision, which details how much we can or cannot use each desire in favor of others, what we do with the part we cannot correct, and how we use it in favor of others, although it is still not corrected. The portion explains how we continue to seemingly correct it.

QUESTIONS AND ANSWERS

We are talking about a process of recognition of evil in Egypt, the entrance to the desert and the land of Israel. Today the people of Israel are already in the land of Israel, but it seems that we still have not gotten into Egypt. There is a big gap between what is happening in Israel and where we are supposed to be. How can you explain this gap?

Today we are in a different situation, which is why we do not need to go through all those degrees. By "we," I mean the group that assembled and connected to Abraham, that went out of Babylon and came to the land of Canaan, and from Canaan—following the degrees of Isaac and Jacob—went into Egypt.

"Egypt" means that we have acquired our big egotistical will to receive, from which we wanted to escape because it was very bad for us. All that is negative in our lives comes to us because we are selfish, because we hate everyone and cannot avoid it. We bring these states on ourselves, although we regret being pulled into these miserable and worthless situations. In this way we actually "finish" ourselves off, wasting our lives on a lowly, animate degree, unable to rise to a higher level.

Initially, we strive for something eternal and perfect, but life in this world leads us into a life on the animate level. It is hard for us to live like an animal, so we cling to the hope that life continues in the next world. If we were certain that there was no continuity, we would not be able to go on living in this world because that would make our lives completely meaningless. This is why so many people believe in the next world, the afterlife.

The incarnations we have gone through have given us the understanding and the recognition. They have given us the drive to escape from Egypt when we wish to obtain bestowal, Godliness, and an elevation of our lives. We have already been through all the stages of scrutiny and correction and have decided that we must exit our egos. We want to rise above and move to another dimension of life.

The reality we live in can be one of reception for ourselves, as we feel it now while we are immersed in receiving more and more. However, there is another reality, where we do not absorb inwards, but rather exit ourselves and transcend the animate degree where we are in a material body so we can perceive what exists outside of us.

It is a special method, called "the wisdom of Kabbalah," and we must learn how to act according to it, how to perceive the out-of-body reality. We still do not understand it, which is why it is called the "hidden world," the "hidden method," or "the method of the hidden." It is a special instruction given to those who truly wish to exit themselves and begin to feel the reality outside of them, which is complete bestowal upon others and love of others. This reality is completely opposite from the one we know today, where we give only to ourselves and love only ourselves, wishing to receive for ourselves and caring only about what is ours.

Achieving this transition requires a process; is this the process described here?

It requires a process of transition. This is why we are called "Hebrews," from the word *Avar* (passing over, to pass over). Our whole work is to pass over.

At what stage is this process now? Where are the people of Israel today in relation to this process?

We have made the passing over; we passed through the desert. The correction was first done by exiting the ego. This is called "traversing the desert and entering the land of Israel." That is, instead of receiving, we began to bestow. We did it as a small country and a small nation that went out of Babylon.

However, to correct the rest of the Babylonians, we had to be broken and go through the ruin of the Temple, meaning to reenter the ego, the will to receive, and be dispersed among the nations. The ten tribes scattered, and today we have no idea where they are, but they are mingled among all the nations, and they are doing their work, as do we, who have now returned to the land of Israel.

Something special is happening here, something that Kabbalists spoke about. We are returning, not in order to live in Tel Aviv, or in some other city, but to go through the stages of rising from the exile, out of Egypt, through the desert, to the actual land of Israel. We and the whole world are in these stages now.

What is happening throughout the world today resembles the time of the Pharaohs. It is written that Pharaoh drew Israel closer to the Creator.* He afflicted them, treated them badly, and threw them away so they would run from Egypt. This is how the Creator worked through Pharaoh. Pharaoh is really the Creator's loyal servant, the servant of the upper force. Today, we are feeling that these forces

* "And Pharaoh drew near, and the sons of Israel looked, and behold, the Egyptians were marching after them, and they became very frightened; so the sons of Israel cried out to the Lord" (Exodus, 14:10).

are affecting us and the entire world. They are truly like Pharaoh, pressuring us, and we have nowhere to run.

The current crisis is putting us in a situation that we cannot overcome or correct as we used to. We also cannot escape from country to country. No place is better or worse because the crisis is happening everywhere at the same time, very clearly and very quickly, so the way up is, "And the children of Israel sighed because of the work" (Exodus 2:23).

We are the same group that already went through this process. We are carrying within us *Reshimot* (recollections) and genes from our previous states. We must be "a light for the nations" as soon as possible. For this reason, the pressure on us will only increase, even more than on anybody else. The faster we pass it on to the world, crying out the biggest cry, the more we will spare ourselves and the world suffering. Our good future depends entirely on our struggle with ourselves, with our own evil inclination, with the world that does not wish to listen, but especially with the people of Israel who do not want to listen. It is called the "War of *Gog uMagog*."

What about the blessing and the curse? What is that mechanism?

These are the two forces by which man advances.

Is it the Creator's doing?

Of course the Creator is doing it. From the very beginning, He says, "I have created the evil inclination," meaning He admits it. Our entire evolution is advancement through the "whip" behind us, repeatedly coming down on us and goading us forward, while we have no choice but to run ahead and advance at its pace.

If we want to advance at the pace of the whip, it is called "in its time." In this way, we advance through beatings. But if we want to move faster than the beatings so they do not touch us, we need to move ourselves a little faster, as in "I will hasten it," meaning we need to rush time, as it is written that Israel sanctify the times, making them shorter.*

In other words, there are two options from the beginning.

Yes. One option is through the curse. This is also a correction because blows are corrections. The other option is through the blessing, when we are drawn forward.

We learn that we need to include all our desires, so what happened at Mount Sinai, when the people agreed to be as one man with one heart?

There is no need for anything more than that. We receive everything else. Of course, there is a lot of work that must be done, but we receive help, support, an instruction called "Torah," a force that is *Moshe* (Moses), which *Moshech* (pulls) us faster forward and thus prevents the blows from reaching us.

For the most part, the Torah speaks of things we go through against our will. It does not say that we can go through everything in a good and pleasant way; it only points to the obstacles ahead, like a guidebook that marks obstacles, problems, transgressions, and so on. If we go through the path according to our nature, without advancing by using the guidebook, we will suffer curses. This is our path: there are curses in it, punishments, and problems, because we are a "stiff-necked people,"** as we have seen throughout the road in the desert. The Torah does not take into account that we can rush ourselves faster than the whip that lashes us.

Is our choice only whether to go through the process favorably or unfavorably?

Our choice is only to run ahead toward the good, toward bestowal and love.

---

* *Masechet Berachot*, 49a.

** Exodus, 32:9.

And we cannot change the overall plan?

No, but we can experience it differently, in a favorable and desirable way, to feel it as a good life. It is like a child who does not want to go to school, so he feels everything as pressure, beating, and suffering, as a hard life.

From *The Zohar*: Know This Day and Reply unto Your Heart

"Heart with a double *Bet* means that the good inclination and the evil inclination, which reside in the heart, have mingled in one another and they are one. "And you shall love the Lord your God with all your heart" means with both your inclinations—the good inclination and the evil inclination, so the bad qualities of the evil inclination will become good, meaning he will serve the Lord with them and not sin through them. Then there will certainly be no difference between the good inclination and the evil inclination and they will be one."

Zohar for All, *VaEra* (And I Appeared), item 90

If Mount Gerizim stands opposite Mount Eival, they are seemingly good and bad, so we will certainly choose the good. In that case, where is the choice?

The problem is that there is concealment. If we know what is good and what is bad, there is no choice here. By Nature, we are drawn to the good and avoid the bad. But if there is concealment, we do not know which is bad and which is good. If one gives you a blessing or a curse, it does not mean that on one corner we have someone who will beat you up, and on the other corner stands someone who will bake you cakes. If that were the case, it would be obvious where you would go because there is no choice here. But in this way, you would be like a puppet on a string, not a human being.

A human being is one who has grown above one's beast, who is not drawn to the good that seems like a cake, nor runs from the bad where there is the curse. Rather, such a person tests him or herself in relation to truth and falsehood. It is possible that what seems like a curse now is actually the truth, and that which seems like a cake is the lie. We need to elevate ourselves above the good and the bad that appear as "gut feelings." We need to raise ourselves according to our awareness by being drawn toward the truth and not toward falsehood. This is the scrutiny that is very difficult for us to make.

What is the truth and what is a lie?

The truth is the point, a degree called "Man," who is similar to *Elokim* (God), where He is the standard, the highest place we must reach, and which includes everything. We need to come to a state that is to us both truth and falsehood, good and bad, where everything connects in one place, as it is written, "I have created the evil inclination, I have created for it the Torah as a spice." It is a place where all the beginnings connect, as it is written, "All my thoughts are in You" (Psalms 87:7).

Why then is it built this way, with all the conditions and concealments?

It is so in order to give people a chance to choose. Otherwise, we would be as machines.

But people neither care nor want to care. They cannot choose anyway, so at least they should have a good life.

No, the whole purpose of Creation is to turn us into human beings. Those who choose regardless of good or bad elevate themselves above the corporeal scrutiny.

If the Creator is benevolent, why did He draw us a path that is not easy, that most of the time is unclear how good it really is?

Assume that a person turns on his vacuum cleaner and walks out of the house, while the vacuum cleaner is cleaning the carpets. This is what we look like today, and it seems as though we want to stay that way, walking around like the vacuum cleaner, like robots hitting one corner and turning to the other. Would we want to have this mechanism that keeps directing us in life this way? If so, where is the human here? We are not; we only *feel* as though we are alive, letting each day go by until we die, as long as we do not suffer.

The Creator's purpose is precisely to show us the most sublime challenge against the suffering, the difficulty, and despite the problems that we experience. Our world is advancing toward a no-choice situation, toward a crisis we cannot mend, and which we cannot exit or survive. Either we take upon ourselves the work of being human, or we will be forced into that position against our will.

"Against our will" means it will be done by blows until we say, "We want it." Therefore, we should learn to agree to the work we have been assigned to do, and then the goodness will immediately open up to us.

Terms

First Fruit

When the will to receive grows, we bring it to correction, to scrutiny. That desire is called "first fruit."

Tithing

The tenth part, ten percent, which cannot be corrected. *Malchut* is the tenth *Sefira* in the structure of our soul. She cannot be corrected because she is the will to receive itself. She must instead be mingled with the first nine qualities of bestowal, and this is how she is corrected.

Because it is impossible to correct the will to receive itself, we give a tithing instead. We simply do not work with the part that cannot be corrected. Rather, we hand it over to bestowal so it will be corrected by itself. Afterward, at the end of correction, it will be corrected.

Altar

An "altar" is the place where correction is made, the contact with the upper light.

Blessing

A "blessing" is the force we receive from above in order to perform acts of bestowal toward others. This force comes after we prepare for it, when we truly want to perform acts of bestowal above, from whatever we will have. When that happens, an upper force comes to us, which is called "receiving a blessing." A blessing is the *Ohr Hozer* (Reflected Light) that we activate, a force from above.

Blessing vs. a curse: a "curse," in its simple form, indicates that a person is not asking for and is not receiving the upper force. On the other hand, a "blessing" is the reception of power from above in order to perform an act with the aim to bestow upon others, wherein we discover that we are similar to the Creator and feel as such.

What Is, "With God's Help"?

All we have is God's help. We can do anything; our actions are not difficult. The difficulty is only in coming to a state of demanding of the Creator to do it for us, and then it is immediately done. This is why everything is easy.

All we need is to make contact with Him and then do everything with His help, the help of the upper force, the upper light. When it comes, it scrutinizes all the details in us, all the desires, giving us strength and correcting us. This is how we discover that we truly are "You have made me from behind and from before" (Psalms, 139:5), and that He does everything for us.

Choice

The choice is to see that in truth, man is not the operator, but the Creator. Man needs only to demand of Him, as it is written, "My sons defeated Me."* By committing Him, "You have made us, help us, and do it on us," we achieve a perfect world.

The meaning of the term "perfect world" is that in all of our 613 desires, which have been corrected, we had a share, as well–we asked for them to be corrected. This is why we see the world as perfect, spiritual, and eternal.

From *The Zohar*: I will bring you out, I will deliver you, I will redeem you, I will take you

"First, it is written, 'And I will bring you out from under the burdens of the Egyptians,' and then, 'And I will deliver you from their bondage.' And afterwards, 'And I will redeem you.' Should He not have said first, 'And I will redeem you,' and then, 'And I will bring you'? Indeed, He first said the most important, since the Creator wished to first tell them the most beautiful–the exodus from Egypt." But "The most beautiful of all is, 'And I will take you to Me for a people, and I will be to you a God.'"

Zohar for All, VaEra (And I Appeared), item 52-53

* *Masechet Baba Metziah*, 59b.

Nitzavim-VaYelech

(Standing-Moses Went)

(Deuteronomy, 29:9-30:20; 31:1-31:30)

Portion Summary

The portion, *Nitzavim* (Standing), deals with Moses' speech regarding the covenant between Israel and the Creator. Moses makes it clear that the Torah applies to the whole of the people of Israel, to every single one, and was given until posterity. Moses stresses the principle of choice: should a person worship other gods, he will be exiled from the land. But if he wishes to be reformed, the path is through repentance. The Creator allows the people to choose between life and death, but commands them, "Therefore choose life" (Deuteronomy, 30:19).

In the portion, *VaYelech* (Moses Went), Moses gives his final speech before the people's entrance to the land of Israel. He reinforces the people's confidence so they will not fear fighting for the land knowing the Creator is with them. He officially hands

over the leadership to Joshua, son of Nun. Moses writes the Torah and instructs the people of Israel to assemble once every seven years to read it. The Creator reveals to Moses that in the future the people of Israel will sin, and commands him to write a song to remind the people of the Creator.

COMMENTARY

It may seem as though portions repeat themselves, but any repetition is at a new degree. The whole Torah deals only with the correction of the soul. It is as if the soul were cut into slices according to the degrees of the great will to receive, which is why it appears to be the same.

Similarly, each day in our lives seems to resemble the next, yet each day feels different, and life consists of many days joined together. The special thing about this process is that it is not about the people of Israel or the desert, but about an individual going through the stages of spiritual development.

Spiritual development is done in two stages. The first is the preparation in Babylon, in the *Bilbul* (confusion). The second stage is in Egypt. In this world, one tries to do as one sees fit, but gives up because this world is leading us into a state where we are not achieving good results in life. The result is a crisis similar to the one the world is in today.

And yet, we do not seek the meaning of life, but money, power, respect, pleasures, freedom, vacations, and we are beginning to understand that it is impossible to have them. Whether due to personal crises or because of the global crisis, we finally come to the fundamental question, "What is the meaning of my life?" We seek satisfaction in life, but we cannot find it anywhere. Therefore, without satisfaction we feel like Prophet Jonah, who said, "It is better for me to die than to live" (Jonah, 4:3).

We seek fulfillment, but we arrive at a situation where there is only one way, which we are discovering these days. Gradually, the whole world is approaching the stage of, "What is the meaning of life?"

Due to the crises, we are all facing a state of bankruptcy. Although it currently seems that only banks and large corporations are moving toward it, in truth the whole world is faced with the questions: "What are we doing with ourselves, with our lives?" "What is it all for?" "What is going on here?" These questions lead us to the answer that everything is happening only so we may rise above the search for satisfaction in our own short lives.

While we are beginning to search for real fulfillment, the eternal and complete one, above this transient life, we go through stages of inner corrections that lead us toward another life, to the spiritual life, the life of the soul. It is as though we acquire another body, an internal one, which is not made of flesh, but is all desire. Our corporeal body, the flesh, is where that desire dresses, and it is called a "soul," which we must reveal and nurture.

There are two stages in the development of that body: the first is called "Moses" and the second is called "Joshua." Moses is called the "faithful shepherd." In that stage, we rise to the degree of *Bina*, to bestow with the aim to bestow. It is a degree that is all bestowal, faith. The degrees where we acquire the quality of Moses, the revealing of the spiritual body, are called the "forty years in the desert."

Following the revelation of the spiritual body—the *Kli* (vessel) of the soul—we work on filling it with light. We acquire the *Kli*, conquer the land of Israel, expel from there what is unfitting and undesirable, and fill our *Kli* with the upper light. This is the degree of receiving with the aim to bestow, the degree of Joshua. It is a higher degree than Moses, an "improved" degree of Moses.

We advance in conquering the land (desire) by working on our egotistical will to receive, which opposes us and tries to make us fail each step of the way. We get stranded, err, and constantly have troubles with the covenant. We must connect with the will to bestow and constantly choose life, as it is written (Deuteronomy 30:19), "Therefore choose life, that you may live, you and your descendants."

We can acquire the additional, spiritual life while we are living in our physical bodies. It depends solely on our correction, on the extent to which we are immersed in the intention to bestow, on how filled we are with the upper light. When we obtain the upper light, we are rewarded with eternal life. This is really our goal; it is the purpose of our lives here in this world, in our physical bodies. This knowledge used to be in the hands of a chosen few unique individuals in each generation, but today the whole world is awakening toward it, and we will all need to reveal our souls.

QUESTIONS AND ANSWERS

The portions that speak of the entrance to the land of Israel mention Joshua's new leadership and new laws. Today the world is also moving into a new stage with new laws. Will explanations about it help, or is it impossible to understand anything until we are actually in the New World?

First, we need to recognize our helplessness and deficiencies, similar to the way it happened in the desert when we faced the entrance to the land of Israel, but did not know what to do and feared entering it. Even prior to that, at the foot of Mount Sinai, there was a problem of great hatred similar to the one that threatens to burst throughout the world today and pull us into a third world war, a nuclear one.

And prior to Mount Sinai, we had to jump into the Red Sea and cross it, despite our very real fear of death. Today, we are feeling the same great obstacles looming before us like impassable walls. And yet, the Torah always opens a door for us.

Baal HaSulam writes about it beautifully in a story about a man who sees a wall with a door. He approaches the door, opens it, and enters. In spirituality, there is a "wall" because we currently do not see anything at all. We still cannot see what is separating us from spirituality. First, we discover the wall. When we want to break in and seemingly bump into it head first, we discover the door and attempt to enter, and the door immediately opens.

We see this many times in the Torah: Near the Red Sea, when Nahshon jumped and the sea opened, as well as by Mount Sinai, and in other cases. We are required to "go for it," to choose life.

From *The Zohar*: Moses Is the Dominion of the Sun; Joshua Is the Dominion of the Moon

"The Creator said to Moses: 'Moses, do you wish for the world to change? Have you ever seen the sun worshiping the moon? Have you ever seen the moon governing while the sun is still present? Rather, your dying days have come; summon Joshua. Let the sun be taken and let the moon govern. Moreover, if you enter the land, the moon will be taken because of you and will not be able to govern. Indeed, the governance of the moon, Joshua, has arrived, and it cannot rule as long as you are in the world.'"

Zohar for All, VaYelech (Moses Went), item 12

These are two degrees. It is impossible to move from one degree to the next without completing the first. We must complete the degree of Moses, degree of *Bina*—bestowing with the aim to bestow. From it, we advance to the degree of Joshua, to receive in order to bestow. This is the conquest of the land, the entrance to the land of Israel—a desire that is aimed entirely toward bestowal.

In other words, the degree of Moses is "That which you hate, do not do to your friend." The degree of Joshua is "Love your neighbor as yourself." It is a higher degree, an extension of the degree of Moses. The next degree is always a step closer to the end of correction, compared to the previous one, and Moses is the fundamental level of all the degrees.

What does it mean that the Creator informs Moses that the people will sin?

There is no other way. We advance only through our sins, through the wicked that appear to us. The Creator says to us in advance, "I have created the evil inclination."

The whole of Creation is the evil inclination. The evil inclination is ill will, an egotistical desire, the opposite of the Creator. It is a desire to receive with the aim to receive, to be contemptuous of everyone, exploit, steal from, and deceive everyone. The Creator does not hide what He has done, but explains that He did all that so we would correct ourselves and rise above that ill will.

The wisdom of Kabbalah is the only one that explains to us how to correct ourselves. One who feels truly deserving of correction must do something with the ego, with oneself, one's life, and find the fulfillment in life. This is when one comes to the wisdom of Kabbalah. Everything else we do in life is mere customs, but they do not correct us or even reveal to us that we are bad.

Before *Rosh Hashanah* (Hebrew New Year's Eve) and *Yom Kippur* (Day of Atonement), a time of introspection and reflection, we say, "We have betrayed." We say that we are wicked indeed, both toward each other and toward the Creator. But were it not written in the prayer-books, who would think that it was so? In fact, even when we read it in the prayer books, we do not really sympathize with it or feel that it is really so.

Why does the Creator have to command us to choose life? Who would choose death?

Our physiological life and death are completely out of our control. Once we are born, there is no question that we will also die. But even the choice whether or not to be born is not in our hands. From the moment we emerge from the womb, we are beginning our march toward death. It follows that the command to choose life has nothing to do with the physical life.

Does the Creator pave a good path and a bad one, and then say "Choose," recommending that we choose the good?

Choosing the good indicates that a person is acquiring the spiritual life while still in this life. "Therefore, choose life" refers to the spiritual life. The choice is whether to end life as an ordinary person would—at the end of physical existence, having lived in order to serve the body, putting it to bed, bathing it, and satisfying its other needs—or to rise to another level while still in the physical body. The Torah is for those who wish to ascend to another degree, as it is written, "I have created the evil inclination, I have created for it the Torah as a spice." In that case, "the light in it reforms them."

When one comes to that Torah (law) of life, to eternity and perfection, that person acquires an additional life during this life. When that happens, one does not die, even when the body does.

These days, we are beginning to feel more like one people. We empathize, and we are beginning to deliberate. Are we faced with a very big move we will have to take?

Now is the first time in history that people do not know what to do with the world. We are discovering that everything we have developed over the years is gradually halting, becoming dysfunctional. We do not know what will work and what will not. Suddenly, everything "slips through our fingers," and leaders do not know what to do, for all their knowledge and advisors.

Is this the wall we spoke of earlier, which we keep encountering in every direction?

Yes, we are discovering that the Godly system is beginning to appear. It is called, "the revelation of the Creator to the creatures." When the Godly force—Godly quality (of bestowal)—appears, it is a system that we do not know how to handle.

Man is the evil inclination. Yet, all of a sudden, the good inclination appears before us. However, we do not recognize it as good. We see that the world is global, integral, and that everyone is interconnected and interdependent, but we do not want to live in that world. This is where we discover that we are made of the opposite material. After all, the Creator says, "I have created the evil inclination" in you, and here a system appears before us that creates the good, where everyone is connected. If you try to adapt yourself to that system, you will find "therefore choose life."

Which Joshua do we need now?

Both of these forces, Moses and Joshua, exist in all of us.

Is there a difference between how people searched thirty years ago, when each was searching personally, and how they search today?

Even when everything was fine, people still needed to answer the question about life's purpose.

But there is a huge difference because today people are not asking what we are living for. The crisis is coming to their doorsteps.

Even today, some people study Kabbalah because they are seeking the meaning and purpose of life, even though they are generally happy. They do not come because of suffering in their everyday lives, but because of the emotional pain of feeling empty. However, those who come to study Kabbalah are about one percent of the global population. The rest come because of the problems in their daily lives.

Assuming one is from Japan and has experienced the earthquake and tsunami, and then the nuclear disaster in Fukushima, would that person not ask, "What is going on here?" "Am I missing something?" Or would that person simply be lost and not know how to cope with the world? Would anyone who sympathizes with him or her feel the same?

Every nation, person, and every part in the world is treated differently. We do not know in what way because it has to do with "soul sentences," but we will *all* feel the immense pressures pushing us toward the entrance to the network of connections between us, the global and integral network that is now slowly appearing, and to which we are not adapted.

Now is the first time in history that we must adapt ourselves to the ties that are appearing between us. Previously, we built egotistical connections between us as we wished. But now we must work to the contrary. The emerging network is "telling us": "You have to adjust yourselves to me, or you will not succeed."

Moses encouraged the people of Israel to be brave because the Creator is with them. From where can such confidence come? Is it because we are marching toward a very bad situation?

It is confidence. It is not a bad situation; it depends on how you look at it. Looking at what is appearing before us, we can see that it is salvation. We are being presented with a beautiful example, an opportunity to connect with everyone. The negative reactions we all feel, the suffering, mayhem, problems, and confusion, are so we will try to direct ourselves correctly through them and try to adapt ourselves to our newly formed connections.

These new connections are the Creator Himself; it is the quality of bestowal appearing between us. Of course we hate it and reject it. We do not understand it, but it is Him. This is called "the revelation of the Creator to the creatures." These are really the days of the Messiah, when that light is gradually appearing, a light of bestowal drawing us from our egos upward.

But if a person has no point in the heart, can you talk to him before he suffers?

No, you can't.

What confidence can we promise? Can we say to him, "Wait, suffer a little more and then we will talk"?

No. Of course he must suffer, but here is where the wisdom of Kabbalah appears in order to explain the reason for the suffering. We need to suffer very little, like clever children who understand and walk in the right direction after the first hint.

Our calendar guarantees that we will achieve all the corrections and abundance by the end of the six thousand years. The question is, "How much will we suffer along the way?" We can shorten these times by ourselves, and not wait another 220 years or so, but rather accomplish it in our current lives.

The end of the portion speaks about Moses being commanded to write a song, to prepare for Israel something that will remind them of the goal. What is so special about the song?

The song is for the future, should Israel sin. It is not like songs we know today, but a special connection between us and the correcting upper force. It is a system of connections by which we evoke within us the power of correction.

Even when we sin, we can be certain that the mechanism that Moses built in us will help. Moses is the force of bestowal within us. It is absolutely clear of reception, and we return to it when we sin so it will help us reform ourselves.

Is there no connection whatsoever between this song and songs we speak of today, with rhymes and melodies?

Of course there is no connection between this song and those with rhymes and melodies. The song we are speaking of is like a book. A book is disclosure, a *Megillah* (scroll, from the word *Gilui*, disclosure).

So it is a spiritual mechanism, like *The Song of Songs. The Song of Songs* is not a song you sing. A musical piece truly has something about it, and a song evokes emotions.

Clearly, we have emotional expressions on different levels. However, here we are speaking of a special mechanism, such as King David, who wrote *Psalms*, Solomon, who wrote *The Song of Songs*, or Moses, who wrote the song we are talking about here. It concerns writing about a special mechanism of connection that helps the next degrees that fall into sin rise again.

We read *Psalms*, or *The Song of Songs*, or Moses' song whenever we need to take something in our hands, rely on something, and thus advance.

The Creator commanded Israel to read it every seven years, once they entered the land of Israel.

Seven years marks a complete degree: *Hesed*, *Gevura*, *Tifferet*, *Netzah*, *Hod*, *Yesod*, *Malchut*.

Once we are in the land of Israel and unite, will we still sin?

Yes, no doubt. From the beginning of the portion, we are told, "Do not be afraid to come in; there will be wars there, but you will be saved."

Israel's wars are only wars with our desires. It is not the land of Israel, where we must conquer seven nations, but our own seven *Klipot* (shells), opposite the seven pure spiritual qualities. The war is with our own will to receive, which is egotistical and is called a *Klipa* (shell). It is the evil inclination that we correct, and thus achieve the conquest of the land, as the desire turns into bestowal, into love of others.

The whole Torah is "Love your neighbor as yourself." This is what we must achieve. Therefore, the system that is appearing before us will eventually compel us to do so, whether we like it or not. Unless we achieve unity with the whole world, to the point of loving every single person in the world, we will not be able to continue; we will have no bread.

When does one become free?

When one decides, "I do not want to do what is coming from within, following all kinds of traits, reactions, and impulses." First, one needs to test the verse, "Therefore choose life." Is it truly for eternal, spiritual life? If it is, one follows it. If not, then he does not. This is one's point of independence.

Terms

The Giving of the Torah

The force around us, which we can draw, is called the "light" that reforms our evil inclination. If we want it, it is ready and we can use it.

Other Gods

God is the governor of man. A person serves other gods when one serves one's own ego. Such a person keeps what he or she says without even thinking about it. We are such loyal servants that we do not even think that we have a master, another god, telling us from within what we should do.

Confidence

This is a special illumination that comes to us. With it, we can go against our nature and remain confident that we will succeed. The Hazon Ish wrote in his book, *Faith and Confidence*, that it is "a subtle leaning from the subtleness of the soul."

Repentance

Teshuva (Repentance) comes from the verse, *Tashuv Vav legabey Hey* (Let *Vav* return to *Hey*),* which means to raise *Malchut* to *Bina*, and thus come to a state where the entirety of the will to receive wishes to bestow.

* *Zohar for All, Mishpatim* (Ordinances), item 237.

Haazinu

(Give Ear)

(Deuteronomy, 32:1-32:52)

Portion Summary

The portion, *Haazinu* (Give Ear), deals with the entrance to the land of Israel. Moses begins with a song that serves as a reminder to the people when they abandon the work of the Creator in the future. The song praises the guidance of the Creator and His choice of the people of Israel, and presents the people of Israel as stiff-necked, and who have turned to idol worship.

Afterward, there is an explanation of the punishment for committing idolatry, and a statement that the Creator will not help Israel against its enemies in such a case. However, to the extent that Israel repents, the Creator will save them from all their enemies.

When Moses concludes reading his song, the Creator commands him to climb up Mount Nevo and look from there at the land of Israel. He tells Moses that he will die and will not be awarded entrance to the land of Israel.

COMMENTARY

The Torah contains all the secrets of the world. The Torah means instruction; it guides us on how we should conduct ourselves in order to advance. The Torah speaks of the whole of Creation and helps us cope with difficulties, showing us what to do.

The big question is why the Torah ends *before* the entrance to the land of Israel. In truth, the struggles, problems, the great dilemmas, and the difficulties of coping with all that awaits the people from that time on– especially in this portion,–are already within us.

The people had reached a state where they were ready to advance and enter the land of Israel, to cope with all the problems and to rise above them. It is precisely through this war that the people acquired the land of Israel. The story speaks of our desires, our forces, which have become corrected through the light, through everything that we have done and went through in the desert in order to be ready to enter the land of Israel.

The song, *Haazinu*, praises the Creator, the force of bestowal. It stresses that we must always remember to interpret what is happening accurately, and to extol the force of bestowal, the value of love of others, which is the great rule of the Torah and for which we do all that we do. "Love your neighbor as yourself" is more than just a maxim; it is the purpose of each and every action, a rule that includes all our efforts.

The song praises the people of Israel–those desires in us that want to rise, to be like the Creator, giving with the aim to bestow or even receiving with the aim to bestow. The song praises all those desires, called "the people of Israel" because they are the greatest and the most important.

Every now and again we should remind ourselves that the Creator supports us only in acts of bestowal. That is, if we wish to receive any support or blessing, we will merit it only if we advance toward the conquering of the land, toward conquering all of the egotistical desires that currently govern us, and turn them into the aim to bestow.

We should see it in our world today, as well. We are being exposed to our own corrupted system, the inclusive global crisis, which can be resolved only through bonding between us. This is the only way we can rise above the overall crisis and build what is called the "spiritual land of Israel."

Exiting the crisis is our own exodus from Egypt—through the great problems we are experiencing, through vagueness, miscomprehension, and disorientation, just as in the desert. We have no idea where to go or how to get there, no clear goals, no idea what we should do, and yet we arrive at the land of Israel. We cross the desert when we give up everything out of the desire to truly be in the aim to bestow, in unity between us. When we begin to connect, we build between us a desire that is *Yashar El* (straight to God), *Ysrael* (Israel).

Eretz (land) comes from the word *Ratzon* (desire). It is *Yashar El* when all our desires aim at one another and the network of connections between us builds the *Kli* called *Eretz Ysrael* (land of Israel).

This is why it is written that once humanity completes the process of corrections and scrutinies, the land of Israel will spread throughout the world as "The land of beauty."* In the end, all the desires of humanity will unite and become one, "as one man with one heart," and this is the main theme of the great singing, *Haazinu*.

If we do not advance toward that, we will face problems and troubles that will not only turn us around and mercilessly direct us back toward the goal and without favorable support, but they will also show us where we are erring each time and how we should advance.

Moses is only an observer. He cannot do more than that, and only makes the general correction of looking at the land of Israel.

* On that day I lifted up My hand unto them, to bring them forth out of the land of Egypt into a land that I had sought out for them, flowing with milk and honey; it is the beauty of all lands.

Moses is called the "faithful shepherd," the pure quality of bestowal. This is why he can only see the land of Israel in the light that is in *GAR de Bina*, by which he will help pave the way for the people Israel, through his gazing.

"Gazing" refers to corrections. Being the *Rosh* (head) of the degree is what Moses does. It is also how we enter the land of Israel, as well as traverse it using Moses' power.

Questions and Answers

The title of the portion is *Haazinu* (Give Ear). What is *Haazinu* and what is singing?

There is no seeing before the land of Israel. All of our *Kelim* (vessels) are *Kelim* of hearing and seeing. Hearing is the degree of *Bina*, and seeing is the degree of *Hochma*. Afterward, both of them rise together to *Keter*.

We ourselves are in *Malchut*, so *Malchut* first ascends to *Bina*. We ascend to *Bina* through the desert, where the force of bestowal walks ahead and we chase it, striving to catch up with it against our will.

That state, that journey, is truly a desert: dry, lifeless, empty, where everything happens with great difficulty. Yet, this is the only way to obtain the force of bestowal above our will to receive.

Man is built to want to enjoy life. This is why we all strive to satisfy ourselves. We do not want to be considerate of anyone, as though our will to receive is telling us, "I want to have the whole world and the next world, and there is no one in the world but me and the Creator, who will serve me."

We have to correct ourselves into the opposite, and advance in such a way that all of our "selves," our desires, thoughts, qualities, and everything within us and about us aims to bestow. These corrections will allow us to connect to the whole of the great *Kli* and discover the spiritual world and our own spiritual lives, where we are included in this immense force called "Creator." Thus, we do not feel that we belong to the animate level, but to another level of existence.

We build what is called the "speaking" by acquiring the force of faith, only to bestow, to connect with others, to find channels of bestowal and connections we are not yet activating.

In the desert, we need Moses' power, which is like the sun. Joshua, with whom we enter the land of Israel, is like the moon. When we rise above Egypt, we face our own egotistical desire and acquire the level of *Bina*, the level of *Ozen* (ear), hearing.

Moses, who began the degree on Mount Sinai, is also the one who now ends it. His last stop is at the entrance to the land of Israel, on Mount Nevo. *Haazinu* is the conveyance of Moses' force, which we acquired one at a time during the forty years of the desert.

"Forty" is the sign that we have risen to the level of forty, the degree of *Bina*. This is why it was said that a man is forbidden to study Torah (Kabbalah) before the age of forty. The level of forty means that a person has not yet acquired the degree of *Bina*, and therefore cannot see. He has not acquired seeing, but only hearing, and the Torah is called the "attainment of the Creator."

Is *Haazinu* a sort of conclusion of the degree of *Bina*?

"Conclusion" means the connection of all the degrees of the desert that are given to the people of Israel together, to prepare them to enter from the desert into the land of Israel.

From *The Zohar*: Moses Revealed on the Day when He Departed from the World

"At the time when Moses said, 'Give ear, O heavens, and I will speak,' the worlds shook. A voice came forth and said, 'Moses, Moses, why are you alarming the world? You are the son of man, and because of you the world will quake.' He started and said, 'For I shall call on the name of the Lord.' At that time they became silent and listened to his words."

Zohar for All, *Haazinu* (Give Ear), item 22

This concludes Moses' role, and he hands over everything to Joshua, the degree of the moon. Joshua is not bestowing of his own, but only of what he received from Moses. Joshua acquired from Moses the force of bestowal only because he was devoted to him. He did not study, but served Moses.

We, too, need to understand that if we serve the world, then we will rise and acquire the whole of Creation. This is the role of the Israeli nation, to be "a light for the nations," to correct ourselves, and to be "a kingdom of priests and a holy nation" (Exodus 19:6).

In the degree of the desert, we correct ourselves and prepare to serve others. In the degree of the land of Israel, we begin to work with the desires to receive and turn them into those that aim to bestow. These degrees testify that we are already working with the nations of the world, meaning with the whole of humanity.

What does it mean that the Creator helps or does not help the nation face its enemies? How does one tell if He is helping or not?

We are always in the state where everything is filled with light and the Creator is ever-present. However, all of it is hidden from us because we are hiding it with our uncorrected *Kelim*, with our desires and thoughts. The more corrected we become–connected among us in bestowal, love, and unity–the more we will discover the force that fills the whole of reality, even now.

Therefore, whether He helps or not depends on our direction. If we are moving toward Him and labor to be like Him to the extent of our equivalence of form with the Creator–according to the laws of equivalence of form–we will discover Him. It is similar to the way a radio receiver operates: When it is tuned to receive the right wavelength, we hear what is aired on that frequency.

Is it enough to want it, or does one also need to carry it out?

We need to perform certain actions, but not in order to say, "I want it," but in order to *really* want it. Therefore, wanting is enough, but it is not simple to say, "I want it." It is not a matter of words. Rather, within that desire there must also be the decision that *all I want is for it to happen.*

For example, if a person wishes to connect with others only to benefit others, in "Love your neighbor as yourself," that person must examine how he or she is trying to use the whole of reality in favor of another, and from there, in favor of more and more people. It is the opposite of the way people act now, when we use the whole of reality for ourselves.

In other words, does the other become more important than the self?

This is the meaning of "as yourself," *more* than yourself. It is just as a mother treats her baby.

Should it be in the intentions? Is it not enough to physically give to others all that I have?

It is not about the physical world, which is completely insignificant here. This concerns the connection of the hearts, our souls, our emotions. The whole of reality—the whole of the matter that has been created—consists of desire. By "desire," we mean its direction and how we use it. We need nothing but to want, as it is written, "The Lord will finish for me" (Psalms 138:8).

The upper force that we discover here among us is what builds the network. This is the work of God. We need not do a thing; there are no actions in us; we cannot do anything but ask that it will be done. We saw it with those who erred in different deeds in the journey through the desert, when they did not know how to ask, how to demand, how to reveal.

There is an element here that seems educational. The Creator is seemingly saying, "I know you will sin in your direction in some way. You will be punished for it and then you will repent." What good will it do?

When you bring up a child, you do not say such a thing, but rather, "Listen, it's best for you to do this or that," while giving a personal example. When the child errs, we let him or her understand that it was a mistake. We do not tell a child, "We know you will make mistakes, so be careful because you will be punished, but then you will repent and you will be fine." These are not helpful words.

We are not required to be good. Rabbi Akiva knew about the ruin of the Temple in advance, so when the ruin finally arrived, he laughed. Jacob wanted to tell all his sons about what was happening to them. Rabbi Shimon knew what sort of book he was writing, and for what times, as well as what would happen along the way, and we, too, need to experience these events. From this time on, we are beginning to discover that everything is right before us and has been prepared for us.

It is clear that we will make mistakes every step of the way, and each of us will discover the sin of *Adam HaRishon* (Adam) in all of our 613 desires. Yet, our mistake will be if we do *not* ask, if we do not request and demand of the upper force, the Creator. Only when we connect with others as much as we can will we discover how we hate and repel them. Therefore, we must demand of the Creator to keep the connection, and not us, or the result will either be corruption, or we will discover that it is the opposite, and flee.

We need not be in fear of revealing the shattering between us, the great ego. We also need not bow to other gods. Rather, we should ask for the correction here, instead of running away.

If we do this, we will do everything correctly and we will not make mistakes. However, in truth, we make mistakes each time because we cannot quite discover our point of contact with the Creator. We must exert in the correct approach, as well, where we try to act like babies. But following great efforts and tremendous work, we must still err, reveal the shattering, and learn that we are incapable. Only then do we discover the right kind of evil.

We discover the evil of the right kind of shattering, the proper one. For that, too, we need the light, the revelation of the Creator. When it happens, we see the place that the Creator needs to fix. We see the great shattering, the great correction, and we receive everything pre-prepared. In fact, we are only present in the process while it is happening, with our great egos, the revelations, and the shattering and its correction.

What is the idea behind the climb up Mount Nevo? Moses went up and gazed, but was not permitted to enter the land of Israel. This sounds cruel because he was permitted to see the beauty from afar, but was not permitted to reach it.

The Creator told Moses in advance that they were approaching the land of Israel and that he was going to die, and that Joshua would replace him. It sounds inhuman, heartless, but the degree of Moses is not directly related to the land of Israel at the end of correction.

Moses represents the whole of the light of the sun, all the light. But for now, the land of Israel needs to be conquered and corrected, and only the force of bestowal can enter the land of Israel, only Joshua, the light of the moon. By letting in and correcting that force–the light of the moon–Joshua's role ends, and only then does the end of correction arrive.

Once the people of Israel have entered the land of Israel, there are only ruins, expulsions, and exiles. After some time there is a return to the land of Israel, and only now are we implementing all the corrections and arriving at a state where there are revelations of the genuine land of Israel, and the desire to receive with the aim to bestow. This is when we come to that state known as (Samuel 2, 23:20) "a valiant man of Kabzeel" (*Rav Pe'alim Mekatze'el*).

All the corrections we have made throughout the generations will come together in a single correction, the network of connections among us, among all the souls, will appear all at once, and everyone will truly be connected. This is when the force of Moses will burst with the light of the sun, together with Joshua, the force of the moon—"the two great lights" (Genesis 1:16)—and we will come to a day that is all good.

Have we made any corrections along the way? It seems that our current situation is worse than ever.

So far, we have only been preparing ourselves. We have made no corrections so far, and we have not revealed all the corruptions. Only now, in this crisis, are we beginning to disclose them. The corruption and correction are close by; they are tied to one another. If we wish, we can do it very quickly because there is no need for the corrections to be lengthy.

Is it up to us? It seems as if the Creator is doing everything.

It depends on our request. We can rush times. It is written (*Masechet Berachot*, 49a) that Israel sanctifies (rushes) times. We must "summon" the Creator to correct. It is the force of bestowal that is among us, the hidden light that is present even now, and which we must summon to correct us.

Terms

A Stiff-Necked People

We have *Panim* (anterior) and *Achoraim* (posterior) sides. The *Achoraim* of the degree are the hardest, most egotistical desires to receive and not give. "Stiff-necked" means great difficulty; these are the biggest desires, the toughest ones, and indeed they are found in Israel and not elsewhere.

Although we see that cruelty exists in everyone, it is far more so in Israel because when we come to these great corrections, we connect and scrutinize the worst *Kelim* (vessels) and become a stiff-necked people. It is impossible to avoid this.

An ordinary person is not considered stiff-necked. Rather, only those who walk on the path of corrections become stiffer, increasingly discovering the evil inclination, as it is written, "He who is greater than his friend, his inclination is greater than him" (*Babylonian Talmud, Masechet Sukkah*, Chapter 5, 52a).

Guidance of the Creator

The guidance of the Creator means that there is none else but Him. Along the way, we only need to bring the catalyst between our actions and His—the demand that it will happen. Without our demand it will not happen, but in truth the Creator begins and ends every situation, and we only ask in-between.

It is not just a request. We need to know what we are asking for and how He executes. This is how He knows we come to know the whole system, as well as Him.

Punishment

A "punishment" is the inability to bestow because there is nothing worse than being denied that; it is similar to the way we consider reception to be the most important thing.

Mount Nevo

This is the place of *Bina*, Moses' place, where this force is found until it achieves complete redemption, and then it appears.

Gazing Over the Land

This is the correction of seeing, called "gazing." *Histaklut* (looking) of *Eynaim* in the *AHP* is what Moses does. This is how he performs corrections over the land of Israel, so the people of Israel can enter the land with his blessing, his force, and can continue the corrections. Joshua is already leading them with the force of Moses.

Idol Worship

When we turn to ourselves or to any other force in the world but the one, giving Force, which is hidden among us and must be revealed, this is called "idol worship." We must turn to it and ask it to be revealed, and this will comprise the correction.

Summary:

We need to make the entire connection of "Love your neighbor as yourself" between us. It is not simple, but it is the great rule of the Torah. Loving others is the whole of reality that must come together. Today, we are discovering that the whole world needs this–it is the only way we will be able to come out of the crises we are in today.

We are truly in a shattered state, which is actually good news, because then we can discover the negative in us. When we do, we need only demand of the Creator, together with our common force, that we connect with others, and then we will discover Him, and discover the spiritual, perfect, peaceful life, in endless harmony for all, here and now.

VeZot HaBracha

(This Is the Blessing)

(Deuteronomy, 33:1-34:12)

Portion Summary

The portion, *VeZot HaBracha* (This Is the Blessing), is the last portion in the Torah. It is dedicated to the greatness of Moses. In this portion, Moses blesses the tribes of Israel and mentions the uniqueness of each tribe and its particular lot.

Moses dies at the age of 120. Before he dies he climbs up Mount Nevo and is buried in a valley in the land of Moab. The children of Israel mourn his death for thirty days and then assume Joshua as his heir.

Commentary

"This Is the Blessing" is the portion that concludes the Torah, and there are new issues in it that are not immediately noticeable. Throughout the Torah, it speaks of one person within us. It describes the correction of our hearts, our desires, our rising above our egos and the work by which we invert the ego, as it is written, "I have created the evil inclination; I have created for it the Torah as a spice" because "the light in it reforms them."

Our entire ego becomes good. Instead of exploiting, deceiving, and stealing from others, we need to act to the contrary—bestowing and loving others. We perceive the spiritual, upper world through the quality of bestowal to others. This is really the entire correction that we need to make on ourselves. It is the process we must go through, which we do in this portion at the conclusion of the corrections that the Torah details.

Throughout the portions, we gradually correct ourselves through the light that we draw from the Torah. It is not a simple thing to do because we need to know how to draw in the light. In the end, when we have drawn in enough light throughout the Torah, having corrected our egos, we arrive at the last stage in which the point in our hearts—the point of Moses, which has accompanied us, prepared us, explained to us, and taken care of us—concludes its work.

There is no death in spirituality. In fact, there is no death anywhere; it is only the way we perceive things. When we speak of someone being "dead" or "alive," it only seems that way, when, in fact, there is renewal of all forms of matter.

Many *Midrashim* (interpretations) deal with the issue of Moses' death not being death. It is considered that he "went up to God." In fact, Moses' "death" is the last degree of the corrections of the desert, which corrected only some of our *Kelim* (vessels), the part called *Galgalta* and *Eynaim*, vessels of bestowal. Now we must rise to the next level of corrections, to *Eretz Ysrael* (land of Israel). *Eretz* comes from the word *Ratzon* (desire), and *Ysrael* (Israel) comes from the words, *Yashar El* (straight to God).

Now we need to correct our heavier desires—the desires of *Eretz Ysrael*—which are at a higher level than the degree of Moses, in a degree called Joshua. Therefore, now a new leader appears in us–Joshua. Previously, he was next to Moses, growing alongside him. Now he is accompanying us and leading us toward the next corrections.

This is also why it is pointless for the Torah to speak of future corrections because we are already prepared for them and will make them; we will achieve the correction of the land of Israel and the entire world. This is the role of the next degree, the degree of Joshua, in which the land of Israel, the land of beauty, is spread to the rest of the world.

Moses' dying means that we have gone through 120 degrees, which are three times forty. These are the forty degrees during which he was reared in Pharaoh's house and a degree called the "evil inclination" appeared in him, the "great serpent," "Pharaoh." He spent another forty years in the house of Jethro, priest of Midian, and led Israel through the desert for another forty years. Altogether, it is 120 years that we need to go through in order to realize the point of Moses in our hearts.

Questions and Answers

The Torah begins with the letter *Bet,* and *The Zohar* writes that it is because *Bet* stands for *Beracha* (blessing). The Torah also ends with the portion, "This Is the Blessing." What is a blessing, and what is so special about it?

A "blessing" is a force from above. When we connect to a higher degree, we obtain the force that corrects us, one that is absent from our degree. Although it seems to us that we can change our world, fix it and make it better, each time we try, we see that we are unsuccessful, to say the least.

This is what many think today.

As we continue to see, economists, financiers, and industrialists still think there is something they can do to correct the situation.

On the one hand, they are helpless and do not know what to do, but on the other hand, they are trying. This is a sure path toward despair, helplessness, and a great cry, as it is written, "And the children of Israel sighed from the work" (Exodus 2:23). It is similar to the situation in Egypt when they built their cities, Pithom and Rameses. When the construction was done, they saw that everything they had been building for so many years was not in their favor.

We are in the exact same situation today. However, finally, the proper degrees are beginning to appear. We are beginning to reflect on our lives, what we need to obtain, how we can progress, and how we can support our souls and our bodies.

We are finally realizing that our goal is simply not within our power, and that we need a higher force to help us. This is why it is written, "I have created the evil inclination; I have created for it the Torah as a spice" because "the light in it reforms them." To succeed, we need guidance, the knowledge of something we do not have. Everyone is helpless, from every world leader on down, yet no one knows why. These people are still running on momentum, trying to do something, but their efforts are all futile.

It seems as though we are in the stage of Egypt. Does that mean that everything has been preordained? If so, what should we do?

Of course it is all preordained; we only need to carry out the plan.

But will it not happen anyway?

When a child goes to school, the curriculum has already been prepared: all the tests, works, and everything the child will learn at school. But the child does not know all that. Everything is still ahead for the child. Once in school, he or she is taught new things each time. New exercises are given, and the child must do them. This is how children grow.

But a child cannot know if he or she will grow up to be an engineer or a doctor, or will drop out in the last year of high school.

Neither the child nor the teacher knows the answer to that. However, if we read what psychologists, biologists, and geneticists write about the child, we will see that they feel quite confident about predicting what will happen to the child.

The fact is, we still do not know all the systems, and yet, everything is already determined in advance, there is nothing new. This is not where our free choice lies; we do not decide anything at any point along the way. Our free choice is only to be in a good environment that will accompany us on the correct, short way toward those states we must experience.

When we look back on our lives, we often feel that we did not really control the situations in our lives.

True. We acted, but things simply happened one way or the other, not always as we wanted them.

Children, too, have no real choice up to a certain age.

It's not only children who have no real choice; none of us determines anything in life, whether we are twenty, thirty, forty, or fifty. The only thing we do determine is our relation to what is happening and where we want to go. This is the only way we can change our destiny. We must go through the various stages of development, but we can experience them as good or not so good.

In other words, does understanding the system and perceiving it turn us into a "giving" person?

Of course, this is how we change our destiny. We feel that we partake in the actions in a meaningful way, entering better degrees and steps that will promote us toward our goal.

For example, when we begin to study, it is clear that we must also complete the studies. It is possible to go through with them suffering "blows," failing tests, and taking extra years to complete them. But it is also possible to go through our studies positively and smoothly, winning praises and awards.

It is all a question of approach, encouragements, and the example that the social environment offers. This is why our best choice is being in a good environment in which we can develop faster and better. Everything depends on our preparation.

These days, many scientists are concerned about the world; they seem to agree that there is an overall collapse. What kind of world are we leaving for our children?

It is called, "And the children of Israel sighed from the work." We have arrived at a situation where we have nowhere to go. All the work we have done with our egos is like the work in Egypt. We wanted to develop systems, design buildings, create cities like Pithom and Rameses. These are beautiful cities for the ego, but the text calls them *Arei Miskenot* (cities of misery), which are both poor and dangerous.* We can remain in them, drown in the dust, and never rise again. And yet, there is a turning point from which we can leap into the next degree.

What is the next degree? Which blessing should we expect now, or which should we summon?

We need to understand that where the wicked fall, the righteous will rise. In other words, it appears that the present point is actually an invitation for us to ascend. We must leave our egos behind, not erase them. Now, we can work with them in a different way.

We need to turn them into "help made against us," to become our assistants against themselves. We need to understand that at this point we are being invited to reach the enlightened world, the next degree.

Our entire world is in our egos, and we need to rise to a world that is entirely above them. It is written, "Love covers all transgressions"

* The word, *Miskenot*, derives from the word *Miskenut* (misery), but also from the word, *Sakanah* (danger).

(Proverbs 10:12). Below is hate, and above is love. If we unite, we will discover the spiritual world between us, one of eternal life, harmony and abundance.

Assuming we can achieve that state, but the rest of the world has not, what will change, if anything?

It is possible to do it individually, as well.

Today we are very dependent on each other, so what does it matter who does it?

We must *all* do it. Those who accomplish it will help others do the same; they will circulate the change and reveal the information everywhere, thus helping to build a new environment.

The first thing that our world needs is an environment that encourages people to unite, that teaches us that we are all inevitably connected, now that the world has become circular. Everyone writes about it. Scientists are addressing this topic and are publishing essays on the internet. However, we are not connected between us, although by Nature we must be connected. A gap has surfaced for the first time between us and Nature, which in *Gematria*, is God.

In other words, the Creator is appearing to us as a general, integral, and global system. He wishes us to connect in order to draw close to Him. The more we unite, the more we will succeed. The lack of unity among us is the problem because we have no desire for it. We detest this bonding, which is why we need to build an environment that constantly influences us into thinking that it is good to be connected.

It seems as if it is one's personal work. But what about leadership? After all, as individuals, what can we change?

We must make it happen. Today we can all be influential because we are all present in the internet, on Twitter, on Facebook, and so on. Today, anyone can make a difference.

But we have become accustomed to being managed, and we are still managed by institutions and authorities.

We see that those authorities cannot do a thing. All the committees, the protests, the organizations that pop up everywhere scream that they have things they want to do. But what are they actually doing? Do they want the same kind of revolutions we had two or three centuries ago? Everyone knows these will not work in today's world.

Is it possible that someone with intelligence will arise and see things in this light?

No, because these people are not studying Kabbalah. For this to happen it must be a person rising out of the circular, integral system. That system exists only in those who study the wisdom of Kabbalah. These students connect with each other in groups and draw the light that reforms to them through their bonding.

These people are making corrections called *Mitzvot* (commandments/good deeds). The word, *Mitzva* (singular of *Mitzvot*), comes from the word, *Tzavta* (together). When they unite and draw the light, the light corrects them, which is the making of the *Mitzvot*. They correct the 613 desires that exist in each of them by connecting with others. When they are corrected, they become tied together.

Each group that is studying the wisdom of Kabbalah becomes a miniature corrected world. When they circulate this knowledge, they carry with them the power to show the world how we should unite and what we need to do.

Does it not say that a new leader will be born, a new Moses? Assume that a leader such as Moses is born now. What qualities would he have so as to help us through the crisis? Or is this a group issue?

It is not a leader or a certain personality type; it is a large group, people with points in their hearts who are connected among them.

They draw the light that reforms, and through them the light traverses to the whole of humanity. This is the role of the Israeli people, to be the "light of the nations."

This is a big responsibility; is it up to us?

We have no choice. Moses, too, did not want the responsibility, saying that he was "slow of speech" (Exodus 4:10). He rejected this hard and committing role, as does everyone else. However, we must carry it out nonetheless.

The world is demanding it of us through its anti-Semitic approach. They are actually saying that they depend on us, and that it is we who are to blame for the world's troubles. And yet, the fact that the world depends on us means that we have the power to change things.

From *The Study of the Ten Sefirot*

"Our sages said (Midrash Raba, Portion "And This Is the Blessing"), 'The Creator said unto Israel: 'Regard, the whole wisdom and the whole Torah is easy: anyone who fears Me and observes the words of the Torah, the whole wisdom and the whole Torah are in his heart.'' Thus, we need no prior merit here; and only by virtue of fear of God and the keeping of *Mitzvot* is one granted the whole wisdom of the Torah."

Kabbalah for the Student, "Introduction to the Study of the Ten Sefirot," item 21

This is the answer; we need nothing else. Fear means that we are trying to carry out a simple order: to want to unite because we have no choice. Today, Nature and the world are compelling us to do it.

To unite, we have to build an environment that educates us through the media, internet, radio, and other means. Soon, millions of people will be out of work; they will need to learn and to receive supplements to their income in return for learning how to unite. Each person will work for 2-3 hours daily because there will not be enough work for more than that. The rest of their time will be spent studying.

Their studies will draw to them the vital force, the power of the light, and through it we will succeed in everything. This in itself will be a job.

According to statistics, today only two percent of the global population needs to work in agriculture, and only ten percent more are needed in industry, commerce, and everything else. When we establish a balanced world and more balanced consumption, when we stop consuming non-essential products, ninety percent of the world's population will have nothing to do.

It sounds ideal; everyone will want to work only two hours a day, study the rest of the time, and get paid for it.

It is not that simple. The study consists of two parts: the receiving of information, and the receiving of social education. In the first section, students will learn about the world and be taught the meaning of an integral system. This will include why the world crisis is happening, human nature, free choice, the purpose of Creation, the correction of Creation, and what we must finally achieve. This is a study about our lives and about the whole process of our evolution.

The social education part will consist of group exercises that enable people to experience our psychology firsthand. They will learn how best to connect with others and discover what motivates us as human beings. In this way, people will learn psychology, and from this they will feel the soul within them.

This is how we will connect through the souls. We will begin by attaining the next degree of existence, the degree of the "speaking," the human degree (Adam), which is similar (*Domeh*) to the Creator, as it is written, "Return, O Israel, unto the Lord your God" (Hosea 14:2).

Terms

Conclusion, or Conclusion of the Torah

"Conclusion" refers to the conclusion of the guidance. It is the end of the first corrections in our preparation, when we acquire the first correction and then enter the land of Israel, where we continue the corrections. At this conclusion, we experience the first correction in our 248 organs and 365 tendons, our 613 desires. It is called "bestowing in order to bestow," or the "degree of the desert."

Blessing

A "blessing" is the pouring down of upper light on our matter (substance), our lives. It is impossible to execute any correction or anything good in the world without the upper light, which is the operator and the doer.

There is a very nice essay in the *Introduction of the Book of Zohar*, called "The Essay of the Letters," which explains that the Torah must begin with the letter *Bet* because only in the upper light that comes from the Creator, the degree of *Bina*, can we make corrections.

Tribe

Just as our bodies consist of different organs such as brain, heart, liver, kidneys, and lungs, the "body of the soul" consists of twelve primary parts, known as *Yod-Hey-Vav-Hey* (*HaVaYaH*), in each of which are three lines. Because *HaVaYaH* consists of four letters, if you multiply it by three lines in each letter, you get twelve parts, known as twelve tribes.

120

"120" is 3x40. Each *Partzuf* (face), each soul, divides into three parts: *Rosh* (head), *Toch* (interior), *Sof* (end). The complete correction in *Rosh*, *Toch*, *Sof*, is forty, which is the degree of *Bina*. We become corrected through the degree of *Bina*, through the blessing.

Death

When a person stops using the current degree and ascends to the next, it is considered "death." The previous degree is regarded as dead because it is no longer being used.

Leader

This is the *Rosh* (head) of the degree, like a head. Israel is called "the leader of the world." Israel contains the letters of the Hebrew words, *Li-Rosh* (I have the *Rosh*). A "leader" is the thought, the intention that leads, and everything is judged according to the intention.

About the Author

Rav Michael Laitman, PhD, is an international authority on authentic Kabbalah. His background is highly unusual for one renowned in the spiritual: he was educated in the sciences, holds an MS in bio-cybernetics, and has pursued a successful scientific career, later turning to Kabbalah to further his scientific research. He received his PhD in Philosophy and Kabbalah from the Moscow Institute of Philosophy at the Russian Academy of Sciences.

In 1976, he began studying Kabbalah, and has been researching it ever since. In 1979, seeking new avenues in Kabbalah, he came across Kabbalist Rabbi Baruch Shalom HaLevi Ashlag (1906-1991), the firstborn son, and successor of Kabbalist Rabbi Yehuda Leib HaLevi Ashlag (1884-1954), known as Baal HaSulam for his *Sulam* (Ladder) commentary on *The Book of Zohar*. Michael Laitman was so impressed with Baal HaSulam's son, that he became Baruch Ashlag's closest disciple and personal assistant, spending the bulk of his time in the company of his revered mentor, and absorbing as much as he could of his teachings.

Today, he is regarded as the foremost authority on Kabbalah, having authored thirty books on the subject, translated into ten languages. His live lessons are broadcast daily on cable and satellite TV and internet around the world. In recent years, he has become a sought-after lecturer in academic circles in the United States and Europe.

Dr. Laitman is the founder and president of Bnei Baruch–Kabbalah Education and Research Institute, which operates the largest and most extensive internet site on the subject of Kabbalah, *www.kabbalah.info.* The website provides unlimited access to Kabbalistic texts and media in over twenty languages, with 1.4 million hits per month. Since the year 2000, the *Encyclopedia Britannica* recognizes *kabbalah.info* as one of the largest internet sites in both number of visitors and quantity of educational and informational materials on the science of Kabbalah.

Further Reading

To help you determine which book you would like to read next, we have divided the books into six categories—Beginners, Intermediate, Advanced, Good for All, Textbooks, and For Children. The first three categories are divided by the level of prior knowledge readers are required to have in order to easily relate to the book. The fourth category, Good for All, includes books you can always enjoy, whether you are a complete novice or well versed in Kabbalah.

The fifth category, Textbooks, includes translations of authentic source materials from earlier Kabbalists, such as the Ari, Rav Yehuda Ashlag (Baal HaSulam) and his son and successor, Rav Baruch Ashlag (the Rabash). The category, For Children, includes books that are suitable for children ages 3 and above. Those are not Kabbalah books per se, but are rather inspired by the teaching and convey the Kabbalistic message of love and unity.

Additional material can be found at www.kabbalah.info.

Beginners

A Glimpse of Light: The Basics of the Wisdom of Kabbalah

A Glimpse of Light: The Basics of the Wisdom of Kabbalah offers selected contemplations from the ocean of wisdom contained in the wisdom of Kabbalah. This book touches upon topics such as pleasure, ego, love, men and women, globalization, education, ecology, Nature, perception of reality, *The Book of Zohar*, and spirituality. Just open the book wherever you wish, and begin to read. Each chapter contains several sections that combine to form a complete picture. This collection will serve you as a "glimpse of the Light," a window into the profound emotions and perceptions we can all attain by studying the wisdom of Kabbalah.

The Spiritual Roots of the Holy Land

The Spiritual Roots of the Holy Land takes you on a wondrous journey through the land of Israel. As you take in the breathtaking views of the holy land, another layer of the age-old country is revealed—its spiritual roots, the ebb and flow of forces that have shaped the curvy landscape that is sacred to billions of people around the world. At the end of the book, you'll find roadmaps of Israel, to help you locate each place you visit, whether in mind or in body, and more details on the forefathers who have made this land the focal point of an entire planet.

Self-Interest vs. Altruism in the Global Era: how society can turn self-interests into mutual benefit

Self-Interest vs. Altruism in the Global Era presents a new perspective on the world's challenges, regarding them as necessary consequences of humanity's growing egotism, rather than a series of errors. In that spirit, the book suggests ways to *use* our egos for society's benefit, rather than trying to suppress them.

...Stating that society's future relies on cooperation of people to work together for society, stating that much of society's degradation in recent decades has been the result of narcissism and greed, *Self Interest vs. Altruism* is a curious and recommended read.

James A. Cox, Editor-in-Chief, *Midwest Book Review*

A Guide to the Hidden Wisdom of Kabbalah

A Guide to the Hidden Wisdom of Kabbalah is a light and reader-friendly guide to beginners in Kabbalah, covering everything from the history of Kabbalah to how this wisdom can help resolve the world crisis.

The book is set up in three parts: Part 1 covers the history, facts, and fallacies about Kabbalah, and introduces its key concepts. Part 2 tells you all about the spiritual worlds and other neat stuff like the meaning of letters and the power of music. Part 3 covers the implementation of Kabbalah at a time of world crisis.

Kabbalah Revealed: A Guide to a More Peaceful Life

This is the most clearly written, reader-friendly guide to making sense of the surrounding world. Each of its six chapters focuses on a different aspect of the wisdom of Kabbalah, illuminating its teachings and explaining them using various examples from our day-to-day lives.

The first three chapters in *Kabbalah Revealed* explain why the world is in a state of crisis, how our growing desires promote progress as well as alienation, and why the biggest deterrent to achieving positive change is rooted in our own spirits. Chapters Four through Six offer a prescription for positive change. In these chapters, we learn how we can use our spirits to build a personally peaceful life in harmony with all of Creation.

Wondrous Wisdom

This book offers an initial course on Kabbalah. Like all the books presented here, *Wondrous Wisdom* is based solely on authentic teachings passed down from Kabbalist teacher to student over thousands of years. At the heart of the book is a sequence of lessons revealing the nature of Kabbalah's wisdom and explaining how to attain it. For every person questioning "Who am I really?"and "Why am I on this planet?" this book is a must.

Awakening to Kabbalah: The Guiding Light of Spiritual Fulfillment

A distinctive, personal, and awe-filled introduction to an ancient wisdom tradition. In this book, Rav Laitman offers a deeper understanding of the fundamental teachings of Kabbalah, and how you can use its wisdom to clarify your relationship with others and the world around you.

Using language both scientific and poetic, he probes the most profound questions of spirituality and existence. This provocative, unique guide will inspire and invigorate you to see beyond the world as it is and the limitations of your everyday life, become closer to the Creator, and reach new depths of the soul.

Kabbalah, Science, and the Meaning of Life

Science explains the mechanisms that sustain life; Kabbalah explains why life exists. *Kabbalah, Science, and the Meaning of Life* combines science and spirituality in a captivating dialogue that reveals life's meaning.

For centuries, Kabbalists have been writing that the world is a single entity divided into separate beings. Today the cutting-edge science of quantum physics states a very similar idea: that at the most fundamental level of matter, we are all literally one.

Science proves that reality is affected by the observer who examines it; and so does Kabbalah. But Kabbalah makes an even bolder statement: even the Creator, the Maker of reality, is within the observer.

These earthshaking concepts and more are eloquently introduced so that even readers new to Kabbalah or science will easily understand them. So if you are curious about why you are here, what life means, and what you can do to enjoy it more, this book is for you.

From Chaos to Harmony

Many researchers and scientists agree that the ego is the reason behind the perilous state our world is in today. Laitman's groundbreaking book not only demonstrates that egoism has been the basis for all suffering throughout human history, but also shows how we can turn our plight to pleasure.

The book contains a clear analysis of the human soul and its problems, and provides a "roadmap" of what we need to do to once again be happy. *From Chaos to Harmony* explains how we can rise to a new level of existence on personal, social, national, and international levels.

Kabbalah for Beginners

Kabbalah for Beginners is a book for all those seeking answers to life's essential questions. We all want to know why we are here, why there is pain, and how we can make life more enjoyable. The four parts of this book provide us with reliable answers to these questions, as well as clear explanations of the gist of Kabbalah and its practical implementations.

Part One discusses the discovery of the wisdom of Kabbalah, and how it was developed, and finally concealed until our time. Part Two introduces the gist of the wisdom of Kabbalah, using ten easy drawings to help us understand the structure of the spiritual worlds, and how they relate to our world. Part Three reveals Kabbalistic concepts that are largely unknown to the public, and Part Four elaborates on practical means you and I can take, to make our lives better and more enjoyable for us and for our children.

INTERMEDIATE

The Kabbalah Experience

The depth of the wisdom revealed in the questions and answers within this book will inspire readers to reflect and contemplate. This is not a book to race through, but rather one that should be read thoughtfully and carefully. With this approach, readers will begin to experience a growing sense of enlightenment while simply absorbing the answers to the questions every Kabbalah student asks along the way.

The Kabbalah Experience is a guide from the past to the future, revealing situations that all students of Kabbalah will experience at some point along their journeys. For those who cherish every moment in life, this book offers unparalleled insights into the timeless wisdom of Kabbalah.

The Path of Kabbalah

This unique book combines beginners' material with more advanced concepts and teachings. If you have read a book or two of Laitman's, you will find this book very easy to relate to.

While touching upon basic concepts such as perception of reality and Freedom of Choice, *The Path of Kabbalah* goes deeper 'and expands beyond the scope of beginners books. The structure of the worlds, for example, is explained in greater detail here than in the "pure" beginners' books. Also described is the spiritual root of mundane matters such as the Hebrew calendar and the holidays.

ADVANCED

The Science of Kabbalah

Kabbalist and scientist Rav Michael Laitman, PhD, designed this book to introduce readers to the special language and terminology of the authentic wisdom of Kabbalah. Here, Rav Laitman reveals authentic Kabbalah in a manner both rational and mature. Readers are gradually led to understand the logical design of the Universe and the life that exists in it.

The Science of Kabbalah, a revolutionary work unmatched in its clarity, depth, and appeal to the intellect, will enable readers to approach the more technical works of Baal HaSulam (Rabbi Yehuda Ashlag), such as *The Study of the Ten Sefirot* and *The Book of Zohar*. Readers of this book will enjoy the satisfying answers to the riddles of life that only authentic Kabbalah provides. Travel through the pages and prepare for an astonishing journey into the Upper Worlds.

Introduction to the Book of Zohar

This volume, along with *The Science of Kabbalah*, is a required preparation for those who wish to understand the hidden message of *The Book of Zohar*. Among the many helpful topics dealt with in this text is an introduction to the "language of roots and branches," without which the stories in *The Zohar* are mere fable and legend. *Introduction to the Book of Zohar* will provide readers with the necessary tools to understand authentic Kabbalah as it was originally meant to be—as a means to attain the Upper Worlds.

The Book of Zohar: annotations to the Ashlag commentary

The Book of Zohar is an age-old source of wisdom and the basis for all Kabbalistic literature. Since its appearance, it has been the primary, and often only source used by Kabbalists.

Written in a unique and metaphorical language, *The Book of Zohar* enriches our understanding of reality and widens our worldview. Rav Yehuda Ashlag's unique *Sulam* (Ladder) commentary allows us to grasp the hidden meanings of the text and "climb" toward the lucid perceptions and insights that the book holds for those who study it.

GOOD FOR ALL

The Secrets of the Eternal Book

The Five Books of Moses (The Torah) are part of the all-time bestselling book, The Bible. Ironically, the Bible is an encoded text. Beneath it lies another level, a hidden subtext that describes the ascent of humanity toward its highest level—the attainment of the Creator.

The Secrets of the Eternal Book decodes some of the Bible's most enigmatic, yet oft-cited epochs, such as the story of Creation, and the Children of Israel's exodus from Egypt.

The author's lively and easygoing style makes for a smooth entrance into the deepest level of reality, where one changes one's world simply by contemplation and desire.

The Kabbalist: a cinematic novel

At the dawn of the deadliest era in human history, the 20th century, a mysterious man appeared carrying a stern warning for humanity and an unlikely solution to its suffering. In his writings, Kabbalist Yehuda Ashlag described in clarity and great detail the wars and upheavals he foresaw, and even more strikingly, the current economic, political, and social crises we are facing today. His deep yearning for a united humanity has driven him to unlock *The Book of Zohar* and make it–and the unique force contained therein–accessible to all.

The Kabbalist is a cinematic novel that will turn on its head everything you thought you knew about Kabbalah, spirituality, freedom of will, and our perception of reality. The book carries a message of unity with scientific clarity and poetic depth. It transcends religion, nationality, mysticism, and the fabric of space and time to show us that the only miracle is the one taking place within, when we begin to act in harmony with Nature and with the entire humanity.

Like a Bundle of Reeds: why unity and mutual guarantee are today's call of the hour

Like a Bundle of Reeds: why unity and mutual guarantee are today's call of the hour explains why unity and mutual guarantee (mutual responsibility) can heal our society and, surprisingly to some, mitigate anti-Semitism. Using numerous quotes and references from Jewish sages and historians, the author sheds light on some of the Jews' most daunting and mystifying questions: What is our role on this planet? Are we truly "the chosen people"? If we are, what were we chosen for? What is causing anti-Semitism, and can it be cured?

The book offers a road map for achieving the desired social cohesion and unity. In the pages within you will read the testimonies of sages throughout time, stating that unity is the key to prosperity. Indeed, unity is the very gift that the Jews can give to the world, and which the world impatiently awaits. When we unite and share our unity with everyone, then peace, brotherly love, and happiness will forever prevail throughout the world.

Unlocking the Zohar

The greatest Kabbalist of the 20th century, Rav Yehuda Ashlag (1884-1954) paved a new way for us by which we can reveal the secrets of *The Book of Zohar*. He wrote the *Sulam* [Ladder] commentary and four introductions to the book, in order to help us understand the forces that govern our lives, and to teach us how we can assume control over our destinies.

Unlocking the Zohar is an invitation to a wondrous journey to a higher world. The author, Kabbalist Dr. Michael Laitman, wisely ushers us into the revelations of the *Sulam* commentary. In so doing, Laitman helps us fine-tune our thoughts as we read in *The Zohar*, to maximize the spiritual benefit derived from reading it.

Dr. Laitman also included numerous inspiring quotes from *The Book of Zohar*, specifically translated, edited, and compiled for easy reading and understanding of this powerful text.

The Point in the Heart: a Source of Delight for My Soul

The Point in the Heart; a Source of Delight for My Soul is a unique collection of excerpts from a man whose wisdom has earned him devoted students in North America and the world over. Michael Laitman is a scientist, a Kabbalist, and a great thinker who presents ancient wisdom in a compelling style.

This book does not profess to teach Kabbalah, but rather gently introduces ideas from the teaching. *The Point in the Heart* is a window to a new perception. As the author himself testifies to the wisdom of

Kabbalah, "It is a science of emotion, a science of pleasure. You are welcome to open and to taste."

Attaining the Worlds Beyond

From the introduction to *Attaining the Worlds Beyond*: "...Not feeling well on the Jewish New Year's Eve of September 1991, my teacher called me to his bedside and handed me his notebook, saying, 'Take it and learn from it.' The following morning, he perished in my arms, leaving me and many of his other disciples without guidance in this world.

"He used to say, 'I want to teach you to turn to the Creator, rather than to me, because He is the only strength, the only Source of all that exists, the only one who can really help you, and He awaits your prayers for help. When you seek help in your search for freedom from the bondage of this world, help in elevating yourself above this world, help in finding the self, and help in determining your purpose in life, you must turn to the Creator, who sends you all those aspirations in order to compel you to turn to Him.'"

Attaining the Worlds Beyond holds within it the content of that notebook, as well as other inspiring texts. This book reaches out to all those seekers who want to find a logical, reliable way to understand the world we live in. This fascinating introduction to the wisdom of Kabbalah will enlighten the mind, invigorate the heart, and move readers to the depths of their souls.

Bail Yourself Out

Bail Yourself Out: how you can emerge strong from the world crisis introduces several extraordinary concepts that weave into a complete solution: 1) The global crisis is essentially not financial, but *psychological:* People have stopped trusting each other, and where there is no trust there is no trade, but only war, isolation, and pain. 2) This mistrust is a result of a *natural process* that's been evolving for millennia and is culminating today. 3) To resolve the crisis, we must first *understand* the process that created the alienation. 4) The first, and most important, step to understanding the crisis is to *inform* people about this natural process through books, such as *Bail Yourself Out*, TV, cinema, and any other means of communication. 5) With this information, we will "*revamp*" our relationships and build them on trust, collaboration, and most importantly, care. This mending process will guarantee that we and our families will prosper in a world of plenty.

Basic Concepts in Kabbalah

This is a book to help readers cultivate an *approach to the concepts* of Kabbalah, to spiritual objects, and to spiritual terms. By reading and re-reading in this book, one develops internal observations, senses, and approaches that did not previously exist within. These newly acquired observations are like sensors that "feel" the space around us that is hidden from our ordinary senses.

Basic Concepts in Kabbalah is intended to foster contemplation of spiritual terms. Once we are integrated with these terms, we can begin to see the unveiling of the spiritual structure that surrounds us, almost as if a mist has been lifted. It is a book for those who wish to awaken the deepest and subtlest sensations they can possess.

Children of Tomorrow: guidelines for Raising Happy Children in the 21st Century

Children of Tomorrow is a new beginning for you and your children. The big revelation is that raising kids is all about games and play, relating to them as small grownups, and making all major decisions together. You will be surprised to discover how teaching kids about positive things like friendship and caring for others automatically spills into other areas of our lives through the day.

Open any page and you will find thought-provoking quotes about every aspect of children's lives: parent-children relations, friendships and conflicts, and a clear picture of how schools should be designed and function.

The Wise Heart: tales and allegories by three contemporary sages

Kabbalah students and enthusiasts in Kabbalah often wonder what the spiritual world actually feels like to a Kabbalist. *The Wise Heart* is a lovingly crafted anthology comprised of tales and allegories by Kabbalist Dr. Michael Laitman, his mentor, Rav Baruch Ashlag (Rabash), and Rabash's father and mentor, Rav Yehuda Ashlag, author of the acclaimed *Sulam* (Ladder) commentary on *The Book of Zohar*. The poems herein offer surprising and often amusing depictions of human nature, with a loving and tender touch that is truly unique to Kabbalists.

Textbooks

Shamati (I Heard)

Rav Michael Laitman's words on the book: "Among all the texts and notes that were used by my teacher, Rav Baruch Shalom Halevi Ashlag (the Rabash), there was one special notebook he always carried. This notebook contained transcripts of his conversations with his father, Rav Yehuda Leib Halevi Ashlag (Baal HaSulam), author of the *Sulam* (Ladder) commentary on *The Book of Zohar*, *The Study of the Ten Sefirot* (a commentary on the texts of the Kabbalist, Ari), and many other works on Kabbalah.

"Not feeling well on the Jewish New Year's Eve of September 1991, the Rabash summoned me to his bedside and handed me a notebook, whose cover contained only one word, *Shamati* (I Heard). As he handed the notebook, he said, 'Take it and learn from it.' The following morning, my teacher perished in my arms, leaving me and many of his other disciples without guidance in this world.

Committed to Rabash's legacy to disseminate the wisdom of Kabbalah, I published the notebook just as it was written, thus retaining the text's transforming powers. Among all the books of Kabbalah, *Shamati* is a unique and compelling creation."

Kabbalah for the Student

Kabbalah for the Student offers authentic texts by Rav Yehuda Ashlag, author of the *Sulam* (Ladder) commentary on *The Book of Zohar*, his son and successor, Rav Baruch Ashlag, as well as other great Kabbalists. It also offers illustrations that accurately depict the evolution of the Upper Worlds as Kabbalists experience them. The book also contains several explanatory essays that help us understand the texts within.

In *Kabbalah for the Student*, Rav Michael Laitman, PhD, Rav Baruch Ashlag's personal assistant and prime student, compiled all the texts a Kabbalah student would need in order to attain the spiritual worlds. In his daily lessons, Rav Laitman bases his teaching on these inspiring texts, thus helping novices and veterans alike to better understand the spiritual path we undertake on our fascinating journey to the Higher Realms.

Rabash–the Social Writings

Rav Baruch Shalom HaLevi Ashlag (Rabash) played a remarkable role in the history of Kabbalah. He provided us with the necessary final link connecting the wisdom of Kabbalah to our human experience. His father and teacher was the great Kabbalist, Rav Yehuda Leib HaLevi Ashlag, known as Baal HaSulam for his *Sulam* (Ladder) commentary on *The Book of Zohar*. Yet, if not for the essays of Rabash, his father's efforts to disclose the wisdom of Kabbalah to all would have been in vain. Without those essays, few would be able to achieve the spiritual attainment that Baal HaSulam so desperately wanted us to obtain.

The writings in this book aren't just for reading. They are more like an experiential user's guide. It is very important to work with them in order to see what they truly contain. The reader should try to put them into practice by living out the emotions Rabash so masterfully describes. He always advised his students to summarize the articles, to work with the texts, and those who attempt it discover that it always yields new insights. Thus, readers are advised to work with the texts, summarize them, translate them, and implement them in the group. Those who do so will discover the power in the writings of Rabash.

A Sage's Fruit: letters of Baal HaSulam

The greatest Kabbalist of the 20th century, Rav Yehuda Leib Halevi Ashlag, who wrote the Sulam (Ladder) commentary on *The Book of Zohar*, had very few students. A prolific writer, he spent almost all of his time at his desk, so the students that he did have were precious. When spending time away from home and from his students, Rav Yehuda Ashlag would write elaborate letters to provide them with guidance and encouragement. Today these letters offer a window into the special relationships cultivated between the great teacher and his devoted students.

A Sage's Fruit: letters of Baal HaSulam is a compilation of those letters, which are now being presented to English speaking readership for the first time. The unique style and tone that Rav Ashlag uses in his letters offer inspiration and guidance to any seeker of spiritual advancement. The nature of this book is such that it changes a person. Regardless of how many times one may read the text, it constantly takes on new forms, as if reading it for the very first time. Now that these letters have been revealed, it is unclear how we could perceive spiritual advancement without them.

Gems of Wisdom: words of the great Kabbalists from all generations

Through the millennia, Kabbalists have bequeathed us with numerous writings. In their compositions, they have laid out a structured method that can lead, step by step, unto a world of eternity and wholeness.

Gems of Wisdom is a collection of selected excerpts from the writings of the greatest Kabbalists from all generations, with particular emphasis on the writings of Rav Yehuda Leib HaLevi Ashlag (Baal HaSulam), author of the *Sulam* [Ladder] commentary of *The Book of Zohar*.

The sections have been arranged by topics, to provide the broadest view possible on each topic. This book is a useful guide to any person desiring spiritual advancement.

Let There Be Light: selected excerpts from The Book of Zohar

The Zohar contains all the secrets of Creation, but until recently the wisdom of Kabbalah was locked under a thousand locks. Thanks to the work of Rav Yehuda Ashlag (1884-1954), the last of the great Kabbalists, *The Zohar* is revealed today in order to propel humanity to its next degree.

Let There Be Light contains selected excerpts from the series *Zohar for All*, a refined edition of *The Book of Zohar* with the *Sulam* commentary. Each piece was carefully chosen for its beauty and depth as well as its capacity to draw the reader into *The Zohar* and get the most out of the reading experience. As *The Zohar* speaks of nothing but the intricate web that connects all souls, diving into its words attracts the special force that exists in that state of oneness, where we are all connected.

FOR CHILDREN

Together Forever: the story about the magician who didn't want to be alone

Like all good children's stories, *Together Forever* transcends boundaries of age, culture, and upbringing. Here, the author tells us that if we are patient and endure the trials we encounter along our life's path, we will become stronger, braver, and wiser.

In this warm, tender tale, Michael Laitman shares with children and parents alike some of the gems and charms of the spiritual world. The wisdom of Kabbalah is filled with spellbinding stories. *Together Forever* is yet another gift from this ageless source of wisdom, whose lessons make our lives richer, easier, and far more fulfilling.

Miracles Can Happen: tales for children, but not only...

"Miracles Can Happen," Princes Peony," and "Mary and the Paints" are only three of ten beautiful stories for children ages 3-10. Written especially for children, these short tales convey a single message of love, unity, and care for all beings. The unique illustrations were carefully crafted to contribute to the overall message of the book, and a child who's heard or read any story in this collection is guaranteed to go to sleep smiling.

The Baobab that Opened Its Heart: and Other Nature Tales for Children

The Baobab that Opened Its Heart is a collection of stories for children, but not just for them. The stories in this collection were written with the love of Nature, of people, and specifically with children in mind. They all share the desire to tell nature's tale of unity, connectedness, and love.

Kabbalah teaches that love is nature's guiding force, the reason for creation. The stories in this book convey it in the unique way that Kabbalah engenders in its students. The variety of authors and diversity of styles allows each reader to find the story that they like most.

CONTACT INFORMATION

1057 Steeles Avenue West, Suite 532
Toronto, ON, M2R 3X1
Canada

Bnei Baruch USA,
2009 85th street, #51,
Brooklyn, New York, 11214
USA

E-mail: info@kabbalah.info
Web site: www.kabbalah.info

Toll free in USA and Canada:
1-866-LAITMAN
Fax: 1-905 886 9697